AMNESIA

AMNESIA

A HISTORY OF DEMOCRATIC IDEALISM
IN MODERN THAILAND

Arjun Subrahmanyan

SUNY
PRESS

Cover image: Army survey department's constitutional parade, 1932. Photo courtesy of the Phraya Phahon Foundation.

Published by State University of New York Press, Albany

© 2021 State University of New York

For information, contact State University of New York Press, Albany, NY
www.sunypress.edu

Library of Congress Cataloging-in-Publication Data

Name: Subrahmanyan, Arjun, author.
Title: Amnesia : a history of democratic idealism in modern Thailand / Arjun
    Subrahmanyan, author.
Description: Albany : State University of New York Press, [2021] | Includes
    bibliographical references and index.
Identifiers: ISBN 9781438486512 (hardcover : alk. paper) | ISBN 9781438486529
    (ebook) | ISBN 9781438486505 (pbk. : alk. paper)
Further information is available at the Library of Congress.

10 9 8 7 6 5 4 3 2 1

Contents

Illustrations

Acknowledgments

Bureaucratic inertia and the insecurity of a twenty-first century academic's career have prolonged the time taken for this book to appear. The political economy of modern academia has pushed me around the world, with the moves prompted by the gnawing anxiety of unemployment. In global terms, the sacrifices are puny and the self-absorption clueless. Moreover, the silver lining of these problems is bright indeed: especially the continuous support and friendship of many people in many places. I am deeply grateful to the people around the world who gave me their time and companionship. In Berkeley, California, where this project began as a half-baked PhD thesis, above all I am indebted to Peter Zinoman for his criticism and support. Also in California, thanks go to Penny Edwards and the late great Jeff Hadler for their mentorship, as well as Amy Pitsker for her friendship and support. Chris Conte and Tammy Proctor in Logan, Utah gave me the chance to teach independently and supported my work. At Binghamton University, Kent Schull encouraged me at a crucial time, and more recently my editor at State University of New York Press, James Peltz rescued my project from two years in the editorial wilderness. In Australia, the current and former Murdoch History colleagues—Dean Aszkielowicz, Michael Sturma, Andrew Webster, and Sandra Wilson— have made the small program a haven in a neoliberal storm. Also in Australia, I am very grateful for the support of Robert Cribb and Craig Reynolds, giants of Southeast Asian history writing, and the friendship of Anne Schwenkenbecher. In Bangkok I quite selfishly drew many people actively or unwittingly into my work. Patphorn Phoothong, above all, a constant help, support and friend who has had the good sense not to go into academia. Many more colleagues in Thailand supported my work, including most vitally Chalong Soontravanich, Thanaphol Limapichart,

Laurent Malespine, Puli Fuwongcharoen, Sittha Lertphaiboonsiri, and Thongchai Likitpornasawan. For the comrades Samson Lim and Lawrence Chua: enough said. Finally, for the love of Mum, Lakshman, and Dad.

Staff at the National Library of Thailand, the National Archives of Thailand, the National Library of Australia, the Murdoch University Library, and many other repositories assisted my requests and suggested new ones over the years.

Readers of various drafts of journal articles and chapters of this book, whom I would name if I knew who they were, have been invaluable in helping turn bad writing and vague thinking into something passable.

An earlier version of chapter 4 was originally published as Arjun Subrahmanyan, "Education, Propaganda and the People: Democratic Paternalism in 1930s Siam," in *Modern Asian Studies* 49, no. 4 (2015): 1122–42, and is here reproduced with the permission of Cambridge University Press.

An earlier version of chapter 5 was originally published as Arjun Subrahmanyan, "Buddhism, Democracy and Power in the 1932 Thai Revolution" in the *Asian Studies Review* 41, no. 1 (2017): 40–57, copyright © 2016 Asian Studies Association of Australia, reprinted by permission of Informa UK Limited, trading as Taylor & Francis Group, www.tandfonline.com, on behalf of 2016 Asian Studies Association of Australia.

Thai Language Conventions

This book adheres to the general phonetic transcription system for most Thai words that is used by the Royal Institute of Thailand. No tonal marks are used. Common English spellings are used for personal and place names that are widely known, as are the owner's preferred transcriptions. The commonly spelled English versions of certain Thai royal names are used instead of their lengthy official titles. Official ranks and positions for government servants are given at the first reference but thereafter are omitted, unless they appear in a quoted source that uses them. Following conventional usage, Thai people are referred to by their personal names and Westerners by their surnames. The Bibliography therefore lists Thai names alphabetically by their personal names.

Introduction

The 1932 Revolution in Thai History

In early April 2017, a near-century-old plaque sunk into the pavement outside the Royal Plaza in Bangkok, Thailand, disappeared. The unremarkable, thirty-centimeter brass marker bore a simple inscription that encircles its rim: "At this spot the People's Party established the Constitution for the progress of the nation." The center read "24 June 1932, Dawn." The plaque's elegant brevity commemorated the beginning of Thai democracy in the 1932 revolution, an event staged by a group of military and civilian commoners from the bureaucracy and known as the People's Party. They toppled the absolute monarchy and introduced a constitutional government that vested power in the people. The 1932 plaque, its words faded over time by foot and car traffic across the Royal Plaza, was replaced overnight that early April with a new plaque bearing a very different meaning.

The new plaque reads, again in a combination of circular and centrally placed text: "Loyalty and love for the Triple Gem, one's clan and having an honest heart for one's king are good. These are the tools to make one's state prosper." Centrally placed, in larger text, it reads: "Forever may Siam prosper" and "Fresh-faced, happy citizens are the strength of the land."[1] The overblown phrases, borrowed from a royal seal created at the turn of the twentieth century to honor the Bangkok monarchy, exhort people to submit and obey. They also mark the latest symbolic attack on human rights, liberty, and democratic rule of law that cemented 1932's place in the history of Thailand. A military dictatorship claiming royal approval today controls Thailand, and the latest war on the country's democratic movement and history has been undertaken in earnest since the 2006 elimination of the last civilian democratic government. Indeed, the plaque's removal

1

is not an isolated event; in recent years shadowy actors have removed a series of icons and monuments to the first Thai democracy.[2] The new millennium political crisis is a regular feature of journalism around the world and a subject of compelling scholarship.[3]

There is a long history to the struggle in a country that as one commentator wryly observes has made more moves toward and away from democracy than perhaps any other country in the world.[4] The country for nearly nine decades has experienced repeated political unrest, coups, and dictatorships. Military and monarchic groups, often relying on each other's capability and ideological strength, have intervened frequently to subvert the democratic rule of law. Those who have tried to build democracy meanwhile remain much less well known. In a region where state-enforced historical amnesia is rife, Thailand has turned it into an art form.

This book covers the first phase of Thai democracy from 1932 to 1949, and argues two main points that rescue the origins of Thai democracy from oblivion. First, the People's Party revolution ignited aspirations among common people for a greater say in government and a more egalitarian society. Making democracy a social good became a task shared by the government and society. Second, people made their history amid changing political alliances and conflicts that both advanced and obstructed the People's Party democracy. In this checkered initial version of Thai democracy, educated "outsiders" to the bureaucratic system—labor organizers, schoolteachers, journalists and writers, Buddhist monks and rural parliamentarians—and state "insiders"—primarily military officers and lawyers trained under the old regime's guidance—together advanced the democratic revolution against a royalist rebellion that asserted the political and cultural primacy of monarchy. This book explains the social impact of 1932 in different political phases—compromise, consolidation, and collapse—of these landmark years.

The Standard View of Thai Democracy: The King's Gift

Removing the commemorative plaque in 2017—as well as other icons of the June 24 movement in recent years—is meant to remove the People's Party from history. The prevailing narrative of Thai history revolves around the moral supremacy of monarchy,[5] and the monarchy's halo illumines what is important about 1932. King Prajadhipok—the king whose absolute power was taken away by the People's Party—is retrospectively credited as the father of Thai democracy. As described by one of his advisers, a man who served both the old and new regimes, the king had a magnanimous plan to introduce democracy but he was preempted by the impetuousness of the People's Party when they presented him with a fait accompli.[6] Still, in the official narrative Prajadhipok was a democrat at heart and, even after the June end of the absolute monarchy, adhered to constitutionalism rather than violently resist it. The most famous photograph of the times, taken at the ceremony introducing the December 10, 1932 constitution, shows the king handing the signed document to his attendant and by extension giving his gift to the nation. Not only the king's personality explains the formal royal bestowal of the constitution, but also adherence to an ancient Thai custom of democratic kingship. The monarchic view of 1932 relies on a presumably unshakable popular loyalty to kings, and also the belief that the Thai king is traditionally a "Great Elect" who has been chosen by popular acclaim since the thirteenth century.[7] This view, in part, is meant to explain the political instability after 1932. According to the monarchic view, the upstart People's Party could not hope to gain the legitimacy earned over 700 years by the kings, and all political crises of the 1930s and 1940s are blamed solely on commoners. According to its narrative, popular vice is the benighted corollary of monarchic virtue: the People's Party was comprised of insincere or duplicitous politicians bent on power, who foisted their authority on a society completely unprepared for, and uninterested in, the revolution. The pro-monarchy, anti-People's Party view of 1932 became entrenched with a series of anti-People's Party writings that accompanied the rejuvenation of royal power after World War II and continues to be influential.[8]

The wave of anti-People's Party polemics in the late 1940s helped rebuild the real and symbolic power of monarchy. At the same time the United States, newly interested in the region, found a rejuvenated monarchy ready to hand as a symbolic counterweight to communist ideology; as security for the money they gave the Thai state to be a good ally, Americans happily believed arguments that the monarchy had always enjoyed strong popular support. The monarchy made Thailand an "oasis in a troubled continent" as the Time Corporation put it, and a place where the continuity of benign kingly rule meant that "Americans could feel uniquely at ease."[9] The hand of royalists in rewriting recent history was thus strengthened. Further, American advisers and academics' fervent belief in modernization theory colored views of the recent past, and marginalized the social and intellectual dimensions of the 1932 revolution. American academics, and often their Thai students, framed this period as above all strengthening,

in the memorable phrase of the leading book on the topic, the "bureaucratic polity." The growth of secular power in the offices of state—needed
by the Thai kings to modernize the country in the face of foreign pressure—eventually curtailed the monarchy's power. But the events of 1932,
ostensibly a reform of unchecked rule, in fact deepened the institutional
power of state officers who were not interested in or answerable to public
opinion.[10] The machinery of bureaucratic power, not people's aspirations
or ideas, explained the revolution. Even radical scholars writing around
the same time viewed 1932 as only important for the "partial, mystified
revolt . . . of absolutism's own engine, the functionalized bureaucracy."[11]

The Revisionist View:
Commoners' Struggle and 1932's Importance Today

The long-standing focus on the monarchy and the bureaucracy is easy to
understand. One is the enduring icon of uncolonized Thailand's political and
cultural life; the other, created by the monarchy as its servant, staged the
bloodless and secretly planned overthrow of the king without any popular
mobilization. But pathbreaking work by Thai and foreign scholars in the past
generation, on which this book builds, has shown three important areas:
public criticism of politics; the revolutionaries' attempts to create a new
moral leadership that resonated socially; and the contemporary relevance
of the revolution. We can now see the revolution as a multidimensional
and complex struggle; Siam/Thailand was not a uniquely calm oasis in
a trouble continent but a country that like its neighbors experienced
profound social change. The People's Party movement stemmed from a
longer social and intellectual transformation,[12] a leading component of
which was an emergent middle-class nationalism that opposed a purely
dynastic state.[13] As a result, the old standby subjects of the times have
been reassessed. We now know that the monarchy opposed, rather than
supported, democracy.[14] Instead of a vague "partial, mystified revolt" within
a politically immature civil service, we now understand much better the
complex social history, and motivations and internal disagreements among
the People's Party and their social backers.[15] Furthermore, cultural history
has enriched our understanding of the revolution, especially by examining
the People's Party's visual and written work as elements of their project
to make democracy part of Thai culture.[16] And, since the 2006 coup that
ended the penultimate civilian democracy there has been a resurgence

of popular and scholarly interest in 1932, as the opening chapter in the story of a popular movement for democracy met by stubborn royalist opposition. It has hence become a symbol of what remains unfulfilled and suppressed in Thai society.[17] Contemporary history has forced a return to the most basic question about Thai politics: whom does the political system represent?

A New Interpretation:
The Insiders and Outsiders Who Made Democracy

The best revisionist scholarship about the revolution explains its social *origins* as much more than a kingly bestowal of democracy. This book furthers the revisionist history of 1932 by explaining the revolution's main *outcome* as a widely inspirational democratic idealism that sank roots after the People's Party took power and amid the political instability of the times. How insiders and outsiders made the revolution against the backdrop of dramatic political contests is the thread running through the six main chapters in this book.

Who is an insider, who an outsider, and what are their places in social history? And what did democracy mean at the time for these two groups?

On one level, insiders and outsiders shared much in common. Both groups belonged to a new intelligentsia, they were products of a state becoming more administratively complex and an economy more closely linked to global capitalism. Middle class—while a "chameleon among definitions"[18] and a term debased by shoddy usage—is a roughly correct description of their social position. They worked at the middle and lower levels of the state service, and also extra-bureaucratic professions. At the time of the revolution, they numbered around 100,000 people among a working population of 6 million. They stood in stark contrast to the roughly five in six of the working population who were illiterate rice farmers. The middle tier of society also stood in obvious difference from the old ruling class of royals and senior, ennobled[19] civil servants at the apex of the social pyramid and who numbered roughly 1,000 in 1932. The middle class lived by their intellectual capability; the peasants by their physical toil; and the royal-ennobled elite lived in idleness, sustained by rents and inherited wealth, or the comfortable salaries given to elite bureaucrats. And in Siam, as in all of the non-Western colonial world at the time, for most of the middle strata it was not literacy per se that distinguished them from the

rest of their countrymen and women but Western-style education.[20] But
their education resulted in far more than a narrow technical training: it
was a character making force, breeding new values and outlooks. Like
others in the Western-dominated world they comprised a small minority
who "discovered . . . the high road of ambition which wore the white
collar of the teacher, bureaucrat or office worker," as Eric Hobsbawm put
it, and became their society's movers and shakers.[21]

But the teacher, petty bureaucrat, or office worker in Siam lived
worlds apart from well-connected officeholders in their access to political
power. Insiders had it; outsiders did not. Insiders staged the 1932 revolt
and directed the post-June establishment of a constitutional system. The
civilian and military wings of the People's Party, representing law and
defense, two central organs of the bureaucratic polity's power, comprise
the core of insiders. Almost all of the People's Party members came from
the central tiers of the state system and made friendships—some long
standing and some dissolving bitterly in the first years after the revolution—through their civil service training and office holding. The Thai
bureaucracy, like all modern Southeast Asian bureaucracies, rested on a
series of patrimonial networks, rather than rationalized administrative
efficiency, for its power.[22] Ennobled ranks, marks of social respect and
state service, privileged the leaders of the People's Party. And while the
revolution was staged to limit kingly power, considerable crossover existed
between the old and new regimes. Patronage bound some People's Party
insiders to old regime officials, producing friendship, enmity, cooperation
and conflict. Some important old regime figures, sympathetic in varying
degrees to constitutionalism but often at odds with the People's Party,
formed a crucial, additional insider cohort under the People's Party regime.
Old regime political and administrative power was especially pronounced
in the first year of the revolution.

Insiders after 1932 moved to the center of state power, Bangkok. The
city's might, wealth and social diversity grew rapidly in the early twentieth
century. The rest of the country funded Bangkok's growth but changed
much more fitfully and unevenly. Aside from an occasional stopover by
a government officer, an itinerant merchant or a holy man, most villages
were unvisited by strangers, and unconnected to larger populations; the
Thai word for "society" (sangkhom) was only invented in the 1930s. In
country areas, there were few books, newspapers or radios. Most of the
outsiders came from this world and became local leaders. All were young
and all shared a common outsiderness, which was not based on a strictly

class consciousness, but an awareness—common in all modern political movements—of being excluded in some way.[23] But they did not just want the wealth or status that the haves enjoyed; they wanted authority to speak and act for their communities. Lower-level civil servants, Buddhist monks, the rural bourgeoisie, lawyers, and teachers are the outsiders most inspired by the People's Party's message. These outsiders initially had no bureaucratic influence beyond the local level, or connections to the old or new regime ruling class. Among those within the civil service, some were ennobled for their provincial government work; most were not. Many state insiders wrote their own accounts of the times, and many others have been written about, often in funeral volumes that highlight their good deeds and moral character.[24] Amid the hagiography, we know their family backgrounds, their work, their foreign education, their beliefs and struggles. Most outsiders did not write memoirs, and do not have funeral volumes. Most have vanished from the historical record. But like the self-designated People's Party, they too became the intellectual and moral spokesmen for the masses who had little share or stake in anything beyond the daily toil of their households.

Their small numbers, the unique quality of their work, and their claims to leadership in a largely illiterate peasant society all linked insiders and outsiders to each other, even if their power was starkly uneven. Insiders and outsiders changed Thai history, and they collaborated and struggled to lead the course of democracy. These two facets of 1932—its idealism and the struggle for hegemony—propelled 1930s and 1940s Thailand and made the long-term importance of the revolution.

Idealism is not used as a reproach. Instead, I refer to a mode of thinking that projected a better or fairer society as a way to judge conduct and as a basis to act.[25] I pose this meaning in contrast to that used in the standard narratives of 1932, which assert that impractical, unrealistic, or wishful thinking doomed the People's Party. As argued in one of the few English language books on 1932, to the misguided People's Party, democracy was "a wonderful system that could work miracles . . . They spoke much about democracy even though they did not clearly know what . . . they were talking about."[26] The People's Party and those they inspired were in this view like the "hot-brained boys and crazed enthu-siasts,"[27] of Europe's long nineteenth century, as a critic of revolutionary politics memorably phrased it.

The historical importance of the 1932 revolution—its novelty, insta-bility, and long-term effect—calls for a better explanation of the idealism that drove the politics of the times. The language and performance of democracy were not mere masquerades through which an opportunistic cabal falsely represented its particular interests as the same as those of everyone else. Instead, the workings of democracy became arenas through which citizens fought for hegemony, a combined political/cultural contest for a new moral and intellectual leadership that appeals to the public and is persistently unstable and unfinished.[28]

But while my use of the word idealism is not meant as a rebuke of people at the time, status and privilege shaped the notions of a fairer or better society, and crucially determined who had the most power to judge success or failure, what was permitted and what was not. The quest to gain moral and intellectual leadership created a paradoxical democracy after 1932. The insiders devised a method of leadership in Siam that still resonates, what this book terms "democratic paternalism," and which has parallels to the way democratic and revolutionary governments the world over have exercised power. It is democratic because its makers justified the revolution on the grounds of popular rule, individual rights and legal equality, and paternalist because they restricted, and at times outright excluded, the political role and responsibility of ordinary people. Hence the new regime often withheld freedom from the people who supposedly already enjoyed it.[29] The contradiction that this produced becomes apparent among outsiders, who resisted the limits to their freedom, and spoke against the regime on behalf of uneducated people. Also, however, the People's Party's paradoxical democracy alienated two large groups of people, Chinese and women, one by law and racism, the other by silence, and in both cases outsiders rarely challenged the Promoters.

As the absolutist kings before them, the revolutionaries were suspicious of the Chinese in Siam—the largest overseas Chinese population anywhere in the world and as in many places in Southeast Asia central to the export and commercial economies. Rulers forged a strategy of division, whereby "good" Chinese—the wealthy, loyal to the king, and assimilated through marriage to Thai women—were rewarded with inclusion. "Bad" ones—especially poor, republican, and/or criminal men and women alike, who raised their Chinese-speaking families without, in the eyes of Thai officials, sufficiently merging into Thai society—suffered discrimination.[30] Hence, not merely antiroyalist thinking, but a healthy dose of anti-Chinese racism also shaped People's Party nationalism. Throughout the 1930s and 1940s, the People's Party government launched a range of legal and rhetorical attacks against the Chinese community to curtail their economic influence and degrade their social position. The irony of the anti-Chinese nationalism of the new regime matched that of the xenophobia of the old regime: much of the insider class in both cases came from Chinese parentage, and under both regimes the Chinese contributed mightily to the modernization of society.

The second major exclusion is starker. While the Chinese "problem" regularly features in the following chapters, there are hardly any women in this story. There were no women members of the People's Party, none in the civilian bureaucratic or military cohorts that mobilized behind the revolutionaries, none in the national assembly, in labor leadership, or among the religious leadership. Some of these groups seem obvious: the religious professional class did not admit women; neither did the military. But the People's Party threw open the national and local assemblies to men and women, and both men and women could vote for their representatives. There were no laws against women attaining high office, in the cabinet or any ministry, or advancing to senior professional work. Thai, and Southeast Asian women generally, have historically had considerable economic clout and social freedom, at least in comparison to great patriarchies like India or China. The traces of women in the revolution, however, are mere glimpses: a photograph of unnamed women volunteers supporting the government against a rebellion, anecdotal evidence of scores of women entering university-level teacher training, or enrolling in the People's Party Association, a widely popular public branch of the Promoters' movement. In all cases, the gaps in the historical record leave us, as often in history, with a knowledge that, as Marc Bloch described it in a classic text, "assumes the rather anemic aspect of a world without individuals."[31] Why were women not an obvious part of the idealistic, freedom-giving revolution, the most important in modern Thai history?

The contest over moral and intellectual leadership that the revolution began was novel, but it also inherited a gendered Thai political culture. Politics—fighting, administering, and deciding who fit where in the social hierarchy—was a man's world, be he ethnically Thai or a man descended from a Chinese immigrant father who rose in society. Whatever his family background, the leader as a "man of prowess"—physically and spiritually powerful, possessing many wives and producing many children—exerted a traditional and continuing appeal as a doer and decider. Behind all of the supposed strength and great deeds, however, were women, whose bodies mediated political loyalty, integrated powerful groups, and maintained political alliances through the production of (primarily) boys.[32]

In this context, the revolutionaries exposed the shakiest aspect of their democratic ideology. While the new regime often overtly kept the Chinese at a distance, it tacitly excluded women via cultural norms inherited from history. It gave an appearance of equality for women that did not really exist; indeed, democracy worked toward the "perfecting of an illusion" of freedom.[33] Ostensibly free citizens, women continued to be subjects of male privilege, and their exclusion from public life stems from the sexualized politics inherited from the old regime. The culture of marriage crystallized women's subordination. Only in 1935 did Thai law recognize monogamy as the sole lawful form of marriage. The law did not make polygyny a crime and the practice remained widespread, as did a man's prerogative to recognize as heirs his children born out of wedlock. Critics decried the sexual indulgence of the royal and ennobled elite in the two decades before the revolution. However, the larger debates over polygyny and womanizing of those years were not clearly mappable along class lines, and instead showed the privilege of the bureaucratic insider over less well-connected men. Polygyny and male sexual primacy became democratized as the bureaucracy encompassed more commoners. While alliance building, the traditional political rationale for a man to have many wives, disappeared with the creation of a modern Western-style administrative state, the male prestige associated with polygyny continued. Insiders certainly continued to benefit from gendered politics, and outsiders were loath to criticize or to really push for a genuine social revolution, that is, one that upended family politics.

Thus, Thai male outsiders—lawyers, teachers, monks—sought to level the playing field, and enjoyed a distinct advantage in doing so. The People's Party drive for hegemony, meanwhile, harmed large groups of people whom society's leaders viewed as untrustworthy (the "bad" Chinese), or incapable (women). These two groups of adults hence were the ultimate outsiders to the entire period: central to the making of modern Siam but unacknowledged; vital to the social and economic power of Thai men but scorned. Notions of the modern free individual after the revolution always attached more to men than women, and more to Thai men than Chinese.

The Book Outline: Forging Democracy amid Political Conflict

Framed by the relationship between insiders and politically active outsiders—and the prejudices and constraints of democratic idealism—this book studies Thai history from 1932 to 1949. We move from the largely painless birth of democracy in a quiet revolt to its bloody demise in a military crackdown. A fleeting period of time, these seventeen years have left a permanent mark on Thai politics and society. Amid a series of conflicts, they foregrounded debates between insiders and outsiders over how democracy could improve society in three main areas: political representation; popular welfare; and moral and intellectual life.

Chapter 1, "The New Regime and the Old," explains how conflict derailed attempts to expand the political sphere. The People's Party's tentative compromise with old regime officials in the wake of the June takeover collapsed in a failed royalist rebellion at the end of 1933. The crises of the first eighteen months of the new order patterned struggles for the rest of the era, pitting commoners against the monarchy and civilians against the military. The chapter also explains that as the new regime consolidated their power from the end of 1933, popular support swung behind the People's Party who jailed and executed their enemies. "Hegemony protected by the armour of coercion"[34]—consent backed by force, popularity by violence—is one of the legacies of the times that put critical but supportive outsiders in a difficult position.

Chapter 2, "A Fragile Alliance," turns attention to the widespread interest in popular welfare that the revolution brought, and focuses on the changing fortunes of labor activists through the People's Party years. The Chinese are central to the story, since they comprised much of the laboring population. Shaken by the crises of 1932 and 1933, and fearing further disorder, the People's Party sought to tame labor through periodic paternalist interventions and also checks on Chinese labor. Thai-Chinese activists, however, emerged during the Pacific War and the early postwar years and contributed to postwar democracy. In response to their influence, factions in the People's Party allied with labor to enhance their own power.

Chapter 3, "Spokesmen for the Peasantry," continues with the theme of popular welfare during the phases of compromise and consolidation, and examines the lives of the peasantry, the vast majority of the population. It discusses the contending arguments for improvement between state insiders and newly empowered outsiders that, while especially acute in the first years of the revolution, roiled debate throughout the People's Party years.

Chapter 4, "Making Citizens," addresses another key debate of the revolutionary years: moral and intellectual development under democracy. The People's Party's reliance on old regime conservatives to govern education in the first years created the "democratic paternalism" that characterized the formal democracy. At the same time, country teachers in particular sought local management freed from the tutelage of Bangkok officials, many of whom they felt were holdovers from the old regime. After the defeat of royalist rebellion in 1933, the People's Party asserted its moral leadership by expanding education for Thais, and also through widespread public relations that stressed the modern regime stood for the people. Outsiders joined with the party to educate people about the new order but also resisted central control. Rural activists, many of whom joined the new national assembly that held its first elections in November 1933, committed themselves to a more vital democracy through education as well as politics.

Chapter 5, Buddhist Democracy in the Revolution," also discusses the cultural force of the revolution, and shows the religious power of democratic idealism. In the mid-1930s a push for greater local authority among provincial monks gained national attention. Religious outsiders, remote from the center of Bangkok's religious power and members of a very old religious fraternity, then gave the People's Party commitment to secular democracy an ironic twist.

Reforms within the Buddhist order coincided with greater People's Party control of the government, but also with the gathering storm of world war. From 1938, military autocracy deepened, and produced a backlash that brought together some civilian members of the People's Party and out-siders who made common cause against dictatorship through the national assembly and the supporters of parliamentary democracy. Chapter 6, "The Revolution Betrayed," thus picks up the theme of political representation and the upholding of the democratic rule of law discussed in chapter 1, and discusses it in the context of the latter period of the People's Party regime when democracy flowered and died. Outsiders, while gaining unprecedented influence in the new regime, ultimately lost as one time military and monarchy insiders, a mixture of old and new regime men, violently asserted their right to rule. The curtain thus descended on the first phase of Thai democracy.

A willed leap into the future that is restrained by the political circum-stances of compromise with the old regime, consolidation of new regime power, and then its collapse, marks the revolution. It is remarkable how much the 1932 revolution changed Thai society given the obstacles facing the People's Party. The revolution to be sure had its limits. But its makers also embarked on the astounding novelty of introducing popular democ-racy into a weakly integrated and young state. The revolution brought a widespread and spirited debate over the social importance of popular rule, and over who legitimately could participate in the new democracy. Better revisionist history belies the old explanations of the period that explain 1932 as a betrayal of kingly goodness, or as a battle for supremacy among a few elites who imposed their will on an apathetic society. We can now explain the social passions and conflicts unleashed by a secretive revolt against the world's last absolute king.

Chapter One

The New Regime and the Old

Compromise, Rebellion, and the Enemies Within

In 1932, Siam was the last absolute monarchy in the world, and the crown faced crisis. Rumors of civil unrest and revolt against the Bangkok monarchy, coupled with widespread popular hardship, fueled an uneasy atmosphere in the beginning of the year. The fall in price of exported rice in the wake of the economic depression[1] that began in 1929 deprived paddy farmers, the vast majority of the population whose labor sustained the elite and underpinned Siam's place in the international economy, of their main income and led to criticism that the king's government was indifferent. At the same time, public gossips criticized the elite for holding tremendous wealth that could have helped the poor at a desperate time. Within the military, rumors of rebellion became common currency, and something of a joke. Beer and whiskey loosened tongues, and drinking buddies among the officers and men in the army and navy would gently rib each other for joining a table of two or three: "You must be plotting something!"[2]

Public speculation had it that the April 6, 1932 celebration of Bangkok's 150-year anniversary as the dynastic capital would be canceled for financial reasons; as spiritually and politically powerful as the monarchy thought itself to be, perhaps it could not pay its bills.[3] Also at the time a prophecy reportedly first made at the city's founding in 1782 that the kingdom would collapse 150 years hence recirculated in Bangkok. In April for the commemoration "blood would pool in the stomachs of elephants, there would be killing for seven days and nights, the earth and sky would change places," and the royals would be killed amid revolt.[4]

At ceremonies on the royal grounds that clear, hot April day, a cooling breeze brought relief to the assemblage of royal-ennobled elite sweltering in their full regalia. And, apart from the winds stymieing the king's repeated attempts to light ceremonial candles—which some people took as a bad omen—the April celebrations proceeded smoothly.[5] The festival of kingship formed the last grand display of unchecked royal power. For a genuine threat existed, as a small group of plotters at that very time honed their plans to end the absolute monarchy. Beginning in the same April, ten men met seven times to work out the best way to end the absolute monarchy with the minimum disruption and violence but with maximum surprise.[6] These men led the "People's Party," a mysterious, secretive group that the public would later learn comprised around 100 young civilian and military state officers.[7]

The leading "Promoters," as members of the People's Party called themselves in echo of a vanguard political strategy adopted from Russia and China, formed a tight-knit group originally of seven young men who came together for the first time in Paris in February 1927 to plan the overthrow of the absolutist system.[8] The foreign students' group grew their network from a middle tier bureaucratic base, and successfully enrolled four senior military officers whose armed support made the plan a reality five years later. The civilian leader of the group was Pridi Banomyong, thirty-two-years old at the time. Born to a Thai-Chinese small farmer and landowner in central Ayuthaya province, Pridi gained a law doctorate at the University of Paris in 1927 where he studied on a government scholarship. His wife, with whom he was related through their great-great-grandparents, came from a well-connected family. In 1885, her grandfather—at the time an attaché at the Siamese legation in London—joined a group of princely reformers who tried, and failed, to convince King Chulalongkorn (r. 1868–1910) to introduce a constitutional monarchy.[9] Phibun Songkhram, aged thirty-four in 1932, was a junior army officer and leader of the middle-tier army cohort. From a family of Nonthaburi province market gardeners, Phibun was born into a sturdy two-story houseboat on a canal not far from Nonthaburi's provincial offices. He graduated at the top of his cadet class at the army staff college and like Pridi then studied on a state scholarship in France. Phibun graduated from the artillery school in Fontainebleau in 1927.[10]

Of the four senior officers, two particularly important in our story are Phraya Song Suradet (1892–1944) and Phraya Phahon Phonpayuhasena (1888–1947). Close friends, the two men were army colonels sympathetic to the frustrations of junior officers who led the military planning for the revolution.[11] Song, of mixed Thai-Vietnamese descent, studied military science in Germany as did Phahon, whose Chinese father rose in the government service and became an ennobled civil servant. Both were linked personally as well to the original Promoters through Prayun Phamonmontri (1897–1982), a former royal page, army officer and then military reservist studying political science in France who came from a palace and government-connected family. Prayun's father had taught Song and Phahon at the military cadet academy in Bangkok, and Prayun's German mother taught German to Song and Phahon in Bangkok before the two left to study in Germany.[12] Phahon also had an immediate family connection to the Promoters through his nephew, Nep Phahonyothin (1900–1946), a British jurist and then student in political economy at the University of Paris who joined the plotters. Teacher-pupil relationships bred loyalty. Song Suradet and Phibun Songkhram in the army college, and Pridi Banomyong in the justice ministry's law faculty, among others, were revered teachers who used their positions to spread the revolutionary message and win supporters.[13]

As the day of reckoning approached, the plotters pushed ahead but remained wary. In the run up to their strike, the Promoters mainly met at Prayun's house; they kept a pack of playing cards on hand as they sat at a table, in case the police paid a visit.[14] Late in June, the Promoters screwed their courage to the sticking place, and changed Thai history. Heavy rain overnight on June 23 relieved a humid evening, during which the plotters finalized their plans. June 24 dawned refreshingly clear and mild.[15] Song, the logistics chief of the revolution, sent armored cars rumbling through the streets of the Siamese capital Bangkok and they quickly surrounded the ministries and palaces that formed the heart of state power, and cut internal communications. On the pretext of a military exercise, the Promoters sent many military units to the Royal Plaza outside the Ananta Samakhom Throne Hall, the premier symbol of royalism where the king ordinarily met with his senior princely advisers.[16] At 6:00 a.m., the group executed a bluff: Phahon announced to the assembled soldiers at the plaza that the old regime had been deposed and a constitutional system established. Cheers went up from the rebel officers, and the soldiers who were led there on the pretext of a training exercise joined in. In the words of a historian, "Everyone thought everyone else had joined the revolution; and none dared think of resistance."[17] Squat and strong, Phahon then discovered the gates to the throne hall locked, but with the help of an iron bar

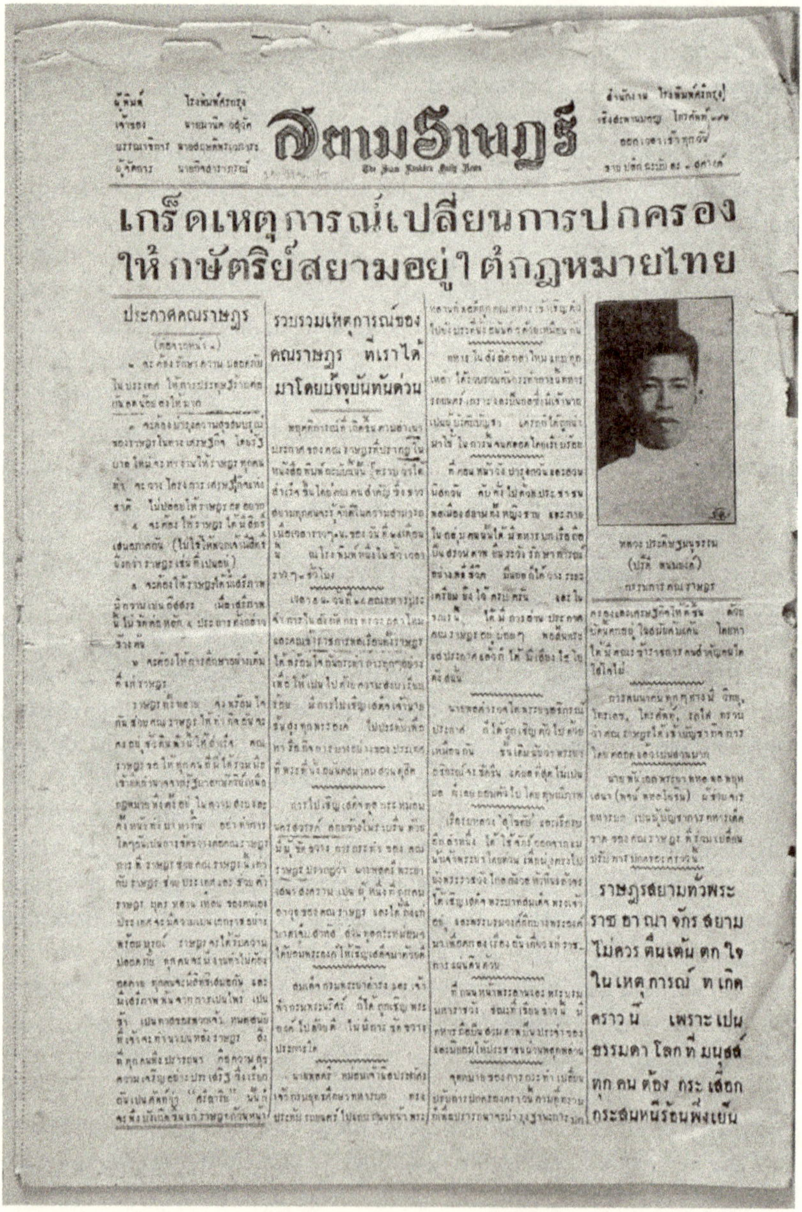

Figure 1.1. The new era: Front page of Siam Ratsadon newspaper, June 24, 1932. The picture shows the thirty-two-year-old Pridi Banomyong, with his official title, Luang Pradit Manudham ("Fashioner of Righteous Men"), and he is listed as "State Councillor, People's Party."

he broke the lock and forced his way into the grounds.[18] The throne hall, seat of royal power, then became the commoner party's headquarters.[19]

Within a few hours, the absolute power of the 150-year-old Thai monarchy had been deposed in Southeast Asia's only independent country. Despite the atmosphere of suspicion of the past few months, the quick strike caught the ruling class unprepared. Many princes were arrested at their palaces, among whom was the interior minister still in his pajamas,[20] and taken hostage along with the senior Bangkok army commanders under the absolute monarchy who were in the city that fateful morning. Remarkably, only one captive was injured in the move against the king and no one was killed. The People's Party established itself at the throne hall that Phahon opened.[21]

Through the afternoon, despite their success, confusion reigned among Bangkok people and civil servants. Nervous soldiers, idled by confusion among the higher ups, whiled away the time drinking and seeking gossip. *Sri Krung* newspaper, one of whose founders had participated in a failed 1912 revolt against the absolute monarchy, became the lifeline for news-hungry Bangkokians. The paper supported the Promoters, and printed flyers free of charge for the group to disseminate; onlookers saw many military cadets racing to and from *Sri Krung*'s offices with flyers for distribution. The editor of the paper that day was as important as anyone in Bangkok, and people crowded his offices all day seeking information.[22]

The People's Party manifesto that *Sri Krung* printed that June morning announced that the king's government had "treated the people as slaves and animals" and intentionally kept them in ignorance, because "if the people have education they will know the evil" that has been done to them.[23] To the Promoters, the world's last absolutist system was an oppressive and embarrassing anachronism in an age of popular authority. They issued a six-point proclamation of their aims: to maintain the country's independence; to maintain public safety and greatly reduce crime; to improve the economic well-being of the people by securing full employment and making a national economic plan; to provide equal rights for all so as to eliminate princely privileges; to give people all lawful liberty and freedoms; and to provide universal education.[24] The People's Party pledged to limit kingly power in the name of popular welfare and empowerment. They proclaimed, "The time has ended when those of royal blood farm on the backs of the people," and "When we have seized the money which those of royal blood amass from farming on the backs of the people, and use these many hundreds of millions for nurturing the country, the country will certainly flourish."[25] Initially, the rebels suggested that a president may be appointed and a republic formed if King Prajadhipok refused to accept limited monarchy.[26] By the early afternoon, the group had consolidated their power. Prince Boriphat Sukhumphan Kromphra Nakhonsawanwora-phinit,[27] a wealthy royal and the most powerful minister in the kingdom, and the man arrested in his pajamas early that morning, acknowledged the group's governance in a public announcement. As interior minister and also military governor of Bangkok, he recognized the People's Party and called on "all military and civilians to maintain public peace and avoid all unnecessary bloodshed."[28]

Other senior royals fled ahead of capture by the People's Party and traveled by train to King Prajadhipok (r. 1925–1935) at the king's seaside palace *Klai Kangwon* (Far from Worry), a few hours south of Bangkok. Playing golf on the palace course that afternoon, the king was surprised by a hurrying courier bearing a telegram notifying him of the revolt. He faced an uncertain future. By midnight on the 24th, the king huddled with senior advisers and family members to evaluate his options. The majority opinion favored a military counteroffensive, comprising four major units that would descend from the provinces on Bangkok and defeat the rebels. They discounted the People's Party strength and avowed that their "will was equal to or greater than the force of arms" against them and that the people of Bangkok were loyal to the monarchy and would fight for it. The minority argued that the People's Party did not mean to liquidate the monarchy, and that the king had two options: to leave the country and negotiate with the rebels; or return to Bangkok and cooperate with the People's Party to govern under a constitution. Senior princes from the military and ministries advised a fight; the king's wife and her parents favored capitulation to the rebels' demands by returning to Bangkok.[29]

The confusion of events vexed the king. He could not be sure whether the People's Party were a small group without larger backing, or whether they represented the thin end of a dangerous wedge of princely resentment against the king and his series of bureaucratic layoffs, meant to balance the government's budget in the depression crisis, which cashiered many elite civil servants over the prior years. What was Prince Boriphat's role in acknowledging the People's Party? An ambitious and powerful man, was he too somehow involved in the plot?[30]

The king recalled that his first instinct was abdication but his father-in-law talked him out of it on the grounds that it would lead to bloodshed and perhaps even invite in foreign powers that would end Siamese independence. Armed resistance, as suggested by the loyal military leaders, was possible but the king thought the People's Party might massacre the senior princes held as captives. "I felt I could not sit on a throne besmirched by blood."[31] Prajadhipok recalled that when he decided to return to Bangkok "[w]e were all quite aware that we were probably going to our death." His wife the queen and her mother both argued firmly for returning: "[T]he ladies preferred death to dishonour and that was enough for me," as the king wrote soon afterward to a nephew.[32]

The king opted to cooperate with the rebels, and within two days agreed to the curtailment of his power. On June 27, a constitution hastily written by Pridi Banomyong vested sovereign power in the people, established an appointed national assembly, laid out a ten-year plan for a fully elected assembly, and guaranteed legal equality, individual freedom and right of association.[33] On the 28th, the throne hall became the seat of the national assembly, and the members arranged in a semicircle facing the assembly president for the first time at 4:00 p.m. that day. Chaophraya Thammasakmonri, a senior ennobled old regime officer, became the president, and appointed Pridi as the secretary to the assembly. Pridi then called for all members to swear an oath of allegiance to the citizenry they represented, and the Promoters' six principles.[34] The People's Party had triumphed, introduced a democratic system, and changed Thai history.

What was the event to be called? Initially, the People's Party lacked a single designation for their historic feat and left an excited public in the dark about what exactly had taken place. The group first that summer used the phrase "change the system of government in which the king is above the law to the system . . . in which the king is under the law."[35] They also resorted to the French phrase "coup d'état," or *rathaprahan* in Thai, to describe their success. Prince Wan Waithayakon, a key old-regime statesman and owner of a widely read Thai newspaper of the times, however, said these formulations were too wordy and formulaic ("change the system of government"), or completely wrong ("coup d'état"), since they did not capture the event's historic significance. Prince Wan, a committed constitutional monarchist but among those princes whom the king suspected on the day he learned of the revolt might be behind the People's Party movement, imagined something much more dramatic. In early 1933, the prince legitimized the event by inventing a new Thai word—*patiwat*—to fix June 24 as a "revolution," which he described as a fundamental, and fundamentally beneficial change to the political system for all the people.[36] This was especially urgent since *kabot*, an illegitimate action, until then

Figure 1.2. A euphoric beginning: A government officer distributes copies of the People's Party manifesto to excited city people on the morning of June 24, 1932.

was still the gloss of the English-language political revolution.[37] While ending absolutism was the immediate aim, Prince Wan's words aspired to something more than legal curtailment of the king's power. Prince Wan's singular designation, also however masked an astoundingly complex and contradictory social result.

The Past as Prologue:
The Rapid Rise and Fall of Thai Absolutism

Members of a young generation born around 1900 are the main actors in this book. They grew up in a recently politically integrated kingdom that experienced rapid and uneven socioeconomic change. And, like neighboring European colonies, the Siamese state was subordinate to Western power. Modern Thai history dates from the 1855 Bowring Treaty, the first of many foreign treaties that the Siamese kings were forced to sign and that mandated trade with low customs dues and diplomatic immunity for foreigners. Western imperialism and capitalism opened the door to Siam and profoundly shaped society, politics and the economy.[38] The kings responded to the power of the West by centralizing their rule in the Bangkok dynasty. Centralization began in earnest in the 1880s under the reign of King Chulalongkorn (r. 1868–1910), the fifth king of the dynasty, and produced a new absolutist state in the 1890s. "Young Siam"—as the cohort around the young king styled itself—was comprised of avowed modernizers. They transformed the country by implementing European-derived techniques of modern commercial law to further economic development, civil and criminal law to forge an international standard legal system, administrative rationalization and mapping, contemporary education, and a modern military.[39] All of these changes directly shaped the People's Party's careers and outlooks.

At the same time, a basic contradiction emerged that inspired the revolutionaries. Legal reforms after 1892 began creation of a common legal regime for all Siamese and shrank the distance between the social classes. The monarchy from the fifth reign popularized the use of *ratsadon*—citizen—as a comprehensive category for the people, the same word the People's Party would adopt for their moniker, and also developed official nationalism that theoretically bound all people together.[40] A discourse from Thai tradition that distanced rulers from ruled, however, accompanied material and politico-legal modernization. The regime pitched its legitimacy not only on Western notions of civility and Western laws and administration, but also revamped indigenous elements that highlighted the ruler's charisma and spiritual superiority (*barami*).

Christine Gray presented this conflicted source of legitimacy as the main antinomy in the historical rationale for Thai kingship, and a damned either way scenario for the monarchs: if they became too Westernized in governance, they lost the link—invented or otherwise—to the sacrality of ancient kingship; if they remained preoccupied with rituals, and costly ceremonies, their Western colonial neighbors viewed them as crackpot oriental despots and they faced potential takeover from the Western powers.[41] A balancing act followed, which the Chakri kings maintained by asserting their *barami*, and also presenting themselves as the most professionally capable. Chulalongkorn consciously advanced his personal moral and spiritual authority, and the importance of bureaucratic-monarchic rituals. The king insisted that high officials attend state *and* royal ceremonies,[42] and one observer remembered that in the fifth reign "few weeks pass without the occurrence of some new festival or ceremony."[43]

The fifth king's appearance and state apparatus put him on a par with European monarchs and statesmen, but around him developed a royalist culture where privilege purportedly stemmed from the aura of the righteous Buddhist kings. The "high" imperialist era of state building produced in Siam an unprecedented mixture of European and local elements of political legitimacy. And while the European states that held colonies in Southeast Asia practiced some type of democracy at home but dictatorship in the region, the modernizing Bangkok state was singularly authoritarian.

The political economy of high imperialism created modern Siam as an absolutist state. As one newspaper writer argued in 1927, there was nothing particularly Thai about absolute monarchy.[44] The short life of absolutism, despite its pretensions of longevity, is remarkable. Rising and falling within forty years, absolutism had an uneven social impact and gives us a picture of an entity powerful and weak simultaneously.[45] On the one hand, in some places absolutism profoundly changed customary politics. On the other, wide swathes of the population were barely integrated into the absolutist state. The roots of Bangkok state "tradition"—absolutism's supposed link with the Thai past—also are superficial. Without an absolutism historically entrenched and far reaching, attachment to the monarchy was limited mainly to Bangkok and its immediate hinterland.

And as it modernized, the state faced a series of political crises that exposed its fragility. In the fifth reign the initial bureaucratic infight pitted the king against senior princes and then later a second tussle developed between elite bureaucrats and the younger generation of commoner civil servants.[46] Moreover, the generation of 1900 found that no sooner had the leaders of their parents' generation begun to remake the country with Bangkok at its center than the changes they initiated undermined the absolutist state's control and produced conflict in a poorly controlled hinterland: the 1893 crisis imposed by France that resulted in the surrender of claimed territory; another reduction in claimed territory in 1907;[47] and peasant and millenarian revolts in 1902 against the fiscal and political power of the new state.[48]

The hybrid ideology of Young Siam thus soon seemed out of date. The threat also came from much closer to home. The 1912 plot from within the military sought to set up a republic.[49] The 1912 plotters directly inspired the People's Party, not least because of their criticism of absolutism's smug princes. Judging by public criticism and recollections by leading People's Party members, the old regime elite in the early twentieth century seemed more interested in patronage than social problems or threats to national sovereignty. The highest jobs in the administrative system established from 1892 went to the royal-aristocratic class and widespread favoritism undermined the supposed meritocracy of the civil service. While nonroyals benefited from the expansion of the civil service, in King Prajadhipok's reign an oligarchy of senior princes closely held power. The most powerful man in the kingdom was not the king, but Prince Boriphat, who adamantly opposed any plan to reform politics.[50]

Prominent People's Party members criticized the way people behaved. Song Suradet remembered that: "Government officials (of the old regime) felt nothing, except that they were appointed to be the masters of the people and they sought the chance to become the king's clients so that he would grant them salary increases and promotions." General disinterest in social problems among those fawning and flattering the king angered and motivated the revolutionaries. For the officials without a social conscience: "The nation's business could wait, and the losses to the country that followed did not shame them."[51] Phahon, the senior most People's Party member, recalled: "In the old civil service senior people and bosses generally did as they pleased. They were not interested in the views of subordinates, no matter how sound or important the issue."[52] Kulap Saipradit, a progressive journalist, supported the People's Party and interviewed Phahon. Son of a railways clerk, Kulap resented the elite privilege that rested on the contingency of high birth. In a newspaper article written just after the June takeover, he summarized much feeling that ran against the old regime and its members who claimed to be extraordinary.

> The royal family may have both smart and stupid people. They may be both ignorant and arrogant. This is what led the absolute monarchy down a hopeless path and led people increasingly to realize that birth had nothing to do with goodness.[53]

Song, Phahon, and Kulap criticized the highest levels of the hierarchy, but many people after 1932 labeled snobbery, fawning, and flattery of any and all superiors as pernicious old regime degeneracies. Such behavior grew from the state's expanding power. Institutional modernization created wide differences in wealth, power and knowledge—as the People's Party manifesto quoted above highlighted—and critics used all three as weapons against a seemingly out-of-touch absolutist system. Moreover, critics would use examples and ideas from overseas in their polemics. Globalized communications made Thais aware of politics in distant countries, and by the

1920s members of the young generation reflected on their situation to a degree unmatched by their elders. Thai "exceptionalism"—the kingly state's supposedly unique, controlled, and harmonious path to modernity—has always been greatly overstated. At no time is this more evident than in the interwar years. As in other societies, the shocks of the high imperialist era affected everyone, and the tools to deal with profound change were borrowed from around the world.

To many in the young generation, socioeconomic change made absolutism an oppressive anachronism. As the People's Party manifesto claimed, it was time to dispose of the world's last absolute kingship. But in a largely illiterate peasant society, state modernization far outpaced the growth of any vigorous social movements or independent institutions that might successfully challenge absolutism. Unlike the social ferment during the long gestations of the absolutist states of Europe, or the long history of peasant movements in China that challenged dynasties, Siam had no political parties, religious fraternities or peasant brotherhoods opposed to the Chakri state reforms. Instead, the social composition of Siam in the early 1930s comprised four main occupational groups: the senior government officers from royal families and those ennobled for state service; the bureaucracy; the middle classes outside of the bureaucracy, especially in commerce and independent professions like journalism and publishing; and the peasant and working classes.[54]

At the top, roughly 1,200 senior bureaucrats held sway over a kingdom of around 12 million people in the early 1930s; one-third or so of this number were politically active.[55] A main bureaucratic driver of the revolution came from the service's middle and lower tiers—which had about 72,000 members in 1932—and especially from the military, law, teaching, and local government.[56] A commercial middle class of mixed Thai-Chinese parentage, around 6 percent of the adult population,[57] managed the economy. Additionally, among these middle classes is the extra-bureaucratic intelligentsia, around 1.25 percent of the population,[58] especially important in journalism and publishing. Print capitalism in the interwar years revolutionized public consciousness. Lone rebels criticized the monarchy from the late nineteenth century, but they were mainly self-published. By the 1920s, however, the press in diverse, often short-lived serials, stood in for political association. Public reading quickly mushroomed. More than 160 newspapers and magazines circulated in the fifteen years of the reign of King Vajiravudh (r. 1910–1925).[59] From 1925 to 1935, 212 papers circulated, with around 50 new papers established after 1932.[60]

The elements of the middle class, in the civil service, commerce and independent professions, lived well. As Marc Bloch described the corresponding class in Europe: "[T]hey, compared to most of their countrymen, lived in relative ease and had a sense of security that no laborer enjoyed . . . Their modern education was usually richer in texture and better in quality than most people's. And by a thousand little details of dress, language and good manners (they show themselves) as among a very special group that enjoys high prestige in the eyes of less fortunate mortals."[61]

Manual work, by contrast, did govern the waking hours of most people. Roughly 83 percent of adults were farmers, and most could not read. The revolution appeared in a fragmented society without much associational life beyond the village. Millions of upcountry people were born, lived, and died in places seldom or never visited by Bangkok officials. Around 2 percent of the working population labored in industry, primarily in Bangkok but also in some country areas tied to mining, forestry, and the like. They too had minimal or no schooling.

The broad support for the People's Party by diverse and unrelated cliques and groups—mainly those living with relative ease, security and prestige—is remarkable. But in addition to the total enthusiasts are the others who supported the ideals of the new regime but not its practices, and those who violently rejected the entire project. Partial, disruptive modernization produced a mosaic of relative influence and wealth within even the same occupational group. In this complex social composition, the People's Party could not control the changes they set in motion.

A Shaky Coalition Forms and Royalists Fight Back

The People's Party, passionate spokesmen for the masses, upended a young absolute monarchy and found support among related groups who also both benefited from and were disadvantaged by the state's uneven modernization. The Promoters faced immediate threats. In the first flush of their surprise victory, old regime enemies rather than newfound supporters greatly concerned them. The Promoters would not have gained power without military support. In addition to imprisoning senior princes, among their first moves the Promoters cashiered all old regime princes who were senior military officers, and restructured the military and police hierarchies to favor the young cohort and centralize power in the army.[62] In a matter of days, the old royalist top-heavy military cohort had been eliminated. People's Party officers moved into the key positions. But other decisions made in the first days of the new regime would profoundly shape the entire People's Party era by leaving royals embittered but not entirely removed from power. Key administrative positions remained with the old regime, and many of the old guard moved into the new national assembly. Moreover, indecision on how to limit the king's power haunted the People's Party.

For the first three days in postabsolutist Siam, the army governed the country, directed by Phahon. From June 27, Pridi's provisional constitution introduced a new administration. On June 26, leading People's Party members went to see the king at his Bangkok palace. They sought his formal, signed forgiveness for the strongly worded attack on the monarchy in the group's manifesto of two days previously, and to present the king with Pridi's draft constitution. The king instantly agreed to and signed the document pardoning them. The group then read to him the constitution Pridi wrote. Prajadhipok replied that he needed some time to read it himself; the revolutionary emissaries told him he had one hour to examine the document and sign it. The king was not cowed by their demand, left the room, and reappeared an hour later asking for some more time to examine the document since he did not understand it all. The revolutionaries gave him one day, by which time Prajadhipok had cleverly inserted "temporary" (*chua khrao*) in the title of the June constitution.[63]

Pridi's constitution is notable for its plain language and democratic spirit. To supporters it embodies the revolution's promise.[64] The preamble explains that the People's Party called for the king to reign under the constitution. The first and second clauses state that supreme power belongs to the people, and that power is exercised on behalf of the people by the king, plainly referred to as *kasat*, the national assembly, the executive People's Committee (Khana Kammakan Ratsadon) and the courts.[65] The fifteen initial members of the People's Committee were Committee Men or Commissars (Kammakan), chosen by the assembly, who formed a politically charged administrative group that did not have clear ministerial jurisdiction. And here lies one of the original checks to People's Party control. Bureaucratic power politics shaped the revolution, and stymied the immediate chances for a socially radical movement to develop from the wellspring of resentment of privilege. To govern effectively, the People's Party compromised with the old regime.

Despite the Bolshevik sounding language of the June administration—which matches the radical tone of the first People's Party manifesto—the committee and the top comprised many old regime figures. The Phraya-rank Manopakon Nithitida, a senior justice ministry officer close to the king became the first premier or Chairman, as he was termed in English. Pridi knew Mano from the law ministry, and thus the choice was a political move relying on a personal connection. The first national assembly (Sapha Phuthen Ratsadon) comprised seventy appointed legislators, more than half of whom were old regime professionals. In large measure, the first assembly became a civil service assembly. In speaking to ministerial heads on the afternoon of June 24, Pridi explained the reasoning of the People's Party.

> Ordinarily a national assembly is elected based on the citizens' wants. We cannot do this right away, and so initially we thought to have the makers of the change sit in the assembly. However, while our group has some education, most still are very young and inexperienced. Hence we decided to invite senior civil servants and other professionals who are concerned about the nation to join the assembly.[66]

Fewer than half comprised the civilian, progressive wing from the People's Party that backed Pridi. To be sure, these spirited democrats were important in countering kingly power. They also demonstrated that the new government was not merely a front for the military group within the People's Party, and that civilians played a key role in shaping the new government.[67] Still, the initially radical language of the government belied a complex arrangement of forces. People's Party, people's representatives, people's committee, commissars: all of these strong, republican words masked a hybrid regime governed by a combination of old-regime titled elites and young radicals and backed by the power of new generation military officers and their networks. Thereafter in the first months of the People's Party era a drafting committee headed by Mano and made up almost entirely of old-regime conservatives, Pridi being the lone exception, wrote a permanent constitution. The December 10, 1932, permanent constitution endured until 1946. Thai historians have well explained that a conservative legal faction exercised great clout in 1932, and they came mainly from British legal backgrounds. These men asserted royal privilege and also attempted to forge the link between Siamese kingly and British monarchic traditions of a customary, centuries old contribution to modern constitutional law.[68] The king, demoted and slighted by the People's Party takeover, regained importance. Mano explicitly stated the reliance on the king in the constitutional process.

> The drafting committee was in constant contact with the king during the process, to the point where you might say that it was entirely a cooperative effort . . . the king's approval (of the document) was not merely an affirmation of what was presented to him, but much more than that it was in agreement with what he desired.[69]

The language of the resulting constitution shows the royalist conservative political counterattack in the few months after the June takeover.[70] *Ponlamueang*—people—instead of *ratsadon*, exercised sovereignty. Using people instead of citizens may sound like a quibble, but actually was a charged rhetorical move; *ratsadon* excludes the monarchy; *ponlamueang* includes it. The king's input into the drafting is clear in other areas. He objected to his demotion in the interim constitution's language to a mere social category, *kasat* (warrior-king), which existed on a political par with the assembly, the executive and the courts in Pridi's constitution. He said this was not appropriate to a spiritually superior monarch. In the December 10 constitution, he was termed as in absolutist days as *Phra Mahakasat* (Great Sovereign) and stands above, and was inviolate compared to, the other organs of the state.[71] The preamble to the December constitution jettisoned the plain language of the June constitution and monarchic status zoomed into the metaphysical stratosphere.

> King Pratchathipok: the great power of the world, a king in the Chakkri Dynasty; the great in the Sun's Dynasty who is God's beloved; a pure descendant of the Kings who are warriors; the great man of the royal family; the king of the world; the great emperor with pure high birth . . . a superb example of men; well-known everywhere; full of merits from the former life; an incarnation of God . . . [i]ncomparably mighty and powerful under the auspices of all the benevolent gods . . .[72]

Apart from spiritually exalting the king, the December constitution also adopted more conservative vocabulary. The permanent constitution created a twenty-person Council of State (Khana Rathamontri) instead of the People's Committee, led by a Premier (Nayok Rathamontri) and the individual members became State Councillors (Rathamontri) instead of commissars. Until June 1933, the Council of State comprised mainly old-regime professionals.[73]

Despite monarchists' gains, they felt threatened still and their bitterness grew. Between December and the early months of the following year the conflict between royalists and revolutionaries deepened. Displaying an impressive hypocrisy, the king's party accused the revolutionaries of ushering in an age of tyranny. As we now well know, the monarchy and royalists from the beginning used the press to undermine the People's Party and contributed directly to the series of crises that emerged afterward and pushed the People's Party further to the "right" as a matter of survival. The king's father-in-law Prince Svasti, who advised capitulation to the People's Party demands in June 1932, secretly supported several widely read newspapers opposed to the revolutionaries, especially the *Bangkok Daily Mail*, *Siam Num*, and *Thai Mai*.[74] A letter to the government from the period reflected what was widely known at the time, and advised keeping an eye on the above three mentioned.[75] Another advised that a plot may be afoot within the shareholders of the *Siam Num* group, under the management of Hom Nilawat na Ayutthaya.[76] These private letter writers echoed what the opposition papers wrote openly.

The People's Party's relative weakness in the first months of the revolution produced a confused public debate on the scope of the new democracy. Whom did the new regime represent? Would political parties be allowed to form? The People's Party transformed itself soon after June 1932, a process that gives a clue how the Promoters saw themselves. They branched out into a bigger organization, but kept real power at the core.

The People's Party in the first months of the revolution occupied an uncertain legal position. As a political and public relations strategy, leading members established the People's Party Association at the end of August 1932 as a juristic legal entity. Soon after the takeover of power, the Promoters encouraged people to join this new association. Ronasit Phichai, a Promoter from the army, appealed on radio for members at the end of June. Beating back public misunderstanding, Ronasit emphasized that the new organization did not employ people.[77] The association occupied prime Bangkok real estate: the king gave it the Saranrom public gardens for its activities at the same time that he gave the People's Party Parutsakawan Palace as the Promoters' headquarters and the new government house.[78] The association pledged to support constitutionalism and realize the People's Party's six principles,[79] and the government announced that once the new national assembly were in place, there would be no need for the People's Party and the association would take its place.[80] Original June 1932 Promoters, leaders of the failed 1912 rebellion, and local civil servant electors "who were not above politics" (i.e., royals) all joined. Additionally, young people between sixteen and twenty could also join as junior members if they had nominees. From Bangkok, the association spread its network upcountry and sustained itself in part with member dues.[81] Nitisat Paisal became the chair, and leading Promoters comprised the association's executive. Nitisat's public life—both monarchist and pro-People's Party—encapsulates the new regime's odd composition. The British-educated lawyer served the old regime as a justice ministry official and was one of the drafters of the permanent constitution of December 10 that gave much power back to the king. At the time of the association's founding, Nitisat was the chief judge of the criminal court.[82] He did not join in the original People's Party cohort, but became a supporter and helped establish the democratically inspired Thammasat University in 1934 that opened higher education to everyone. After the revolution, Nitisat argued first on radio and then in a book that opposition parties were contradictory to social stability since they would automatically adopt an antagonistic position to whatever the ruling party does. In a frequent refrain heard in many periods of modern Thai political history, Nitisat argued that there were more pressing issues—security, economic development, foreign affairs—that would not be solved if interparty conflicts festered.[83]

Under his stewardship, as a leading scholar of the period explains, the association functioned as a microcosm of the People's Party government and the Promoters dominated its management. Between September and December 1932, the association expanded into the provinces, enrolled new members, opened provincial assembly halls and engaged in philanthropy, for example, donating new robes to the Sangha. By the end of 1932, the association had 14,000 members in thirty provinces, nearly half of the country. Initially the only revenue came from sales of Nitisat's constitutional primer, but in ensuing months the association diversified revenue into issuance of commemorative coins, fees collected at democratic fairs, and constitutional celebration festivals.[84]

Pridi stated that people joined the association out of democratic fervor. The expansion into the many thousands is astounding, but we know almost nothing about why people enrolled. Why, for example, did many professional women join the group? Here and in some other cases, a scant historical record offers general information without individual stories, and frustrates a better understanding of what people wanted from, or imputed to, the new political system. Scholars thus have focused on the association's elite. Thamrongsak termed it a "civil service party." In this view, even though the association was very large, it revolved around government officers from the senior administrative service: provincial governors, judges, magistrates, senior educational officers, and police chiefs.[85] Accordingly, it is difficult to tell the government and the association apart, ordinary people had a limited role, and through the new outfit the Promoters colonized society. It is likely that many joined for career security. Two leading ministries—defense and interior—encouraged their civil servants to join, and many probably signed up for fear of losing professional opportunity and political favor.[86]

Indeed, the educated public complained in some cases that the association was a sham. Phra Dunyaphak Suwaman (1894–1982), for example, worked in 1932 as the chief judge in Nakhon Sri Thammarat province in the far south. Dunyaphak was a committed constitutionalist who went on to serve many administrations, and a man whose morality stemmed from committed Buddhist practice. He became good friends around this time with Buddhadasa Bhikkhu, destined to be Thailand's most famous intellectual monk of the twentieth century. Dunyaphak's personal decency aside, his route to career advancement involved the People's Party network. He became chair of the Nakhon Sri Thammarat provincial sub-committee of the association via a hidden process. Ostensibly elections chose management of provincial branches, but to critics the choice, like that of Dunyaphak, seemed to be predetermined by insiders. Opponents of the People's Party used his case and that of others to allege that the new democracy was an oligarchy.[87]

The high number of new regime-connected elite civil servants who benefited from the association aggravated opponents, and was duly exploited by old-regime reactionaries. *Thai Mai*—one of the newspapers supported by the king's father-in-law—accused the People's Party Association of being a privileged power in the provinces.[88] The likewise royalist-backed *Bangkok Daily Mail* waxed about political ethics and expressed the worst possibility.

> It is only from the juxtaposition of the thoughts and actions of men that communal wisdom arises. If there is but one party, there can be no democracy, there can only be autocracy and demagoguery. We are forced to continue to believe that the People's Party Association has all the potential evils of a fascist organization.[89]

After the government introduced the second constitution in December 1932, royalist opposition to the People's Party coincided with other challengers. In the latter part of 1932 Luang Wichit Wathakan, a thirty-four-year-old intellectual polymath, announced plans to form the Samakhom Khana Chat—the Nationalist Party Association (hereafter, the Nationalist Party or the Khana Chat). Wichit had worked in the foreign affairs ministry, lectured in history at Chulalongkorn University and was editor of *Thai Mai* newspaper. While still a young man, he already had years of experiences as a writer and public intellectual. Just before the revolution he had started his own newspaper, and filled it with history, philosophy, and politics. In August 1932, he resigned from government in protest at the People's Party's closure of *Thai Mai* for criticism of the new regime.[90] From a middle-class Chinese trading family, and through ambition, talent, and patronage, he rose from a humble background to become one of the leading intellectual figures of the times.[91] Wichit worked in Paris in the 1920s as an assistant to the secretary of the Thai Legation. There he met and became friends with Pridi and Phibun.[92] He was a political chameleon; and like Nitisat Paisal and other leading figures after the revolution, he both supported and criticized monarchy, and applauded and censured the People's Party. In the latter 1930s he strongly supported Phibun's military wing in the People's Party, and then continued making a career backing autocrats in the middle of the century. In this initial phase of the revolution, he wrote several books that asked compelling questions about the scope of the democracy and he challenged the People's Party to expand popular rule. In November 1932, Wichit in his book *Kanmueang kanpokhrong Syam* (*Siamese Politics and Administration*) argued that it was the citizenry's right under the December constitution's article 14 to form political parties. Just before then, in October Wichit had resigned from government service and found allies to set up the Nationalist Party. Some came from journalism, for example, Luen Saraphaiwanich and Luy (Louis) Girivat, two writers and editors from the *Bangkok Daily Mail*. Others were senior titled civil servants from the old regime, including Phraya Sena Songkhram—the only casualty of the June takeover—Phraya Thephasadin na Ayuthaya and several other men.[93] Phraya Thonawanikamontri, one of the founders who had studied in the United States and held a senior position in an old-regime ministry, explained the rationale.

The founding was to fulfill complete legislative governance of the democratic system. That is, a party that was elected to the minority would act to check the majority party, and not allow the government party to exercise power solely as they saw fit, which would be counter to the interests or welfare of particular groups.[94]

Many of the founders would later join in the ill-fated Bowondet rebellion,[95] but at this stage they sought a peaceful route to power. In January 1933, the Nationalist Party applied for legal recognition. It termed itself a Nationalist Party to distinguish it from the "citizen" party that was the People's Party, a name that hinted at both a broader and a narrower member base. It included and aimed at royals who were explicitly banned from politics by the constitution's article 11, and it also imposed high membership fees that kept out modest commoners.[96] The founding statements submitted to the government reiterated the People's Party agenda: maintaining the kingdom's sovereignty and independence, protection of the constitution and the monarchy, and support for the peasantry and labor, for example. It also stated, however, that it would train people in political education, support them in elections and form a government if elected.[97]

The People's Party divided on the issue. Pridi met with Wichit in January 1933, and endorsed the establishment of the Nationalist Party. Nitisat, by contrast, argued against recognizing the new party since in pending elections he warned the People's Party might lose the vote to the nationalists.[98] Sim Wirawaithya and Sanguan Tularaks, two radical members of the People's Party who did not come from the civil service, criticized the nationalists via their *Sajjang* (Truth) and *24 Mithuna* (June 24) newspapers. Mano styled these two as Pridi's Moggallana and Sariputra, after the two intensely loyal disciples of the historical Buddha. Mano also saw their newspapers as the *Pravda* of Siam.[99] *Sajjang* pronounced that the "Nationalist Party is a party for a small number of rich people. It is a party dangerous to the workers and peasants."[100] Under the criticism, the Khana Chat remained in legal limbo but was nonetheless a political reality.

A study of the problems with the People's Party revolution argues that Pridi and Wichit—two prominent public figures with influential supporters, the Thomas Jefferson and Alexander Hamilton of Siam—missed a golden opportunity to establish a two-party system that could have put Siam on the road to democratic viability.[101] The point is interesting food for thought, even though modern history of supposedly mature Western democracies shows that often established political parties undermine rather than strengthen the system. And, given the developing climate of antagonism and the gains made by the king's party under the December constitution, the choice and the responsibility did not rest with these two men alone. Not only the People's Party, but King Prajadhipok and Mano too were ambivalent about the Khana Chat's purpose and utility. The iconic view of Prajadhipok highlights his democratic aspirations, most notably expressed in the historic abdication statement of March 1935, where he expressed a willingness to surrender power to the people as a whole but not to an oligarchy.[102] And during the drafting of the permanent constitution in November 1932, Prajadhipok gave a speech championing the formation of political parties as an essential part of democracy.[103] But Prajadhipok like his father and half-brother who sat on the throne before him had long doubted the suitability of representative politics for Siam.[104] Prajadhipok's optimistic speech in November 1932 perhaps reflected a belief that with a renewed monarchic power anticipated under the December constitution he could control politics. But by early 1933 he had tempered his enthusiasm.

The king, Mano and the king's close advisor Phraya Sriwisanwaja met in late January, and Prajadhipok decided that no parties should form until the people were better educated. In a cabinet meeting the following month, Mano instructed, and the majority endorsed, decertification of the legal status of the People's Party Association. Mano stressed that all bureaucrats and assemblymen must resign from the association within a two-month grace period. In April 1933, a major crisis erupted over a socialist economic plan that Pridi drafted; the plan horrified the old-regime elites in the government, the wider royalist network, and even generated hostility within the People's Party. With the king's backing,[105] Mano prorogued the parliament, and the government also disbanded the People's Party Association.[106] During this time, however, the cabinet did not discuss the status of the Khana Chat. It seems that the latter was to be a sacrificial animal for the dissolution of the People's Party organization: Wichit told the National Assembly that Mano instructed Wichit, much to the latter's dismay, to fold the Nationalist Party and Mano would then dissolve the People's Party.[107]

Mano and conservatives feared that Pridi's economic plan would become a political party campaign platform that would be endorsed by his large following in the National Assembly. Further, Mano and his supporters feared that if, as Pridi wanted, the status of the People's Party Association should be decided by the assembly then it would endure as a political machine. Puli explains that this accounts for the cabinet-directed dissolution of the association. The day following Mano's proroguing of the assembly his government amended the civil law to ban formation of any group that "posed a threat to the nation." The broad wording targeted the association and set up a no-party political system. Nitisat Paisal, head of the association, was soon thereafter demoted from his directorship of the criminal court and the Association's members pressured to resign.[108] Mano's decree effectively wound up the association. In its place thereafter, a People's Party Club (Samoson Khana Ratsadon) emerged as a tame, apolitical social network mainly of Bangkok citizens. At its height membership was around 1,000. It had no upcountry network, and the government closed it at the end of World War II.[109]

From April 1 until June 20, the Mano government ruled by executive branch and royal decree. There was no assembly. With government by decree under Mano aimed at destroying the People's Party organization, "die hard royalists rejoiced in their belief that the days of the absolute monarchy were returning."[110] Pridi went into exile in Singapore and his followers kept a low profile; Sanguan Tularaks for example shelved his journalist and political careers and became a farmer in his home province for several months. A Prajadhipok loyalist told Prayun Phamonmontri, one of the original Promoters who became the deputy chair of the People's Party Association, that the royalists had planned to execute the People's Party leaders in this period. The bloodletting was planned for June 24, the first anniversary of the revolution, when sixty People's Party members would be decapitated and their heads placed on spikes in public.[111]

The Bowondet Rebellion and the End of Conciliation

During this heated period, Prajadhipok wrote the following from his Hua Hin palace in March 1933:

> They (the People's Party) say they "love the nation," and reserve power to themselves. They pocket money for themselves. For my part, if I "love the nation" I have to give up my power, and become a slave . . . I want to do something really extreme but am afraid that the lords will all have their throats cut. But people's sacrifice has a limit . . . We here (at Klai Kangwon) have lots of plans, but we do not disclose them for fear that they will get out. But we will put up a damn good fight before we easily submit to our capture.[112]

The fight soon came. On June 20, 1933, the original four senior military commanders of the People's Party staged a coup against Mano and the royalists. Despite the inner conflicts among the plotters that accompanied the June coup,[113] its success saved the revolution. Mano was removed from power and the assembly reinstated but with more new regime supporters and the old guard largely removed. Despite their obvious political power, the military faction in the People's Party felt they lacked policy and purpose, and the cabinet decided to recall Pridi, the intellectual driver of the revolution, from exile when they met in mid-August 1933.[114] Pridi returned to a raucous welcome at the end of September.

An emerging political crisis exacerbated the main problem of the first phase of the People's Party era—the scope of democracy and the role of political parties. Things worsened. The end of the Mano government prompted old-regime military elites and royalists in July 1933 to try and topple the government by force.[115] A meeting of the plotters—the Khana Ku Banmueang (Party to Rescue the Country)—chose Prince Bowondet as leader of the rebellion in October just before the rebellion broke out and the revolt has ever after borne his name.

The origins of the revolt lie in both political and personal conflicts. The leaders unanimously hated the People's Party and viewed Pridi as a communist who would destroy the monarchy.[116] To further the complexity, Bowondet was personally disaffected from many royals and his old-regime fellow plotters.[117] Various elements of the rebellion, especially the Bangkok contingent, did not trust Bowondet. Phraya Srisitthi Songkhram, one of the prime movers of the plot and a colleague of Phahon who also had trained in Germany (and declined an invitation to join the People's Party before June 1932), assured the others that his faction would dispose of Bowondet after victory.[118] According to the later recollection of Queen Rambhaibarni's brother Suphasawat the two different factions belonging to Sitthi and Bowondet hated each other, an enmity that undermined the entire rebellion.[119]

The rebellion spanned October and November 1933, and has been well told in Thai historiography.[120] Before his departure from the northeast garrison of Khorat, where he assembled his soldiers, Bowondet told the Khorat provincial governor that the government was communist, and held a religious ceremony in which Buddhist monks blessed the rebels. By the evening of October 11, Bowondet and Srisitthi's forces had converged on Don Mueang aerodrome and Bang Khen outside Bangkok. Srisitthi wrote to the government that the *Khana ku banmueang* acted because the government was indifferent to public criticism of the king, allowed Pridi to return without clearing him of a charge of communism, which amounted to an agreement with communist ideology. A crisis point had been reached, the letter stated, and the *Khana ku banmueang* could not take any more.[121] They dropped leaflets by plane over the city, the first of several rebel and government airborne propaganda campaigns, which claimed the government was a communist tyranny and that the People's Party would abolish the monarchy and establish a republic.[122]

From Don Mueang aerodrome on October 13, Prince Bowondet wrote to Phahon, informing him of six rebel demands, and also air-dropped the statement over the city. Among the main demands were: restoration of maximum monarchic authority under the constitution; rule by law not threat of arms; permission for political parties to form; removal of civil servants from political positions; and redistribution of military resources evenly among the provincial garrisons.[123] The government ignored the demands, and went on a public relations blitz to win popular support. They issued twenty public announcements between the 11th and the 15th, including a point by point takedown of Bowondet's demands, and more than forty in total by the next week. Wichit Wathakan, from the failed Nationalist Party, now turned against his former party comrades and played a central role writing the communiqués for the government.[124] The government accused Bowondet of lies and deluding his followers, and also reprinted one rebel communiqué where Bowondet criticized the king for being too soft and advanced himself as a more capable monarch.[125] The government offered astounding rewards for information leading to the capture of the leaders: 10,000 baht (about $3,730 at the time[126]) for Bowondet, and 5,000 baht (around $1,865) for Srisitthi.[127]

The first military propaganda campaign in Thai history found widespread support in the press. Managers of large publishing houses, and widely read daily newspapers that printed and distributed many government communiqués, happily waived payment for their work and supplied the government with free newspapers that they could send to the troops fighting the rebels.[128]

October 14 and 15 saw the heaviest fighting of the main crisis of the People's Party years. Participants experienced the continuous roar of battle on the 14th, a noise heard as far away as Pathum Thani and Ayutthaya. On the 15th, Bangkok citizens thronged the Sanam Luang in Bangkok, eager for news, but the government shooed them away since it needed the field as an airplane landing site. Others climbed the Golden

Mount—the highest point in Bangkok—from where they observed and heard the destruction of the battle in the northern suburbs of Bangkok around the aerodrome where Bowondet had camped.[129]

Phibun Songkhram—a Promoter put in charge of suppressing the rebellion—advanced on rebel positions along the rail line outside Bangkok amid monsoon-flooded fields. Soldiers recalled tough-going advancing through sometimes chest-high water.[130] The railways became the means of death. On the 15th the rebels sent an unmanned rail carriage barreling into the government lines at Laksi on the outskirts of Bangkok that killed several soldiers. The episode traumatized participants on both sides. Phibun pushed through, however, and the following day Bowondet led his forces out of northern Bangkok. When the government occupied Laksi they found only corpses and ruin.[131] The climactic battle of the rebellion happened at Hin Lap in the Dong Phrayayen mountain pass in the northeast. The rail line to the northeast had opened the area to swift traffic earlier in the century and forced reconciliation of the northeast to Bangkok's growing power. Now, as in outer Bangkok, the rails became the means of destruction. Bowondet entrusted Srisitthi with the defense. Srisitthi set up his defense from the surrounding heights that looked down upon the pass and rained fire from hidden heavy and light gun emplacements on the government for the entire first day. The battle raged until after dark when the government broke through, having traveled two kilometers from where they began that morning. Srisitthi was killed in the fight, his body photographed and taken back to Bangkok as evidence of the government's victory. The rebels fled back up the line to the northeast without Bowondet's permission, their passage hampered by civilian assistance to the government in sabotaging rail lines.[132]

The rebellion killed fifteen government soldiers, one civilian, one Buddhist monk and eight rebels.[133] These figures roughly correspond to the nineteen killed among the Siamese Expeditionary Force in Europe during the Great War. In a century of unprecedented global brutality, they are trivial. But the psychological and political effect was profound.

Before the rebellion erupted, Prayun Phamonmontri traveled to Hua Hin to meet the king. Then secretary to Mano, once a royal page and a close friend to many royals, Prayun recalled being challenged by royalists. They told him that he and the People's Party would see the power of monarchy very soon, and they all would be beheaded. One called out as he was leaving the palace to return to Bangkok: "Hey, where should we send your head?" Prayun replied that they should wait and see how the rebellion turned out.[134] And indeed the rebellion marked the end of political compromise with the old regime. Bowondet fled to Indochina, and Mano also went overseas. Medan in Sumatra became the center of royalist politics in exile from January 1934, when the king, many senior royals, and an additional two-dozen-plus lesser royals moved there. As Nakharin remarks, it was likely the largest final gathering of royals in Thai history.[135]

The rebellion failed due to internal division among the rebels and poor coordination, undersupply of food, water and ammunition, low morale among the foot-soldiers, and the swift action of Phibun Songkhram and his army.[136] Additionally, popular support for the government doomed the rebellion. The rebellion provoked a widespread reaction against the plotters. Secret communication from sympathetic station masters and rail officials, some far upcountry behind Bowondet's lines in the northeast, greatly helped the government's field operations. So too did sabotage of rail lines ahead of retreating rebel forces.[137] Crucial support came from people in the central province of Lopburi, according to the government,

Figure 1.3. The new regime's unsung heroines: Civilian women volunteers during the Bowondet rebellion, October or November 1933. Photo courtesy of the Phraya Phahon Foundation.

in the form of news sent about rebel movements and transport of stores and munitions.[138] Sanguan Tularaks and Sim Wirawaithaya led a civilian logistics contingent in the field to assist the troops.[139] Volunteer brigades reported to the government for military service but were politely refused. University students helped the police with surveillance of suspected rebel sympathizers, and law students helped the police arrest rebels fleeing from Don Mueang.[140] Labor in a range of industries sought a fighting role. Prajadhipok declared this should not be done, and feared that once the masses had finished with the rebels, they would turn on the lords. A 3,000-strong labor contingent's service was politely refused by Phahon.[141] Labor instead, under Thawatt Rittidej, mobilized in support of the government by forming urban peace and order squads.[142]

Popular support for the government included donated food, money, clothing, medicine, matches, and tobacco. A range of people pledged support. A judge, and former army chief warrant officer from the mid-southern province of Songkhla signed over title to his Studebaker, valued at 900 baht, for the army's use.[143] An Uttaradit province collection yielded nearly 1,500 baht, and included donations large and small, from a

Figure 1.4. Mobilizing support: Mr. Bun Thiam, a People's Party backer, collects supporters to donate to the government cause during the Bowondet rebellion, October or November 1933. Photo courtesy of the Phraya Phahon Foundation.

prince's gift of 150 baht to pennies offered by schoolgirls; and a similarly organized Trang provincial committee forwarded small donations from teachers, farmers, and traders.[144] Some loyal civil servants offered parts of their government pensions.[145] One poor but well-meaning citizen offered his lottery ticket, with the pending draw perhaps garnering 40,000 baht for the government![146] Hospital patients and even prisoners also pledged material support.[147] Big donors, meanwhile, included the wealthy and famous, large businesses like Siam Cement or Sri Krung Press, and the People's Party Association.

The national archives in Bangkok have preserved evidence of very strong popular support for the regime during this major rebellion of the 1930s. Popular backing for the regime appears more as tribalism than democratic enthusiasm. Once Srisitthi's photograph was published, people in the provinces people struck it and tore at the picture. Phahon publicly condemned widely distributed lampoons of Prince Bowondet as a fat man riding a pig into battle. Some people advised all-out war on the royals. A writer from Bangkok wrote to the government advising that the People's Party should not rest but pursue other royalists in the state ministries who were being funded from the royal network in the Dutch East Indies.[148] The surveillance and vendetta advocates echoed a muscular aspect of popular support for the revolution that appeared soon after June 24.[149] How the times have changed. As with so many aspects of 1932's memory, the contemporary junta has upended history. In late 2019, the prime minister formally opened the "Phraya Srisitthi Songkhram and Bowondet" room in the army museum to praise these men and to honor the current king. Srisitthi's relatives are central to his rehabilitation: his grandson Surayudh Chulanont engineered the 2006 coup and is a privy councillor today.[150]

With full spiritual solemnity, the People's Party commemorated the government's victory and the sacrifices of commoners in the struggle. In February 1934, the government held a cremation ceremony at Sanam Luang, the royal field outside the Grand Palace, for the fallen soldiers and police. The ritual marked the first time in Bangkok's history that commoners were accorded such respect, which the government publicized widely, including by a government magazine devoted to the ceremony.[151] The government issued commemorative medals to the forces and planned a three-volume printed set that included chronicle of the events, eyewitness accounts and government documents with the assistance of pro-government newspapers. The editor of *Sri Krung*, a man who also was an assembly representative, undertook to lead the work.[152]

The People's Party Turns on Its Enemies:
Prisoners in the Wake of Bowondet

The government also took more directly repressive measures, and moved unyieldingly against rebellion.[153] In the wake of the rebellion's crushing, the government resurrected a 1927, absolutist law, that targeted the "Crime of Speech and Actions Causing Hatred of the Government." The assembly—fully appointed since the June 1933 toppling of Mano's executive dictatorship—unanimously passed a Special Courts Act.[154] The act allowed a special court to decide all cases involving the rebellion, whether military or civilian.[155] This tribunal was exempt from the normal judicial process; it fell under the ministry of defense's control, allowed only court-approved defense counsel (but often no counsel was provided), and barred appeal.[156] The 1933 special court became the first of three military courts in the 1930s that tried regime opponents. The 1933 court tried more than 300 people allegedly complicit in the rebellion; it sentenced 47 to life in prison.[157]

The military was the prime mover, but did not act alone. To its aid came state legal insiders and the appointed assembly. Pridi devised a Defense of the Constitution Act that passed the national assembly in 1933.[158] In 1935 Rene Guyon, one of the founders of Thammasat University, wrote the second special courts act to try a new round of enemies from within the noncommissioned officer ranks. Other Thammasat lecturers served on the courts but none protested against these exceptions to the constitutional rule of law. Parliamentary opposition to the slide into dictatorship developed over the course of the 1930s, but the appointed assemblymen backed the executive's tribunals. In late 1938, the last of the special courts met to decide the fates of alleged antigovernment conspirators, and handed down their verdicts in 1939.

The 1933 trials swept up not only Bowondet rebels. They also charged the leaders of the still born Nationalist Party, and writers from the Siam Free Press group that formed an informal opposition to the People's Party. Luen Saraphaiwanich, forty-two years old at the time of the revolution, managed the Siam Free Press and also was a member of the Nationalist Party of early 1933. In his telling of the People's Party years, Luen was a patriotic democrat; to the government he was a rank royalist reactionary. As in many cases, retrospective prejudice in the historical record makes it difficult to uncover the truth. On the one hand, Luen made no secret of his happiness at the demise of the People's Party Association, and indeed many saw the aim of the Nationalist Party not to open the political sphere but to end the People's Party.[159] On the other hand, Luen's possible democratic contributions were closed off by the enmity between new- and old-regime actors. Luen claimed constant harassment of his newspapers, and two major ones, the *Krungthep Daily Mail* (Thai) and its English partner the *Bangkok Daily Mail* were closed for good in November 1933.[160] Luen and other old regime loyalists frequently used newspaper censorship as a prime example of how the new regime flatly contradicted the free speech guarantees in the December 1932 constitution and the spirit of democracy.

Luen Saraphaiwanich claimed to have nothing to do with Bowondet's rebellion. When the rebellion began in October, Luen was in the middle of campaigning for a Bangkok seat in the planned first parliamentary elections promised by the government. The police issued an arrest warrant for him as a conspirator. Anticipating the trouble he was in because of his prior criticisms of the government, he destroyed his campaign flyers and fled by train to the south. Disguised in dark glasses and as he put it "as a Chinese," he avoided detection on the train when police boarded looking for rebel sympathizers that they had identified. He arrived in Hua Hin eventually where he stayed with Krom Luang Singhawikromchai, former minister of defense under the absolute monarchy and Luen's one-time commander when he was in the army. His patron went with Prajadhipok, also in Hua Hin, and others to Songkhla in the south but Luen refused the invitation to accompany them. After being bitten by a dog in Hua Hin, which he took as an evil omen of his fate, Luen was eventually arrested and sent to prison.[161]

Luen's story is a vivid picture of the collateral damage of the civil war, the solidarity of the prisoners and the extrajudicial use of law by the government in their pursuit of an idealized new order rid of traitors. His wife Mom Luang Chalong and son were also arrested, and his wife died prematurely in jail. Luen attributed this to mistreatment. Before her jailing, Chalong tried to get her husband released by bringing a case against the interior ministry, Phahon, and several arresting police officers on the grounds that the government violated his right to liberty guaranteed under the constitution. While the case was in motion, the assembly passed a law that retroactively protected government officers discharging their duty in suppression of the rebellion. Anticipating that cases such as Chalong's may multiply, the government used the law to protect its officers from trial.[162] After ten months held in detention without charge, Luen along with Louis Girivat, also of the Siam Free Press group, So Sethabut and four others were charged with conspiring to topple the government and restore the absolute monarchy. Luen claimed the prosecutors used manufactured and/or unsubstantiated evidence against him and suborned perjury from witnesses. He was sentenced to life imprisonment.[163] In 1936, Chalong died. The prison warden allowed Luen to attend the funeral in April, which gave some emotional relief, but also led to Luen's greater estrangement from the government. On the way to the temple, Luen's transport changed at Bangkhunphrom Palace. Luen protested the stop, asking that they just proceed directly to the ceremony. Prince Boriphat gave his palace to the People's Party before he went overseas. Seeing it brought back a flood of memories to Luen: meeting his wife there for the first time and gaining the friendship and patronage of Prince Boriphat. Amid his revelry, a prison official pointed to the palace and exclaimed: "This place was built with money squeezed from the blood of the people." Luen listened in stunned silence.[164]

Here we can look at the fate of two additional prominent critics of the time—Choti Kumphan and Thephasadin na Ayutthaya—to show the wider effects of the elite conflicts. Both Choti and ri were supporters of constitutionalism but critics of the People's Party, and the government targeted both using ordinary and special courts.

Choti Kumphan was a well-known public figure and veteran of World War I. Among the first foreign PhD recipients, Choti gained a doctorate in economics from Leipzig University. In August 1933 he presented a nationalist economic agenda to the premier. He asked that the government set up a "Thai Commercial Company" to cut out foreign (i.e., Chinese) middlemen in control of the rice trade. He articulated a familiar theme: regardless of ideological orientation, all nationalists saw the holy grail of economic health in a strong state hand. He proposed that half of the company's shares be government owned, and half sold to the public.[165] A board of supervision could be created consisting of himself and like-minded business nationalists Mangkon Samsen, Wichit Wathakan, and others. He also proposed that consuls be eliminated in countries where the government could instead station a commercial representative (for example, in Java, Hong Kong, and Holland).[166] Choti's economic nation-alist ideas were common currency, but he was an outsider to the circle around the Promoters. After the Bowondet rebellion, he ran afoul of state insiders because of his outspoken criticism of state planning. The law held him in its net for most of the 1930s. Choti told his fellow prisoner Nim-itmongkol Navarat that he always thought that sooner or later he would be sent to prison, and he and seven others were jailed in 1934 under the constitutional defense act for five years' upcountry imprisonment as antigovernment criminals.

Choti Kumphan's friend Thephasadin na Ayutthaya[167] sent an appeal to Phahon on his behalf in August 1934. Thephasadin, one of the members of the Nationalist Party, had studied in France for eight years and for officer training in Belgium for four more. He commanded the Siamese Expeditionary Force in World War I sent by King Vajiravudh to support the allies and win diplomatic favors for Siam.[168] He was one of forty members of an elite council that King Prajidhipok established to advise on government affairs in the 1920s.[169]

After the revolution he was variously president and deputy of the assembly, an elected representative for Bangkok from the first elections that came in the wake of the Bowondet rebellion in 1933, owner of a dairy farm, and a prominent public figure who often spoke on topical issues.

In defending his friend, Thephasadin took the constitutional high ground by claiming that Choti's imprisonment was illegal because the government held him without charge.[170] As with Luen's case, the constitutional high ground washed away in the tempest of emergency governance. The head of the Santiban (police special branch) wrote to the deputy police chief that the constitutional defense act allowed for preventive detention without charge when a case was being investigated. The police special branch chief added, for good measure, that Thephasadin had insulted the integrity of the Santiban and was not interested in the other people who were arrested with Choti, although as a Bangkok representative in the assembly he also represented them. The special branch's overtly political role here is extraordinary. So too is the government's reason for denying Choti bail in October 1934; the court claimed that the case was too important politically. On October 8, Choti and eight others were sent into internal exile, termed "restricted residence" in Tak and Mae Hong Son provinces far away from Bangkok. Later that month, some of Choti's associates were charged with fomenting rebellion and given five years upcountry exile, consisting of freedom in a limited area, accompanied by their families.

Choti was not a rank reactionary, bent on destroying the People's Party regime. Instead like other educated critics of the government he sought democratic and material development for the country exactly as the Promoters avowed. In ordinary times, criticism would have ostensibly strengthened civil society's push for government accountability. But these were not ordinary times, and especially after the Bowondet rebellion suspicion ran high among insiders about any threat to their power. Thephasadin na Ayutthaya himself was swept up in the antigovernment cases and arrested on October 1, 1934.[171] R. D. Atkinson and Victor Jacques of Tilleke & Gibbins, a prominent Eurasian law firm in Bangkok established at the turn of the century and close to the old regime, represented Thephasadin.[172] Prominent figures with high priced legal counsel received slightly better treatment than average citizens; Thephasadin was let out on bail. Atkinson argued in November and December 1934 that Thephasadin, as deputy speaker of the national assembly at the time, was immune from prosecution. The court rejected Atkinson's defense, and pursued a criminal case, based on articles in the penal code and constitutional defense act that criminalized Thephasadin's alleged subversion. The state claimed that in August and September of that year Thephasadin and his cohort claimed that the government was inclined to communism, had no economic plan for the country, and used taxes as a way to enrich themselves.[173] The court also heard that Thephasadin and company called for a forceful overthrow of the government. The defendants denied the charges and claimed that their grievances about the economy were submitted in a petition from locals in the capital who sought their support.

Thephasadin defended himself on grounds of constitutional protection for free speech in a trial that packed the courtroom with interested citizens. When he was first arrested in October, Thephasadin claimed a double standard in treatment of critics. He asserted that when Pridi had been charged with communist subversion over his economic plan the previous year, the state dismissed the charges since he was a valuable insider. Thephasadin, however, was dogged at every step and complained that "[i]t was not amusing to have to go around everywhere accompanied by the police."[174] He admitted to being against the government on what he saw as its misuse of power. On December 25, he received two years' imprisonment, and officers from the criminal investigation division handcuffed him and led him out of court.[175] Soon, however, Thephasadin was freed, when the appeals court in early 1935 reversed the prior decision. He did not, it found, compose a critical document and did not incite the people to revolt.[176] On February 1, 1935, Thephasadin returned to applause at the assembly, and later in February the assembly granted him a leave of absence for "nerves."

The state did not forget about him, despite the appeals court decision. During the 1937 lands scandal that temporarily ended Phahon's government and that is discussed in chapter 6 at greater length, Thephasadin was back in the news. He claimed to have been again tailed by the police and harassed for supposed involvement in the insider dealing. He said the police were determined to do him harm and were trying to prevent him from participating in the pending elections held at the end of the year.[177] He returned to prison.

Phibun's Rise:
The Military Takes Power and Stages Show Trials

As Thephasadin recalled in 1945, he was extremely naive to think that since he had done nothing wrong justice would prevail according to the rule of law. Indeed, the 1939 trial of a range of the new regime's enemies came after several years of budding autocracy that flouted the spirit of constitutionalism and consolidated most power within the military wing of the People's Party. Phibun Songkhram played the starring role. He had become defense minister in 1934 after his success in the Bowondet rebellion and in subsequent years faced a range of challengers.

Phibun's star rose after the Bowondet rebellion. Aside from crushing the revolt and gaining the defense portfolio, Phibun gained from the king's exit. King Prajadhipok, dispirited by the political turmoil and ill, abdicated the throne in March 1935. In January of the previous year, he left the country, traveling initially to Medan to join Prince Boriphat, and then going on to Europe. In making his decision, Prajadhipok highlighted the range of new policies that curtailed his power. The government sent officials to England, where the king now lived, and they "attempted the impossible—that is, to try and prevent the king from abdicating and at the same time to turn down his proposals in the most tactful and polite way."[178] Initially keeping the news from the public, the government eventually published a large report on the proceedings that sought to legitimize the Promoters' right to limit kingly power.[179] After complicated discussions over which royal family member should become the new king, the national assembly endorsed the government's decision and invited Ananda Mahidol—born in Heidelberg, Germany, nine years old at the time and living in Switzerland—to become the next king. Since he was a minor and per the constitution, the national assembly decided on a three-man regency to decide on royal affairs for him until he gained his maturity.[180]

Amid a friendly regency council governing for a pliable boy the Promoters, and Phibun especially, continued to face down threats. In August 1935, the government arrested noncommissioned officers planning a revolt, and thereafter established the second special court to try the suspects. Taken from their families and banned any further contact with them, the accused were held in the Defense Ministry building for three weeks before trial, where the authorities tried to establish their link to Song Suradet. Phibun and Song's relations soured after the Bowondet rebellion, and Phibun and his cohort frequently alleged Song as in on a range of plots against them.[181] Song was thus tied in to the government's allegation that the conspirators sought to kill Phibun, Pridi, and others, invite Prajadhipok back to Siam, and dethrone the boy king.[182] An English barrister expressed an interest in representing the defendants, but he backed out when he discovered the military's dominance of the trials and the lack of protections for the accused. One man was executed, despite pleas from his wife, and twelve others sent to prison.[183]

At the end of 1938, Phahon was pushed out of the way and Phibun gained the premiership. On route, he had survived three assassination attempts: failed shootings after a football match in February 1935,[184] by his valet before a dinner in November 1938, and another failed dinner party killing, this time by poisoning, in December 1938. After the last attempt, Phibun retreated from public appearances, even as one week later he became premier.[185]

Reeling from threats against him and determined to assert his power, Phibun used the 1939 tribunal to get rid of a range of challengers. The court alleging fourteen different groups of plotters had hatched conspiracies. The government targeted royalists and alleged conspirators backing Song Suradet.[186] The verdicts announced that from the start of the new regime, its enemies sought a return to the old. It concluded there were plans to topple the government and "deal with" Phibun, Pridi, Phahon, and other leaders of the People's Party.

Thephasadin in his account noted, however, that he never faced a "gestapo" state that held his mere existence as enough of a crime to warrant punishment.[187] Like the others Thephasadin had no defense counsel. He noted the stark discrepancies in accounts among prosecution witnesses about who visited him and what they discussed. Prince Rangsit, a fellow inmate also accused in the trials that year, echoed the role Song was supposed to be playing when he termed Thephasadin the "truffle" of the group: the World War I military commander was the main ingredient mixed into every other fanciful plot. Thephasadin, when allowed to cross-examine the witnesses, exposed their staged presentations to the court but the judges took no notice. The accused was adamant that the witnesses for the state were paid thugs.[188] Thephasadin's long conflict with the government culminated in his conviction in the November 1939 trial that convicted two of his sons, and three associates as well. The conviction rehashed the older subversion claims and expanded them, alleging that between November 1934 and January 1938 Thephasadin and his plotters sought to overthrow the government, and in October 1938 assassinate Phibun.[189]

Choti, meanwhile, was accused in a separate group of eight plotters of also defaming and scheming against the government and, ironically, encouraging communism from late 1936 to 1938. Choti's real crime was his friendliness with Song Suradet. When Phibun moved against Song, Choti's Song connection was used against him. During the 1939 trial, a police sergeant who knew Choti during his upcountry imprisonment and afterward testified to Choti's antigovernment politics and his loyalty to Song. After his early release from Mae Hong Son imprisonment, Choti stayed upcountry. He wrote considerably—on banking, finance, trade, employment, cooperatives, and communications. He finished a book on labor and economics dedicated to Song entitled *Patiwat achip* ("The Vocational Revolution"). In the latter 1930s he was in contact with Thephasadin, Song, and Phraya Udomphongpensawat, the latter man another member of the 1933 Nationalist Party and a Song ally, with whom Choti stayed in Bangkok for a few months. The police witness testified that Choti said he, Phraya Udomphong, and the group wanted to depose the government, and that afterward Pridi, Phibun, and the others would be killed.[190] The special court sentenced Thephasadin to death in 1939, but his term was commuted to life afterward by Phibun. Choti received a life sentence.

Thephasadin encapsulated the anger against the government for its subversion of the constitutional rule of law. The government spared himself, Prince Rangsit, and Chamnan Yuthasilp. But he remarked,

> It appeared at first that people needed us to die . . . (But then) what did it mean . . . that Field Marshal Phibun commuted three people's sentences to life imprisonment? That the court had freedom per the constitution? Or that the court had to accept a report on how it was to judge ahead of time? If the court were free to judge according to justice and the law, how did it happen that Field Marshal Phibun had a voice to decide who died and whose life to spare?[191]

The court did not spare Thephasadin's two sons. In 1939 both fell among the eighteen shot on the court's order. An eyewitness to the executions recalled a cold morning in late November 1939. An array of warmly clad police regular and special branch officers, interior ministry officials, and the prison warden and provincial governor stood in the stillness awaiting the execution. Wearing sarongs or thin Chinese pants and thin tops, the prisoners shuffled out to the firing ground in shackles. A monk from the nearby temple delivered a sort of last rites where he implored the men waiting to die not to feel hatred for those doing their duty. The witness noted the quiet and stoicism of the Thephasadin brothers, even as in the final moments they quietly choked their tears back knowing they would not see each other again. The prisoners were tied to cross posts, like a Christian crucifix, with cotton straps and blindfolded. Executioners fired their rifles from about six meters amid the quietly onlooking crowd.[192]

Malai Chupinit wrote that the execution of the eighteen charged in the 1939 case weighed more heavily on Phibun than any other action of his government. In their conversations in 1945 after Phibun had fallen from power, Phibun quietly deflected blame from himself and cleansed his hands of the victim's blood by claiming that Adun Decharat, the chief of police, forced him to sign the death warrants. Adun only agreed to the three commutations for Thephasadin, Prince Chainat, and Chamnan Yuthasilp. When Adun came to Phibun's house with the paperwork, Phibun claimed to be suffering from nerves and exhaustion. Presented with the warrants, Phibun vomited and was overcome with sickness at the prospect of the executions. Adun, however, would not leave, according to Phibun, until he signed the orders.[193] Phibun's deflection of responsibility onto Adun's shoulders undermines Phibun's wartime claim to be the great leader, accepting all sacrifices to protect the nation from its enemies. It also does not explain why the farflung court accusations generated a momentum of their own.

We can close with another constitutional monarchist prisoner of the 1930s whose fortunes and public role sank amid the polarization. Prince Nimitmongkol Navarat wrote extensively in English and Thai in the 1930s and his writings and life further highlight the dilemma facing all not in the daydreamer royalist camp described by Suphasawat. Nimitmongkol went to jail after the Bowondet rebellion in the first wave of arrests because he happened to be at the Don Mueang aerodrome in early October 1933. In his own telling, he had scant regard for the rebels. Bowondet, he says, was unpopular and an incapable military strategist. The origins of the

Figure 1.5. Government troops on the way to battle against Bowondet's forces, October 1933. Photo courtesy of the National Archives of Thailand, Department of Fine Arts.

rebellion he opines lay in vague mutterings over a bottle of whiskey at a provincial army club.[194]

In prison Nimitmongkol edited *True Blue*, a pro-monarchy newspaper that was smuggled out of prison by friends and relatives who visited. He noted that the special court, as Thephasadin noted, acted arbitrarily depending on Phibun's influence. Nimitmongkol recalled that two junior alleged conspirators were freed when Phibun turned up at a court hearing and ordered their release. Many prisoners thereafter hoped that Phibun would intervene to rescue them.[195] In 1937, while Phahon was still premier, Phibun gave a newspaper interview where he commented that if he were premier he would allow political parties to form. By then, Nimitmongkol had been released from prison and wrote a book on political parties. While Phibun's comments seemed to signal a friendly atmosphere and freer politics, Nimitmongkol discovered that the opposite was true. He was jailed again after the police raided his publisher's store and confiscated printed copies of the book.[196] The government charged Nimitmongkol with conspiring with Choti, Phra Sitirueangdetphon—a military officer under Song's patronage—and others. Nimitmongkol had not seen Sitirueangdetphon in twenty years and did not know most of his alleged co-conspirators.[197] Sitirueangdetphon defended Bangkhen for the government during the Bowondet rebellion but later told Nimitmongkol that he wondered whether his imprisonment came from that action. He opined that Phibun resented him taking the initiative and also never trusted him since he was Song's friend. Sitirueangdetphon remarked to Nimitmongkol that they arrested him as a stand in for Song.[198]

One of Nimitmongkol's coprisoners in the 1939 trial recalled that the organization of the court made him feel like an amateur fighting the American champion Jack Dempsey.[199] In Nimitmongkol's recollection, the prosecution's witnesses were remarkably well informed about times, places, and people allegedly conspiring, but were vague or could not recall details when defendants had the rare opportunity to cross examine them.[200] He concluded the trials were a pack of lies and lost interest. He was not alone; at one point he glanced at Thephasadin who was sketching a lampoon of the judge.[201]

Conclusion

Government forces destroyed the royalist threat at the close of 1933, and ended their compromise with the old guard. Apart from the government's, and especially Phibun's, initiative, the rebellion floundered for its own reasons. In addition to poor coordination and personal conflicts, the Bowondet rebellion failed because of its political incoherence. The rebels' political aims ranged from an absolutist restoration, to Bowondet as a new king, to constitutional, multiparty democracy under a (new or existing) king. There were thus contradictory strands of royalist opposition to the People's Party throughout the 1930s and 1940s.[202]

Prince Suphasawat—King Prajadhipok's brother-in-law—recalled that in the 1930s one type of royalist group were feeble, superstitious, and hoping in vain for a restoration of their glory. He contrasted these relics with "conservative" monarchists who looked to a future of robust constitutional monarchy and democratic governance. The outsiders discussed in the following chapters did not form a social category; the status rested on inferiority in different fields of power: economic, ethnic, administrative, regional, and cultural. Where did these "conservative" royalists fit? Did they share in one or more of the disadvantages with other outsiders? Did they feel any commonality to others? Or were they uniquely entitled, substituting a quickness to take offense and readiness to declaim from the moral high ground for any real grievance, and are they hence debarred from the same historic category?

In the 1930s, the coercive armor of People's Party hegemony—exercised via the military's growing influence—partly elides the historian's questions. The critical journalists, writers and long-serving public officials were among many others who suffered in this dark time due to their ideas and the contingencies of their friendships. The stark opposition of monarchists and People's Party, used by Nattapoll to cut through the historical fancies of monarchic nationalism and greatly help us to understand the counterrevolution, at the same time does not serve us very well to account for the middle ground, or shared optimism about democracy. Luen, Choti and the others all supported a mixed regime of monarchists and commoners living under the constitution. With the rebellion, however, the Promoters became more skeptical than ever about the circles of critics. The People's Party in the 1930s created a long-standing resentment among conservatives, and also gave birth to the rise of military politics. And the poison spread. In the early postwar period when democracy flourished, these men emerged from prison embittered and angry. They entered the fractious world of parliamentary politics and helped to dismantle a popularly chosen government and trash constitutional democracy.

An important book about the era, heavily critical of the People's Party, is entitled *Sat kanmueang*—political animals, or animal politics: 1930s politics was an all out war of survival and power. There were no ideals. But describing the dual aspect of the new regime as a centaur, or hybrid of idealism and force, is a better metaphor than as an instinctual, mindless beast.[203] The regime gained popularity as it consolidated power, and the triumph over Bowondet seemed a victory for commoners over princes, one that promised a popular state. Phibun's idealized new regime pushed forward the goal of a society without lords and their retainers. The king and his men became to the governing commoners like the "stranger(s) in our midst" as Saint Just concluded during the revolution in France.[204] After Phibun's ascent to the premiership the government banned people from hanging Prajadhipok's picture in their houses, and encouraged them to display the heroic commoner Phibun's image.[205] On the tortuous way from their ideal of a republic in all but name to a new reality, the Promoters after Bowondet did not surrender to rank nihilism but found the peril of their political position imposed limits to what the revolution, and democracy, offered. The danger in part led to the arbitrary exercise of law. The regime shelved plans for expansion of the political sphere, and one of the original six tenets of the People's Party—public safety and security—severely limited another promise—to ensure individual liberty and freedom. The tensions, embodied in dual leadership of consent and force, endured through the People's Party era.

Chapter Two

A Fragile Alliance

The Working Classes and the People's Party

The revolution produced a wide-ranging debate over the ethics of wealth and poverty, the ease of the leisured, and the toil of workers and peasants. Economic nationalism fueled and sustained the revolution in tandem with the demand for political rights and freedoms. Initially, the monarchy suffered the most drastic change in their circumstances. After the revolution, people gossiped that royals possessed vast wealth in fixed capital and savings. Newspapers claimed huge sums banked by royals exceeded the national wealth, and papers printed names and the supposedly correct amounts of their wealth.[1] In the initial euphoria, the People's Party manifesto claimed that the millions in royal wealth would be distributed for popular welfare. They did not do so. But while the fabulous fortunes of the royals were not expropriated, as many among them feared, the People's Party moved decisively to manage royal wealth. In the first year of the revolution, the new regime slashed by one third the royal budget, and by 1938, it had been cut by 80 percent compared to the 1931–1932 expenditure.[2]

The wealth of nonroyal privileged people, also, came in for public criticism. Institution of an inheritance tax on the rich became a popular idea after 1932.[3] The high incomes of senior bureaucrats, also attracted public attention. Before the revolution, a senior civil servant earned about 200 times more than junior ones,[4] and the gap did not shrink substantially after 1932. In assembly debates over the annual budget, outspoken members criticized the government's high expenses as stemming largely from inflated civil service salaries, outlays for which dwarfed spending on social welfare.[5] The rector of Thammasat University in Bangkok, established by the People's Party in 1934, made around 1,000 baht per month; a clerk typist about 20 baht per month.[6] One writer to the new government asserted that government pensions for senior officials were regularly in the range of 600 baht per month, three times what should be given.[7]

Petitions to the government show what some people saw as more appropriate distributions. One writer to the government wrote that a sufficient salary for anyone of the rank of deputy director or higher in a state office should be 60 to 100 baht per month.[8] For Mr. Chamras, this contributor, salaries of 200 baht and above should be abolished.[9]

The People's Party established a base of thirty baht per month for government civil servants. While a far cry from the 200-plus times higher salaries of senior officers, nonetheless white-collar work for anyone was reasonably secure and easy. This chapter by contrast looks at the world of urban labor and their struggle for a better life under the new regime. Urban labor toiled for a fraction of white-collar wages, and in fact had no guarantee of any income at all. Bangkok was the political heart of the country, and the scene of the commoner-monarchy conflict of the 1930s and 1940s. The city also was the economic lever of national wealth. The global economy transformed Bangkok in the age of high imperialism and produced the commoner poverty that accompanied elite commercial and administrative wealth. As in the countryside, centripetal administrative reforms had a centrifugal socioeconomic effect. While outsiders upcountry grew up hundreds of kilometers from the economic and political center of the country that governed these changes, some of their fellow outsiders lived in the city only a stone's throw from the corridors of state power. An ethnic division of labor accompanied the spatial difference. The rural economy relied on primarily Thai and Lao labor, both components of a long-standing demographic expansion into wet rice-growing lands. In the city, on the other hand, Chinese labor largely drove commerce in the early twentieth century. Early in the new regime, they found Thai spokesmen who campaigned on their behalf as part of a pan-ethnic worker movement. But while the People's Party pledged to represent all common people, as we will see their nationalism shaded into ethnic chauvinism. Eventually by the war the Chinese had to stand up for themselves, and they thereafter contributed much more forcefully to the People's Party's popular platform and to a broader, integrated labor movement.

Figure 2.1. The consummate old regime insider: His Royal Highness Boriphat Sukhumphan Kromphra Nakhonsawanworaphinit. The most powerful old regime officer, and one of the kingdom's wealthiest men, Boriphat went into exile after 1932, leaving his palace for the People's Party's use. Photo courtesy of the National Archives of Thailand, Department of Fine Arts.

Bangkok: The Growth of a City and the "Bad" Chinese

In the first decades of the twentieth century, Bangkok and its commerce grew enormously. It is estimated that Bangkok's population trebled in a generation, from about 365,500 in 1910 to more than 700,000 in 1929, and 890,000 in 1937.[10] By the 1930s, the Bangkok population numbered about one in fourteen of the kingdom's total population. Most industrial labor concentrated in the city. As a whole, in Siam those in "industrial pursuits" in 1929 numbered around 165,000 people, roughly 2.2 percent of the total working population of the time. The majority of this vague category would have been the proletariat, but the census of the time makes it hard to gauge how many.[11] By 1937, urban manufacturing accounted for around 52,300 people; with an additional 26,600 in transportation and communication. While some of the latter included office work, in telegraph or telephone exchanges, for example, most of this type of service was in urban transportation, rickshaws, buses, trams, and the like. Together these two categories accounted for around 22% of the urban working population. A large number of these people were very young; the census data counts workers as young as ten years old.[12] Women accounted for roughly one in four manufacturing jobs, and one in three of all the urban working population. The biggest laboring occupations in the city that employed (mainly, but not exclusively) men were: rice mills (around 5,000 workers); printing (nearly 3,000); saw mills (roughly 2,400); and construction (nearly 2,000).[13]

Bangkok until after World War II remained largely a Chinese city. During Chulalongkorn's reign in the late nineteenth and early twentieth centuries, Chinese labor dominated in urban rice mills, mining, railway construction, transportation, and the port.[14] Travelers spoke often of their presence. A French Indochinese colonial officer drolly lamented in 1911 that a Bangkok visitor's first desire was "to see the Siamese people, and (their) last regret on leaving is of not having found them."[15] Above all, the visitors saw poor laborers—roughly seven in ten arrivals up until 1932.[16]

Amid high immigration and a changing socioeconomic prominence in Siam, Chinese society in the first twenty years of the century became publicly visible, and well organized.[17] A major strike in 1910 against taxes on the Chinese community, backed by criminal gangs, caused much of the Thai public to lambast the Chinese as irredeemable troublemakers. But it also formed a turning point for the Chinese in Siam from a world of secret societies, thuggery, and criminality to recognized speech and regional associations. Politics also changed. The local Chinese population enthusiastically greeted the success of Sun Yat-sen's movement.[18] Sun Yat-sen visited Siam in 1908, and local supporters established a Siam branch of the Kuomintang. Siao Huat Seng—a pioneer of Chinese journalism in Bangkok who published both Chinese and Thai-language papers—became Sun's main ally and for decades worked in Siam on behalf of the KMT. Siao's fascinating life and work shaped Thai public life, and indeed the public merged into the private as well: he was Phahon's wife's uncle.[19] The newly formed Chino-Siam Bank and Chinese Chamber of Commerce channeled support for Sun's party, including prominently rice mill owners, who played a central role in the Thai economy. In the teens and 1920s, Chinese republicanism flourished, and influenced overlapping generations of intellectuals from the 1912 plotters to the People's Party. Chinese schools and newspapers emerged in numbers from the 1910s, and served the needs of a growing population infused with overseas immigrants.[20]

From the end of World War I until the depression, strong growth in the rice, tin, and rubber trades attracted an unprecedented wave of Chinese immigration. The Chinese population of Siam reached its all time high in the revolutionary year: around 12 percent of the total population, with over half of these being *lukjin*—Thai-born Chinese. The numbers of *lukjin* grew over the decade, while overseas-born numbers shrank.[21] *Lukjin* then became a central component of Thai society, and contributed mightily to politics in the People's Party era. Most Chinese were concentrated in Bangkok and nearby provinces, around four in five of all Chinese in the kingdom. Chinese numbers upcountry also grew in the same years as transportation improved and hence so did Chinese commercial interests. Numbers nearly tripled in the north, and by fourfold in the northeast.[22] A high prince toured the rail lines in the northeast in 1928 and wrote to King Prajadhipok that the railway zones looked like Chinese colonies.[23]

Numbers—of workers and immigrants, or both as a percentage of the kingdom's, and especially Bangkok's population—give an impressive if impersonal outline of Chinese society in Thailand. What was life like for most of them? A glimpse into their working lives is given below. Politically, under the People's Party *lukjin* were second-class citizens, and, even worse, overseas born. Thai elite consternation over the 1911 Chinese revolution persisted into the 1930s; the new regime tacitly allowed Chinese to take part in the revolution, but also discouraged them. The 1911 revolution prompted the absolute monarchy to pass a citizenship law that gave any Siam-born person Thai citizenship, regardless of ethnicity, in the hopes that this would sever Chinese loyalty to the mainland, and especially to its republicanism. At the same time the 1913 citizenship law gave Thai citizenship to children of any Thai father who was also a citizen, regardless of where the child was born.[24] But nervousness about Chinese agitation, and unmanageability, persisted in the 1920s and 1930s.

King Prajadhipok's ambivalence toward democracy and political parties shared the attitude of his brother and father before him that Thai people were too immature for self-rule and that political associations would create disorder. But fear of Chinese organization, not just native naivete, informed much of this attitude. In his well-known "Democracy in Siam" article of 1927, Prajadhipok wrote a "real democracy" was very unlikely to succeed in Siam, because as he explained "the parliament would be entirely dominated by the Chinese Party."[25] He in the same years wrote that the immigrants of the day—the boom years—were "real Chinese," that is, without any tie to Siam, and that the growth of Chinese education—and the radical ideas introduced in schools—created a large minority hostile to the kingdom.[26]

As it happened, the absolute kings did not have to face a Chinese takeover of politics. Neither did the People's Party. No Chinese political party formed after 1932, and the People's Party purposefully limited the Chinese community's role in post-1932 public affairs. Political circumstance doomed Wichit's Nationalist Party; racism doomed the Chinese. Anyone of Thai citizenship who had foreign parentage faced tough obstacles to vote for candidates, or run for a seat, in the preparatory local councils or as provincial representatives to the national assembly. All such people had to prove they had a Thai-language secondary education, had completed military service or had been a salaried government clerk for five years. Most *lukjin* could not meet such requirements, and no overseas-born Chinese could.[27]

City Labor after 1932 and Their Spokesmen

Laborers worked long hours for little, and there was no Thai labor law to guarantee rights, provide insurance, or mediate disputes consistently. While Siam joined the International Labor Organization in 1919, it is not clear what impact membership had, since Thai government representatives told the League of Nations that it did not need labor laws because Siam was an agricultural country.[28] Before the revolution in Prajadhipok's reign Prince Purachatra, the powerful minister of commerce and communications, asked the king to consider labor protections. The king replied that there was no need for labor laws, minimum wages, or enforcement of eight-hour working days for Siam, and that they would open the door, better left shut, to labor organizations and trade movements.[29] The government urged management and labor to come to agreements over pay and conditions; the hands-off policy unsurprisingly favored capital.

Before the revolution workers and organizers repeatedly agitated for better pay and conditions in a range of key industries. The government's response often highlighted the alleged communist or Chinese criminality behind the scenes.[30] After the revolution, the same grievances persisted to motivate labor and their spokesmen and a series of strikes and campaigns in Bangkok marked urban transportation, construction, rice milling, textile factories, and, in the southern peninsula, mines.[31] In the new regime, the government's promises of a better life for common people gave a new energy to the articulation of long-standing grievances.

Chinese rickshaw pullers kindled the first major labor movement of the People's Party era. While in China around the same time the exhausting work of pulling a rickshaw became a symbol of national weakness and shame, and a driver of urban politics,[32] and in contemporary Singapore and Vietnam a rallying cause for anticolonialism,[33] in Siam rickshaw labor highlighted foreign labor's alienation and their voicelessness in a changing political order.

In 1930s Bangkok, many urban people used rickshaws, but the transport's heyday had past. While facing competition from automobiles, buses, and trams, 3,000 rickshaws per shift nevertheless plied the streets and their use returned handsome profits for the owners. A Chinese bourgeois cartel, organized in an association, controlled the business, and rented rickshaws per day to pullers. The cost of a rickshaw's construction— around 50 baht—could be recouped with a little over two months' rental; in a year, the 3,000 rickshaws netted more than 700,000 baht in profits. Pullers meanwhile, renting the conveyance for 40 satang per day and 35 by night—roughly one dollar and ninety-three cents, respectively—were largely at the mercy of the owner's cabal. Owners blacklisted debtors, and cast them out of work. After a long shift, pullers earned between 1 baht and 1.25 baht; owners claimed about 80 satang of the earnings—20 to 45 satang a day, then, for food and other necessities.[34]

In early August 1932, 6,000 pullers struck against the rental rates. Pullers were desperate but intimidated by management. There were no heroes in the clash but plenty of stubbornness and fisticuffs. After several days of bad feeling fermenting, the strike began at a single rickshaw outfit on the fourth and the protesting strikers called for their fellows to join, sometimes threatening scabs. On the morning of the fifth, around 230 pullers set out for work—around 8 percent of an average morning's hire—but returned soon under warnings from strikers. It is not clear who led the movement. The action on August 4th seems to have been planned ahead of time, but whether an organized strike force led the way is unknown. Instead, groups of pullers fanned out across the city and prevented other pullers from working under threat.[35] A temporary lull in the conflict ensued later on August 5th, with owners pledging to reduce the rental rates but then reneging. Thawatt Rittidej, a young journalist and spokesman for various commoner causes, appealed to the chief of police, whom he knew from a pawnshop workers' strike in 1931, to intervene to force a firm owners' commitment, but to no avail.[36] Midday on August 4th, two police went undercover, as a rider and a puller, to try and suss out the leadership, but were recognized and threatened by laborers. While they arrested one man as a leader, police soon released him since they could not tell what role the man played.[37]

On August 9th, around 2,000 rickshaws assembled outside Parut-sakawan Palace. The coolies wanted the government to guarantee the owners' spoken commitments to reduce the rent on the conveyances. A tense atmosphere prevailed; many police of different units, as well as People's Party members, circulated outside the building to calm people's nerves.[38] When queried, the strikers said they had no leader and acted spontaneously. People's Party members found seven men amid the Chinese throng who understood Thai well, and brought them into the palace to discuss the group's demands. The following day, a Thai police officer represented the workers in a meeting with the Chinese bosses. The meeting on the 10th, convened under the pressure of the People's Party via the interior ministry that controlled the police, succeeded in forcing the owners to agree formally to rent reductions.[39]

The strike lacked natural leaders, and no laws governed how strikes should be resolved. Bereft of the spirited activity of "organic intellectuals" from the workers who could articulate class grievances and link them to larger economic problems or labor laws, the rickshaw strike ended when the People's Party and the police intervened. This peculiarity of the People's Party era—what a contemporary Western observer termed the "spasmodic paternalism" of the new regime[40]—would repeat in many strikes and workers' causes that did not have their own leadership. Newspapers came closest to the role of a public persuader. All major papers of the time followed the strike closely, and all sympathized with the coolies' plight. *Sri Krung* newspaper had a strong People's Party link; as we learned above one of its founders was a veteran of the failed 1912 military revolt, and a man honored by the Promoters as one of their inspirations.[41] The paper frequently championed the new order. In this case, showing a grand leap of faith in the level of working-class consciousness, the paper opined that the strike ended without serious violence because the coolies believed in the People's Party's democratic ideology.[42] The *Bangkok Daily Mail*, meanwhile, while no friend to the People's Party, also highlighted the coolies' hard lives and recommended the government do more to help poor people. The rickshaw pullers, the paper argued, formed the poorest of the poor, fighting for daily survival and treated like beasts of burden. The paper argued that the coolies were not forgotten people; no one knew or cared about them in the first place.[43]

The state insiders from the People's Party and their collaborators from the old government who together governed Siam in these years became prominent public figures of the day, and scholarship and sometimes public memory preserves their importance. By contrast, biographies of the poor do not exist; the *Bangkok Daily Mail* is correct. The Chinese proletariat were among the ultimate outsiders: poor, unlearned in Thai letters, and without any political voice. Of the seven Chinese men who entered Parutsakawan we know their first names only: Sui, Jijeua, Hia, Huaheng, Hai, Chai, and Leng. Where they came from, how they fared after the rickshaw revolt, and how they died are unknown.

Others in our story of outsiders by contrast are public men. And around some have developed small cults of personality that have preserved them as heroes. Thawatt Rittidej (1893–1950) was the chief spokesman for labor in the kingdom in the early People's Party years, and because

Figure 2.2. The unknown men: Rickshaw pullers on strike, August 1932, hear from a police officer about the government's plan to help them. Photo courtesy of the National Archives of Thailand, Department of Fine Arts.

of his writing and activism we know more about him than many other outsiders. While far removed from the powerful elite, Thawatt like many commoners within and without the bureaucratic system who rose in life also had some elite connections as a young man that educated and directed him. Thawatt was born in Samut Prakan province, just outside Bangkok, the son of a market gardener and district officer. His father had no title, but the family enjoyed reasonable comfort from their commerce and the father's government salary. He entered the civil service in the naval supply department in 1917, under the patronage of a noble from Thawatt's home district whom his father knew. Thawatt spent four years in the civil service before resigning to seek opportunities in the growing newspaper business. He established *Kammakon* (Labor) weekly in January 1921.[44] Thawatt exploited Siam's semicolonial position to his business advantage. During the period of extraterritoriality treaties, foreign nationals were immune to Thai law. Many newspapers took advantage of this lucky situation. King Vajiravudh at the time lampooned the general situation where the enrollment of foreign-born gardeners and servants as editors; to him the practice seemed a ridiculous abuse of the extraterritoriality privilege. In a single year, Thawatt registered five different foreign nationals as editors of *Kammakon* to evade censorship.[45] Thawatt was clever, but also impassioned. In an early edition of *Kammakon* he explained the idealism that would guide his activism for the next fifteen years: to preserve the liberty and rights of labor, to encourage them to awaken from their slumber, to liberate them from slavery, and to resist the corruption of the lords that he felt ruined the country.[46]

Thawatt's interest in labor reflected his social views, informed by reading about world history and a healthy self-confidence that he understood how to solve the problems of modern Siam. The modern economy created the material conditions of urban labor, and labor's "awakening" as Thawatt put it depended on a sociopolitical transformation. In a March 1922 article, he wrote the following:

> People will have liberty to the extent of the global progress towards civilization (*siwilai*) that has taken place. The final result of this process is human equality . . . Labor in England have tremendous power and are equal to the high class. Now, the Labor Party's power has enabled them to found a government, and we cannot doubt that the future of this power will expand to the highest level.[47]

Thawatt's faith in British socialism as a harbinger of universal freedom conveys the Occidentalism that frequently underlay Thai democratic
propaganda. As with many in the 1900s generation, Thawatt perceived
Siam as backward. He also anticipated the post-1932 debate over wealth
and used the topic to argue that people are born free. In a February 1921
article he wrote,

> Believing that wealth or social rank can deny the rights and
> liberty of poor people or workers is illegitimate . . . wealth and
> ranks can disappear at any time, but people's rights never do.
> As long as there is life, there are rights. Bosses and employers
> should always hold to this principle of justice.[48]

Throughout the 1920s, Thawatt continued in newspaper publishing,
writing, and social activism, and his acumen attracted the attention of
both common people and the government. In 1921 and again in 1923,
Chinese tramway workers struck and paralyzed the urban railway for several months. Strikers demanded a better agreement with management that
would guarantee their pay and conditions, and they approached Thawatt
to advance their cause. He became known as an eloquent and forceful
petitioner on behalf of common's people's rights against employers and
state claims. He also became a thorn in the government's side. The police
jailed him for three days in January 1926 on charges of defamation of high
state officials, but the government lacked corroborating evidence and had
to release him. He soon wrote a fiery editorial in *Pakka Thai*, a new paper
he established to succeed *Kammakon*, that pledged to "kill the corrupt
elites (*ammat*) who steal from the people, to slit them from ear to ear
with his sharp pen."[49] Thawatt's polemics continued through the twilight
of the absolute monarchy. On the eve of the revolution, he attacked King
Prajadhipok for the £250,000 allegedly spent on the king's eye treatment
in the United States, which Thawatt read about in the *Penang Gazette*.
He also frequently wrote the government on behalf of the peasantry, for
example, in January 1931, representing 1,000 farmers from Minburi and
Chacheongsao provinces on the eastern seaboard who sought tax relief
and credit amid the depression.

Thawatt met Pridi and some leaders of the People's Party for the first
time after 1932. But the revolution's idealism dovetailed with his own, and
gave him a new ideological platform to make sense of the experience, as
he saw it, of the silent masses. Thawatt, moreover, had help from a friend,

Wat Sunthonjamon, who worked with him in his newspapers. Wat, forty years old at the time of the revolution, worked upcountry in the police force after graduating from the police cadet academy. After four years in the force, he ran afoul of powerful old lords in Lampang—whom he hated, as Wat's biographer puts it, because they "oppressed the people without humanity"—and was forced out of the police.[50] He journeyed to Bangkok in 1921, and there studied law and also wrote for, and for a time owned, newspapers. Wat also opened his own law firm; he advertised his firm in newspapers as an ally for the poor and oppressed and pledged himself to work pro bono. After 1932, Wat became personally loyal to Pridi and supported him in the coming years. In 1939, Wat graduated from Pridi's Thammasat University in law, and established a new law office just before the war some colleagues. Pridi's imprimatur stamped the firm: the *Manutham* Law Offices, named from part of Pridi's official government name, *Pradit Manutham*, shaper of righteous men.[51]

In addition to helping the Chinese rickshaw pullers, Thawatt and Wat, soon after the revolution represented a railways organization that sought the constitutional government's intervention in a labor dispute. Just before the rickshaw strike, a labor group of around 700 workers within the state-owned Makkasan railways petitioned the government for removal of the director of the railways. The charges they leveled reflected a new 1932 spirit that decried management's behavior as antidemocratic. The group accused Phra Suwaphan of incompetence, of only listening to flatterers, and ignoring workers' complaints and mistreating the Thai people. Moreover, he governed in secrecy; the group claimed their hours had been reduced without a clear explanation.[52] By the end of the month, the group's activism bore fruit. A government committee investigating Phra Suwaphan recommended his removal from the railways on grounds of incompetence.[53]

The Makkasan movement encouraged labor in other industries to organize and assert their interests. The 1932 constitution enshrined the right to assembly and association. While political parties failed to establish despite the constitution's tacit approval, labor organized into formal advocacy groups. Establishment of a legitimate tramways labor organization in October 1932 followed the opening provided by the Makkasan campaign. The Siamese Tramway Workers Association, following the opening provided by the Makkasan campaign, emerged in October 1932 and pledged to seek better working conditions, better pay, and to be a political voice for city workers. It became the first labor organization in Thai history. The founding members asked Thawatt to be chairman; and he and Wat also established at the same time a worker's welfare organization, with Wat providing legal advice, which they hoped would encompass labor more generally.[54] In January 1933, Thawatt composed a long list of grievances on behalf of the association that included reinstatement of several workers who had been fired for attempting to organize the workforce, and fairer working conditions.

Workers accused Phra Suwaphan of mistreating Thai-Chinese labor, as noted above. Before and after the revolution critics attacked such people for meekly serving Western capital, which critics associated not only with poverty but a loss of sovereignty as well. Like others, Thawatt's populism attacked the semicolonial position of Siam and blamed the old regime for selling out the country. The Siam Electric Corporation (SEC), majority held by Europeans, owned the tramways network. Like many other economic nationalists, Thawatt asserted the constitutional revolution as a passage to national independence and used this to pressure the new government into greater social responsibility. In a letter to the premier Mano in early 1933 he argued that

> Siam is called a sovereign country but the people have long been governed as if it were a colony . . . Siamese labor are slaves of their employers, and this is especially true in the case of labor working in foreign firms . . . The People's Party change of rule that has introduced a constitution has been a tremendous boon for the Thai people and has given the opportunity for the Thai people to possess liberty and freedom as they should . . . the new government is pledged to mediate between labor and employers and is the enabler of justice for us.[55]

The People's Party Cautiously Supports Workers

The tramways strike was among the largest labor actions of the 1930s. It disrupted urban lines for several months and 200 workers participated. The new government, meanwhile, occupied an uncertain middle position between labor and management and hesitated to act decisively. On the one hand, the Promoters pledged in their initial manifesto to ensure secure livelihoods for all citizens, and they also pledged to abolish the remnants of extraterritoriality that bound Siam to the West. Urban labor, while small in number, formed a prominent group in Bangkok that the People's Party could not ignore. Further, the People's Party saw the emergence of organizations that supported the new democracy as proof that the old regime did not care about people. Finally, banning such an organization would be taken as antidemocratic.

On the other hand, however, political-economic stability, and the royalist threat, concerned the new government. And while the new regime committed to making a fairer society and achieving full sovereignty, it feared antagonizing foreign governments and businesses, or of giving the impression that it wanted to up end the status quo in Siam. Amid the tramway workers' turmoil, the government faced criticism that they favored the tramways company, a foreign company (the SEC), over a Thai-owned bus company that sought to expand its network, due to the government's agreement with the SEC to manage competition. The government received a healthy return on their favoritism for the SEC.[56] Hence political and economic calculus, here as in many cases, tamed the revolution. Phraya Chasenyabodi Sriboribal, born in 1885 and the first interior minister after the revolution chosen for his long service in the ministry and for his closeness to Mano, described the problem during the tramways strike.

> This company (the SEC) was legitimately established. The demands of the workers cannot be met. It is as if they wanted to establish workers' control over the employers, or as if they (the workers) wanted to become the directors of the company. If the government becomes too involved, it will have bad effects and this should end now.[57]

Legitimate establishment meant foreign ownership by law under foreign treaty stipulations, which trumped worker demands and controlled their fate. Government involvement would give workers the false idea that they were masters of the situation. And foreign capitalist interests, the minister warned, would view government involvement as socialism. In addition to foreign considerations, the strike occurred during the struggle between Mano and the king and their parliamentary backers on one side and the People's Party and their supporters on the other, and while the government divided internally and argued over an economic plan. Prajadhipok, Mano and other conservatives in early 1933 fought with Pridi and his backers over Pridi's national economic plan that called for large-scale collectivization of agriculture and state control of the economy.

While the plan will be covered more in the following chapter, here we can focus on labor's impact on the conflict.

Pridi and some among the civilians in the People's Party were sympathetic to the workers, and the group was concerned with closing the gap between the government's charged democratic and economic nationalist rhetoric and the inconsistent backing it gave to popular movements. In Pridi's economic plan he referred to the tramways strike as the outcome of private ownership of industry, which brings "turmoil and disaster to the country."[58] Royalists were horrified that this plan signaled a local replay of the radical hatred for monarchy that ended Tsarism in Russia seventeen years previously.[59] The plan caused a political storm. Backers of Pridi and his opponents heatedly argued over the plan in the government.[60] The king's men also published 3,000 copies of a kingly rebuttal on the same day that Pridi went into exile because of the crisis. The king's rebuttal was widely read, while Mano banned Pridi's text.[61] The next chapter will discuss the plan in more detail. In criticizing Pridi's plan, Prajadhipok wrote that its alarmist tone over Thai labor relations misread the real situation: "That the tram workers have stopped work is not because of any genuine hardship. Instead, someone [i.e., Thawatt] has stirred them up so that he can organize an association, become the leader and obtain a comfortable income."[62] In September 1933, around six months after the April crisis and just before the Bowondet rebellion erupted, Thawatt petitioned the assembly to consider his case of defamation against the king. Thawatt felt Prajadhipok had ruined Thawatt's public standing by referring to him as a troublemaker.[63] Chasenyabodi Sriboribal died in early 1933, and his successor as interior ministry was another senior old-regime figure. Phraya Udompong Phensawat, born in 1873 from a minor royal line and who had served in government since King Chulalongkorn's reign, wrote to Phahon of the public clamor over Thawatt's charge.

> Many newspapers have written about Thawatt's accusation against the king lodged with the national assembly. I think this is . . . an event of completely unprecedented danger to the king.[64]

What so alarmed Udompong? Thawatt's move crystallized a clear trend emerging in a time of transition. In the move from absolutism to constitutionalism, from lords above to lords under the law, a much larger social force emerged, one that was seen as a danger: public criticism that reduced the king to the level of a citizen. The economic hardship of ordinary workers developed into a criticism of the Lords of Life, as the Thai kings had styled themselves. But in the conflict of the time between the People's Party and the old guard, only a partial solution emerged. The assembly did not take Thawatt's case against the king, and indeed one assemblyman, the prominent businessman Mangkon Samsen, countersued Thawatt for lèse majesté.[65] Still, the labor movement aggravated the tension in the government. Thawatt knew the People's Party ambivalent, and tried to force their hand in the labor dispute. The nervous government sent interior ministry officials to observe and report on the activities of the strikers continuously.[66] In this turbulent period, Promoters sought a quick solution that would allow them to concentrate on the insider struggle that threatened the government. The government ordered Prayun Phamonmon-tri, the secretary to the state council, and the metropolitan police chief to intervene with the foreign directors of the SEC. The latter agreed to the workers' demands and reinstated the fired workers in November 1933.[67]

The government's spasmodic paternalism resolved the tramways strike amid a larger conflict—culminating in the Bowondet rebellion of October—between commoners and the monarchy. And the strike had an electric effect. Many other organizations formed to campaign for their rights in the coming years, including rice coolies, taxi drivers, Makkasan railway workers, and social welfare organizations.[68] As with the tramways strike, such activism put the government in a difficult position.

A strike by rice transport coolies in early 1934 became the largest labor disruption of the People's Party era. Again, the voiceless immigrant Chinese found Thawatt as their patron. At the end of 1933, eight Chinese leaders representing 3,000 rice coolies from thirty-two city mills approached Thawatt on their behalf. The main grievance was mill owners' violation of a longstanding customary payment of three baht per cartload to rice coolies who transported paddy from buyers in the countryside to urban mills. By custom mill owners withheld this money from shippers who brought rice to the mills, when it would then be redistributed to coolies. The customary payment for the backbreaking work of paddy shipment formed a staple of Chinese coolie income during the harvest season. In late 1933, the mill owners cut the payment to coolies in half—thus keep-ing half for themselves—and then reduced it further without warning or explanation to sixty satang, just over one-half baht, per cart. In a letter to the government in January 1934, Thawatt wrote that the coolies "could not take the mill owners' injustice any longer."[69] In the ensuing fight over workers' compensation, unelected assemblymen and other conservatives in government backed a pro-business solution. Over the prior two months, the People's Party gained stronger control of the government. While the balance of forces tilted in favor of the Promoters, capital-owners' conservatism worked against the working class, and put the party on the back foot. Mangkon Samsen, a Sino-Thai businessman and appointed parliamentary representative for Bangkok who had lodged a lèse majesté charge against Thawatt as mentioned above, weighed in on the side of the mill owners. In an echo of Prajadhipok's criticism of Pridi, Mangkon claimed in a letter to the government that the protesters had been excited by democratic rhetoric but were not actually coolies. Instead they were paid stooges of a greater, sinister power. What was this power? Chinese secret societies? Disgruntled thugs, ready for a fight? A different, murky subset of the Chinese commercial class also losing money due to the rice mill owners' retention of the payment? We can speculate that Mangkon was grandstanding, since he did not say who was to blame; the specter of Chinese troublemaking, perhaps he felt, worked well enough. Mangkon also asserted that the three-baht payment was never customary. In fact, he asserted, the payment rested on encouraging hard work, and the market should operate that way: the just payment was whatever any mill owner decided as a sufficient incentive.[70]

In late January 1934, the rice coolies struck. They soon thought that their demands had been met, when the chair of the Chinese Chamber of Commerce in Bangkok intervened. The government requested the chamber's help, since the body carried weight: legitimate, respected and now established after twenty-some years of standing for Chinese interests. The mill owners agreed to cease collection of the three-baht fee from boat owners and to establish fixed wages for coolies. But in a confused situation, labor's victory soon unraveled and conflict ensued for the next several weeks. Amid the tension, five coolies were stabbed in clashes involving the workers.[71] Both the government and the mill owners reverted to a position against the coolies. Thawatt and his colleagues discovered that the government would not contradict big (Chinese) capitalists and that the new government firmly aligned with the latter when push came to shove. The government arrested thirty organizers, including Thawatt, and deported seven of the Chinese activists to China. These men suffered amid the ethno-legal politics of the time; they were born in China and did not come from any Siam-born family. The strike's size and Chinese composition greatly concerned the government, and led to a total reconsideration of foreign labor in Siam. The number and importance of Chinese labor gave these workers, as Thompson blandly put it, "the power to create an unpleasant situation."[72] Moreover, Thawatt's optimism regarding the populist policies of the People's Party, that is, toward the working population as a whole, largely evaporated. He wrote in February to Phahon, the senior People's Party member who became premier in June 1933 following the exit of Mano. Thawatt seemed resigned to failure. He wrote that after the Chinese leaders' banishment.

> (We) accepted our fate, and this incident showed that wealth governed Siam, and the People's Party had no (popular) support. They were like water lettuce floating alone in the middle of a pond.[73]

The People's Party did have popular support, contrary to Thawatt's claim, but it was lodged between labor and capital. The government leaned on mill owners to compromise but they refused. In late February 1934, mill owners closed their mills for four days rather than pay coolies what they demanded. The state largely withdrew from direct involvement in conflict in March, with the state council secretary writing to the economic affairs minister that "the government has no legal basis to get involved in this matter" and, lamely, from the perspective of Thawatt and like-minded advocates, added that "in this case when we have tried to effect a reconciliation but could not, our duty is finished."[74] The conflict dragged on. At the height of the rice mill strike of April 1934, the government appointed a commission to devise ways to handle labor demands, with Thawatt and four of his parliamentary allies playing key roles on the panel.[75] They proposed labor protections and material support, including work relief funds as a budgetary staple. These proposals gained some traction in the government but did not really change labor relations. Periodic state interventions in labor conflicts continued, while the national assembly in 1938, and the government in 1940, rejected comprehensive labor laws as unnecessary since, they asserted, management treated workers fairly, like a father would treat his children. And men alone benefited from gains made in various labor disputes. The labor of women and children remained entirely unregulated throughout the decade.[76] Labor candidates stood in late 1930s national assembly elections, with some limited success. Critics, however, echoed Prajadhipok's earlier disapproval, claiming that labor was not a suitable occupation for the country's "apprentice politicians" in the assembly.[77]

Anti-Chinese labor policies, meanwhile, became much more apparent after the Promoters consolidated power in the mid-1930s. In 1935, the government targeted rice mill labor, backbone of the export economy who struck with Thawatt's support, by requiring that one-half of mill workers be Thai citizens. The move came clearly in response to the perceived threat of Chinese labor activism. Phibun's ascent to the premiership in late 1938 accelerated the pace of anti-Chinese policies. By the beginning of 1939, the "dream picture of Thailand for the Thai began to be painted in bold brush strokes,"[78] as the government pursued Thaification of the economy in earnest. The Phibun government soon demanded that Thai labor comprise three-fourths of all workers in public and private industries.[79] Enforcement was spotty, but the atmosphere caused widespread confusion and fear. Major and minor industries both came under scrutiny, and affected not only unskilled labor but the range of Chinese-dominated trades. Some cases seemed silly, but affected thousands of people. Pettiness could produce major chaos.[80] In the run up to the war, the national assembly passed many measures that reserved a range of jobs for Thais.[81]

What had labor gained after 1932? Harsh working conditions and poor pay drove the labor struggles of the 1930s. The government's promises after 1932 to be of and for common people further excited and encouraged labor to make their demands. Labor found in Thawatt a keen backer, a relatively privileged spokesman-publicist who made his living from words. Thawatt articulated the struggles based on his hopes for the new regime. Critics, meanwhile, labeled strikers as delusional or hoodwinked by sinister forces; and their experience, however difficult, distorted by the language used on their behalf. Activists faced interwoven challenges—especially hostility to resident Chinese, conflict within the government and lack of clear labor laws. Paternalism further enveloped or blunted worker's consciousness and limited their autonomy. The opening chapter of labor in the new era, thus seems a half-finished picture, an incomplete emergence of a new social movement. For Thawatt Rittidej too, the first era of activism ended in disappointment. He largely disappeared from view by the end of the 1930s. Among his last public causes was a personal fight, akin to much of his activism on behalf of the poor against wealthy: he appears among many commoner tenants whom Prince Chula Chakrabongse evicted from land the prince owned and wanted to develop.[82]

Wartime Labor:
The Promise and Peril of Japanese Power

As everywhere in Southeast Asia, the coming of Japanese power to the
region changed Thai history. The war bolstered and endangered labor's
hand, and their goals evolved from fatherly protection to self-protection
and a much larger goal: saving the country from fascism. In the process, a
new breed of labor organizers introduced more sophisticated and effective
means to defend workers, and the Thai-Chinese took center stage in the
struggle. While Phibun Songkhram's brand of popular nationalism during
the war pledged to protect common working people and safeguard national
independence, he and his cohort had to contend with Japanese wartime
labor demands and the reality that Thailand was not really independent
and had to conform to a new power. *Lukjin*-led labor, of both Thai and
Thai-Chinese workers, by contrast radically opposed Phibun's compromise.

Initially, local labor welcomed the arrival of the Japanese. The Japanese
alliance worked initially not only for Phibun and the army, but also for
common people. The Asian superpower arrived in Thailand ambitious to
employ thousands of people on its infrastructure and industrial projects
and had the money to pay them. In 1942, employment boomed on the
now infamous Thai-Burma railway and supporting projects. The scale
of the labor involved, especially regarding Thai workers, is not known.
The Thai government claimed the ninth railway regiment—the Japanese
regiment tasked with completing the rail line—commanded 100,000 total
laborers on the Thai side of the rail line, of whom 40,000 were said to
be Thais. Another Thai government estimate puts the number at 40,000
to 60,000 Thais.[83] Wages the foreign army offered drew thousands of
people to the area. By late 1943, for example, the Japanese offered three
baht per day to unskilled workers for railway labor in Kanchanaburi at
the origin of the Thai-Burma railway, compared to just over one-half
baht per day paid by the Thai government for the central and northern
railways,[84] and three times the unskilled daily rate from the 1930s. In the
early days of the project in June 1942, many more Thai laborers sought
work at Ban Pong in Kanchanaburi province—the beginning point for
the railway—than the Japanese could employ.[85] While many found work
with the Japanese, the sheer numbers meant many others went to work,
at lower wages, for the Thai rails department excavating along sections
of the line, or on roads work in Kanchanaburi and beyond. Still others
worked as motorboat operators transporting materials for the Japanese

and Thai operations along the lesser Kwai and Mae Klong rivers that ran through the area. By a government account, 3,500 boatmen, many of them Chinese, came up from Bangkok alone.[86] Indeed, the Japanese presence stimulated a miniboom in the regional economy.

Over time, however, ready cash paid by the occupiers was not enough for many Thais. As conditions deteriorated on the planned railway line and worksites moved into forbidding, disease-ridden jungle farther west, many fled their worksites and returned home.[87] The Japanese ninth railways regiment, moreover, treated local people and imported labor poorly. Above all, the petty day-to-day mistreatment and arrogance by the Japanese bred discontent. On occasion, their coarseness produced violence. A major clash erupted between Thai labor and the Japanese in November 1942 at Photaram district just to the south of the railhead at Banpong, and then a major fight broke out in the following month at Banpong after a drunken Japanese soldier assaulted a Buddhist monk. Several Japanese soldiers were killed in the skirmish.[88] After the Banpong melee, Thai laborers abandoned the Japanese projects in the area in fear for their safety. The Japanese suspected that the Thai government had instructed laborers not to work for the Japanese there, a claim the Thai government denied.[89] Japanese reports from Banpong confirmed the depth of resistance by Thai laborers. An intercepted Japanese message to Tokyo described a series of attacks on Japanese soldiers by Thai laborers. The message claimed that much of the antagonism stemmed from workers' resentment about their abuse by Japanese soldiers, who treated them the same as prisoners of war.[90] A later report alluded not only to fighting between the Japanese and Thais, but the tearing up of railway ties on a section of the track northeast of Banpong.[91] A Japanese officer noted that local people became openly hostile, with armed Thai men attacking Japanese soldiers and women throwing stones at them in the period after the main fracas.[92] By the end of that year, many Thais had soured completely on the Japanese alliance. As a result, workers sourced from British Malaya increased dramatically, and many became public examples of misery.[93]

The Japanese turned also to another source of labor in early 1943. They relied heavily on the resident Chinese, whose work, channeled through the Chinese Chamber of Commerce and independent labor bosses, draws a complex portrait of Thailand's semicolonial status under the Japanese and their ambiguous relations with the resident Chinese. Above all, it shows that the hypernationalism of the wartime state, and the danger it faced, warped the government's democratic rhetoric of standing for all people and wrapped the new regime in a snug blanket of ethnic chauvinism that endangered the ultimate outsiders: the Chinese.

In the first months of the Pacific War, the old guard of Chinese leadership that organized much of the Thai economy collapsed in disarray. Amid attempts to Thaify the economy as mentioned above, Phibun's government saw a tandem, budding friendship with Japan endangered by local Chinese activism. Beginning in 1937, Chinese secret societies—violent, intimidating players in labor organization—combined with KMT and communist anti-Japanese groups to organize boycotts of Japanese goods and collect funds from local Chinese to send home. Both activities were illegal, but astoundingly successful in damaging Japan's interests in Siam. By the end of 1937, no Chinese would openly trade with Japanese interests and the boycott a near total success.[94] Major police raids followed, and Phibun's government arrested, imprisoned, or deported leading members of the Hainan and Teochiu associations, the two largest language associations, before and after the Japanese attack on Pearl Harbor.[95] A police dragnet in August 1939, as the most prominent example, netted hundreds of suspected anti-Japanese activists, and reams of paper detailing anti-Japanese plans and calling for Chinese labor strikes.[96] Amid this, gangs killed bosses and workers who disobeyed orders. The violence affected not only anti-Japanese work, and stemmed from a range of local turf fights and score settling. Sixty-one Chinese merchants were assassinated around the turn of the decade.[97] State mistrust of the Chinese received a jolt when the chair of the Chinese chamber of commerce and the treasurer of the Teochiu association were assassinated in November 1939. Witnesses at the January 1940 trial of the men who killed the chamber of commerce head revealed the power of the secret societies. The confessed murderers added to the portrait of a society out of control when they stated that the chamber head himself ordered many merchants killed for political or economic reasons. As a final bloody insult to the whole affair, secret society assassins later killed the father of one of those on trial.[98]

With the war, the government redoubled its persecution of resident Chinese.[99] But amid such a heated and hostile atmosphere, the Phibun government still needed Chinese workers for the Japanese, and especially the Japanese rail projects. Four major enlistments of Chinese labor followed between 1942 and 1944, which concluded in May and August 1943, and July and December 1944, respectively.[100] One estimate claims nearly 37,000 Chinese workers traveled to Kanchanaburi and the Thai—Burma railway as a result.[101] Another estimate puts the figure at around 29,000.[102] In either case, the total of Chinese was likely much higher if private hires and the Japanese working independently with the local Chinese population—both of which regularly featured in wartime hiring—are included.[103] To a large extent, the Thai government acted to protect Thais from Japanese labor recruitment by redirecting the burden to the Chinese. At the same time, in management of the labor recruitment drives, the Chinese Chamber of Commerce negotiated high wages for the laborers from the Japanese.

In March 1943, Phibun stated in two documents that the kingdom's Chinese should help shoulder the burden of Japan's labor requests, especially given the hardship imposed on the Thai farming community from the foreign occupier.[104] While the subsequent Chinese labor mobilizations stemmed from this generally phrased Thai government exhortation, a confused route led to their employment. The Thai government resisted efforts by the Japanese to dictate policies regarding the Chinese in order to maintain national sovereignty, but at the same time turned a blind eye to Japanese enlistment of the Chinese workforce. This became apparent in the period around Phibun's end-of-March recommendations. When told that the Thai government did not want any more Thais enrolled as labor, the Japanese believed that the Thais could force the Chinese chamber to cooperate. The Japanese also believed that the chamber itself had absolute authority over the Chinese working population. The Thai side refuted both of these assertions, and denied they could act thusly. First, they refused on the grounds that they could not command a civil organization to do their bidding. Second, the Chinese chamber was not an independent legal authority that had exclusive power over the working population.[105] Confusingly, however, the Thai government told the Japanese they should work out their own arrangement with the Chinese, independent of the Thai government.[106]

An extraordinary situation, then, for a semi-independent Thailand and its Chinese workers unfolded initially in the spring of 1943. In early April, the Chamber of Commerce chair reportedly informed the Japanese that a deal needed to be worked out between the Japanese and Thai officials prior to direct negotiations.[107] Nevertheless, direct Japanese-Chinese chamber talks went ahead; the Japanese did not inform the Thai government of the content of the discussions.[108] At the end of March the Japanese ninth regiment called on the Chinese Chamber of Commerce to recruit 10,000 workers, and would pay them from 2.7 to 3.5 baht per day. Although skeptical about the conditions offered, the Chinese agreed to set up a recruitment committee.[109] In this case, Thai officials sought to reinforce

the cooperation of the Chinese Chamber of Commerce, which met in
early April after the Thai police came to see the chamber representatives
to determine the quota of Chinese to be raised from various provinces.
The Chamber of Commerce set up an employment committee, and in
Bangkok, Chinese assembly halls, business associations and contractors
supplied significant numbers of laborers. Workers were attracted by daily
wage rates substantially higher than average, including a minimum daily
rate of 3.2 baht for laborers.[110] According to a Thai interior ministry report,
initially the Chamber of Commerce agreed on two baht per day, but then
discovered that Chinese laborers at Don Mueang airport were being paid
three baht per day. The Chamber of Commerce and Chinese labor then
demanded and received from the Japanese three, and eventually 3.50 baht,
at Kanchanaburi.[111] In a tangled administrative scenario, the Chinese chamber managed the logistics and kept the Thai metropolitan police and the
Bangkok governor—whose city supplied most of the labor—informed.[112]

The Chinese elite intervened and managed Chinese labor, according
to their own later explanation, because the Japanese mistreated Chinese
workers everywhere in 1942.[113] By one measure, they succeeded astoundingly. Their bargaining produced higher wages than the Japanese told
the Thais they were willing to pay. The Chamber of Commerce refused
the Japanese side's vague health, sickness, material provisions and other
stipulations and won concrete benefits for their workers.[114]

It is probably unfair to hold a wartime government in crisis to
account for changeable, contradictory or hypocritical social policies. Still,
the Phibun government's anti-Chinese chauvinism and callous disregard
for citizens' and residents' welfare flagrantly contradicted much of the
post-1932 claims to a new social compact. In the war, the Chinese commercial class acted where the government would not. Further, a parallel,
Chinese-driven movement to the Chinese chamber's role in mediating
labor problems upcountry emerged the during the war. A rejuvenated
communist movement organized labor and guided strikes in new Thai
state enterprises and also in Japanese factories.

Lukjin Labor become Thai Patriots

Nationalist mythology lionizes the Seri Thai (Free Thai)—a politically
diverse coalition of anti-Phibun, anti-Japanese groups led mainly by Pridi—
as wartime heroes who fought off the invaders, deposed dictatorship, and

saved democracy. In fact, the communists alone effectively resisted the Japanese and channeled a new wave of popular activism that contributed to postwar democracy.[115] Their popular political influence and support to the civilians in the People's Party after 1945 is an ironic outcome enabled by the war. The war years turned an alien movement into a Thai one.

A communist party operated in Siam from the 1920s and until the revolution overseas Chinese and Vietnamese dominated. They did not publish in Thai and directed their activity mainly to their home countries.[116] The few occasions before 1932 when communists called for revolution in Siam caused great alarm, and the king for one took the threat seriously. Responding to one detailed Chinese text distributed in 1930, Prajadhipok wrote that the work should be read by all of his ministers, and that it "was very well written, and not the work of someone foolish . . . If the . . . document were disseminated among the agriculture classes in Siam, many might find it quite convincing."[117] The party pledged after 1932 to expand its work among Thai people—a communist document from September 1932 listed 325 party members, none of whom were Thai—but faced persecution from the new government. The new regime sent hundreds to jail and, while a minirevival of the party's fortunes occurred in the mid-1930s, by later in the decade the party faced its extinction.[118]

In the 1930s, communists and the People's Party mistrusted each other. In English, Thai and Chinese leaflets that it distributed in the autumn of 1932, the party denounced the new regime as fake revolutionaries, and a disgruntled elite that took power from the king out of self-interest, not as they claimed to help the poor.[119] Communist pamphleteering was a feature of Bangkok life for the first four years after the People's Party took power, and spread to provincial towns, including a marked presence in the northeast from 1934 until the first half of 1936.[120] The Promoter's faced a twin fight in the early phase of the revolution, against royalists and communists alike. Communist rhetoric as just described matched the royalist criticism of the People's Party almost note for note. In a delicious irony, those from the two extremes of the political spectrum not only spoke the same way about the Promoters, but Communists and those suspected of helping the counterrevolution also often became jailhouse friends. Luen Saraphaiwanich, among others, fondly recalled the mutual support and stimulating conversations among these strange political bedfellows.[121]

Prison became one of the key sites through which *lukjin* made their "detour to Thai-ness" as Kasian puts it. Thaiifying communism occurred among a young cohort of radicals from mainly well-to-do *lukjin* commercial families who gained good educations, became highly critical of Thai and Asian affairs, and eschewed comfortable careers to raise the political consciousness of ordinary people, Thai and *lukjin* alike, amid the danger of war. Phibun's political and economic assault on the Chinese had largely destroyed the overseas Chinese communist cohort in Siam. A movement to rejuvenate the party in 1940 or 1941 resulted in a new "Thai Department" comprising mainly *lukjin* comrades.[122] The Japanese arrival in Thailand, following as it did Phibun's assault on the Chinese, coincided with a fresh communist party attempt to mobilize Thais and resident Chinese against the war, and gave a golden opportunity for a cosmopolitan class to become Thai patriots and remake politics.[123]

The colorful biographies of two founders of the rejuvenated party—Si Anothai and Jit Lehawat—show how the times changed labor leadership, as Thai-Chinese came to the fore. Si Anothai was a northerner born into a mixed Chinese and Tai minority family in 1921. His wet nurse, a slave in a lord of Phrae's household, fed not only his body but also his resentment of the powerful. She regaled him with tales of feudal exploitation under the old upcountry rulers. A precocious youth, he attended Assumption in Bangkok, one of the city's premier schools patronized by many Thai-Chinese commercial families as well as upper-class Thais. Mangkon Samsen, the Thai-Chinese businessman who entered the national assembly and sued Thawatt for his attack on the king, was one of his elders and made a strong impression on Si when Mangkon led a student strike against high school fees. (Assumption expelled Mangkon as a result.) Si's precociousness allowed him to complete high school in two years. He learned to read English well, and was impressed by Marx's *Capital*, the *Anti-Duhring*, and the *Communist Manifesto*. He also translated Lu Xun's classic novella *The Real Story of Ah Q* in Thai from Chinese. When his father pressured Si to study law at Thammasat, he rebelled and studied railway engineering within the rails department and graduated in 1943 at age twenty-two. In the meanwhile, Si and other well-off students from good schools in 1940 established the Khabuankan Thai Issara (Thai Independence Movement) to combat the growing Japanese menace in Asia, and entered major industrial plants—tobacco, rice and sawmills, a liquor distillery, the Bangkok docks and the Makkasan rails—as laborers to organize other workers.[124]

Jit Lehawat, a Thai citizen born in 1910, spent time in prison in China and French Indochina during the 1930s and 1940s for his involvement in communist and anti-Japanese work.[125] Jit was born in the central province of Suphanburi to a father from a Teochiu commercial family of herbal apothecaries, long resident in Siam, and a Mon mother. At age four, he accompanied his father to China.[126] He remained there to study through high school. He then passed into a teacher training school in Nanking before studying at an art college in Shanghai. As a teenager, he joined the Chinese communist movement, and at twenty-one he participated in the September 1931 protests against Japan's invasion of Manchuria. The nationalist government sent him to prison in 1934 on communism charges. After his release two years later he returned to Siam where he taught in a Chinese school in Khon Kaen in the northeast, and then in Bangkok in the main school funded through the Chinese chamber of commerce. He also became a leader in anti-Japanese politics.

Amid anti-Chinese politics on the eve of war, Jit feared for his family's safety and sent them to live with his father in Suphanburi while he himself traveled to French Indochina as part of his work in the anti-Japanese movement. There he campaigned against fascism and was again jailed, this time by the French authorities in Lao in December 1939. After four months in jail, Jit gained release and went to Phnom Penh when the Thai-French war erupted in May 1940. He returned to Bangkok in June 1941.

Jit's practical experience overseas contributed to the small group's interest in the political theory, and publicity, of resistance, and complemented Si's learning. Damri Ruangsutham and Wit Udomprasert—two additional founding comrades—asked Jit to join their political-economy study group after he returned from Phnom Penh. The group adopted the communist party's "semi-colonial, semi-feudal" designation of Thai society: that is, a society partly controlled by the West and partly by traditional lords.

The new Phak Khommunit Thai (Thai Communist Party), at its first party congress in December 1942 issued a policy platform that relied on mainland Chinese communist arguments for their raison d'être: drive out the Japanese bandits, cooperate with the Allies, end discrimination against the Chinese in Thailand. They also espoused, as the Chinese communists did, establishment of democracy, freedom of speech and association, and improvement of popular welfare.[127] While mirroring their great neighbor's language, these demands also echoed the republican rhetoric from the People's Party before the hypernationalism of Phibun's government. The party also continuously chronicled their struggle. In contrast to the Pridi-led Seri Thai movement that grew through the bureaucracy, the communist movement spread through publicity and journalism.[128] The *Mahachon*

(The Masses) newspaper began in 1942 in both Thai and Chinese, and the inaugural issue appeared on May Day.[129]

Practically, the party focused on organizing workers within Thai and Japanese factories. The war changed the mood considerably from Thawatt's early days: the party channeled labor militancy, not only moral appeals or self-help, against owners and organized not only strikes and slowdowns, but also machine breaking and destroying products to impede the war effort.[130] Meanwhile, the party organized violent anti-Japanese action; in the south, the party worked in coordination with the Malayan Communist Party. Party support in the south stemmed from the concentration of unskilled Chinese workers in the rubber and tin industries; in Bangkok Thai labor had entered the labor force in larger numbers and there the party worked through a dual ethnic and occupational frame. While the 1930 document that troubled Prajadhipok detailed the peasant's misery, Maoism with its rural focus lay in the party's future. At the time it focused on the proletariat.[131]

During the Japanese period, Si Anothai and the others organized labor on the Bangkok docks, the tobacco monopoly, the Makkasan rail that Thawatt had patronized earlier, and sawmills and large urban rice mills, among others. Their work mobilized overseas and locally born Chinese and Thai labor. In some cases, they tapped into an already active laboring class. In 1941, for example, workers struck at the Thai Tobacco Monopoly—a Phibun enterprise that superseded the old semicolonial British-American Tobacco Co. Workers from the Electricity Board, another state enterprise, joined them in a 1,300-strong worker strike. They succeeded in their demands for higher pay and welfare provisions from the government. The leaders of the two organizations also combined to form a state enterprise welfare association under labor's direction. Pridi's backers helped the group, including Sanguan Tularaks—a radical whose 1930s newspaper *Sajja* Mano labeled the *Pravda* of Siam—who was the head of the tobacco monopoly.[132] Soon after the 1942 congress, the party sent Si into the state-owned tobacco factory to further the workers' aid association work.[133]

Labor organizers and strikers faced constant threat. The Thai government arrested many communists and fellow travelers in early 1942; some gained released soon after arrest, others languished in jail for the rest of the war.[134] In 1943, the Japanese—working with the Thai police to identify troublemakers and seeking information on the anti-Japanese underground—arrested and tortured the two elder sisters of Wit Udomprasert, one of *Mahachon*'s founders who borrowed money from his family to begin the newspaper.[135]

Wartime hardship prompted waves of labor activism and planted the seeds of panethnic working-class consciousness in the kingdom. In this environment, in 1944 the party set up the Saha Samakhom Totan Yipun—the Anti-Japanese United Association—and in the middle of that year assembled various Bangkok workers' organizations into the Saha Samakhom Kammakon Krungthep—the Bangkok United Association of Workers.[136] Seven Bangkok workers' assemblies joined to establish the group, and by the end of that year and in early 1945 the group sent people into Japanese factories to disrupt production and organize workers.[137] According to an organizer, the anti-Japanese resistance directed more than 170 strikes from late 1943 to late 1944. In addition to strikes over wages and conditions, the communists encouraged strikes on patriotic grounds: thirty-five of the strikes happened at Japanese armaments and war materiel factories.[138] Economic failure could turn into political success. At a Japanese shipbuilding site in the middle of 1944, 1,000 Thai and Chinese laborers demanded higher wages and better health and safety protections. The Japanese in response sent in the army to surround the yard, and arrested and interrogated many. A large worker protest resulted and in a tense situation the Japanese backed down and released the prisoners. They did not, however, meet the wage and other demands of the workers.[139] Political awareness—and tactical progress—was forged at Thai sites also. Workers led by women struck at two large match factories under Thai-Chinese ownership in August and September 1943. Seven hundred workers, including children, struck against long hours toiling for meager wages—from forty to sixty satang per day. Management told the workers that wages could not be raised since profit margins were too low in a Thai-government controlled industry. They also threatened that if the workers did not return to work the Japanese would forcefully intervene. Three women organizers, active in the anti-Japanese resistance, forged a coordinated strike at both factories that publicized their plight to students, women's groups and wider society. According to Damri, their work became a template for subsequent broadly pitched labor activism.[140]

Labor 1945–1947:
Civilian Democracy and the Legacy of the War

The anti-Japanese and labor groups worked underground during the war, and it is hard to say how many members they had. But many in these groups entered the postwar labor movements, where they gained legitimacy not only for fighting for ordinary workers but also because of their politics as the prime wartime nationalist, anti-Japanese force. The organizations stood for both Thai and Chinese labor, which bucks the conventional wisdom that the communist movement was entirely a Chinese affair. Moreover, as anticipated above in the activism at the Thai Tobacco Monopoly, communist labor leaders developed good relations with the Pridi factions in the government that worked against Phibun, an alliance that endured until the 1947 coup ended both group's political clout.[141]

The largest postwar labor organization grew from wartime communist-sponsored groups. The old Saha Samakhom Kammakon Krungthep after the war gained legal recognition in 1946 as the Samakhom Saha Achiwa Kammakon haeng Prathet Thai (United Labor Association of Thailand); 40,000 people attended its formal opening on January 1, 1947.[142] The group helped establish a new rice mill workers union in 1946, which within the year had over 5,000 members from all of the major Bangkok rice mills: fifty Thai-Chinese owned mills and nineteen owned by the Thai Rice Co. Ltd. Bunsong Wijarana, born in 1923, led the rice labor movement. He grew up in the rice labor trade amid a life of toil, with no days off apart from Chinese Lunar New Year—when the Thai-Chinese managers went home to their families—and no health insurance or benefits. Bunsong's group won health cover, paid leave and double pay on Sundays for rice workers.[143] By the summer of 1946, strikers led a range of actions, encouraged by the Saha achiwa, in the tobacco monopoly, the Thai rice company, among state airways technicians, and in the Makkasan rails.[144]

The June 1946 Makkasan railway strike reestablished rail labor as a major activist group. In the new atmosphere given oxygen by the democratic spirit after the war, the group claimed a major victory when the state enterprise became the first government firm ever to grant health insurance to workers.[145] Wisit Sripatra became the head of the Makkasan rail labor organization that year, and his colorful life is a fitting comparison to others during the first chapter of modern Thai labor history. Thawatt, for example, came from some privilege, so too did Wisit, but in a more dangerous guise; Thawatt's career from journalism, Wisit's in the rice trade; Thawatt's firmly a product of the new economy, Wisit is a seeming throwback to secret societies and their rough justice. Wisit was born in 1911; his father was a gambler, alcoholic, and opium addict. From an early age Wisit worked in an opium den, where he took a great interest in reading because addicts would often arrive with newspapers and books to while away the time. In his teens he worked for a wealthy Chinese rice miller and his Thai wife, a lady who owned extensive land in the Rangsit district north of Bangkok. Wisit threatened people for a living at this time; he was a hired gun at the mill. In an abrupt about face, he then chose a path of peace, and lived for one month as a monk during the monsoon season (known as a rains retreat). Thereafter, Wisit embarked on a short-lived career in the naval survey department and worked in the south. But still only in his twenties, Wisit lost his position when the government arrested his superior for alleged complicity in the Bowondet rebellion. During the war, Wisit joined an anti-Japanese group that was independent of the Seri Thai but perhaps communist led. In the flux of Thai politics after the war his career blossomed and died. He gained renown as a skilled advocate for labor via the Makkasan work, and for the few years of thriving civilian democracy played a key role in labor activism. In 1948, however, as the government swung against civilian democracy, Sangh Patanothai, one of Phibun's supporters who took over leadership of a government-backed labor organization, accused Wisit of communism and he was imprisoned. He helped establish a socialist party in the late 1950s, but the military dictatorship at the decade's close ended their fortunes. Thereafter, in the 1960s Wisit was in and out of jail.[146]

The civilian government's postwar relations with labor were complex. By the account of a police special branch officer, part of his unit frequently intervened in disputes. The police, unbeknownst to workers, leaned on capital to compromise with labor.[147] Pridi, who was premier briefly in 1946 but behind the scenes the leader of postwar democratic governments, directed the special branch to support labor.[148] After his resignation, special branch help continued. In 1946 major strikes erupted among rice coolies. In one, the state railways authority fired five workers who transported rice at Bangkok Noi station and who led demands for better pay and conditions. In solidarity with the fired workers, rice transporters, working on the Battambang-Bangkok rail line to fulfill British demands for rice,[149] struck; the railway authorities fired seventy of them. Additional workers from waterways rice transport units joined the strike. In distress over paddy sitting idly at Bangkok rail stations, management fired many of the strikers and hired replacements, which in turn produced a tense confrontation between the two workers' groups. Finally, police intervened and separated the two to prevent violence.[150] Management's scab solution did not work out according to plan. When the replacement workers transported the paddy to urban mills, mill workers refused to take the paddy. A widespread urban mills strike ensued.[151] Prompted by the government's worries over the British reaction to the emerging labor movement, the ministry of interior arranged meetings between the labor leaders and the rail authorities. The latter refused to compromise, however, or to reinstate the five workers fired from Bangkok Noi station. The police special branch intervened and made secret payments to the five until they found new work.[152]

A sorry ending for these five highlights the complexity of postwar labor politics and the fragility of civilian democratic government in a chaotic time. The five initially found work at the Saphahan organization, a government body set up by Thongplaeo Chonlaphumi in collaboration with a French legal scholar who worked at Thammasat. Thongplaeo, born in 1912, graduated high school three years before the revolution and became a Promoter. In the 1930s, he worked in finance and customs for the government, obtained a law degree, and then a law doctorate in France. He remained in government during the war where he joined an expanding cohort of Pridi people who opposed Phibun's growing dictatorship, and was secretary to the national assembly—and also an assemblyman—until Phibun terminated his appointment in 1943. Through these years, and until the right-wing coup of 1947, Thongplaeo lectured in economics at Thammasat.[153] Among many other civilians from the People's Party, he highlighted economic welfare as a key postwar problem. His Saphahan began with good intentions as a mechanism to distribute consumer goods at a controlled price, and a fat budget of 50 million baht. In time corruption swallowed the Saphahan, and Thongplaeo himself asked the special branch to close it. As a sign of the group's powerful stakeholders—who personally benefited—Thongplaeo had to ask the police for help. Chiap Amphunan, a special branch officer who assisted labor at the time under Pridi's direction, in response pointed to the group's political clout. He told Thongplaeo that the police could not close the Saphahan but only rein in some of its more obvious fraud.[154]

Eventually, the Saphahan closed, and the five workers sponsored by the special branch lost their jobs. Chiap gave them a letter to take to the Saha achiwa that asked the latter to help the five. The Saha achiwa refused since the workers were not dues-paying members. Chiap lamented that Saha achiwa's reaction showed their elitism, and their lack of support for workers they pledged to protect.[155] Chiap also expressed the more likely explanation for the Saha achiwa's wariness: crackdowns, round-ups of leaders, mixed with spasmodic paternalist support for workers. Earlier in

1946, Chiap had visited Tianthai Apichatbutr, Saha achiwa's leader, and offered special branch help in worker disputes. Tianthai was a young jack of all trades from a prosperous commercial family. After graduating from Assumption, Tianthai in the 1930s worked for foreign businesses, was hired into the customs department of the finance ministry, lectured in law, and then became a labor activist during the war.[156] He was part of an active Pridi network, and had collaborated with Thawatt Rittidej's friend Wat Sunthonjamon in establishing the Manutham Law Office in 1939. Now, Tianthai, surprised by Chiap's offer, refused. Chiap at the time found this reasonable, albeit disappointing, since the special branch, and the People's Party government generally, had a checkered relation with labor. Tianthai hence was rightly suspicious of Chiap's friendliness.[157]

Conclusion

Pridi argued that the People's Party chose "people" (*ratsadon*) for their group's name because they were identical to most people, and lacked any advantage or privilege. As Pridi explained it,

> At the time most of the population (*ponlamueang*) under the governing power called themselves "*ratsadon*" . . . for example when recalling some hard times, the people would say "the commoners suffered every step of the way." This shows the characteristic life of people under the absolute monarchy. For that reason, we chose People's Party, to show the directness of our position with the people's needs.[158]

Labor history tells a much more complex story, in which the People's Party became a new elite whose interests sometimes joined and sometimes diverged from the working class because of political circumstance, ethnic prejudice, and war.

Partly the hesitant intervention in labor disputes resulted from conflicts in the government, with the People's Party weakness limiting their ability to push through radical change. The People's Party also, in their optimism about what the revolution could accomplish, misread the difficulty of changing old regime mentalities. Pridi remarked fifty years later that when old-regime officers were brought into the government after June 1932, he "hoped that they would be more progressive than they acted."[159]

But Pridi also offered ideas on a captive mind syndrome of absolutist Siam that arguably applies equally to himself and his group as it did to people he came into conflict with. In the same piece of writing Pridi argued,

> The party or revolutionary movement to establish a new society is . . . comprised of people who were born in the old society. They form a progressive element, who forsake their standing in the old system and devote their lives to establish a progressive new society. But as this progressive element is born and lives in the old society, they carry the residual vision and habits of the old society embedded within themselves.[160]

The "progressive" element did not forsake the standing from the old system that gave them an advantage, and their drive for a new society proceeded irregularly with their attempts to control and lead. Additionally, the People's Party cohort and their wider relationships were multidimensional, pro- and antimilitarist, populist and authoritarian, sympathetic and hostile to the Chinese. Moreover, the entire constellation of relations changed dramatically with the various crises, especially the royalist rebellion of the 1930s and the Pacific War. In addition, the "people" in this chapter's story comprised a fluid and multifarious mosaic: overseas Chinese labor, ethnic Thai labor, Thai-Chinese capitalists, popular Thai advocates, popular Chinese advocates, monarchic and republican spokesmen. In the charged war and postwar atmosphere, when state-labor relations featured wars of position and influence, the larger pattern of a growing popular demand for welfare emerges clearly. The People's Party revolution put in motion forces that the Promoters could not control.

Chapter Three

Spokesmen for the Peasantry

The Revolution and Social Welfare

The absolutist state existed for only four decades, from Chulalongkorn's reforms of 1892 to the 1932 revolution; its champions avow it put the country on the road to modernity and reformed centuries-old features of Thai society. King Prajadhipok—Chulalongkorn's son—and Prajadhipok's nephew Chula Chakrabongse—Chulalongkorn's grandson—cast Chulalongkorn's reforms as the real revolution of modern Thai society.[1] A popular Western historian wrote that the king "took his generation and his country by the ear and flung them outward into the world. His rare understanding of both what it meant to be modern and what it meant to be Thai and the skill with which he manipulated the power at his command meant for his country the preservation of its independence and the creative shaping of its modern identity."[2]

The "Chulalongkorn view" favorably contrasts absolutist Siam with its predecessors.[3] The old Siam of decentralized and arbitrary power, purely local economies, slavery, and forced labor, tax "farms"—skimming operations for wealthy people to trade in important commodities—all survived the growing intrusiveness of Western economic power. It took a new state to abolish old Siam, centralize power in the capital and govern through institutions borrowed from the West. The country became tied to international commerce to a degree never before experienced in the late nineteenth century and social mobility allowed people to take advantage of new economic opportunity. By the turn of the twentieth century, the absolute monarchy governed a theoretically unified state.[4] The dominant narrative of Thai history since the early twentieth century has asserted that the kings and their entourages ensured harmonious Thai social development and national freedom during the era of Western imperialism.[5] Consensus under kingly rule, not conflict, is the hallmark of standard history. Great men relieved the stresses of modernity and resolved the difficulties of forging a unified state and society.

In the first half of the twentieth century, however, reality was much more complex and fraught. In the countryside, broadly speaking, two Siams existed. One depended on the world economy. The export-driven, monetized society developed mainly in the central plains to the north of Bangkok, the tin and rubber-producing regions of the south, and some forestry areas around Chiang Mai in the north. A small bourgeoisie—mainly of Thai-Chinese descent—attained tremendous wealth that they used to enjoy cosmopolitan lifestyles and sometimes forge political influence high in the government. At the same time, these areas tied closely to the modern economy had the greatest wealth inequalities, the highest levels of debt and tenancy, and the least stable incomes. Within this zone, Bangkok and the central plains to the immediate north of the city also produced much of the new intelligentsia that staffed the civil service, commercial firms and the independent professions.

People in the other Siam lived largely from subsistence farming, had little use of money and less debt. Class differences were much less pronounced here than in the capitalizing areas. People were less familiar with the wider world, and ambitious young people especially had limited opportunity to improve their position. Most people lived in small communities, often insecure and diseased. Here Siam's greater integration into the global economy resulted in poverty, powerlessness, and isolation. Also, however, educated outsiders in remote provinces that had been subordinated to Bangkok remained stubborn voices advocating a measure of independence from central power. The northeastern plateau was the largest area in this Siam, and its population the least integrated into the national state. And here a young generation expressed itself most forcefully.

The twin forces of international capitalism and domestic political integration—even though always uneven and irregular in their impact—shaped household economics and mentalities. Critics of the old regime referred to twin worlds in their attacks; one developing too quickly in the wrong way and the other not developing at all. From one, they pointed to the exposure to the world economy and unregulated capitalism resulting in exploitation. From the other, they identified isolation and backwardness.

The social fragmentation that the People's Party inherited continued to stymie their attempts at national integration and affected their political control. It also produced a desire for a better life.

Before the revolution, Pridi argued consistently to his fellow Promoters that a parliamentary system must be introduced to alleviate rural poverty and insecurity.[6] The perception that Siam's backwardness stemmed from the old regime's weakness fueled the revolutionary fire. This chapter gives a snapshot of rural history, and then we hear the popular clamor for reform that the revolution produced, and the struggles among state planners to deal with rural poverty. In an ironic twist, we will see that right-wing, hypernationalist state policies under the Phibun government from 1938 echoed elements of earlier, tarnished left-wing dreams for a collective economy, and that motley elements of state planning continued as core parts of the popular clamor for rural welfare.

The Stable Disorder of Agrarian Semicapitalism

The government elite before the revolution held conflicting opinions about rural Siam's developmental needs. Despite the obvious hardship of the Great Depression, at a Bangkok Rotary Club talk in 1931, a foreign adviser to the government portrayed the peasantry as happy living their simple lives. Chinese exploitation, in this telling, posed the main obstacle to rural welfare. Similarly, a French Indochinese official with ties to the government wrote in a Bangkok newspaper that pre-1932 Siam was a tropical arcadia, with Chinese troublemakers alone responsible for trying to stir up grievances.[7] Apologists for the good old days found Chinese exploitation a powerful polemical weapon, as they did the lost rusticity of traditional Siam.[8]

But for the modernizers of the People's Party and people enthused by the revolution, nostalgia was not what it used to be. They looked forward instead to a better life that could be brought with state-mandated material progress.

For the revolutionaries and other critics in absolutist years, the government elite directed the exploitation but were not the sole actors or beneficiaries. Public opinion also identified Western and Chinese commercial men as reaping the fortunes of the Thai economy. Since the 1920s, the segments of the popular press that criticized absolutism alleged that the political elite worked hand in glove with the Chinese merchants and foreign firms to purposefully squeeze the peasantry in single-minded pursuit of profits. Critics of the old regime used a clear binary of producer/parasite to frame injustice in the period. Exploitation as the reason for peasant poverty was a powerful trope repeated in attacks on the old regime before and after the revolution. In reality, the picture of Thai farming and peasant livelihoods is very mixed.

Rice is the staple food that sustains Thai life, and more than any other commodity, paddy generated the surplus revenue that maintained the royal-noble elite, and then the People's Party, in power. The value of rice exports roughly equaled, and in some years exceeded, the total national budget over the 1930s.[9] The censuses of 1929 and 1937 counted roughly 6 to 8 million people as farmers, and rice farmers accounted for more than four-fifths of total labor in the kingdom in these years.[10] From the late nineteenth century, the rice frontier expanded continuously into undeveloped areas. The area of paddy cultivation in the central region doubled in the period between 1905 and the Pacific War, and the profit-seeking expanded elsewhere as well with all other areas having a fivefold increase in the area under cultivation.[11] The main expansion in the first half of the century was in the central plains, where farmers and investors steadily drained the Chaophraya River delta—a vast expanse of swampland infested with crocodiles and traditionally home to bandits and others avoiding the state—and cultivated the new fields. Peasants in the central plains initially and then elsewhere—"like water rising on an uneven surface"[12]—took advantage of the state's abandonment of the old forced-labor obligations to the lords, in the twin forms of slavery (abolished in 1874) and corvée labor (1905), and seized on the cash opportunities of the commodity export economy.

Capitalist transformation outstripped the legal regime that regulated the economy. Laws issued in the first decade of the twentieth century regularized the agriculture ministry's use of land titles and cadastral surveys to determine land ownership, but these regulations only applied to Rangsit and other major canal tracts where since the late nineteenth century the royals had bought land. Everywhere else, as the 1909 Land Act confirmed, the practice of "hold and reserve" and tax payments sent to the Ministry of Finance sufficed to claim de facto ownership of farm-land.[13] Pridi and other People's Party lawyers, experts in administrative and commercial law, sought a legal revolution to help govern the country's economy. Their efforts, however, met the inertia of ad hoc arrangements that had been used over decades. Land title remained a fuzzy concept until well after the war. By the 1950s, a cadastral survey covered only 5 percent of land outside the central region. Remarkably, in the mid-1960s land deeds covered only 35 percent of all land in the kingdom and most of these were central lands.[14]

Chinese middlemen linked the nation of smallholders to the global market. The lower Chaophraya River delta, the hub of agricultural capitalism, had no roads, and small Chinese traders traveled the watery landscape in small boats buying rice from independent farmers and selling foreign goods. The thousands of boatmen mentioned in the last chapter who traveled up to Kanchanaburi to exploit market opportunities offered by the Japanese came from a much longer lineage of riverine traders. By the early 1900s the small Chinese trader reached anywhere commerce was possible and dominated trade in all provincial market towns. Critics ignored Chinese industry's role in modernizing Siam, and they viewed the immigrants in much more simplistic and scornful terms. The salience of Chinese in commerce, and their relative wealth in contrast to the peasantry, created a perception that they lived easily off of others' hard work. In the depression, Thai nationalists—some in the bureaucracy, some in the popular press, and some failed businessmen looking to assign blame for their problems—targeted the Chinese as sucking the life out of a naive and powerless peasantry. But in fact as highlighted by Carle Zimmerman and James Andrews, two Harvard University academics hired by the government for rural surveys in 1931 and 1935, paddy buying was very competitive and exhausting work, and the web of world market forces caught both paddy dealers and peasants at a disadvantage. Neither, Zimmerman and Andrews concluded, had an effective form of self-defense.[15]

Moreover, blithely accusing the Chinese as alien parasites falsified the reality of how rural debt occurred. Farmers used whatever means of credit and security they could, and sought loans first from relatives or villagers since such money could be gained informally and with little or no interest. People known to each other arranged most debt in Siam in the 1930s, and according to a contemporary observer Thai women were much better at and more interested in lending money at interest to their fellow villagers than their men.[16] Andrews found that debt to relatives accounted for nearly three-quarters of all debt in the northeast and more than four-fifths in the south. These figures accord with the low commercialization in these areas. Predictably, surveys discovered lower amounts of kin debt in the center (just under half owed to relatives) and north (one-fifth). And the most commercially oriented pockets in each region had the highest debt to strangers. Where loans exceeded debts, villages had more wealth and villagers lent more money to outsiders; where debts exceeded loans, villagers were poorer and people borrowed more from outsiders. So in Khorat, the gateway to the northeast region and the launching pad for the Bowondet rebellion of October 1933, commercial agriculture in a small area around the town brought higher incomes and more wealth, and poor neighboring villagers had to borrow from townspeople they did not know.[17] Again, Phibun's ban on Chinese in key northeast towns during the war reflected the region's commercial dynamism even if the remedy did not match the problem. Lenders in Khorat as elsewhere may have been Chinese, but equally could have been wealthier Thai farmers who had no other money-bearing outlet for their wealth. The high tenancy areas of the central plains carried the greatest debt burdens, but predatory Chinese were not the cause. Thai farming, as Andrews noted in the mid-1930s, inevitably entailed debt because of the work's periodicity. Especially in the commercialized areas, farmers needed loans at planting time and hoped to pay the debt at harvest. In countries with well-developed financial markets, these funds came from credit institutions and banks, that is, from strangers. In poor countries like Siam, farmers relied on other farmers with whom they had a personal connection through kin networks or cooperative societies. Both capitalist and traditional Siam had only rudimentary financial markets. A variety of circumstances such as bad family or village relations forced people to borrow from moneylenders. Faced with the insecurity of their loan, the lenders sensibly sought to maximize the terms to their benefit.

Political appeals rarely target their listeners' coolheadedness. Talk of exploitation offered a simple explanation of mistreatment by an elite working with a parasitical middle class that also happened to be foreign. Chinese traders, moreover, were the agents of consumerism. Neither necessities nor luxury items would have reached rural areas without them. Carle Zimmerman, a Harvard academic hired by the government for a rural survey in 1931, found village self-sufficiency a thing of the past. Income growth in the twentieth century from rice exports turned farmers and landowners away from the other crops—tobacco, sugar, and cotton—that they had previously cultivated for home use. In common with many other colonial economies, households in the Thai central plains sold one major commodity to (mainly Thai-Chinese) middlemen and bought foreign goods for all other aspects of life. The Chinese in Siam then sold imported cotton, cigarettes, and sugar from the UK, India, Japan, and

Holland, and these had replaced local products by the interwar period.[18] All areas of the country that had a nearby sizable market town turned increasingly to rely on foreign manufactures in everyday life.[19]

Especially, the central plains became the commercial center of the country. On the one hand, peasant ownership and greater income are central parts of the emerging agricultural capitalism. At the same time, landlessness and the resulting ties of rents, taxes, and debts also bound large swathes of the population and especially those in the center of the country.[20] Capital accumulation drove the aggregation of larger farms in the Chaophraya valley than anywhere else in the kingdom. Zimmerman found that farms in the central plains were much larger than elsewhere.[21] Also, on average, more than one-third of central plains families surveyed owned no land. Landlessness encompassed more than three-quarters of the population of greater Bangkok villages surveyed, and almost all in the irrigation district of Rangsit.[22] By the early 1930s, the Rangsit area had the highest tenancy rates in the kingdom, with more than four in five people renting land and having often poor relations with their land-lords.[23] Absentee landlords here invested nothing but raised rents on the tenants if the latter developed the land for better returns.[24] Unsurprisingly, tenants rarely made the effort. Ramshackle huts sprawled along the canal banks, housing the migrant population that moved to the area. Many of these immigrants came from the northeastern Lao-speaking population.

As critics frequently remarked, greater integration with the world economy did not bring technological improvement. Even as many determined, or desperate, farmers and industrious merchants sold on the modern world market, traditional modes of agriculture prevailed all over the country. With some rare exceptions, farmers did not irrigate in any systematic way, used manure rarely, and harvested and threshed rice by hand.[25] Plowing was poor, rarely breaking the ground to more than three inches deep (and hence exhausting the soil quickly) and, along with indifferent seed selection, this limited production per *rai*. Rangsit farmers in the most commercialized part of the country, and remote upcountry farmers both relied on age old techniques. Plows seemed to be relics from the ancient tales: a wooden shaft and tip, with iron tips less commonly. Some areas lacked plows until the twentieth century; an old villager in Trang province in the south explained to Chatthip Nartsupha, a prom-inent Thai political-economic historian, how farmers chased buffaloes around a field to break up the earth. Plows arrived there in 1903.[26] Carts in the northeast in the 1930s were "of an ancient style with a roof, and an ungreased wooden axle. Wherever there are carts, their singing noise is heard long distances away."[27]

Zimmerman's northeastern surveys covered arguably the poorest and most remote parts of the kingdom. An estimated 2.58 million people,[28] around a quarter of the kingdom's population, lived in the lower half of the northeast in the 1930s, the home of many of the leading voices for rural welfare. The region—while remote, ethnically complex and with a long-standing streak of independence—still showed economic similarities to other parts of the country. Agricultural technology, as Zimmerman noted, was primitive. Rainfall, irregular and unpredictable, was usually the only the source of irrigation.[29] Rarely did farmers enjoy two consecutive years of good crop yields in this environment. Overcoming agricultural backward-ness—with new crop strains, better education, and more credit—required always scarce ready money. Additionally, as in other regions the legacy of laissez-faire expansionism limited the spread of farming cooperatives since few people had clear land titles.[30] Popular mobility marked peasant life. Northeastern people moved to the central plains for opportunity, and to the Rangsit development as mentioned above. Within the northeast as well sometimes entire villages would decamp to a promising farming area, and then return from whence they came depending on the available work.[31]

The northeast was not trapped in a time warp. By the late 1920s, had thirty rice mills, and the next largest town in the region at Ubon had an additional five.[32] The growth of mills showed the penetration of commercial agriculture and also the importance of railway expansion in linking the region to the world. The rails enabled the 1933 rebellion, and also the growth of regional commerce. Railways enhanced the appeal of local mills since they eliminated the processing fees paid to Bangkok millers and also allowed transport of greater volumes of rice to the city.

What applied to the northeast applied everywhere: international demand fueled capitalist expansion. In the 1930s, farmers exported about half of all rice grown, and rice accounted for around 70 percent of all exports before the war.[33] But the boom also fueled resentment of the costs involved. The revolutionary generation born around 1900 grew up with a metaphor and image for official exploitation of the peasantry. The People's Party manifesto issued on the morning of the revolution accused the old regime of "farming on the backs of the people," a phrase used by petitioners seeking government relief going back to the sixth reign (1910–1925), and which especially appeared frequently among central plains boom areas like Rangsit.[34] Pridi and others turned it into a national metaphor. Pridi recalled decades after the event the indignation he felt at the plight of the peasantry under the absolutist system and the realization that a new political regime was needed to abolish their misery.[35]

In 1930, Prajadhipok labeled the lack of agricultural modernization as "criminal neglect of an obvious duty." In response to recent agriculture ministry proposals for application of agricultural science, he wrote on a report that it "should have been done 20 years ago."[36] But at that time under his father Chulalongkorn's reign, geopolitics and domestic calculus steered money away from the countryside. Additional aspects of state policy account for Siam's underdevelopment, and make inadequate the laments of people like Prajadhipok. Siam was bound by an international system that worked against the interests of most people, and the elite ignored the problems of rudimentary credit and primitive farming techniques so long as the rice trade boomed.

Outsiders Clamor for Rural Improvement

The revolution's effects on the anarchic rural economy were complex and contradictory. Soon after the June takeover, the new government reduced or abolished a range of regressive taxes that fell on the peasantry. The People's Party's declarations of the need for rural improvement as a core mission of the revolution also stimulated rural leaders to demand change. It occasionally inspired local revolts. In May 1933, 400 Nakhon Nayok peasants backed by a policeman demanded that the government cancel its debts and expropriate land from the wealthy for its use. In early 1935, hundreds of peasants from fifteen provinces arrived in Bangkok en masse and protested credit arrangements at the economic affairs ministry; in August 1937, 800 hungry rice farmers stormed a Chonburi rice mill seeking food.[37] Over the decade, peasant life came into national consciousness as never before. At the same time, a hostile reaction from both old-regime conservatives and some elements in the People's Party doomed any drastic reforms. Above all, Pridi Banomyong's radical, idealistic economic plan of March 1933, discussed below, plunged the new regime into a crisis that directly fueled the Bowondet rebellion, permanently alienated many old-regime civil servants, and for Pridi's haters, forever marked him as a communist. The People's Party government thereafter abandoned any grand plans to reform the economy. But the demands for improvements in rural welfare continued right through the 1930s and 1940s.

The country's first parliamentary elections in late 1933 returned many provincial advocates for economic reform. The elections of November that year sent seventy-six elected members to Bangkok as one-half of the national assembly. Subdistrict (*tambon*) electors, themselves chosen from village meetings, voted for provincial representatives. The assembly thus was heavily circumscribed and expected to ratify People's Party executive decisions. (And, as we learned, election law pretty well banned Chinese participation.) But elected assemblymen often spoke out for rural improvement and became an important force in national politics. Thawatt Rittidej's activism, as described in the last chapter, relied on his writing flair, and he became renowned as a passionate petitioner and newspaper writer on behalf of poor people. Petitions and newspapers were decades-old vehicles of protest. The assembly offered a new vehicle for expression of popular grievances.

Assemblymen's ideas to improve the rural economy ranged from traditional tax relief to more public spending on infrastructure and technology. A desire for modernity governed all the claims, with modernity associated directly with rural improvement and equality. While some old-regime figures yearned for the supposed simplicity of past times, young people from the provinces wanted riddance of yesteryear. Key assembly debates about rural improvement highlight the tenor of the reform proposals given by commoners outside of the corridors of power.

In 1935, Phra Phinit Thanakon, an elected representative from Chiang Mai in the north, proposed a new rural survey to understand poverty better. Phinit disbelieved the placid, optimistic conclusions of Zimmerman and Andrews on the rough egalitarianism of rural life, or that the Thai people could count themselves fortunate given the country's level of development. For Phinit the modern economy overtook whatever village harmony existed. Phinit viewed village life as hidebound. He compared Siam with the United States on a spectrum of development: a wealthy country like the US still had "poor laws," as he put it, so why would a poor country also not have them?[38] Luang Narin Phrasatawetch, an assemblyman for Chantaburi on the eastern seaboard echoed Phinit. Narin claimed Thai peasants lived an entirely natural life. The half-baked Rousseauism of the elite insider variety did not form his opinions; instead, like Pridi, he viewed rural life as a deplorable Hobbesian state. The people lived as savages: bodies, livelihoods, dwellings all stood or fell at the whim of fate. Narin claimed one doctor served for 30,000 people on average, and the old, handicapped, or impaired were usually abandoned. As many rural voices would both then and now, Narin contrasted life in Bangkok to the countryside—like sky and earth.[39] Liang Chaiyakan, a representative from Ubon in the northeast, explained that prior to the constitutional era, royal policy consisted of only one strategy: "collect as much tax and other revenue from the people as possible."[40] He argued that there was no question whether the state should help the poor or not; rather, assemblymen should ask why nothing had been done.[41] Mongkhol Rathanawichit from Nakhon Sri Thammarat in the far south reiterated Liang's point: "From the time we changed the political regime to a democracy, I have not seen anything done by the government or this assembly to directly help poor people."[42]

Thong-in Phuriphat a young elected assemblyman from Ubon whom we will discuss in more detail in later chapters, stated in a 1936 assembly session: "If we do not find a way to give the citizens relief, their hardship will redouble and the fruits of the new regime will not be gained."[43] He echoed a familiar metaphor of the times, claiming that the center treated his province like a minor wife.[44] Treated as inferiors, the local people paid for servitude with a revenue drain, both a cause and effect of poor infrastructure.

Vorasith Darunawethya from the remote Mekhong River province of Nong Khai in the upper northeast weighed in on the unfairness of tax in a region where most families practiced subsistence farming. They could not make money from the export economy, but still had to pay tax.[45] Thongmuan Attakon from Mahasarakham, another Mekhong province, expressed the bias of many rural assemblymen that "everyone knows that the current tax (akon) system is unjust, and against the principle of equality."[46] Vorasith reiterated the point by asking whether the People's Party leadership that tasked the legislature with passing laws thought the current status quo fair. If they did, farmers were in trouble. Manun Borisut, a representative for Suphanburi in the central plains reiterated in that session that the government was not looking after people, but leaving them at the mercy of corrupt kamnan-tambon leaders appointed by the government—for land revenue assessments that the kamnan overvalued to give himself a bonus. Manun claimed that many farmers lost land as payment for what was owed, and that land became concentrated in wealthy hands.[47] Manun represented a fertile central province closely tied to the export economy.

The People's Party committed to road expansion to link the rail lines and shrink the spatiotemporal asymmetries of upcountry Siam. Only with the revolution did the government allocate money to highway construction.[48] But competing budgets, and the prominence of military expenditure after the Bowondet rebellion, limited funds available for road development. Kenneth Landon, in the late 1930s, observed that still no roads linked Bangkok with anywhere. A tyranny of distance cut off much of rural Siam. But simultaneously what Penny Edwards terms the "tyranny of proximity" describes the changes brought to provincial Siam as railways progressively extended to upcountry areas in the first half of the twentieth century. In the case of colonial Cambodia, Edwards describes how French road building brought a spatial reorientation of culture and community.[49] This same dynamic occurred in early twentieth-century Siam. New infrastructure severed old cultural and political ties, and formed new ones. People living close to the rail lines felt the Bangkok state's presence, through teachers, tax officers, and soldiers sent from the city. Commerce grew quickly at these nodes, and news from the capital traveled quickly.

Luang Voranit Pricha, an ennobled civil servant of the same rank as Pridi and Phibun, worked as a judge and in 1933 became an elected representative for Sakon Nakhon. The northeastern province had poor communications with the wider world, and for much of the year its people lived enclosed in their world of mountains and forests.[50] Voranit advocated persistently for local development after the revolution. All good things come from infrastructure: road and rail expansion bring markets, wealth, agricultural diversity, education, and democracy to the villages. The status quo in the upper northeast around this time in which "isolated citizens practice only self-sufficiency" must be overcome, since "the absence of communications means that all the things that should be done and expanded are on hold."[51] He argued that Udon monthon, the circle to which Sakon belonged, had road connections between districts, but needed to be sizably expanded at the tambon level and below. Economic life, and civilizational improvement, would advance. As it is, people could only travel the roads in the dry season. He argued that the government needed a "Yeneral Plan" (General Plan) for road development that would be disseminated everywhere in the kingdom to all provincial and subprovincial officials, and that would be consistently followed even as individual officials came and went in ensuing years. As things stood, the Siamese could only envy the development in neighboring Indochina.[52]

Like officials in other provinces, Voranit opined that the lack of market access denied any ambitious farmers the opportunity to market their produce. Understandably, they shied from hard work since there was no reward.[53] Voranit remarked approvingly that land values rose dramatically when the government surveyed the area in Udon for planned rail expansion; when this ended, the area lapsed into noncommercial apathy.[54] More approvingly, he noted the dramatic expansion in commerce when the rails came, which in a space of four years he noted produced a commercial hub in Udon. He also welcomed the prevalence of strangers in Udon when the rails came. Gone, with good riddance to this modernizer, was the insular society of the old villages. Infrastructure development would streamline governance. Voranit frequently advised a consolidation of the monthon system into fewer divisions that mirrored the military's division of the country into four regions. (His wish came true when the monthon system was abolished in the mid-1930s.) Instead of intermediate fiefdoms between the central government and local areas, Voranit advocated direct province to center relations such as the parliament exhibited. Voranit argued that in addition to the problem of distance and time—with only weekly mail delivery—local officials had difficulty coordinating their work, for example, in his field of law. Unreliable communications with the outside world made court judgments, the calling of witnesses, transport of the accused, and the calling of hearings largely hit-and-miss affairs.[55]

Thong-in and the other elected assemblymen discussed above were all to the "left" of the state insiders they criticized. Their distance from Bangkok, and their local focus, produced a conflict with state conservatives. But prominent voices for rural development came also from more conservative and well-to-do roots. Prince Sittiphon Kridakon, a royal and the brother of Prince Bowondet who led the 1933 rebellion, was the best-known and most vocal advocate for agricultural development. In 1927, some senior teachers at the Bang Saphan agricultural training school in the midsouth approached him at his nearby Bang Bert farm about their idea for an agricultural science newspaper. He supported them and became the paper's editor. His criticisms of government policy thereafter brought rural poverty to widespread attention for the first time and undoubtedly inspired subsequent People's Party rhetoric about popular welfare. Prince Kridakon's proposals for rural credit and modern farming techniques in particular became part of the public discourse. But the old regime state generally ignored his proposals; even as Prajadhipok complained that agricultural modernization was long overdue, Kridakon's ideas did not gain official support. Moreover the polarizing Bowondet rebellion ruined his career. Suspect as the ringleader's brother and accused of plotting a royalist return, the government imprisoned him with others in 1933. Sitthiphon languished in jail for many years and reemerged into public life after the war.[56]

Among the tragedies of the People's Party years is the collateral damage done by the fight between the Promoters and royalists. Am Bunthai, who joined Thong-in as an elected assemblyman for Ubon in 1933, was among the most articulate new generation voices silenced in the repression that followed the Bowondet rebellion. Am studied at a Bangkok teachers' school for agriculture and finished first in national teacher qualifying exams. As a mark of the recognition he gained at an early age for his promise, his May 1924 wedding ceremony was attended by some of the provincial bigwigs, including elite northeastern monks, leading civil servants, and middle-class tradespeople (*khahabodi*).[57] Like other provincial advocates and contrary to the sleepy and naive country bumpkin stereotype that prevailed, Am was articulate and headstrong, and by his late twenties had been repeatedly warned that he was too outspoken and critical of his superiors. He opened agricultural boarding schools in seven northeastern provinces, which brought him recognition as did his ability to win prestigious scholarships and his high academic achievements. Just past his thirtieth birthday, police arrested Am for alleged complicity in the Bowondet rebellion. He was accused of royalism, in part possibly because of his criticism of large state-sponsored cooperatives such as Pridi recommended. He also sought establishment of political parties, which the Promoters viewed as a challenge to their stewardship of the new political system. Am spent most of the last seven years of his life in difficult prison conditions. He did not see his family again. Briefly released in 1934, he was again charged with antigovernment conspiracy in a December 1935 criminal trial. He received twenty years. A newspaper columnist, commenting on the sentence, wrote,

> So, the criminal courts are under the control of politics, with the result that this defendant is given 20 years? . . . Hitler raised a force in Munich to force the government to resign, and fomented deadly violence to achieve his end. He received nine months in prison. (Am Bunthai) sought only to form a civilian association like the government's Constitution Society, which in future may form the basis for a political party.[58]

On August 1, 1940, Am died, one week short of his thirty-eighth birthday, probably of untreated abdominal dropsy. Like many outsiders to the 1932 revolution inspired by the promise of democracy, Am's life shows the contrast between state ill-treatment and local importance and respect.

Am wrote one of the period's outstanding outsider texts in 1933, a book that worked as an extended campaign manifesto, policy paper, and philosophy tract. It appeared a few days before the Bowondet rebellion broke out. Am regarded material, moral and political progress as a continuum. Representative for a poor agricultural province, Am argued in his tract for the greater development of farmers' cooperatives to produce wealth. Thai cooperatives had been officially sponsored by the absolutist government since 1916. While never becoming the dominant vehicles for production, commerce, or credit in the freewheeling rural economy, they always had high symbolic value as embodiments of the community cohesion and joint work ethic that supposedly marked rural Siam.

From their establishment in 1916 until 1932, the kingdom had only 150 cooperatives, all of which raised capital only. The People's Party government frequently advanced an identity between the ethics of democracy and cooperatives on the basis of free association and equality, and cooperatives mushroomed in overall number and diversity of services. By 1933, the number had nearly doubled. By 1935 there were 440, and by the end of 1940 nearly 2,370 cooperatives pooled resources and helped farmers around the country.[59] There were perhaps 10,000–15,000 members by the Pacific War. The rules for cooperatives mandated that all members be from the same village, know each other, be of good standing, and be mutually responsible for each other. Some of the membership also had to be literate.

The number of cooperative members formed a mere a drop in the peasant demographic bucket. But cooperatives had a precious political and moral appeal. Am Bunthai's advocacy for cooperatives reflected his belief in a communitarian, moral economy as most suitable for the underdeveloped countryside. Am advanced the common wisdom of the day among critics of the agricultural and economic status quo that the middleman creditor and paddy buyer had too much power. But he argued against state socialism and pursuit of a rural utopia as the way forward. Unlike grand state schemes, Am envisaged the cooperative economy as a local initiative focused on specific benefits.[60] The national government in his view would mainly act as a market facilitator and source of cheap money. With better local education, in turn, Thai farming could advance to a higher stage, which would push out the middleman and allow buyers and sellers to transact their business directly. He argued that agricultural schools—much like Prince Kridakon—had to accompany the growth of cooperatives to make them viable. In this endeavor, he contended that representatives acted as the enlightened vanguard introducing knowledge.

He styled this privileged group "evolutionaries" (*nak watta*). Am wrote glowingly of the Danish example, a country where 30 percent of representatives came from the agriculture sector and whose local knowledge created prosperity.

Am discussed the Danes and other foreign examples frequently in his pitch for attention to rural livelihoods. Like others discussed in this book, Am valorized the aspects of Western history that buttressed his political claims for the revolution's importance at the local level. The science of Danish farming and animal husbandry, Robert Owen's work to create markets with fair prices at the New Lanark commune, and the German cooperative pioneer Friedrich Wilhelm Raiffeisen's credit initiatives all feature in Am's vision for Thai agriculture. He also suggested that Ubon should adopt the Gary Plan, the progressive era American educator William Wirt's scheme that identified productive work and study as the backbone of rural welfare and character development.[61] The plan as Am envisaged it would use schoolroom study in the morning, and then related exertions—with farming, crafts, and athletics figuring prominently—in the afternoon. Skilled teachers should be hired for these specific projects, and he called for parliamentarians to petition the government for this approach.

This inspirational jumble—American, German, Danish, and British—shows the intellectual heterogeneity of a young activist after the revolution. Am's diverse influences carried weight because of their Western origins, but were unmoored from their historic background. The young generation's generic mantra of "progress" ignored the very different conditions between 1930s Ubon and nineteenth-century Europe or America. Especially striking is that Ubon lacked entirely the industrialization and urbanization that produced all of the neotraditional attempts in the US and Western Europe to reintroduce rural simplicity. Am wanted progress to proceed from local industry and initiative, a grassroots conservativism that did not seek to revolutionize existing hierarchic relations and or level property holdings. In both of these ways his vision reflects wider colonial mentalities, akin perhaps to Gandhi's admiration for John Ruskin's notion of a "social economy" based on mutual cooperation and benevolent guidance. But neither did Am's goals match royal conservatism's timid vision of progress. He like others argued against its main tenet: preservation of Bangkok's power, reliant on a reasonably productive, naive peasantry living docile lives of bucolic simplicity.

I have foregrounded in this chapter the provincial advocates for rural welfare and the socioeconomic conditions of the countryside that propelled them to speak out. But the political circumstances in which they worked powerfully shaped their careers. These men all emerged from the country's first parliamentary elections in 1933, in the aftermath of the new regime's crushing of the Bowondet rebellion and the People's Party's drive to consolidate their power.

The end of the rebellion also gave the military a strong political position. In late 1933, the assembly that included all of the popular voices just described also featured an appointed component controlled by military appointees. After the first parliamentary elections that took place in November, the ratio of appointed assembly members from the military rose from one-fifth before the crisis to more than three out of five.[62] Appointed representatives—from June 1933 through the rest of the decade—rarely said anything in parliamentary meetings.[63] For critics of the People's Party cast into the wilderness after Bowondet, the new regime thus revealed its insincerity, or the perfecting of its democratic illusion. The new regime's true colors in this reading emerged initially in the first post-Mano, June 1933 parliament of "yes-men" put in place after the coup that ended Mano's government, and endured ever after.[64] And still to later observers of the period, even those sympathetic to the People's Party voiced this concern. Given the constraints on politics imposed by the appointed assemblymen, the absence of political parties and the recourse to extraordinary extraparliamentary moves to ensure stability, the parliamentary system of the day appears as democratically meaningless.[65]

Indeed, the People's Party should not be let off the hook for stifling the voices of change. And part of the problem came from old regime players who still remained influential in economic affairs even after the rebellion reduced the old regime's political role, and whose opinions at times matched appointed assemblymen chosen by the People's Party. Phraya Sorayutseni, an absolutist-era figure who became the economic affairs minister for a time after the revolution, for example, rejected Phra Phinit's calls for a new rural survey as repetitive and pointless.[66] Sorayutseni echoed the opinion of Phra Phisai Suntharakan, an appointed assemblyman for Phuket in the south that the Harvard surveys sufficed, not least because the surveys championed the status quo. In the same vein, Khun Semah-anhitakhadi, the deputy minister of the treasury, said in the assembly that contrary to the assertions of the rural representatives, it was difficult to define what was meant by poverty, and to determine who was poorer than whom. Surveys, he added, patterned certain behavior. Ask a farmer about debt, for example, and they will claim a crushing debt burden since they

think you are going to do something for them.[67] Phra Phisai claimed that
the poor of Siam would be wealthy in Europe, since the Thai peasantry
he asserted had land unlike their destitute European cousins.[68] With the
"hold and reserve" system, people freely occupied vacant land. He added
that things could not be that bad since those seeking good karma spent
freely. When temples needed renovation for example, common people
willingly donated their labor and money. Such explanations did not satisfy outsiders. Phra Phisai came from a wealthy province, and some saw
his lack of concern as showing his ignorance. Voranit Pricha from Sakon
Nakhon in the northeast criticized Phra Phisai for not understanding
rural conditions in poor areas like Voranit's home province.[69] Phra Pisai's
attitude, Voranit claimed, suggested that there was no need for any representative assembly at any level of the government. Similarly, Thong-in
Phuriphat criticized Khun Semahanhitakhadi. Thong-in opined that the
minister, interested in sending his sons overseas for education and then
placing them in the civil service, lived in a different world from farmers
who had none of that type of luxurious worry. They wanted above all to
be able to provide for their families in daily life. "Your status has made
you conform," Thong-in said.[70]

Bureaucratic resistance, partly resulting from a shaky post-Bowon-
det coalition that sought to maintain the economic status quo, certainly
posed one obstacle to economic reform. But a major fault lies within the
People's Party own early radicalism. Here we return to a political fight the
civilian wing initiated in early 1933 before the Bowondet uprising that
would have long-term consequences.

Pridi's Utopian Solution

Pridi Banomyong is perhaps best known not for fomenting the revolution
as a Parisian student but for his heady dream to nationalize the economy and enlist the masses of peasants as state employees. His national
economic plan discussed in the cabinet, and among the wider public, in
early 1933 caused a political storm. The king and many royalists accused
Pridi of communism,[71] and Pridi was forced overseas from April to September 1933. The fallout from the plan fractured the government, gave
Mano the pretext to prorogue the assembly and govern by royal decree
between April 1 and June 20, 1933, and ultimately led to Mano's own
political demise in the June 1933 coup. It also encouraged Bowondet

and his rebels to stage their putsch in October 1933, since Pridi had just returned from exile and the Bowondet group feared that the government had become communist. While much has been written about the plan, two points command stand out. First, Pridi's scheme sought to create a utopia by force. It would have had a radical effect on peasant life but none on the middle or wealthy classes. Second, the plan's utopic imaginings turned out to be a major historical blunder that doomed any chance of socialist reform and encouraged critics to attack anything hinting at such an attempt as communist.

The civilian wing of the People's Party behind the bloodless 1932 revolution harbored utopic visions of a radical change in Thai socioeconomic relations, a commitment that they viewed as important as legal equality under constitutionalism.[72] When Pridi drafted the economic plan that became public in March 1933 is not clear, but he had circulated some kind of document to colleagues before revolution.[73] Khuang Aphaiwong, who joined the People's Party in Paris, recalled jokingly much later in his life that people nicknamed Pridi the "teacher" (*ajahn*) not for his learning but for the profusion of grand plans he concocted as a young man.[74] Khuang's attitude was much more serious when Pridi circulated the grandest of his plans in the early days of the revolution. Khuang and others met the strategy with dismay. "*Ajahn*, what have you brought us? This is a ticket to gaol," Khuang reportedly said when the group met at his house for tea and Pridi introduced his plan.[75] In cabinet meetings in December 1932—at the time when the king's party drafted the constitution to protect royal power—Pridi called for control of all land and production via work units that resembled cooperatives.[76] The plan also envisioned state employment for most people, higher tariffs, demotion of the alien middleman from the center of economic exchange, and state-directed industrialization that would free Siam from its colonial economy.[77]

A vision of a Buddhist heaven dances through the outline. In the plan's conclusion Pridi wrote,

> When government runs the economy like this, it will successfully achieve the objectives of the People's Party's six principles, as announced to the people. The contentment and progress to the highest level which everyone desires . . . *si-ariya* . . . will arise for everybody with no exception. Why . . . hesitate to lead the people further to the *kalapaphruk* tree where they can reap the fruit? This is the fruit of happiness.[78]

Figure 3.1. Men of the people: Pridi (left) and Phahon (center) at a village rice harvest ceremony showing their solidarity with the peasantry. Year unknown. Photo courtesy of the Phraya Phahon Foundation.

The imagery of heaven (*si ariya*) and its mythic tree that satisfied all wants (*kalapaphruk*) linked the mundane plan with the transcendental order in Buddhist cosmology. But the plan also shows the tenor of his formal French education and the influence of his teacher Charles Gide and others who championed "solidarism." Pridi studied in a Third Republic that transformed France into a modern state. His French instructors fused three planks of modern life—constitutional law, representative politics. and state economic planning—into a grand plan for social well-being. Solidarism claimed to combine both moral demands and scientific analysis into a new social philosophy and argued that people were mainly mutual debtors who cooperated to build a just society. What was just could be determined through analysis of objective laws. It also believed that public consent created political forms as quasi-contracts. Societies drafted laws that directly reflected their mutual interdependence and solidarity.[79] Pridi's plan showed his belief that a mutual debt compelled people to work together, and that he directly rebutted the perceived libertarian anarchy of rural agriculture that allowed the wealthy to exploit the weak. The state would ostensibly act as a benign force providing the elements of collective welfare that would be fused by the people.

Buddhism and solidarism were not the only philosophies in the plan. The Buddhist utopia, freedom from all wants, and solidarism, a path based on cooperation, were mixed with an ideology of force. Pridi's eclectic socialism, for one, contained elements of not only the Third Republic but also Friedrich List, the German nationalist whom Pridi wrote understood the need for state economic planning in the competitive and unstable world of early-twentieth-century global capitalism.[80] And there is a further aspect: a Thai paternalism that may be a "traditional" inheritance of kingship that viewed poor, common people as incapable of acting in their best interests, and privileged a powerful and wealthier elite. Pridi's plan would coerce the poor into freedom, while the better off would be left alone. The plan—ostensibly a forcing house of improvement and freedom—protected the independence of those who could demonstrate their productivity and those practicing a "liberal profession" like law or journalism.[81]

Pridi's scheme protected only privately owned movable wealth, which poor people hardly possessed. Moreover, the land reform did not target big landlords—who were a small group in Siam and largely connected to royalty—but the welter of modest peasant farms. While Zimmerman's 1931 survey and Andrews's survey in 1935 asserted that a rough egalitarianism prevailed in smallholder society, Pridi's gave a decidedly negative appraisal. He viewed the preponderance of small holders as a national failure, which resulted in meager or nonexistent savings, indebtedness, and low productivity. Private landowners used their land inefficiently, according to the plan, and most farmers wasted their time outside of planting and harvesting cycles in idleness.[82] The state did not require the consent of landowners for purchase of their land. The forced sellers would be given a bond instead of cash payment since the government did not have enough money.[83] Pridi viewed smallholders as selfish. "Don't worry that the landowners will be dissatisfied," he answered Sakon Voravan in a cabinet debate discussing the plan in March 1933. "We proclaimed such law of compulsory purchase (of land) only to prevent people being unruly (*kere*) and refusing to sell or demanding expensive prices."[84]

The plan concluded that the constitution had advanced Siam down the path to civilization,[85] but Pridi felt people would never attain such a condition if left to themselves. The state would improve material life so that it was "equal to that of civilized countries" from a condition, Pridi lamented, in which most villagers lived in "huts or farmhouses which are like those of jungle dwellers in Africa."[86] To refine people the government had to act decisively. Part of the civilizing process meant new work for most workers. Once the state took their land, the peasantry would then be forced into non-farmwork, building roads, for example, or "according to whatever the national plan specifies."[87] Compulsory labor was an old practice that went back centuries in Thai history. The bringers of constitutional liberalism, like ancient kings, relied on forced labor for production. Before the revolution, Pridi lectured in administrative law at the justice ministry, and here as he notes he took the opportunity to teach about the freedom-giving boon that was modern democracy. He also, however, in the same lectures argued for labor levies as a necessary part of modern, state run economies.[88] "Yes, when the government runs the economy itself, it is a reduction of freedom," Pridi wrote in the plan, "but this reduction of freedom is to enable the people to have full well-being."[89] Thawi Bunyaket, a Pridi supporter in the state council, opined in a March cabinet meeting, "I do not see any great loss if we force people born in misery and destitution to attain happiness."[90]

Many years later Pridi recalled a lack of practical expertise among the People's Party, for which they overcompensated with theory.[91] As a young cohort of would-be revolutionaries, Pridi and his group's vision would mold reality. As Somsak puts it: "Reading the Plan, one gets the impression of someone highly confident and enthusiastic for certain *ideals* of what should be done, without having much regard for the existing situation."[92] The influence on Pridi of his teacher Charles Gide accounts for some of the zeal, and his focus on the peasantry rather than capital owners. In his 1904 book on cooperatives, Gide argued that the state should expropriate and collectivize land, since unlike capital land could not reproduce itself, and the cost of buying parcels was prohibitive.[93] But Pridi wanted an immediate agricultural revolution, whereas Gide conceived expropriation as gradual.[94] Gide's work also relied on more detailed surveys of cooperatives' historical impact in Europe and their effects on rural life. While he criticized the existing rural surveys as incorrect, Pridi's plan lacks an understanding of the complexity of rural history or any assessment of existing socioeconomic conditions in the countryside. Pridi's scheme is largely fact-free.

Pridi's goals of expanded cooperatives, peasant control over commerce, and state investment in agriculture and rural infrastructure all resonate with previously discussed criticisms of existing state policies. Both the state plan and the various outsider policy suggestions reflected wider aspirations among the young intelligentsia for a fair economy that protected ordinary people. So too the idealized portrait of how rural life would improve—and a lack of explanation for how the changes would be funded—is echoed in, for example, Am Bunthai's book. Also in common is the education and status of the spokesmen. The legal training of Pridi and Voranit Pricha, or Am Bunthai's wide reading, partially detached them from the peasant world that they represented. But Pridi's heady dream to create a new economy under a strong state stands apart from the calls for economic reform from outsiders for two reasons: the plan's radicalism and Pridi's political stature. Pridi's insider power allowed him to advance the adventurous plan, but the plan's radicalism doomed its chances since at the time the People's Party faced stiff opposition among other insiders with power, especially the old regime elements in the bureaucracy. Pridi's adventurous plan is of tremendous long-term importance. It fomented anticommunism for the next fifty years as a consistent feature of royalist ideology, and collapsed the distinction between socialism and communism. Both were branded both as foreign ideologies unsuitable for Siam.[95] Primarily, those elements of economic policy that predated the new regime were legitimate. Mainly this meant British inspired liberalism with an admixture of cooperatives.

Economic Nationalism and the Status Quo

Three main groups of economic planners emerged after 1932. A status quo ante group of liberal royalists; socialists, the most politically adventurous; and, by the Phibun government of 1938, an economic nationalist group in the bureaucracy. Of these three, the first group, while seemingly cast aside in the era of popular government, still influenced economic policy; the second failed to implement its plans; and politically well-connected fractions of the third succeeded to an extent in determining government policy by the Pacific War.

The first group centered on Mano, the first premier after 1932. As we learned, the Promoters, and Pridi especially, chose Mano because of his royalist connections, which it was hoped would ensure a smooth political transition to People's Party democracy. His cohort, a group of conservative British-trained barristers, provided continuity with the old regime to show

the world that Siam was not a threat to Western capital. In the immediate aftermath of the revolution these men argued for continuity of the
fiscal and land policies devised by the monarchy in the interests of social
stability and foreign approval. The Mano group was closest in outlook to
the British advisers that influenced foreign and economic policy before
1932.[96] While not beholden to British interests exclusively, their approach
reflected British advice: the sanctity of private property, low tariffs, continued Chinese control of trade, minimum investment in industry, balanced
budgets, and adherence to the international division of labor. All of these
policies guaranteed continued markets for foreign firms.[97]

Still, the conservative group did not govern as if nothing had changed
since the fifth reign. The impact of the depression, especially given public
criticism of the government, warranted action. Their action, however, did
not get much beyond commissioning plans. In 1933 Phraya Komarakulamontri, graduate of the London School of Economics, finance minister
before 1932, and the minister for economic affairs in Phahon's government
until 1934, devised a general program that mandated setting up more
rural farming cooperatives, closer credit market management that would
release the peasantry from debt to middlemen, and create government
buying schemes that would ostensibly give the peasantry better prices
for their products than middlemen offered.[98] Additional plans called for
investment in agricultural experimentation stations, much as Sittiphon had
espoused several years earlier, more irrigation, and integrated waterways
networks that would bring far-flung regions into the modern economy.[99]
But a more assertive state role did not materialize. Writing from Britain
in 1934, King Prajadhipok lamented the following:

> I have heard from many quarters people both in Siam and
> abroad are anxious to know what economic policy will be
> pursued by the Government. I think that it is very import-
> ant some definite announcement should be made as soon as
> possible. It is quite evident that the programme drawn up
> by Phraya Komarakul[amontri] is dead. Nobody now knows
> the real intention of His Majesty's Government. Hence great
> suspicion and suspense, [and] a policy of compromise and
> delaying of any decisive action is worst of all.[100]

The economic orthodoxy that had prevailed during the absolute monarchy's
heyday was on shaky footing by the 1930s, and came under attack during

the Depression. But amid the political tumult, Pridi's plan was shelved, and Komarakulamontri's proposals failed to have an economic effect. In the mid-1930s, the king's lament went unheard.

Economic nationalism, however, one of the Promoters' founding principles, remained politically potent. In 1938 and 1939, while he vanquished his rivals through the special courts and clamped down on the Chinese, Phibun's government pushed new policies and founded new firms that pledged to create a new economy for the Thai people. Pridi played a leading role in the effort. After returning from temporarily exile, Pridi served as interior minister from 1934 to 1937—then foreign minister, and

Figure 3.2. The rural utopia as depicted in a government magazine, 1942.

finally then in Phibun's government, he became finance minister at the end of December 1938. His supporters valorize his diplomatic skill and the economic policies he championed during these years as serving the interests of common Thai people. To supporters, despite the attacks on his economic plan and his political exile, Pridi finally realized two pillars of the Promoters' vision, national independence and an economy for the people, by the end of the decade. First as interior and foreign minister, Pridi renegotiated Siam's debt with foreign lenders on favorable terms, and then as foreign minister, he traveled the world working out the final abolition of the extraterritoriality treaties that had for eighty years economically and diplomatically subordinated Siam to foreign powers. Last, as finance minister he helped build a national economy to benefit poor people.[101]

A foreign observer of the times wrote that by the end of the decade, with the Phibun government unleashed, "[t]he forgotten man was now the focus of every political eye. If he was a peasant, he was to be delivered from the "blood-sucking Shylocks." It did not matter whether or not he knew that he was downtrodden or wanted his life transformed. The social revolution had begun."[102] Rhetorically overexcited, perhaps, but big changes did take place. With Pridi as architect from his finance portfolio, in January 1939 the government announced new economic policies—part of a plan that extended like the spokes of a wheel in every direction—which would redraw the tax regime in an effort to ensure social justice. The long-resented capitation and land taxes were finally abolished and replaced by new taxes that targeted the privileged—mainly the Chinese, in other words. Income, stamp, and a range of business taxes followed revised alien registration fees from the prior year's budget to tap Chinese wealth. The financial plan passed a rushed reading in the assembly in March 1939, and members searched to prevent details of the plan leaking to the public.[103]

While the government opened a range of state enterprises,[104] its role in the rice trade gained the most attention. The Thai Rice Co., discussed above as a vehicle of labor activism after the war, was established in late 1938 and bought paddy from farmers for milling. We saw that it moved into owning mills directly, which became sites of labor protest after the war. After its establishment, the government encouraged prisons, hospitals, and the military to buy from the company. In clarifying its rationale, in March 1939, the economic affairs minister explained the following on the radio:

> I have been asked what kind of trade this is—is it free trade?
> Or socialist? Or communist? Or protectionist? Or what? My

answer is that it is Thai-ist. This is a word that you will not find in any dictionary but its meaning is obvious. It is a system to help the Thai . . . Naturally there may be some loss to aliens.[105]

The right-wing nationalists repackaged what Pridi had earlier proposed on the grounds of solidarism, unaware, or uninterested, in the irony of the situation. Pridi too pursued policies after the new revenue code of 1939 that he had first wanted six years earlier, and echoed laments he had used then about the laziness of the peasant and the need for a strong hand to push rural people into thrift and hard work. Old wine, stale and sour, tasted much better in new bottles.

Conclusion

Labor—one in fifty of the working population—fought for workers' rights and protections abetted by middle-class spokemen, communists, and state actors. They lived mainly in the bustling, dirty city, and without any respite from toil. The peasantry—more than four in five of working adults—remained largely quiet after the revolution. Their seasonal work, in a country where free land abounded, was carried out amid the Thai countryside's lush and fertile landscape. Landlordism and abject poverty, tragic drivers of revolutions in China, Russia, Vietnam, and Mexico in the period contemporary with the People's Party movement, did not revolutionize peasant consciousness. The myth of a tropical arcadia in part spread from this organic world.

But labor's plight did not much interest the Thai public, primarily because people viewed it as a Chinese affair, while the peasantry and their Thai world became a major social topic in the early twentieth century. The government before and after the revolution drafted plans for the countryside, one of which—Pridi's plan—became in Kasian Tejapira's words "the first great contest of ideas and policies in modern Siamese history."[106] Most assemblymen came from a world of rice fields and market gardens, and strongly criticized policies that grew the economy on the backs of the rural poor. Critics decried the capitalism of the expanding rice frontier and the bewildering variety of scales of production, tenants and small-scale owners bridged by Chinese middlemen, and a variety of credit and marketing structures. They also criticized the subsistence agriculture that prevailed everywhere outside of the lower Chaophraya delta as a relic of backwardness, isolation, and even native's laziness. Bangkok, the axis mundi of Thai life, beginning in the nineteenth century reoriented all of the upcountry areas to itself. The city-based governors' wealth and ease, above all else, produced the idealistic quest for a better way. The state had a moral obligation to look after people. The revolution took place in the city, not upcountry, but both urban and rural voices for change tasked the elite with bringing the peasantry into the modern world. A plank of People's Party nationalism lay in their pledge to abolish wide income and wealth gaps and create a strong union. The pledge was unevenly fulfilled, and the response by outsiders spirited.

Chapter Four

Making Citizens

Education and Propaganda in the New Order

On the eve of the People's Party takeover, education minister Prince Dhani Nivat proposed an overhaul of the school system to cement loyalty to the throne. Dhani, inspired by Benito Mussolini's plan for national education, wrote glowingly of the fascist way to Chaophraya Mahithon, the head of the Royal Secretariat.[1] Mahithon forwarded the letter to Prince Boriphat. Underlining sections on the absolute obedience that fascism required, Mahithon wrote the following in the margins:

> Will we be successful in teaching Thai people that the absolute monarchy is superior to all other administrative systems? I highly doubt it. To begin the process now is too late. It is impossible to restore the old reverence for the monarch because the fathers of the children currently studying have long been accustomed to, and enjoy, talking badly about the king.[2]

Mahithon's pessimistic conclusion shows the frailty of absolute monarchy's ideological power, and the swell of criticism of the old regime in its twilight. But while capitalizing on old-regime weakness, the People's Party revolution did not dismantle absolutism's institutional power or vanquish old social values. Mahithon, Dhani, and Boriphat all lost their positions once the People's Party took power, and yet an authoritarian culture and patrimonial networks continued to shape education after the revolution. Schoolteachers in the People's Party era criticized the lingering intellectual and bureaucratic influence of the old guard, while the People's Party's ambitious attempts to remake the kingdom's education foundered partly because of this influence.

The People's Party made the introduction of modern, universal education central to their plans for the realization of Thai democracy. The last of their six principles, disseminated in paper and broadcast on radio the day they took power, mandated that the state must provide full education to the people. Moreover, the provisional and permanent constitutions stated that the parliament, initially partially appointed, would become a fully elected body when more than one-half of the population had attained a basic education, or at latest within ten years of 1932.[3] In the context of Thai history this was an ambitious and novel program, and the intelligentsia responded enthusiastically. The inability to reach most people in a poorly integrated state created differences between two broad categories of the "people," the clumpish term in whose name the People's Party staged their revolution. The first category comprised the always remote and largely illiterate peasantry, five out of six Siamese people at the time[4] who were ostensible subjects of the new regime but for whom state projects were likely irrelevant to their lives or incomprehensible. The second category of "people" is the outsider intelligentsia—estimated at 1 percent of the population.[5] The regime found a willing reception for their ideals among the 1 percent, and tasked them with relaying democratic ideology to the illiterate masses. The new intelligentsia also on their own initiative sought to create a more inclusive society especially a system of meritocracy instead of personal favoritism in educational advancement and rural empowerment to better diffuse modern teaching. In the process they asserted youthful élan against the enervation of age; and free thought against customary obedience. People's Party democracy became in its formation circumscribed and legalistic; the new intelligentsia's "thicker" and less tidy interpretation aimed at a broader transformation of social values.

Young Teachers Attack the Establishment

About a year after the revolution, amid the struggle between the Mano government and the People's Party, young upcountry teachers argued that the education ministry was failing the People's Party pledge to enfranchise and enlighten ordinary people. These young activists were members of the nationwide Teachers' Association—an old-regime body that comprised thousands of teachers. They claimed that the new regime allowed old has-beens, incompetents, and bullies to teach and administer. Organic or rhythmic metaphors were popular at the time in social descriptions; in this case, the teachers used a pendulum to make their point. The drag or the dead weight of fossils from a bygone age retarded the natural movement of education toward democracy.[6] The rhythm of generational change is evident in their aspirations: Young Siam had made similar arguments against the provincial lords and proclaimed a similar vitality in their late nineteenth-century remaking of Siam as a centralized and modern state. But now, with the new political rhetoric of democracy and the People's Party's commitment to remake education, provincial schoolteachers raised under the absolutist system used the same rhetoric against their old-regime-installed elders.

In August 1933, teachers at a school in Lopburi province—around 100 miles from Bangkok—submitted a letter to the government criticizing the provincial education head. They labeled the fellow in question, Wichakam Piset, a man of low learning who "does not want to express his opinions for fear of making mistakes."[7] He only attained his position, they contended, because of his friendship with Prince Dhani Nivat, the above mentioned last education minister under the old regime. In addition to his ignorance, Wichakam's laziness and disinterest limited educational advancement in the province. Education in Lopburi, they asserted, had not improved or changed since the old regime; in other words it remained poor. Wichakam's example discouraged independent initiative but encouraged flattery and kowtowing, which the petitioners wrote perpetuated a model completely unsuited for the democratic age.

Teachers in the northern province of Pichit reported similar problems with their local masters. In July 1933, a group there followed up on a letter that they had written to Bangkok the previous August about the Pitsanulok circle[8] education head, a Phra Sawat.[9] As with the Lopburi case, the teachers in Pichit accused their superior a man of dubious morals. Phra Sawat only liked flatterers and he harassed his subordinates, especially if they crossed him. The group portrayed Phra Sawat as an autocrat governing his fief with impunity. In a later letter to the government, the group claimed that a senior civil servant before 1932 knew what was going on with Sawat but important old-regime officers spun a tight web of influence.[10]

Additional, high-level education officers became targets of these campaigns against malpractice and the cases gained national attention. At the beginning of September, the *Chalerm Prades* newspaper published a list of the accused and its correspondent wrote that the teacher's group embodied the democratic spirit.[11] A 187-member teacher's group explained in a letter to the premier around the same time as the provincial revolts that five senior figures in the ministry were old, useless, and stood in the way of democracy.[12] Indeed, the attack on the old-regime hangovers became personal when the teachers attacked Naga Thephasadin, the nephew of the education minister Thammasakmontri. They claimed the government promoted Naga to assistant head of the ordinary education department over many other more qualified candidates. He studied in England because of family connections, they contended, but was a failure and had to return to Siam. Democratic enthusiasts often criticized old-regime bureaucrats and the elder generation in the early years of the People's Party, and many like the teachers paired youth with democratic thinking in direct rebuttal of the immaturity argument. An additional, grievous charge labeled one senior officer as an enemy of democracy: Phraya Wisetsuphawat, head of the common education department, allegedly convened a meeting of students to protest against the People's Party's takeover in June 1932.

Unfortunately for the activist teachers, the coalition of People's Party and old-regime bureaucrats did not take up their complaints—the first public criticism of the new regime's educational system. Thammasak-montri read the news reports with contempt. In August 1933 after the storm broke, he wrote to Phahon, the senior most revolutionary plotter and the successor premier after Mano's government was toppled at the end of June. Perhaps the perceived failure to properly respect Thamma-sakmontri's family with the attack on Naga Thephasadin contributed to his anger. Thammasakmontri asserted that these elements in the Teachers' Association could not be taken seriously. The malcontents were young and easily led astray by troublemakers with an ax to grind. Thammasakmon-tri speculated that the hidden hand belonged to *ang yi*—Chinese secret societies.[13] Thammasakmontri regarded their suggestions for replacements as completely unsuitable. Regarding one, he wrote that if the man were appointed the "world will only laugh, and look down on us; in Thailand is education only worth a pittance?"[14] Conservative newspapers echoed the government's line. One summarized the government's objection that a bad precedent would be set if the conflict became a public issue: "(I)t is not good policy to allow clamor by several hundred people to have any weight."[15] The government deferred to Thammasakmontri's judgment and none of the accused officials lost their positions.

Why did Thammasakmontri's position carry the day? Why was there no cultural revolution in schooling? As with much in the People's Party administration, the answer lies in the legacy of the absolutist state, the compromise forced on the People's Party and their skepticism about outsiders' suitability for politics.

Old Regime Education: Subjects First, Citizens Second

The 1932 constitutionalists inherited a system that did not offer modern education for the vast majority of the population whose lives were tied to the agricultural cycle. Royal schools, elite-patronized temples, and Christian missions offered the best education for the high born and the well connected. In the fifth reign, King Chulalongkorn and his Young Siam fellows created good schools to train elite sons for service in the government and also to infuse attendees with a developing absolutist ideology of loyalty and obedience to the Bangkok king. Suan Kulap (1880), the Military Cadet Academy (1887), the Law School (1896), Ratchawitthayalai (King's College, 1897), and the Training School of the Civil Service (1899, renamed the Royal Pages School in 1902) were the key institutions. All of these were initially completely elitist, for example admitting only certain high-born families or charging fees to keep out poor people. In addition, well-regarded Buddhist temple schools in Bangkok—Wat Thepsirin and Wat Patumkhongkha especially—became training grounds for well-off young men to enter the civil service. Last, missionary[16] or private schools with more democratic admittance policies (Bangkok Christian and Assumption in the former, and Sunanthalai and Ban Somdet Chaophraya in the latter being the most famous) trained aspiring civil servants.[17]

The high road of white-collar ambition that led young men through a Westernized education at government ministry, missionary or private schools did not strand them in a politically stultified cul de sac of state employment. Indeed, the People's Party emerged from two key arms of state education: the military and law. Moreover, by the 1920s many in the new generation attended the mission schools and better temple schools and then entered commerce and journalism. We saw above that the *lukjin* labor leaders during the war came from mission school training. Aek Wisakul, thirty-five years old at the time of the revolution and a prominent Thai-Chinese journalist who coestablished *Thai Mai* newspaper, estimated that one-half of Bangkok Christian and Assumption graduates in the period entered the independent professions, especially in commerce and journalism.[18] The absolutist government responded to the growing influence of the independent professions by establishing its own commercial and technical schools. Partly driven thus by independent schools, the state developed a technical education favoring certain useful areas of knowledge that facilitated state power.[19]

Elite education comprised the slimmest of fractions of Siamese schooling and the graduates of the above schools numbered a small percent of the bureaucracy. Chulalongkorn and his reformers needed more to meet the times. As Young Siam consolidated its power, it expelled many older bureaucrats who were not well educated and whose loyalty was suspect. The fifth reign saw the first plans for mass education. After the fifth king's death in 1910, discussion of a national educational law gained momentum. In 1912, the minister of public instruction Chaophraya Wisut Suriyasakdi (Pia Malakul), an ennobled commoner who rose high in the government of the sixth reign, proposed compulsory education for all children aged seven to fourteen, but the government rejected his proposals claiming a lack of money. Prince Chantaburi, the finance minister, contended that funds were needed for national integration and communications. At the same time the war minister, Prince Pitsanulok, garnered annual increases for his ministry's budget in the range of 1 million baht from the finance ministry. He justified the sums on the grounds of national security, an irony since by this time Siam faced no external enemies or serious internal rebellions.[20] As with agriculture, the absolutist state sacrificed social spending for palace and military outlays.

The impetus to mass schooling in the old regime, and the subsequent People's Party attempt, was the work of Chaophraya Thammasakmontri. Khru Thep (Thep the teacher) as he was familiarly known in 1916 became the public instruction minister after his patron Wisut retired (he died the same year). Thammasakmontri was born Sanan Thephasadin na Ayutthaya in Bangkok in 1877, the eighteenth child of thirty-two in the family of Phraya Chai Surin, the agriculture minister and also minister for finance until his death in 1885. The Thephasadin na Ayutthaya clan comprised one among the elite nonroyal families that maintained their positions by aligning with Young Siam in the administrative revolution of the late nineteenth century. Many rose to power in modern Siam; among them was Phat Thephasadin na Ayutthaya, whose fraught relations with the People's Party we discussed in the first chapter. The tangled relations of polygyny made Phat Thammasakmontri's half brother, but also his nephew.

Thammasakmontri's family was poor despite the father's high position. In a situation repeated among important but impoverished ennobled families, women provided for their sons. Sanan's mother worked as a seamstress to look after the young Sanan and his brothers. Then, intelligent and lucky, Sanan studied at an advanced level in Siam and attended a teacher training school near London beginning in 1896 under the patronage of Robert Morant.[21]

Under the patronage of then Prince Vajiravudh, Thammasakmontri and his brother joined a small group that observed Japanese education in 1902 while accompanying Vajiravudh back to Siam from England. The Japanese plan became the basis for Siam's national education scheme. Thammasakmontri had studied education policy in India as well as Japan, and eagerly used both countries' inspiration to advance a more modern educational system for Siam. He continued the drive for compulsory primary schooling that Wisut had initiated.[22] Thammasakmontri also targeted the higher levels of education and reorganized the civil service school that would form the basis for Chulalongkorn University, which was created in 1916.[23]

Thammasakmontri viewed existing education as quantitatively pitiful and woefully underfunded.[24] The minister argued that the neglect of education exacerbated two crucial social problems that ensued from fifth reign reforms. Development of the market economy led to the first: an uneducated and naive peasantry found themselves at the mercy of unscrupulous foreign or Chinese middlemen. Not only were the peasantry easily duped, but their unfamiliarity with modern commerce prevented emergence of a native middle-class that could challenge foreign control. Second, while the reforms of the fifth reign had released rural people from the feudal burdens of debt bondage and forced labor, they also generated new, more mysterious forces in the form of laws that poor people did not understand. As with the market society that introduced business opportunists and conmen into the peasant's world, modern law brought shady dealmakers and lawyers into their lives who manipulated popular ignorance for their own gain.[25]

An obsession with bureaucratic careers posed another social problem that a better educational system could cure. Young men seeking to rise in society under the reforming state sought government clerkships above all as the easiest route. Indeed, Pridi's failed economic plan of 1933 sought to exploit the preference for government work as a way to enroll thousands in the machinery of the planned economy.[26] But Pridi sought a way around this predilection by claiming that most officials came from families who farmed the land in prior generations, and that contemporary civil servants still had a strong affinity for and love of the land.[27] Part of King Prajadhipok's criticism of Pridi targeted this assertion. In his rebuttal, the king wrote,

> For the (people in general) "government employee" means those who work is to give orders: to direct, or those who are clerks, sitting at desks, sipping tea, doing light work . . . Again, let me emphasize that the Thai people do not wish to be government officials at all if it means that they have to use their labor hoeing or ploughing land instead of sitting at a desk and giving orders. That they wish to do such hard work is out of the question, for they usually have expressed dissatisfaction at just being transferred to the provinces.[28]

According to the king and other prominent critics, Pridi's optimism, or convenient twisting of social values, was bogus. Like many, Thammasakmontri believed most people viewed government work as leisure, not labor. For Thammasakmontri this mindset hindered the development of a skilled business class and produced a lazy, status obsessed younger generation too reliant on the state. Thammasakmontri thus identified the roots of the insider mentality in the growth of the "bureaucratic polity" to put the structure in Fred Riggs's classic terms. Interestingly, Thammasakmontri believed office seeking a uniquely Siamese problem. But despite his valorization of some of Siam's colonial neighbors in their educational achievements, the absolutist state mirrored its colonial neighbors in its production of a new social class that aspired to civil service rather than commerce. An intelligentsia unrepresentative of any social class, and standing only for their own interest, featured in all colonial societies.

At least compared to many other elites, Thammasakmontri had progressive views on education. But he was not a radical educator. Like other state insiders, he worried about the consequences of the peasantry getting ideas above their station in life and believed them doing anything but tilling the land posed social dangers that were best avoided. He sought to use education to save the old social system, not fundamentally change it. And politics was not a part of the curriculum, unless political instruction meant learning obedience to the state and one's betters. Thammasakmontri envisaged the strengthening of the absolutist state through expansion of

basic education, as well as the development of higher education that produced the technical skills that the few elite schools and ministry schools
offered. The remedy for the bureaucratic and anticommercial mentality
applied mainly to well-off people, not to the vast majority who were
farmers. In a 1919 national education plan that he submitted to the government, Thammasakmontri proposed a two-tiered vision of education:
primary for the vast majority of the population, and secondary for those
select few who had the necessary intelligence, financial means, and social
status. The latter then obtained the technical skills needed to manage an
exchange economy.[29]

The government rejected Thammasakmontri's 1919 proposal but soon
passed a primary education act in 1921. Ten years after Thammasakmontri's
triumph, primary education remained scattered and of varying quality. It
still relied, as Thai and other Southeast Asian Buddhist societies always
had, on a Buddhist temple system that taught basic letters and morals.
The Thai absolutist state, however, modernized the ethical training for
its new needs. Manners and morals comprised a mixture of Western
derived bourgeois ethics and Buddhist teachings, and constituted a key
aspect of education under the old regime that would continue after 1932.
Thammasakmontri's patron Chaophraya Wisut's 1906 text *Sombat khong
phudi* (Virtues of the Good Person) was the first definitive statement of
the absolutist quest for intellectual and moral hegemony in education,
and remained in use for most of the twentieth century. This work reinforced a concern with proper deference to social superiors and refined
behavior that ensured social harmony under Bangkok's direction. The
Western element also played into the mix, with ethics of punctuality,
thrift, honesty, diligence, and neat appearance buttressing social order.
Both the ethics-based and upper-level highly restricted technical education
excluded politics, a modern subject that the elite regarded as dangerous
and potentially inflammatory in a society unfamiliar—so they thought or
hoped—with ethics of individuality.

The new order by contrast advocated politics as participatory. But
they while promoting it enthusiastically, the new regime also applied it
temperately, a salient feature of the social program. The abrupt change
in political language brought with the new regime masked a deeper continuity in official attitudes. And while Dhani Nivat lost his position after
1932, Thammasakmontri as education minister in the first two years of
the new regime ensured that an experienced old-regime authority continued to steer policy. Thammasakmontri's paternalist educational views

shaped how democracy should be taught, and above all his view that a very few qualified people spoke legitimately about politics and instructed the people accordingly prevailed.

Weak national integration limited the spread of the People's Party program, and primary and secondary education relied on the curriculum inherited from the old regime. The scheme of learning continued to employ Thammasakmontri's *Thammacariya* (Ethics) textbooks as the foundation of instruction. Thammasakmontri wrote six volumes for this series beginning in the fifth reign, with the intention that they would be used over six years of schooling. Two aspects stand out in the texts: submission to authority and the importance of consensus, both founded on a sense of community that subsumed the individual.

New Regime Ethics, the Expansion of Schooling, and the Chinese Problem

After the revolution and amid the political crises that threatened to topple the People's Party government in 1932 and 1933, People's Party education added democratic ethics to Thammasakmontri's foundational values, and in terms that reinforced deference and promoted obedience. A series of classroom manuals and guides for teachers circulated in the government in these years, and these texts give us the main insight into the government's project in democratic guidance. The lessons mix morals and manners training, Buddhist-inspired teachings on mental independence, which were popular because of their adaptability to notions of the rational democratic subject, and Lincolnesque platitudes about popular sovereignty. Most striking is the close reliance of a good political system, that is, a socially harmonious one, on individual realization of the obligations entailed by different social positions.[30]

The new democratic education targeted secondary school attendees, and their indoctrination largely revolved around ethics instruction that expanded on Buddhist principles inculcated at the primary level to include key aspects of modern citizenship. The budding democratic subject was inscribed over the Buddhist personality, and both discourses highlighted duty to others and self-control. Upper-secondary education, for those who made it that far, offered further training in the social graces. The teachings stressed the virtues of a gentleman, with diligence in giving up vice and maintaining virtue a core principle. Virtue linked to a more developed "understanding of worldly Dhamma," that is, a righteous political system that would emerge from the virtuous setting proper examples for others.[31]

The manuals explained something new in Thai society: how people should evaluate their assembly representatives. But while the notion of political representation was new, the standards by which candidates should be judged relied on older, gendered interpretations of power. Candidates' ethics and comportment guided the people in their choices as much as qualifications. The manuals advised people to vote for candidates with graceful manners, goodwill, and the qualities of "manliness." The new normative political subject was a man. The drafters of this manual apparently forgot that the People's Party constitution and election laws guaranteed the equal rights of men and women to vote and to run for office, provided they met the same age and educational qualifications. The traits of manliness included warm-heartedness, the just treatment of others, and self-control. Additionally, the ideal representative worked for the interests of society and sacrificed for the common good. While these values may have resonated because of their long association with a type of Southeast Asian strongman or "man of prowess"[32] whose character attracted followers, the texts advised people to free themselves from the bonds of patronage. They should not feel compelled to choose village heads, district leaders, or provincial governors as their representatives.

The People's Party pledged to make democracy a new social value that would govern all customs. In a compromise with regressive political forces, however, the worldly Dhamma that described democracy borrowed from preexisting social ethics. The primacy of moral exemplars as guarantors of a righteous political order could have been taken straight from the *Thammacariya* series. Graceful, mannered people—with grace and manners most developed in men—should become the new moral elite via representation, for example, and democracy should establish social harmony, not lead to the assertion of particular interests. The state advised people to independently choose their democratic representatives, but according to state-imposed notions of virtue. Moreover, the People's Party tutelage model contained a doubtful proposition: that the mentors of democracy would willingly accept their political extinction. After being instructed in the new philosophy by Party and bureaucratic spokesmen, the people would perhaps vote these patrons out of office.[33] But the crisis of these years made this a frankly impossible outcome of the early democracy.[34]

State officers wrote the ethics manuals for teachers, on whom the People's Party relied to spread the democratic message. Youthful energy propelled the outspoken criticism of the educational hierarchy in the provinces, and also prompted the ministry to disallow young teachers too much independence. The authorities were mindful of many teachers' naivete. Educational inspectors who traveled upcountry lamented the instructors' meager learning, which is not surprising given the low secondary school enrollment and graduation numbers, and also the fact that most teachers were only slightly older than their charges. Amendments to the 1935 education act stipulated that ordinary teachers must be at least fifteen years old, have a teaching certificate, and have completed three years of high school. In areas where no secondary education was possible, the law required an exam demonstrating the equivalent of four years of primary schooling. Headmasters had to be at least twenty years old, and possess a teaching certificate and a high school six education. They also were required to have at least one prior year of teaching experience. It is not clear how thoroughly these standards were met.[35]

Popular callowness reinforced the new regime belief that not only the peasantry but also members of the new intelligentsia were too immature for democracy and must be led. When challenged by young upcountry teachers, the authorities who had been trained under the old regime argued that the young were immature. People's Party discourse frequently reiterated that independent judgment of merit, not birth or connections, determined status in a democracy. But their rhetoric met a political necessity that gave to the wise men alone legitimate interpretation of democracy. The state advised people not to bow to authority when choosing representatives. Then in a particular case where young teachers claimed a democratic right to reform their institution, the authorities said they were troublemakers.

Following their consolidation of power in late 1933, the People's Party pledged a fast track to popular enlightenment. A new education act (1935) and additions to it (1938) followed plans made in 1932.[36] The government managed a collection of different types of schools. Four coexisted: government schools, local, municipal, and private.[37] Of these, the new regime introduced municipal schools in 1936–1937, and the others stemmed from the old regime.[38] Government schools often were the only government secondary education offered upcountry, while private (*ratsadon*) schools comprised the above-mentioned Christian schools that attracted the upwardly mobile, and comfortable, young generation, as well as Chinese schools, which will be discussed below.

The vast majority of students attended local (*prachaban*) schools that fell under the immediate control of local officials and committees with the education ministry, via the 1935 education act, exercising ultimate authority. Most *prachaban* schools were thinly updated temple schools; over the course of the 1930s temples housed about four in five primary schools.[39] Primarily through *prachaban* schools, the People's Party maintained an eight-year course of study devised by Thammasakmontri; primary education entailed five years at a minimum for boys and three for girls. Up to three further years of secondary school was possible in some places, and usually in government schools. These eight years prepared students, in Thammasakmontri's and then the People's Party plan, for entry to a profession and/or university.[40] Democratic paternalism helped the authorities to mold the curriculum and censure young schoolteachers. It also produced a marked expansion of the educational system. As in the first decade of compulsory schooling in the 1920s,[41] the most dramatic growth after 1932 occurred at the primary level within *prachaban* schools. The People's Party government managed to roughly double the number of schools, the student population and the teaching ranks in the decade.[42] And, a real accomplishment of the revolution, girls fully participated in schooling equally with boys. Schools became coeducational.[43]

According to the education ministry, by 1937 all parts of the country had some type of schooling available. But as in the first decade of Thammasakmontri's reforms, truancy or simply an inability to reach a school kept many children away. In 1934–1935, for example, the government calculated that about 1.75 million primary school-age children should have been in school; about 1 million actually attended. And despite the great increase in schools and enrolments, the government's ambitious plan to educate at least half the population at the primary level remained out of reach. In 1937, one district officer estimated that 10 percent of children had completed primary schooling; a high-ranking government official more generously estimated the figure at one-third.[44] Young people of an age that democracy could inspire remained tied to the land and did not attend school. About three-quarters did not study beyond the first two primary school grades, and numbers fell off drastically at the higher levels. While about 1.1 million children studied in *prachaban* schools in 1937–38, just under 46,000 attended government secondary schools, and an additional 30,000 or so attended *ratsadon* (private) secondary schools.[45] Few graduated from high school year six—considered a largely complete education even without the final two years of the complete educational plan. For 1939, the ministry's research department calculated that about 5,400 people graduated at this level.[46]

We must here address another aspect of education that loomed menacingly behind the People's Party's democratic paternalism: the "Chinese problem." Both old and new regime educators thought that a naive peasantry retarded national development, while an educated Chinese population threatened to destroy it. Although lodged within the racial politics on the eve of the war, Phibun Songkhram did not conjure his anti-Chinese policies out of thin air. Discrimination, and skepticism about Chinese loyalty to the Thai state, went back to King Vajiravudh's reign at least. And Vajiravudh, the master anti-Chinese polemicist, spoke to a wider racism.

And yet the Promoters, according to a leading historian, were much more hostile to resident Chinese than the old regime. The Khana Ratsadon government banned the Kuomintang from forming political associations, and banned a popular account of Sun's Three People's Principles written by a journalist associate of Thawatt Rittidej.[47] In part, the Promoters reacted to changing demographics. The Chinese community between the wars became part of the mainstream of Thai society, thoroughly organized, politically astute and assertive. From the 1920s, as part of the decade's Chinese immigration boom, the number of Chinese women arriving in Siam grew markedly: the decade saw a 140 percent increase in Chinese women arriving by the time of the 1929 census compared to its prior count in 1919. By the 1937 census, a nearly 70 percent occurred over 1929.[48] The growth in all-Chinese families, rather than Chinese men marrying Thais, accelerated the growth of Chinese schools. In the first half of the 1930s, Chinese schools accounted for roughly 200 to 250 out of a total 1,100 to 1,300 *ratsadon* schools. Bangkok contained the majority, with 160 in 1936 and 1937, and another 12 in neighboring Thonburi.[49] Chinese private secondary schools were few. Of over 700 *ratsadon* schools in Bangkok in 1937 to 1939, for example, around 10 were Chinese secondary schools, compared to more than 200 Thai and around 20 American and European secondary schools.[50]

But the government targeted Chinese schools, not Western ones. English was an approved language, Chinese was politically suspect. Moreover, while Western schools conformed to mandated set hours of Thai-language instruction, Chinese schools flouted Thai education. In the late 1920s, King Prajadhipok toured Chinese schools and learned from provincial inspectors that the Chinese schools ignored state mandates on language, and resisted control generally.[51] Thai teachers in Chinese schools were marginal to pedagogy, and underpaid: those hired to teach

Thai received around 15 to 30 baht per month, while Chinese teachers earned on average 40 baht per month. Some received as much as 150 baht. The Chinese teachers and management also excluded Thais from school administration and any important decision making.[52]

The 1921 primary education law introduced gradual enforcement of the new rules on schooling. The law did not apply to Bangkok, and Chinese schools largely continued their own programs. In March 1933, the government mandated Bangkok as subject to the act, and nearly overnight Chinese schools had to adhere to strict rules on language use and were harassed by new regime officials.[53] The state's aggression set a bad precedent; at the end of the decade in Phibun's crackdown on the Chinese, education ministry officials carried guns on their inspections of Chinese schools.[54] During inspections in 1933, People's Party officials found that most students at Chinese schools did not attend afternoon sessions, when teachers taught in Thai. Indeed, inspectors found many students could not speak the national language. The government mandated Thai language instruction most of the time, and severely curtailed the use of Chinese. The Chinese community pushed back. Nine Chinese leaders drew up petitions protesting the crackdowns, and asked that more Chinese-language time be allowed. More than 6,100 parents and 332 business firms signed the petitions, but the education ministry refused to accept them.[55] Amid the tense atmosphere of 1933, the Chinese tried a variety of techniques to get around the rules, including at one school installing alarm bells that alerted people when inspectors were about to enter.[56] The government closed seventy-nine Chinese schools between March 1933 and August 1935,[57] and seemed to be waging all-out war on Chinese education: a Chinese newspaper decried the moves and stated that no government anywhere in the world treated the Chinese community as poorly as the Thai administration.[58] A temporary lull followed, and by 1938 around 500 teachers taught nearly 17,000 students in over 230 Chinese primary and secondary schools around the country.[59] At the close of the decade, the government renewed its attacks on Chinese schools. Whereas previously Chinese teachers marginalized Thais, by the late 1930s the situation was reversed: only one or two Chinese-language teachers survived professionally by the end of the decade in each school. In the first half of 1939, the government closed twenty-five schools, and sixteen more soon followed. The reasons for the crackdowns expanded. Government officials closed schools not only for violating educational law, but also for allegedly printing and spreading pamphlets that called for resistance to a range of government policies, and encouragement to workers to revolt.[60]

Many young, educated people learned politics on the street, so to speak, in the labor activism of the war period. Many others joined in Pridi's anti-Phibun movement. But two main problems challenged popular enlightenment: continued official ambivalence, at best, and exclusion at worst, of Chinese, and the paucity of secondary school graduates. In the early postwar years, democracy reemerged from the military autocracy, remarkably perhaps: in 1947 around one-third of the population above ten years of age had a primary education only, around 3.25 percent finished year six, that is, basic high school equivalence. Around three in 10,000 people had studied through university.[61] Again, however, the talented minority shaped social values, and changed politics. We can discuss briefly now the new university that the People's Party established, and its spirited commitment to the new regime's mission.

Thammasat: The People's University

After Pridi returned from his overseas exile in late 1933, he played a key role in domestic education. As interior minister, he accomplished a historic project, the founding of the state's second university. In the declaration of its principles, the government stated: "Now that there is a Constitutional form of government, [we will] expedite the measures taken to develop the study of Moral and Political Sciences in order to attain the same standard as the Universities in the civilised countries and to achieve rapid progress."[62]

Duen Bunnag, Pridi's French-trained apprentice who also taught at Thammasat, in 1934 wrote the new regime's constitutional law textbook used by all university law students. In inspired passages that echoed some of the language used in compulsory school textbooks, Duen wrote that constitutional democracy awakened people. "People who are awakened [sati sampachanya] . . . are their own masters. . . . If they have to rely on the minds of others to show them the way . . . [then] they are like dolls or puppets. Democracy aims to have everyone be in charge of themselves. . . . It makes everyone know how to use the power of their own minds."[63] Universities anywhere build their reputation initially with words, and soaring rhetoric especially aims to highlight their exceptionalism. Chulalongkorn University, established in 1916 largely on Thammasak-montri's initiative, consolidated the former civil service school and was named for the country's great modernizer. A great man's name did not legitimize Thammasat; the founders chose an ideal instead. Thammasat's claims were revolutionary but so too in large measure was its physical establishment. Chulalongkorn held extensive property, verdant and architecturally impressive, east of the old royal city. In contrast to Chula's landed wealth, Thammasat initially occupied the old law faculty housed in a foreign department store building on Rajadamnoen Avenue, and then gained the title to riverside land the army fourth infantry division had used.[64] Unlike the royal endowment that Chula enjoyed, Pridi established Thammasat to be self-funding. Economically modest, Thammasat also became practical, or cunning, in stabilizing its finances. Thammasat charged tuition and exam fees, and Pridi exploited an Asian crisis to fund the university. After Japan's invasion of China in 1931, Chinese wealth transferred to the embattled Chinese nationalists grew considerably and concerned the Thai government. After the People's Party revolution, the government banned local Chinese overseas transfers. The Overseas Chinese Banking Corporation (OCBC) in Bangkok, however, continued as the main financial channel to China and the police charged it with violating the law. The bank liquidated its assets and Pridi established the Bank of Asia from 20,000 baht in Chinese wealth. Thammasat became an 80 percent shareholder in the Bank of Asia.[65] Pridi's financial shrewdness, and ability to exploit the opportunity offered by the OCBC's political entanglement, was supplemented by charity. Thammasat relied on contributions from prominent citizens. Money to support the first boarders at the university was put up by Pridi, Phibun, Phahon, Chaophraya Yomaraj, a politically powerful man in the sixth reign related to Pridi's wife, and a French lecturer and friend of the Promoters, Rene Guyon.[66]

Guyon—drafter of the special courts act after the 1933 rebellion—gave a Gallic facade to Thammasat's mission. And of nine founding professors, three were French. But modern law more broadly became the premier "moral science" among young intellectuals, and seven of the nine had law degrees or were registered barristers. In addition, in the first year there were twenty-two lecturers for the delightfully named B.M.Sc. degree[67]—the Bachelor of Moral Sciences—and an additional five lecturers by 1938.[68]

Rural people often avoided or were unable to attend school because of work, family, or distance. And only a few thousand young people attended secondary school in the entire country. But a new generation enthusiastically greeted the founding of Thammasat, with more than 7,000 students attending in its first year.[69] This figure is astounding, even by today's standards of mass education. At the time it was completely unprecedented. Chulalongkorn in 1935 had 756 students enrolled.[70] The university allowed broad qualifications for entry and offered correspondence education, which partly explains the high enrollment. The diverse routes for admission included foreign education and government service. Distance learning allowed people upcountry to complete assignments and take exams in their home provinces and have them reviewed by Thammasat lecturers. Regrettably, there appear to be no records of how many students learned via the correspondence system. The figure would have been high, however, because of the limited dormitory space at the riverside campus and most people's poverty. Thammasat presented the first opportunity for people of modest means to get an advanced education, and it also marked the first time that national higher education with a standardized curriculum became a possibility. Unlike the chaotic situation in secondary-school learning, where a range of texts and approaches existed, all Thammasat students within their disciplines followed the same course of study.

The obstacles facing the new university should not be overlooked. While its student population dwarfed Chulalongkorn's in the same period it many fewer professors and lecturers. Still it made two landmark changes in Thai education and society: it trained new regime parliamentarians and civil servants and it gave a home to democracy activists fighting against dictatorship. Many assemblymen of the new generation studied at Thammasat, as did the intelligentsia more broadly. In time, Thammasat law graduates became the majority among the elected members of the parliament. Thammasat law graduates accounted for nearly 70 percent of elected members in the 1948 and 1952 elections, and around half in the following elections in February and December 1957.[71] Royalists and the army—both enemies of the People's Party—gained political power during these four postwar elections, which makes the strong showing of the Thammasat contingent all the more remarkable.

Pridi looms large over Thammasat's formative years in the 1930s and 1940s. And right through the People's Party years, Pridi's democratic paternalism shaped the mission of the university. Thammasat's "moral sciences" framed the teaching of the techniques of modern law, administration, and so on through an ideological link between official virtue and popular welfare. In addition to the ennobled titles most of them enjoyed, the state gave Thammasat's scholars particular names that affixed Buddhist virtue to their official characters. Pridi's official name was Luang Pradit Manudham, "Fashioner of Righteous (Dhammic) Men." Sanya Dharmasakdi, his younger colleague

Figure 4.1. Center of worldly Dhamma: Thammasat University's dome and main hall, with Pridi's statue in the foreground. Photo by the author.

and a legend in Thammasat University politics of later years, embodied "Guarantor of Energy of the Dhamma." Phraya Nitisat Paisal, the "Exalted Scholar of Law," became the secretary of the People's Party association and was among the founders of Thammasat in 1934. After 1932, as part of their obligation, these officials regularly gave lectures to young justice ministry bureaucrats that combined the Dhamma and constitutionalism—universal, eternal law and secular, modern law—in a metaphysical explanation of the basis for self-cultivation and as a way to be a good citizen, which meant primarily a free thinking but dutiful individual.[72] Their work and characters would guide people in the new politics, fulfilling a "Platonic guardianship with Theravada characteristics," as Federico Ferrara styled the trajectory of Thailand's experiments with democracy.[73]

The Platonic analogy should not be carried too far, especially because Plato's political idealism offered women a prominent place. On the one hand, the revolution undoubtedly advanced women's schooling. Primary and secondary schooling for girls expanded steadily. Higher education also had many women entering nursing, teaching, and medicine degree programs. Given the popularity of these three fields at Chulalongkorn, women comprised a large part of the 1930s student body there.[74] One observer at the time remarked that probably all future schoolteachers would be women, since so many enrolled in the teaching program.[75] On the other hand, however, Thammasat in particular was a male fraternity. Women numbered only 91 out of 6,129 students enrolled in the bachelor's degree in 1938; and only 4 graduated with a degree. Compared to 153 male master's degree law students in 1937, 1 woman sat in the program. Master's in political science and political economy, also, had 1 woman in each program, and roughly 40 and 85 men, respectively. No women taught at Thammasat at the time.[76]

Men therefore dominated the teaching and learning of the Dhammic constitutional regime. For a time, they also created a "Cinderella" mythology; a depiction of women as at their best nubile heroines whose beauty brought credit to the nation. Thammasat published an eponymous monthly journal during the People's Party period that explained modern rights and freedoms, Thai constitutionalism, world affairs, politics, economics, and the like. The journal also featured on its cover and inner pages photographs of naked women, smiling, relaxing, or exercising outdoors. The health and happiness motif—mirror image of women's bodies as beautiful boons to the nation—in part derives from the concurrent eugenic movements around the world. It also, in the colonial context signals Siam's modernity as conceived by the Promoters. *Thammasat* journal published such photos along with a range of other newspapers and magazines at the time.[77] Simultaneously, *Thammasat* and the other publishers of these images did not discuss women as men's equals, or constitutionalism as a bringing a regime of such equals; advice on love and relationships prevailed, not politics.[78]

If romantic, gendered abstraction infused the moral sciences, political commitment marked the young men's university cohort. And like the theory, the political practice of Thammasat scholars buttressed state power. World War II fractured the People's Party, and state institutions became central to the conflict. Thammasat formed a key basis of support for Pridi's mainly civilian Seri Thai—an antimilitary, anti-Japanese movement that emerged from the middle of 1943. An Office of Strategic Services wartime report noted that the Seri Thai existed more as a government bureaucratic conspiracy than as a popular resistance movement,[79] and the campus itself and the network of its students, graduates, and associates formed the key supports of Seri Thai power. In the postwar backlash against the People's Party Thammasat came under the control of reactionary military and monarchist groups. In a 1949 revolt against the conservatives staged by Pridi backers, Thammasat again took center stage for a bureaucratically connected rebel organization. Many Thammasat students were brought in for questioning after the government crushed the rebellion. In the next army coup of 1951, the army occupied the campus on the pretext that it needed the land to combat the navy faction that staged the revolt that year. In October of that year, about 3,000 Thammasat students mobilized a protest against the army demanding the return of the campus. The military gave in but subsequently changed the name by removing "political science" from its designation and appointing Phibun as the rector of the university.[80]

Propaganda: Democratic Paternalism on Tour and on Air

The new regime used much more than schooling to spread their message. Especially given schooling's limits and the country's poor infrastructure, the People's Party eagerly adopted new methods and technologies to disseminate democratic ideology. Rural lecture tours and radio broadcasts, in particular, became the primary accompaniments to the educational system for advancement of the message: an imagined community of equals living under the constitution and the People's Party. Like the school and university system, the propaganda drive advanced the new regime's idealism and also sought to control reception of the message.

The government's propaganda efforts began in earnest in the wake of the Bowondet rebellion. The People's Party realized that upcountry support for the rebels was still strong after the government victory,[81] and they targeted first civil servants. In December 1933, Phahon established the Constitution Society—another People's Party-directed group that complemented the People's Party Association—to rally public support for the new regime. As Murashima puts it: "In semi-coercive fashion the society enrolled the first-category members of the assembly into its membership."[82] Like the Promoters' association previously, in 1934 and 1935, the Constitutional Association opened provincial branches that featured provincial chief justices, governors, and other important provincial officials as leading members.[83]

But the government pursued more direct popular contact also. The new regime claimed superiority over the old. Its spokesmen clearly articulated the inherited problems of exclusivity and elitism in Thai society. Ronasit Phichai (1889–1973) was an army officer who had taught in the military cadet school under Song Suradet before the revolution, and also was editor of the army's flagship journal. He brought in many cadets to the revolutionary cause in 1931 because of his persuasive oratory,[84] and became chief propagandist after 1932. Ronasit insisted that in the new era: "It is necessary that common people's knowledge expand to include the entire country and for provincial people to feel as if they are one, and not left out of the commonality as before."[85] He argued that the politics of inclusion would resonate with the population but that much work had to be done to convince most people that democracy would better their lives. He asserted that 25 percent of the population believed in democracy, 15 percent were against the new order, and the remaining 60 percent did not understand the new regime or its ideology and felt that it had no relevance for their lives.[86] For national unity, as well as the good of the regime, democracy mattered.

Both the People's Party government and the absolute monarchy before them were keen students of foreign models of state modernization provided by the Western powers, their colonial administrations, and independent Japan. The Thai government established a publicity bureau in the premier's office in May 1933 that it closely modeled on a Nazi example, and the office later became a department. The propagandists formed a modest group; in 1934, the bureau had twenty staff in total, with ten of these in the lectures division.[87] But the cohort had an ambitious mandate and especially after the suppression of the Bowondet rebellion constitutional propaganda flourished as a means to solidify government power.[88] In a program very similar to the Japanese Meiji model fifty years before,[89] lecturers toured the countryside throughout the 1930s to spread the constitutional democratic message. They commonly traveled several months in the dry season, giving talks throughout a particular region. In a sixty-three-day tour on the eastern seaboard provinces at the end of the decade, for example, a committee visited nearly 55,500 people in forty-four places. Officials distributed 1,500 pictures of the Constitution and an equal number of copies of the document, and they handed out 2,000 printed lectures and 1,500 collections of the premier's speeches.[90]

Most people, as Ronasit remarked, did not understand constitutional democracy. The government advised speakers therefore that for maximum impact the quality of listeners mattered more than the quantity. It counseled that only people with a minimum of four years' primary education be allowed to attend. Children and old women were ostensibly banned.[91] The 1 percent, the educated middle strata of society—civil servants, monks, the rural bourgeoisie, and teachers—formed the core audience, and the intelligentsia ideally would return to their villages and towns to spread the new democratic gospel.

What did the publicists discuss? Initially, officials scrambled to give a clear answer. Rural experience, and particularly the peasantry's sometimes impolite reception of the new ideology, gave an urgent impetus to the government's publicity drive. In 1934, an assemblyman for Petchabun province informed the government that he tried to explain the new order to local people but quickly found they did not understand him, and that perhaps he did not know what he was talking about. Others found themselves confronted by uncomprehending or hostile crowds more interested in solutions to their economic problems than listening to political abstractions. An assemblyman for the northern province of Lamphun, for example, garbled an explanation of tax obligations in a democracy and found local tobacco farmers refusing to pay the tax at all.[92] This irritated the interior ministry, which wanted civil servants to stick to an approved script.[93] In 1934 in Nakhon Pathom—a central province near Bangkok—lecturers found that local people, who like the Lamphun peasantry interpreted the new freedom under democracy as a license to ignore authority, had seized land from wealthy landowners and capitalized on its rental. The lecturers instructed local officials that any further Soviet-style land expropriation could not be allowed. Soon after these cases, the publicity bureau sought message consistency in the lecture circuit and a focus on the new political principles. Lecturers most often promoted the new order by discussing two topics particularly: popular sovereignty and rights of the citizenry.

The Promoters cherished the idea that they empowered the "people" and gave them rights; notions that, like any democratic assertions, were broad and vague enough to be defined in different ways. In brief, the state expected speakers to explain that the people before 1932 had no role in the administration of the country. One spokesman explained that rights and power were almost entirely one-sided; an elite class had them, the masses did not.[94] Another accused the old regime of never explaining what rights the people had.[95] After 1932 the government advised that the people should be informed that masters and servants no longer existed.[96] A heady assertion indeed, one contradicted by the bureaucracy's dominance in the new system but also a source of inspiration to many people because of its frequent reiteration in official language.

The lectures divided individual rights into equality and liberty.[97] Most importantly, legal equality for the first time obviated the privileges of ranks, titles, and class that buttressed the royal-aristocratic social hierarchy of the past forty years. The state cautioned speakers to make clear that equality before the law did not entail material equality or wealth redistribution, given peasant attitudes mentioned above, "moral economy" notions and millenarian movements espousing them under the old regime,[98] and the political backlash against Pridi's economic plan of spring 1933 that sought collectivized agriculture and state-owned industry. With judicial equality, the courts judged the disputes of all citizens equally. (The military, of course, had their own courts, as we have seen.) The new legal regime discarded class and family influence when passing judgment. The speakers used historical context to explain the magnanimous freedoms enjoyed under the new regime. Spokesmen described personal liberty as a fundamental condition of modern society, and speakers explained that progressive countries—which now included Siam, since it advanced from autocracy to democracy—are those that do not allow slavery or the loss of autonomy, which is "very similar to the state of a savage beast." Furthermore, popular sovereignty meant "[w]e do not live in a savage country."[99]

As did the activist upcountry teachers, some regional civil servants interpreted popular rule in a different way than high state officers. And the limits to People's Party governance enabled a contest over the practice of democracy. Provincial assemblymen who emerged as a new class of political advocates after the first elections in 1933 often gave lectures on the new order at the state's request. But this new class among the rural intelligentsia challenged the state's democracy from the above model and took seriously the rights in the constitution just enumerated. In the northeast, the poorest region of the country where popular democracy became a powerful force, publicity officials in 1935 criticized provincial representatives who spent more time tackling local problems than following the official message that the state democracy protected and empowered everyone. Thong-in Phuriphat, an Ubon province representative, gives the best example of the new class's contribution to democracy and their impatience with the pace of change under the People's Party.

Thong-in—two weeks shy of his twenty-sixth birthday, when the People's Party deposed the absolute monarchy—became an Ubon assemblyman in 1933, with the first elections. Like many of the politically engaged intelligentsia, Thong-in studied law—and passed the bar exam in 1931, after completing his legal studies with the Ministry of Justice by post—and worked as a schoolteacher. Thong-in studied for a time in Bangkok. Like heroes in a fable, young men who traveled to the capital for education at the time were greeted as stars upon their return. The prestige of having a metropolitan education was one aspect, but also the mere fact that the prodigals survived the journey at all. He became a secondary school teacher at age nineteen, and in addition to his teaching and legal work also became a district officer.[100] He embodied Thai virility, being a skilled boxer and father of a large family. Thong-in's independent streak irked the government. He served in every assembly until 1947, when a military coup deposed the People's Party. Two years later he was killed with three others in police custody. From the state's point of view, Thong-in was an untrustworthy propagandist. He appeared to them as stubbornly resistant to their directives, and also competed with other local politicians. While competition was perhaps an inevitable part of the incipient democracy, the government sought consensual relations, between the center as master and the periphery as docile apprentice. Thong-in had his own ideas about the relationship. He resented the local presence of Pairoj Chaiyanam, a leading Bangkok official sent upcountry to lecture in 1934. Pairoj and his brother Direk were close to Pridi and rose to prominent work in Thammasat University, and in government. Pairoj was a Party insider from Bangkok who, in this instance at least, viewed popular rule as a limited democracy under the People's Party. Thong-in apparently said that Pairoj should not speak about democracy since he gained an education under the old regime and thus was politically suspect, and in any case Pairoj did not understand northeastern affairs. State officers disliked Thong-in's attitude, and viewed his independence as treason. Pairoj thought Thong-in dangerous because he refused to stand up for a toast to the People's Party at a civil servants association dinner given one night.[101]

Thong-in relentlessly criticized the government over its restraints on democracy, and he condemned the hijacking of the new order by cliques and factions. To his impatient young mind, any compromise with authoritarianism—even or especially in the form of the People's Party—threatened to strangle Thai democracy in its cradle. Late in the decade, Thong-in wrote in a newspaper article that the protection of sovereignty and nationalism had to be popular movements, and people should mistrust any group that claimed to stand for the nation as a whole.[102] Thong-in's idealism should be contextualized. Governance worked through cliques and factions in the absence of political parties or mass organizations, and Thong-in banded together with other northeastern representatives to advocate for regional interests throughout the era. But his public sentiments irritated Bangkok insiders, especially, and his critique aimed at the heights of the bureaucracy.

Thong-in's conflict with Bangkok's paternalist democracy shows the limits to People's Party hegemony, and especially the challenge posed by a new class of rural leaders who spoke independently to their constituents. Radio, the wireless "magic device" that presented an exciting new option for publicity, accompanied lectures as an additional but more closely controlled forum in which the contest occurred. While more easily policed than rural lectures, radio programming similarly reached a limited audience. Prince Sakon Voravan, like his brother Prince Wan, a People's Party advocate, estimated in 1933 that there were 16,000 radios in the country; the following year Ronasit Phichai figured there were 25,000, with most in Bangkok. The 50-percent-plus increase in a year is impressive, but Ronasit estimated that this represented only 2.5 percent of what was needed to reach people.[103] Transmission capacity and staffing posed additional problems. In the early 1930s, Phraya Thai station in Bangkok was the only transmitting station, had power for only two or three hours of programming a day and the ten-kilowatt signal often disappeared outside of the Bangkok area. By one estimate, the signal traveled well for about 300 kilometers. Receiver quality upcountry was another issue. Many of the cheapest sets, that is, those within the financial reach of country people, had only intermittent reception.[104]

The state censored all content prior to airing. While the government created a participatory environment and encouraged educated people to contribute to certain radio programs, as we will see below, only certain government officers were permitted to speak when it came to state affairs and the meaning of democracy. Moreover, such discussion meant the approved script from the publicity bureau that focused only on administrative topics and constitutional nuts and bolts, and not debates on the practice or philosophy of politics.

Even so the regime could not completely control the discourse, especially when parliamentarians, given the minimal staff of the publicity bureau, were drafted to speak about their provinces. Some, for example, a Chiang Mai provincial representative in 1933, related glowingly their people's loyalty to the new regime and village harmony.[105] Indeed, avowals of peasant docility and naivete were common, either from the speakers' genuine belief, elite condescension, or flattery. Undoubtedly such talk would have pleased the publicity bureau. But others, akin to Thong-in in Ubon, legitimized People's Party talk of democracy as the right of commoners to air their grievances and empower them to take charge of their affairs. Many spoke forthrightly about the problems they faced at home. The assemblyman for the northern province of Pitsanulok, for example, opined on radio that government indifference to the lives of people in his province had reduced the place to the status of "an unwanted child of a minor wife."[106] The central province of Chaiyaphum's representative claimed that urban people would have trouble understanding local conditions, which were "as different from Bangkok as the palaces of the gods are to the huts of the destitute."[107] Liang Chaiyakan and other northeastern assemblymen spoke directly about regional poverty.[108]

Parliamentarians were not the only extra-bureaucratic voices. As Ronasit Phichai explained, the People's Party quickly discovered it did not have enough qualified people to speak on additional broadcast topics that were intended to create a more informed and socially engaged citizenry. The new regime thus allowed suitable people of any class or background to deliver lectures in their areas of expertise, however, provided that politics did not form part of the agenda. In the mid-1930s, such topics included: health, provincial history, sports, hobbies such as photography or music, and morals. Like the educational system, radio broadcasts frequently described moral rectitude as fundamental to social welfare. The ethics espoused to produce social harmony relied on traditional religion, and the state invited well-educated Buddhist monks to the radio programs.[109] Like young teachers and rural assemblymen, many young monks were excited by the empowering promises of democracy. Government stated explicitly however that politics could not be broached in Sangha affairs, monks on radio could not criticize people or groups, and sermons could not cover worldly topics. Instead, the government suggested monks focus on the old standbys of religious and moral education: the Sangha administration, the history of Buddha images or particular temples, and the morals espoused in the tales of the Buddha's prior lives (jatakas).[110]

Old-fashioned homilies or temple histories were one thing. But the state's public relations innovations also introduced a new type of discourse: public debates. The government frequently reiterated free speech as important to democracy, and the new forum allowed people to practice oratory and persuasion. In the mid-1930s, the government's Fine Arts Department sponsored a range of debates, broadcast on the airwaves, which quickly became popular with listeners.[111] Hundreds of people attended the exchanges and applied to participate, and the recounting of debates featured in daily newspapers. The government banned from the exchanges not only discussions of political philosophy, but also any discussion of government policy. Such urgent issues as the need for agricultural improvement in an economy dominated by peasant smallholders, or social problems like prostitution were off limits.[112] Instead, the premier and other cabinet ministers spoke positively about administrative change, social issues, and national progress more generally in annual radio broadcasts that the newspapers reprinted.

The participant radio programs by contrast invited people to show their skill in debating things such as: heat is better than cold for health, cigarette smoking is better than betel chewing, strength is more effective than virtue, women of old were better than those today, or beauty contests do more good than harm. Despite, or because of, the vagueness of these topics the censors reined in speakers if they discussed sensitive issues.[113] A debate on beauty contests, for example, flouted on-air politeness codes when some participants started attacking women as a whole. One competitor, arguing against the contests, asserted that beauty contests were immoral since all entrants, everyone knew, worked as prostitutes.[114] The state aimed, then, at apolitical, intelligent, and polite speech. For critics, such an attitude stood in the way of democracy. Newspapers, mainly privately owned by this time, criticized public affairs much more than state-owned radio. Anecdotal evidence shows many were not terribly impressed with government radio, with columnists labeling the radio programs boring, patronizing, too propagandistic, and insufficiently informative. They blamed the new regime for not allowing free expression.[115]

Making the Constitution Sacred and Profane

The government's stress on docility over willfulness, conformity over provocation, did not stem from an innate authoritarianism among the People's Party. Instead the rebellion of 1933 complemented their sense that new regime values had to reach a wider audience. Beginning in 1934, the regime went all out in promoting the symbols of constitutionalism as a new faith. I will conclude this chapter by detailing another approach taken by the Party: presenting the constitution itself as a sacred object embodying universal law. The government celebrated the anniversary of the revolution each year with public commemorations of the progress the country had made under the constitutional order. The government frequently likened the constitution to the Dhamma. These celebrations encouraged people to have faith. If they could not understand abstract democratic principles, then perhaps seeing was believing. The image of the constitution atop its pedestal, governing mundane affairs from above, was the highest profile public artifact of this era and continues to be the image most closely aligned with People's Party democracy.

The People's Party came to power in an age of new media that ambitious regimes around the world used to instill nationalism. The Thai cohort also inherited a visual and performative culture that mixed Thai Buddhist ideas of power with Western liberalism. In all, there was a fertile ground to advance their ideology. Fascinated with photography and wanting to rule as an approachable monarch, King Chulalongkorn and his men created powerful images that brought the monarchy into high profile.[116] His two sons—the sixth and seventh kings—also avidly consumed modern visual culture and presented themselves as worldly moderns and nationalists like their father before them. At the same time, the awe-inspiring aloofness always associated with kingship tempered the sense of national identity created by the new technology's mundane imagery—kings surveying rural townships, watching military parades or opening new bridges or highways. A spectacle's awesomeness points to a central aspect of kingly imagery: the unidirectionality, or monologue of power, from regime to the people. The People's Party inherited political supernaturalism, and added a democratic form. Puli Fuwongcharoen argues that for the People's Party the constitution functioned as a "traditional totemic object, as opposed to a modern piece of legislation."[117] Ever after, the government used the picture as a way to legitimize and sacralize the constitution. The king's role in blessing the constitution is important. King Prajadhipok suggested that the constitution be written in a thick accordion-style codex like traditional religious scriptures so that it would appear "mystical."[118] And the photograph of the king handing down the signed constitution to a supplicant in a December 1932 ceremony highlights the charter as a gift from on high. New regime officers, even when omitting mention of the king's role, spoke of the constitution as a talisman and spiritual power. In 1934, Phahon declared the constitution to be a sacred object;[119] two years later, Pridi declared it the highest form of the Dhamma;[120] and in 1934, the secretary of the Constitution Society that propagandized the constitution declared that "those who see our Constitution as Lord Buddha's scripture are absolutely correct."[121]

Figure 4.2. Justice enshrined: An iconic constitutional image on the cover of a periodical, 1940. Photo courtesy of the Original Press Library.

December 10th became Constitution Day, the center of a series of festivities that celebrated the new order and its freedom from the old ways in ceremonies that evoked traditional high religion. The British Minister in Siam viewed a local Constitution Day ceremony in Lopburi in 1934, and was amazed to see that the constitutional replica altar dwarfed the other two main altars in the pavilion devoted to the Buddha and the king. He opined that

> semi-divine honours were being paid to the Constitution, in the hope, presumably, that the simple-minded Siamese peasant would be induced thereby to regard it as a real entity upon

which he could lavish some of that personal devotion which he had reserved hitherto for the monarch of the land.[122]

Local officials enthusiastically championed the ceremonies and the symbolism. The December constitutional celebrations in Bangkok were replicated all over the country in provincial capitals. Some parliamentary representatives complained that one replica per province insufficient, and many rural areas used substitute images of the constitution to anchor their own Constitution Day celebrations.[123] After 1932, constitutional imagery was widely in vogue. Many newspapers carried the symbol of the charter on its pedestal in their mastheads. Many government offices at the local level adopted the image in their seals. Some entrepreneurs adopted constitutional motifs in their sales pitches and branding.[124] Through the work of both central government and provincial actors, the regime's democratic paternalism materialized before the public.

December 10th became Constitution Day, the center of a series of festivities that celebrated the new order and its freedom from the old ways in ceremonies that evoked traditional high religion. The December rituals continued right through the 1930s and early 1940s. The events of 1934, the pioneer celebration, became the template. On December 8, 1934, a ceremony featured monks chanting over and blessing the constitution. The government presented thirty monks from Bangkok and Thonburi with new robes. On the following day, Brahmin priests blessed the constitution and anointed it with holy water. The constitution was then placed in the throne hall, where kings had been crowned and now the People's Party had its headquarters.

Twin blessings—Buddhist first, Hindu second—took place also on the 10th after a constitutional procession of honor around Bangkok. Delegations of the new people actually and symbolically empowered by the regime—the military, businesspeople, labor, farmers and various people's associations—accompanied the constitution on its tour. The four-hour public journey through the old city culminated at Sanam Luang, where schoolboys and -girls and the Tiger Cubs association flanked the final approach to a ceremonial hall erected for the purpose. Brahmin priests strewed popped rice—traditionally used in religious blessings—and flowers around the hall, a *pipat* orchestra played and then the Constitution Society was finally entrusted to municipal officers. The blessings took place at five in the afternoon. At precisely 5:18 p.m., a procession of planes flew overhead and dropped garlands of flowers onto the site.[125]

And, as with the Thammasat University cohort who associated constitutional modernity not only with sacrality and a new nationalism but also the making of Thai Cinderellas, beauty pageants formed a core of the official push and popular enthusiasm for the constitutional celebrations. The solemn Buddhist and Brahmin ceremonies were a start, but more was required. For additional psychological and material benefit, the government held the first-ever Siamese beauty contest in the 1934 festivities. A writer with a Chinese newspaper at the time wrote that modern, educated people should not be ashamed of their bodies. Upcountry girls from modest backgrounds could potentially earn great fame, he argued, not for themselves but for their hometowns. The judges in the first incarnation in 1934 were all men.[126] The beauty contests—whose judges chose "Miss Siam"—arguably formed the mundane heart of the constitutional celebrations.[127] In 1934 and 1935, the interior ministry chose all participants, but thereafter private interests also advanced their candidates. Despite the above encouragement for provincial girls, the contests had strict rules that barred any working women, and all contestants had to be "respectable." Elite women, as well as men, judged later contestants, people who presumably could discern respectability from sloth. Ironically, as Barmé points out, judges decided the winners as those with the fewest flaws from a checklist of undesirable traits, rather than the most beauty.[128]

In addition, contests of *takraw*, chess, and other pastimes; a lottery; food and drink; and toys all made the three-day event a family affair. Further, the fun had to be a paying concern. The lottery, like the beauty contests, required a fee. The government used the entry fees for the beauty contests to buy weaponry for the military, fund constitutional publicity, and for poverty relief. The government exploited people's acquisitiveness: first prize in the lottery won the tremendous sum of 10,000 baht; the pool totaled 25,000 baht. The festivals interwove material and moral incentives.

Conclusion

Critics who wanted a more democratic system doubted that constitutional festivals marked an improvement over the old sacred rituals of monarchy. Like Thong-in Phuriphat, Thawin Udon represented a northeastern province and challenged the emerging status quo of democratic paternalism. He argued in the late 1930s that people lighting candles and incense for the constitution and regarding it as holy was no different than grannies going to listen to sermons at the temple in order to make merit. Neither group took in the message, he contended. Attendees at constitutional fairs were the equivalent of these old women, who slept through most of the delivery, then woke up at the end of a sermon shouted *sadhu* (amen) a couple of times and fell asleep again until the next intermission. Real democracy, he asserted, was different. It was active, contentious, and lived in the villages and rural towns, not in state-sponsored festivals and passive acceptance of what was presented.[129]

The hegemonic effect of democratic paternalism was uneven because of material limits to state power—money, transport, and books. And prejudice as well; not everyone was welcome to participate in the training. Chinese schools remained under threat through the 1930s; the gains that the Chinese community made came from self-initiative, not government support. The government encouraged Thai teachers to explain popular sovereignty to their pupils as markers of a new freedom and civility, but suspected that Chinese teachers broached the same topic to bind their students to a foreign government and undermine Thai culture. Women, by contrast, were not persecuted under the new regime, but neither did the new government offer them much. Basically ignored, or put on a pedestal and exhibited as constitutional window dressing, women's role in politics and education lagged far behind the men with whom they shared equal protection and opportunity under the constitution.

Democratic paternalism also was limited because many educated people who grew up in the 1930s became frustrated with the boundaries imposed by the Party's paternalist attitudes. They wanted a more active democracy. Many educated outsiders also complained that the new regime remained under the sway of old-regime thought and old-regime actors. The intellectuals' criticism of the system remained consistent throughout the People's Party era, and a range of critics—outsiders across the political spectrum—espoused clear-headed thinking, not propaganda, and adherence to the rule of law, not the rule of men.

Simultaneously, the Promoters' commitment to their sixth principle to expand education resulted in much more, and much less, than a tepid offering of formulaic principles that some critics felt did not change people's attitudes or even interest them. Notwithstanding the problems at the secondary level, schooling expanded dramatically, for boys and girls, and Thammasat, a new university, enrolled thousands more young people than the established university. Thammasat's admittance policies and distance learning brought a new generation into higher education. Many of them entered the Seri Thai resistance to the Japanese, and then the postwar national assembly and government when democracy bloomed anew after military dictatorship.

Chapter Five

Buddhist Democracy in the Revolution

At the time of the 1932 revolution, Thai Buddhism was in ferment. In northern Thailand, the charismatic monk Khruba (teacher) Srivichai, born in 1878 in Lamphun province, had thousands of loyal followers who saw him as a "field of merit" (*tonbun*)—a spiritual power who exercised real-world force. Believing that his power helped them to a better present and future life, villagers throughout the north country lent their labor and material support to his causes. Northern Buddhists—products of a very old independent regional tradition—had long been resistant to Bangkok power and resented the claims of Bangkok authority. Khruba Srivichai posed the gravest threat to Bangkok's power over religious administration in the 1920s and 1930s. He stubbornly flouted Bangkok's rules by conducting unsanctioned independent ordinations, and his large popular backing—whom he led in many temple restorations and public works' projects and which one scholar terms his pursuit of "active utopianism"[1]—made state officials suspicious. A Bangkok official in 1932 wrote to the government that the Khruba was more powerful than any secular lord.[2]

In Bangkok itself, Narin Phasit, a spirited, arrogant, and stubbornly independent lay Buddhist born in 1874, sought to revive the female order of religious professionals (*bhikkunis*), women whom society would accord the same status as Buddhist monks. In one of his numerous writings, Narin compared an independent female religious order to the freedom of neighboring countries from Western imperialism. In 1928, on his own authority, Narin ordained his two daughters as the first *bhikkunis* at his own temple, Wat Nariwong. Narin's ambitious cause failed; his daughters were arrested and he also spent time in jail. The case became a public sensation. Some of the reading public admired his mission; others thought he should be executed. The consummate educated outsider, who like Thawatt Rittidej started his own newspapers and self-published scores of social and political commentaries, Narin made a constant spectacle of himself. He shaved half his head, and took to wearing an image of Christ around his neck, a man whom he identified as a fellow martyr.[3]

In the midsouth, one month before the People's Party revolution, a twenty-six-year-old monk established *Suan Mokkhabalaram*—the Grove of Liberation—as a new temple dedicated to the revival and promotion of *patipattidhamma*: the righteous and emancipatory practice of meditation and self-control in speech, body, and mind first taught by the historical Buddha. He and his lay brother grew the temple and its publicity arm, a monthly magazine, and took religious names of Buddhadasa, slave of the Buddha and Dhammadasa, slave to the Dhamma. A young provincial monk of a commercial family, Buddhadasa became known. His energetic propagation of *patipattidhamma* brought him new friends in Siam's intellectual elite, including Pridi, senior justice ministry officials, and the leaders of the Sangha. Buddhadasa declared his temple's opening a fitting coincidence to the People's Party revolution.

> The history of Suan Mokh is a thing that is easy to remember, encapsulated as it is in the short sentence: "[Founded] the same year as the change of regime." We took this as an auspicious omen of the changes happening in a new era, and as a chance to make (the world) better as much as we could.[4]

In addition to the legacy of Bangkok's state and scholarly Buddhism, Buddhadasa and his brother read widely in global Buddhism and foreign influences prominently influenced them. They pitched their journal, *Buddhasasana*, to monks and a growing class of intellectual laity who were interested in meditation and the scholarly traditions of Buddhism. The laity grew markedly; religious exams, the most rigorous option for those seeking detailed knowledge of textual Buddhism, were introduced for laypeople in 1929. Their popularity thereafter—with examinees reaching nearly 55,000 by 1933—points to the growing popular demand for spiritual education, and the young generation's demand for more diverse avenues of knowledge.[5]

Revolutionary Idealism Finds Fertile Ground

A traditional and regional challenger to Bangkok's religious authority, an outsider intellectual's social crusade, and modernist meditative reformers within orthodox Buddhism all shaped the country's cultural life in the 1930s. All of these causes grew independently of each other and all shared the milieu of socially activist Buddhism. At the same time, the People's Party revolution unleashed a distinctly political Buddhism that is the main subject of this chapter. Some of the politics reflected an ephemeral excitement. Soon after the 1932 revolution, stories circulated of junior monks forming parties and rebelling against their abbots and elders.[6] The anecdotes, covered in newspapers in the autumn of 1932, point perhaps to youthful exuberance and the eternal conflict of generations. But also the news of young people speaking their minds and acting out were signs of a society changing more fundamentally. And in Buddhism much more dramatic and fundamental change was afoot than rebellious teenagers speaking out against an abbot. By the mid-1930s a major revolt among the largest community of Buddhist monks in the kingdom, those belonging to the Mahanikai, or "Great Order," showed the effect of the People's Party message on a preexisting religious conflict.

The Mahanikai and the People's Party movements was comprised of the same generation of young commoners, born around the turn of the century, who grew up under the absolutist state whose institutional reforms bound their professional horizons. The Promoters chafed under old-regime control of the civil and military elite, and so too did the Mahanikai resent the status quo religious elite's dominance. Sangha governance in the 1930s remained tied to a dual system inherited from the absolute kings. A Bangkok dynasty-founded elite monastic order (*nikai*), the Thammayut ("Yoked to the Dhamma"), enjoyed higher prestige and more wealth than the muchlarger residual order, the Mahanikai, which comprised diverse lineages of upcountry monks, most with no ties to royalty. While how much control the Thammayut actually had over the Mahanikai is a thorny historical problem, Bangkok's growing power in the countryside under Chulalongkorn's reforms in the late nineteenth century elevated the Thammayut over the Mahanikai.[7]

When the People's Party declared that the revolution meant a new beginning, the Mahanikai sought parity with the Thammayut. The Mahanikai explicitly tied the spirit of the People's Party with the spirit of Buddhism.

They claimed a return to old socioreligious values of equality within the Sangha—purportedly existing among the Buddha's original followers—that was compatible with the revolution's accomplishment. Religious partisans asserted that revolutionary new beginnings in politics—the People's Party *patiwat*—demanded a religious restoration, or *patisangkhon*, and that Buddhism and a thick version of democracy were intimately linked. The movement sprang from a different social base than the civil service, the urban intelligentsia or the urban economy. Provincial, educated Mahanikai monks and their networks—outsiders to the mainly Thammayut elite-state nexus of religious authority—challenged the palace *nikai* before the 1932 revolution, but then asserted their case with renewed energy in the People's Party era. Their aspiration also became politically focused and gave credence to the idea that there was a "Mahanikai" with a genuine identity. They were their own makers, and not merely a lumpen, passive group thrown together by the powerful for better control.

Mahanikai monks found that their outlook was shared within the larger social movement of educated people in the same generation. Assemblymen responded to the call for representative politics; teachers for democratic ethics; and journalists to the defense of speaking truth to power. All of these gained power from the People's Party secular platform of political liberty and socioeconomic development. Religious reform, however, did not form a part of the People's Party agenda. Pridi rejected a clause to uphold and defend Buddhism among the Promoters' six principles, explaining to the assembly in August 1932 that the secular government's principles forbade privilege of any faith. People were free to believe in anything they chose, or nothing.[8] The revolutionaries often used Buddhist language and symbolism to advance democracy but did not intervene in monastic governance, Buddhist practice or move to confiscate temple wealth or land. Partly their conservatism was a legacy of Thai history. Thai kings had traditionally patronized the Buddhist order and gained legitimacy from it. Unlike neighboring colonies in Siam, there was no radical decapitation of traditional authority political and religious legitimacy remained interlinked. Indeed, King Chulalongkorn and his half-brother Wachirayan deepened the interdependence by administrative reform of the monkhood. Unlike, then, the determined native Catholic priest movement in the Philippines, Islamic political parties in Dutch Indonesia, or the Buddhist, Hoa Hao, and Cao Dai movements in French Indochina, the Thai religious fraternity did not become overtly political or challenge to secular authority. The People's Party also chose their battles. Facing a counterrevolution, the new regime largely ignored religious governance and deferred to the Sangha elite in the Council of Elders, a group of old men that had been appointed under the old regime and who continued to direct Buddhist affairs through most of the People's Party era.

Ordinary monks intervened where at least initially the People's Party would not. And the Buddhist movement of the 1930s is distinct; it shows that the democracy, conventionally understood as a secularizing process, also grew to challenge the religious infrastructure in Siam.

The Thammayut power created a wider outlook and greater political ambition for educated country people, and the institutional structure of state Buddhism was a character-forming as much as repressive power. The careers and aspirations of educated monks show that the "traditional" village of the prewar years did not exist in a time warp, and its leaders were not merely otherworldly spiritual seekers, wholly disinterested in social or political concerns. The effects of state building affected religion profoundly. The professional religious career offered a similar type of opportunity—Eric Hobsbawm's "high road of ambition"—as the modernizing economy, expanding public sphere and growing civil service gave to young people. But travelers on the spiritual high road did not wear the white collar or tropical suit and polished shoes, but orange or reddish-brown robes and walked barefoot. They did no labor, did not study law, made no money, and did not write reports or opinion pieces. And their motivations did not include escaping poverty, or owning an automobile, land, or solid, respectable furniture. The religious movement complements and complicates the story of state-society modernization. Understanding social pressure for change and state response then is akin to fitting interlocking pieces of a puzzle together rather than putting misshapen pieces into disjointed opposition.

Cultivating a Rural Elite:
State Buddhism's Local Impact

Recent religious history shows the complex relationship between local religious authority and state-sponsored ecclesiastical hierarchy in modern Siam. The tension between the two marked the entire transition from autocracy to state democracy and spurred Mahanikai activism in the Sangha. Three things stand out: the traditionally high degree of local religious autonomy; the growing influence and power of the Thammayut upcountry beginning in the late nineteenth century; and the accommodation between local and state Buddhism that was sometimes uneasy but also showed a mutual influence between government and locality.

Networks of teachers and apprentices that over generations transmitted a medley of teachings and practices formed customary religious authority and knowledge. Among the traditions scattered around the country, there was often little, if any, familiarity with original Buddhism, if this latter is conceived of closely adhering to the Pali Canon, and relying on scholasticism and a thorough knowledge of Pali.[9] In this heterogeneous and heterodox world, religious authority was local and largely face-to-face: monks lived close to their parishioners, shared their passages through life, and played an immediate and tangible role in local spiritual and moral welfare. This spiritual/moral authority also historically had a secular component: because they were among the few lettered people in a village, monks were looked to for guidance, and with village leaders created community and consensus.

Throughout history, membership in a local elite and in networks of masters and pupils, the latter bound to each other through religious socialization, have been facets of customary Buddhism that represented Thai religion for the majority of the population. Khruba Srivichai, the northern spiritual hero, came from a long lineage of regional monks who learned and transmitted what their masters taught them; a lineage that spanned modern-day political boundaries. The Mahanikai movement of the 1930s, as we will see, sprang from a specific place—the eastern seaboard provinces—but all of these factors are important here as well. Also, however, the state religious apparatus by our time was a local force that did not produce a unilinear hostility, even though the state authority had an uncertain claim on village loyalties.

The institutional power of the Thammayut and the palace-derived order's disciplinary and intellectual appeal to educated monks are vital forces that shaped the religious fraternity's enthusiasm for the 1932 revolution, and perhaps in unexpected ways. Under the 1902 Sangha Act that sought to control every Buddhist monk in the kingdom, religious power theoretically became centralized in the Council of Elders, a select group of senior Bangkok monks under a Supreme Patriarch. Thammayut monks tended to dominate the Council. The Thammayut also gained autonomy within the Sangha, with the 1902 Act creating four areas (*khana*) of governance: three regions (center, south, and north) and one order (the Thammayut).[10] The act was largely devised by the Thammayut monk

Prince Wachirayan[11] (1860–1921): half-brother of King Chulalongkorn (r. 1868–1910), abbot of Wat Bowoniwet (the temple most closely aligned with the royal family), and the dominant religious professional at the turn of the century. Wachirayan and other central Sangha leaders delegated Thammayut monks from the leading Bangkok wats to travel upcountry and oversee provincial religious practice.

After the 1902 Act, Thammayut monks moved into leadership of most regional ecclesiastical authority. Hence, the Thammayut had influence over Mahanikai monks, but also governed itself. Over the first decades of the twentieth century, within the formative years of the revolutionary generation, Thammayut influence spread persistently, even though they still represented a very small group in a larger fraternity. Numbers tell some of the story: by the mid-1930s, there were 17,305 Mahanikai temples in the kingdom, compared to only 260 Thammayut wats.[12] Exact figures of monks in each group are difficult to pinpoint, but one historian has estimated the ratio of Mahanikai to Thammayut monks at around sixty to one in mid-decade.[13] The impact of this thin population of Thammayut *bhikkus* is a remarkable aspect of the growth of the Bangkok state; very few state religious emissaries managed, or were seen as necessary, to assert Bangkok's leadership.

Historians sympathetic to the Mananikai who first interpreted the events of the 1930s that we will discuss have presented Thammayut expansion and the 1902 Act as blanket state domination of local Buddhism, with a clear binary emerging: royal-elite, urban, dominant versus commoner, rural, subordinate.[14] From a different historical perspective, however, the voluntary intermediary role of local authorities clearly emerges. To further extend their control, the expanding Bangkok state and its Thammayut monks convinced venerable local monks to become Thammayut. There were some notable evangelical successes, especially in the northeast.[15] The process was dialectical. It is highly likely that in the early 1900s the Thammayut provided an inspirational example to textually or ascetically inclined upcountry *bhikkhus*, and shaped how the latter conceived their true calling. The reverse is also true. As Thanissaro Bhikkhu notes, northeastern ascetics offered disciplinary and philosophic inspiration to the state order, which in his argument by the 1920s had lost some of its dynamism as the group's power became routinized. Taylor also in his study of the forest meditation tradition and its history in the northeast explains the interactive reliance, and respect shared, between the Bangkok Thammayut and rural meditation masters.[16]

Throughout the period of Thammayut expansion upcountry, Thammayut-Mahanikai power relations were not purely unidirectional in the
provinces or at the apex of the Sangha hierarchy. The leaders of the royalist
order often sought to maintain harmony with the much larger Mahanikai.
Implementation of the 1902 Act was handled in stages—in some cases,
it was not implemented for twenty years after its passage[17]—and the
balance of power at the regional level concerned Thammayut elites and
their emissaries who did notwant to be seen as lording it over respected
Mahanikai monks.[18] Also, the 1902 Act pledged not to allow interference
in internal nikai affairs, and protected customary practices that honored
the seniority of local monks and consensual decision-making between the
local Sangha and villagers to choose local temple leaders. These customary
practices continued to manage relations on the ground to a great extent,
and a failure to uphold them caused friction in the 1930s. Further, from
the founding of the Thammayut order in the 1830s and the ascension to
the throne of Mongkut in 1851 (he ruled until his death in 1868), the
reformist order sought to maintain unity in the larger Sangha through
careful selection, or vacancy, at the top.[19]

Enforcement of Wachirayan's textual and scholarly standards is a core
dimension of the expansion of Thammayut influence, and education a key
part of the palace-derived order's centralizing thrust.[20] The reception of
these educational reforms, however, is not often addressed, and the attrac-
tiveness of the new learning is central in explaining the religious legacy
of Bangkok's upcountry expansion. While for most villagers the monks'
moral authority did not require the stamp of ecclesiastical authority, among
young religious professionals of a certain temperament, the educational
effect was profound. The young Mahanikai monks who demanded autonomy after 1932 did so as advocates for other locally venerated (and older)
Mahanikai monks who may have avoided Wachirayan's educational system.
But the young Mahanikai members were also men of the first upcountry
generation whose mental horizons were extended beyond the village by
the power that, to an extent, subordinated them, as they gained literacy
in the Pali language and knowledge of the orthodox faith. Most of them
raised their professional status, and were admired for their discipline,[21]
as a direct result of the exam system designed by the Thammayut. This
supra-local aspect to their authority enhanced their local role. It also created a self-confidence that they too, not only the Thammayut, understood
of what "true" Buddhism consisted.

The Mahanikai monks' gloss of original Buddhism as democratic
had no doctrinal quarrel with the Thammayut. Judging by their *parian*, or

scholarly, ranks, many of the Mahanikai activists excelled in the received scholastic training. They asserted, however, that the Bangkok-imposed sectional preference enjoyed by the Thammayut had led to abuses, and the two *nikai* arrangement was a corrupted addition to original Buddhism. In customary Buddhism, a monk or temple's stature always relied on popular endorsement. In their anti-Thammayut polemics, Mahanikai monks used the language of this traditional thick democratic morality in village religion, but also exploited modern administrative knowledge for use against the authority under whose guidance they matured. Their knowledge of the doctrine and rules of the state religion pushed them to seek more self-control within, not apart from, the system that shaped their outlook. They were, thus, a part of two worlds, both of which contributed to their activism.

Country Monks Demand the "Restoration" of Buddhist Democracy

In January 1935, 400 monks from upcountry and Bangkok met in the capital to seek redress of local Sangha grievances through the formal democratic system. They styled themselves the Khana Patisangkhon Kan Phrasatsana (the Religious Restoration Party). *Patisanghkon* is an old word that generally refers to temple repair or restoration, and the group used it to explain what they conceived as an historical recurrence to the original spirit of Buddhism.[22] The restoration was now paradoxically enabled by a contemporary political revolution.[23] Young educated monks led the movement. The twenty-two-year-old *parian* three monk Phra Maha Phrayat and twenty-six-year-old *parian* six Phra Maha Sombun, both from Wat Udomthani in Nakhon Nayok where they also were primary schoolteachers, spearheaded the movement. Phra Yan Naiyok (Pleum), a senior monk at Wat Udomthani whom we will meet below, was their mentor and had brought them together. The two young men traveled to the city to solicit the help of Phra Jan Sukhuma, a friend of Phra Maha Phrayat when the two studied at Assumption College in Bangkok, and also a Nakhon Nayok native son and disciple of Pleum. At the time Phra Jan was a monk at Wat Suthat, one of Bangkok's oldest temples, and his family's reasonable wealth (his father owned a pharmacy) helped the group with its initial costs to expand the network.[24] In small stages these three men built a network of other young monks similarly inspired, out of friendships and fraternities in Bangkok's Mahanikai communities.[25] The most prominent in the group were: Phra Mahasanit, a twenty-three-year-old *parian* seven scholar from Wat Chetuphon; Wat Mahathat's Phra Mahasombun, a twenty-six-year-old *parian* six monk; and Phra Mahayaem, a *parian* nine scholar from Wat Phakinath, also age twenty-six. The various networks came together in the January 1935 meeting at which the movement was launched.

The immediate history of the organized resistance to Thammayut control rests on three cases from Nakhon Nayok, a lower east-central province about 120 kilometers from Bangkok. While travel in the region was still difficult at the time, the eastern seaboard provinces were not the back of beyond often described for the upper northeast or the north where resistance to Bangkok's directives was more spirited. Further, while the Thammayut was relatively thinly spread here, the impact of its reforms was noticeable and key Thammayut monks exercised power in a way that brought them into conflict with the local Mahanikai. In December 1934, the Sangha committee for three districts in the province wrote a long, detailed letter to the education minister in Bangkok who oversaw national religious affairs. Representing more than 500 Mahanikai monks at 43 wats and nearly 2,000 villagers, they asked that 2 Thammayut monks—Phra Muni Naiyok, the head of the Nakhon Nayok provincial Sangha and his superior Phra Ratchakawi, the head of the Prachinburi monthon[26]—be prosecuted.[27]

The two accused Thammayut authorities were sent to the area by the Sangha in Bangkok and had been in their positions for about four years. In this time, they had overturned local religious customs. Phra Ratchakawi, the Mahanikai monks argued, had unlawfully elevated a relatively inexperienced Thammayut *naktham*[28] instructor—hence, someone inferior to the group's leaders and also to local Mahanikai authorities in the province—to preceptor[29] status at a local wat. Soon thereafter, the inexperienced instructor was made abbot of a large, important Mahanikai temple, over the protests of Phra Yan Naiyok (Pleum), the patron of the main founders of the Restoration Party and the Mahanikai head of the provincial Sangha prior to the appointment of Phra Muni Naiyok. But following local custom, the petitioners argued, a local Sangha meeting had already reached a consensus that a resident monk should be interim abbot of the temple in question. Further, this junior Thammayut monk also became the *khweng* or district level authority, without first occupying the most basic leadership positions in the hierarchy.[30] The administrative details here should not cloud the central issues of the protest: that the Thammayut allegedly contravened local custom and also the national

Sangha's own rules, and took advantage of its national power to run roughshod over local people's wishes. From the beginning of the Sangha reforms at the turn of the century, the Bangkok state had been sensitive to the Thammayut's potential violation of local custom and perceived slights to local authority as it moved into authority positions upcountry. Monks such as Ratchakawi and Muni Nayok gave local people adequate ammunition to claim bias, and now as in the People's Party era justification for redress rested on a thick interpretation of democracy.

The petitioners in the December letter also protested the dismissal of Phra Plek Amaro, acting abbot at a nearby Mahanikai temple, by Phra Muni Naiyok with Ratchakawi's approval. The two Thammayut monks alleged that Phra Plek Amaro was unsuitable and in the previous few years showed his arrogance by allegedly lording it over local villagers. Soon after he was dismissed, Amaro was forbidden by these men from giving any statement about what had happened. The vagueness of the charge and seeming arbitrariness of the punishment irked local monks and laypeople: in May of that year a large group of monks and laypeople petitioned Phra Muni Nayok to explain Amaro's case. Muni Nayok stated: "He has not done anything wrong. It is just that he cannot get along with people in Wat Tha Chang village very well, so we held that he is lacking ability."[31] This nonexplanation did not satisfy anyone and instead reinforced the feeling that personal dislike governed their decision. Later, Phra Muni Nayok refused to allow some petitioners from Amaro's temple to see the order relieving him. Revealing the real reason for his dismissal, in June Phra Muni Nayok showed Amaro a letter from Ratchakawi to the local Sangha committee in which his superiors alleged that Amaro did not listen to authority and should be relieved.[32]

Unsurprisingly to the Mahanikai monks, the Thammayut Phra Muni Nayok became the abbot of Amaro's temple after the latter's dismissal. Again referencing a local Buddhist politics, the Mahanikai group contended that such high-handed treatment of Amaro went against the general practice in which local people and monks together decide the abbot by a majority vote.[33] Later, in an apparent attempt to silence any opposition, Ratchakawi forbade any new ordinations or overnight visits by nonresident novices to Amaro's temple.

The Mahanikai monks in their petition also raised Pleum's case, the third and arguably most grievous case of injustice from Nakhon Nayok. Pleum had a thirty-year religious career, and was the abbot of Wat Udomthani in Wang Krajom district, where he mentored the founders of the

Restoration Party. The Sangha higher-ups in November 1931 stripped Pleum of his ecclesiastical ranks and position as head of the Nakhon Nayok Sangha, and installed Phra Muni Nayok in the latter post. As with the Amaro case, the cause for his demotion was murky, and to the Mahanikai seemed contrived to get rid of an outspoken and locally venerated monk. Pleum ran afoul of Ratchakawi since he protested actively against one of Ratchakawi's men acting as a preceptor at a local temple on the grounds that the preceptor was poorly qualified. More damaging perhaps, an anonymous letter circulated publicly prior to Pleum's removal alleging that he had had physical relations with a local woman and stolen temple funds. If true, this charge would have meant his expulsion from the order. In late November 1931 the provincial civil court heard a case against one of Ratchakawi's entourage, an abbot whose name surfaced as the likely author of the letter against Pleum. Ratchakawi's group deeply resented the unusual secular intervention—a violation of Sangha custom whereby all disciplinary issues were to be handled internally—which Pleum sought. Pleum reasoned he had no other choice since his reputation suffered without restitution so long as the Thammayut group controlled his ecclesiastical fate. Three years later, in November 1934 local civil officials and the Thammayut-dominated Nakhon Nayok Sangha met to discuss the Pleum case anew and decided that while Pleum made them look weak, his local standing made it difficult for the authorities to end his career. In the end, Pleum was not evicted from the Sangha due to his long-standing service to the community. According to the Mahanikai petition, however, local villagers were very bitter and shocked at the disrespect shown to the lifelong monk.

The petitioners in December 1934 asserted that these cases revealed a distinct double standard. Phra Ratchakawi and Phra Muni Nayok promoted their fellow Thammayut monks and themselves, and demoted Mahanikai monks like Amaro and Pleum who stood in the way. The Restoration Party leaders knew that the 1902 Sangha Act only allowed general, that is, neutral, governance of Sangha affairs in a particular jurisdiction by provincial or monthon heads, and they claimed in this case the act had been (mis)used to favor the Thammayut. To the Mahanikai activists, since their order was powerful in this province's hierarchy, the Thammayut offenders reshuffled the bureaucracy for better control. The law had thus been ignored, and the Mahanikai activists asserted that in the hypothetical scenario where Mahanikai monks held greater national power they still would not have been allowed to interfere with Thammayut temple affairs or their monks.[34]

From local requests that the heavy-handedness and partiality of the Thammayut in Nakhon Nayok be stopped, the Mahanikai protest criticized the national status quo in the Sangha. They claimed that while the 1902 Act had been abused and hence was not entirely to blame, in any case it was out of step with the times. The group thus added the notion that democracy was an outcome of social development to the previous assertion that local Buddhist politics had always been popular. In April 1935, Phra Plat Jek, a leading member of the Khana Patisangkhon, used these twin inspirations to explain the feelings of the Mahanikai.

> In truth, if someone asks why was it that before you were ruled thusly, I would have to respond that the administration of the country then was absolute [English transliteration], so we had to put up with it. Even if we raised our voices no one dealt with it. The fact that we're speaking up now is because we see that the government is a real democratic one. If we speak of the administration of religious affairs, Buddhism has always been a democratic religion. When the secular power changes and adapts itself to become a democracy, then the religious realm must also turn accordingly. This is the main aim of the group to reform Buddhism.[35]

Among its flurry of petitions and letters to the government in 1935, the Restoration Party made the bold decision to draft a new Sangha Act—a radical move for subalterns in the religious hierarchy, and one that in 1932, the first year of the revolution, would not have gained an audience. The group's draft act mandated the end of Thammayut management of the Mahanikai, the eventual unification of the orders, and free movement in the interim—that is, a Mahanikai monk who wanted to become Thammayut would not have to reordain.[36]

In these first months of 1935, the Mahanikai movement grew to larger networks of monks, some directly linked to the original protagonists and others inspired by their activism. On the same day, the group submitted their act; a letter representing 800 monks at 110 wats in fourteen provinces arrived on the education minister's desk, and a few weeks later he received another two letters—one representing seven provinces, and nearly 1,200 monks from 92 wats; the other twelve southern provinces, 368 wats and more than 2,000 monks—in support of the group's proposed reforms.[37]

Despite the group's gathering momentum, the government opposed the Restoration Party and deferred to Sangha elders who backed the Thammayut monks in Nakhon Nayok and had scant regard or respect for the petitioners. Sangha elites tried to get abbots to chase out offending monks.

Those accused of fomenting trouble were treated harshly; they were kept in isolation and denied food and water. Civil officials who got involved also mistreated the accused. Some forced the monks to sit or stand at a lower position than their interrogators—an unthinkable inversion of the etiquette governing lay-religious interactions—and spoke rudely to them. Mahamakut Academy, the premier Thammayut college that Wachirayan had established in 1893, issued statements that banned promotion of those associated with the movement. Senior figures seen as closet members of the Party were pressured to resign from their positions. Most seriously, Sangha leaders alleged that the "miscreants" committed treason (*kabot*).[38] Under the old regime, where absolute monarchy was the only legitimate authority, *kabot* covered all political challenges to the establishment. The new formal democracy ostensibly empowered all citizens as legitimate critics, but the gravest of crimes under the old monarchy still resonated in a society grappling with the meaning of the new post-1932 politics of popular rule. Phra Sasanasophon, the deputy chair of the Council of Elders and the abbot of Wat Mongkutkasat, a leading Thammayut temple established by King Mongkut, opined that "[T]here are only a couple of people working behind the scenes for them . . . [W]e request that the ministry reject any further troublesome monk issues." Early in 1936, the education minister explained to the premier that the Council of Elders had rejected the arguments of the Restoration Party, using Phra Sasana-sophon's opinion as explanation.[39]

Sasanasophon's language perhaps betrays the persistence of an old-regime conceptualization of popular politics: troublesome people misled by a small coterie of rabble-rousers were bent on destroying the established hierarchy. Officially labeling the activists as deluded rebels and troublemakers was an attempt to destroy their legitimacy, deny that they understood what they were doing, and also deny that the Restoration Party had any larger backing. However, in addition, Sasanasophon's opinions reflect a deeply held tenet of Sangha management and Vinaya discipline, that fomenting schism in the Sangha was among the gravest of offences and potentially grounds for expulsion from the order. Thus the events also show the collision of conceptions of authority. Thammayut elders in the council did not unswervingly stick by Phra Ratchakawi because he was Thammayut, but saw what the Restoration Party claimed as their mandate for restoration as a violation of the disciplinary system. For the leaders of the Sangha, the Sangha Act of 1902 guaranteed "democracy" in the religious order and stemmed from long-standing commitment to the values of consensus, harmony, and meritocratic advancement. To the institutional authorities, these thick values were already the core of what the Mahanikai wanted to overturn.

Phra Ratchakawi's liberal use of his power beyond the cases raised above illustrates the leadership's complexity and the struggle to prevent inner conflict from spiraling out of control. In 1937, Phra Ratchakawi accused Mahanikai monk Phra Wimonmettajan, the seventy-three-year-old head of the Trat province Sangha, of disrespect and slander at a Sangha meeting, and that the Trat Sangha was in disarray. Phra Wimon responded spiritedly that Ratchakawi's recent move to install Phra Mahatawan, a seventh-grade parian scholar and Bangkok pupil of the senior-most Thammayut monk Somdet Wachirayanwongse, as Phra Wimon's deputy was a thinly veiled ploy to engineer a Thammayut takeover of the Trat Sangha. "Would I be so stupid," Wimon asked, "as to request . . . a Thammayut monk not under the control of Trat province to become the deputy provincial head?"[40] Wimon later wrote that in his long career he had seen seven heads of the *monthon* Sangha come and go; now Ratchakawi, the eighth such official, was bent on destroying harmony in the local Sangha but would fail.[41]

Ratchakawi did not shy from the fight. Soon after he learned of Phra Wimon's accusations, Ratchakawi requested that the Council of Elders investigate Wimon.[42] In a victory for local Mahanikai monks Phra Phutthakosajan, the elders' chair and the patron of Ratchakawi from Wat Thepsirin in Bangkok, refused his pupil's request. Unsatisfied, a disappointed Ratchakawi threatened to raise the issue with the head of the Thammayut order—Phra Wachirayanwongse—but Phra Phuttakosajan and the council seem to have been tired of hearing from him and he was rebuffed.[43] This case both shows the legitimacy of Mahanikai grievances in neighboring Nakhon Nayok—with Ratchakawi clearly attempting to exploit his Thammayut affiliation to expand his local power—and also that the Bangkok elite monks were caught in an unwelcome position and did not always come to the defense of their pupils.

The Government Enters the Fray: Reform, Symbolism, and the Limits of Religious Activism

Internal Sangha relations, then, hinged on an attempt to ensure discipline through the established rules over networks of masters and pupils as much as manage smooth Mahanikai-Thammayut relations. After the political revolution, however, the Mahanikai group's activism resonated outside the Sangha because of the assertion that the struggle was not against personalities but antiquated structures. Thammayut-Mahanikai relations formed part of the national debate about democracy's importance for a new society. The Mahanikai group forged parliamentary contacts, all rural democracy activists, who brought the topic to the floor of the assembly. From the first elections in November 1933, the lower house of the assembly became a vocal force in Thai politics. The Sakon Nakhon representative Voranit Pricha was among the first approached by the Mahanikai because of his known sympathy to the movement; Mahasarakham representative Thongmuan Attakon and Thong-in Phuriphat from Ubon, both outspoken democrats, also pledged to support the group.[44] Earlier Phra Thamma Woranaiyok and Phra Mahaphrayat, the disciples of Pleum who helped found the movement, had met Pridi via the labor activist Thawatt Rittidej. Thawatt was also personally known to the group since he was friendly with Mahaprayat's father. Initially Thawatt—who had ordained as a youth in a Thammayut temple—refused to get involved, saying that religious issues were not his area. He relented, however, and took the men to meet Pridi.

For his part, Pridi claimed to have already known about the Mahanikai group through the police special branch that was organized after the revolution. Pridi told them they had his support for a new Sangha act. Thawatt and Pridi's backing was a success by one measure, giving the group crucial support outside the order and among the revolutionaries, but also fed the commoner-monarchy antagonism of the 1930s. Princes Damrong and Narit—two royals at the heart of the post-1932 network of monarchic support who went into exile in the late 1930s—opined that the Pridi association confirmed their suspicion that communists directed the Mahanikai group.[45]

An official change in relations between the two Sangha orders became a national concern in the summer of 1938, and the ensuing debates divided the parliament. Some representatives felt that the status quo should prevail and argued that the secular authority should not interfere in religious issues; the Council of Elders' prior decisions on Thammayut/Mahanikai issues should be final. Another group, however, contended that government intervention was necessary since the perceived imbalance between the two orders contradicted the spirit of the young democracy, echoing Phra Jek's opinion quoted above. The education minister, the ultimate state authority on religious affairs, offered the assembly several possibilities: return to the arrangement "in the Buddha's time," which in this case meant merging the orders under a single administration as the Restoration Party wanted; maintain the orders' ordinational independence but create an overarching administration that removed Thammayut self-governance and its de facto control of the Mahanikai; or maintain the status quo of Mahanikai subordination to the Thammayut. In the end, no one voted to maintain the status quo and the second option of a newly devised authority governing both of the orders equally gained the most votes.[46]

Parliamentary support in the middle 1930s, product of a changed political climate after the Bowondet rebellion, ensured the political success of a religious movement that began as a strictly internal Sangha affair. The assembly, however, faced a turbulent political situation amid the crisis brought by the eruption of war in Europe and the rightward tilt of the People's Party government. More pressing political issues delayed passage of the Sangha Act, but it was not forgotten. Phibun became simultaneously premier and defense minister in December 1938, and attained the height of his power when he became Field Marshal in July 1941. Sangha politics, which had been transformed by the Mahanikai, became a key component of his populism and in 1941 the government issued a new Sangha Act that superseded the 1902 law.

The government's initiative corresponded with Phibun's belief that an opportune moment now came to eliminate royalist opponents in the Sangha elite and send a message to the old palace-connected establishment that their glory days were over. The government introduced the act in the wake of two years of hectic nation-building that sought to legitimize Phibun's power. Beginning in 1939, he changed the country's name from Siam to Thailand, to cement the ethno-nationalism of his regime, and established June 24 as National Day.[47] He introduced state mandates on dress and behavior, to give citizens and public life a Westernized, regimented, organized appearance; and recalibrated the calendar to begin the new year on January 1, casting aside the old system where years began on April 1. Phibun simplified the Thai language to eliminate most royal language, streamline spelling and eliminate the complex signifiers of hierarchy among speakers that came from the old regime, most recently, and ultimately from ancient Khmer. New democratic aesthetics emerged in art, sculpture, architecture, and theater.[48] On June 24, 1940, he opened the Democracy Monument in the heart of old Bangkok to commemorate the constitutional democratic regime, and at the same time laid the plaque on the Royal Plaza to mark the dawn of Thai democracy—the plaque that was removed in 2017 and with which we began this book.[49]

In this climate the Mahanikai's activism had finally born fruit. The core issue of equal treatment and governance of both orders within the Sangha was now law, and its details substantially followed the draft act submitted by the Restoration Party several years earlier. The new act also used the language of representative politics that closely mirrored the People's Party's civil administration. The Council of Elders was abolished, and instead the Sangha now had a Sangha assembly (Sangha Sapha) of forty-five members as the legislative branch, a limited term cabinet (Khana Sanghamontri) and Sangha premier (Sangha Nayok) as the executive, an ecclesiastical court system as the judicial branch for all monks regardless of order, and a reorganization of the national administration into four functional departments that treated both orders equally. The supreme patriarch position still existed, but the new act expressed the holder's authority as parallel to the king's titular position in the constitutional system, here as a signatory to Sangha business decided in the Sangha assembly and cabinet.[50] Reorganization of the national hierarchy, and especially the introduction of the assembly and cabinet, favored Mahanikai interests because of their vastly greater numbers. Further, a 1943 addendum to the 1941 Act mandated a national Sangha meeting that would work out a unification of the two orders. State religion—traditionally relying on the sacred and institutional power of kings—had been officially turned on its head and now relied for legitimacy on popular sovereignty, and its institutional structure mirrored the structure of the postabsolutist state.

In 1941, the government also established Wat Phra Sri Mahathat, or Wat Prachathipatai (Democracy Temple), in northern Bangkok as the first joint Mahanikai-Thammayut temple and showcase of official religious harmony. The temple initially housed twenty-four monks, twelve from each order. In July 1941, Phahon became the first monk ordained. Now fifty-four years old and suffering from a range of health problems, the former premier had largely retired from politics but maintained an aura of high moral conduct and was beloved by the public for his sacrifices for the nation. Clad in the white cloth of an aspirant to the professional religious life, Phahon alit from his black automobile outside the temple and ascended the steps amid a solemn atmosphere. Buddhist relics had been borrowed from the British Indian government to honor the ordination and were prominently displayed inside the temple. All senior People's Party members still active within the movement were present.[51]

The next year on the tenth anniversary of the end of the absolute monarchy, the government held a formal opening of the democratic temple.

The Phibun government envisioned Wat Phra Sri Mahathat as a testament to democracy but also as a premier symbol of official nationalism and its commoner heroes. In the internal discussions for its construction, Wichit Wathakan explained that the government wanted a "Panthéon of Siam," consciously borrowing from the French Revolution's reapplication of the Church of Saint-Genevieve as a reliquary for the republic's great citizens, to house the ashes of the leading members of the People's Party. The new order would have a holy site permanently commemorating what they brought to Siam that, like the constitutional festivals described previously, cast a sacred halo over the revolution. But its sanctity drew from the dignity of ordinary people. The temple embodied commoner life: unlike all Thai temples the *cedi* was hollow, and allowed ordinary people to walk very close to the Buddha relics housed there.[52]

Sacred, and enduring as well. Wichit Wathakan warned that the temple could not fall prey to party politics, as had happened to the Panthéon in France, where remains had been dug up and cast out when different groups took power and reconsidered the historical contribution of their enemies. Legislation and control were needed, he argued, to prevent the tarnishing of the memory of great men.[53] This is a prescient observation given the bitter backlash against the People's Party after the war and again more recently. Under attack were not only People's Party leaders' reputations but also new order symbols, like the People's Party plaque with which we opened this book. Enemies saw People's Party architecture—plain, unadorned lines and angular structures—as ugly and spiritually bereft, and hence completely contrary in both ways to the royal style. In the event, no one attempted to dig up any remains from Democracy Temple and it remains a well-endowed temple in Bangkok's northern suburbs. Still, like the parliamentary movement of the 1930s, the religious split and the People's party era, Wat Prachathipatai faded from political prominence. Tisso Uan, a Thammayut elder from the northeast who had been among the first converts to and evangelists of the royal order decades earlier, became the abbot of the Democracy Temple and the Thammayut, ironically or depressingly, governed the temple in the postwar years.[54]

People's Party hegemony, as we have described, was a process, rather than a finality, incomplete rather than all powerful. Phibun's wartime popularity faded afterward due to his association with Japan and because of royalist and civilian enemies that resisted the military during the war. Also, however, his ideology dissolved because it was never the all-encompassing tyranny its opponents alleged. Religion shows its limits clearly. While motivated by the democratic spirit in the Mahanikai movement and among its social backers to enact new programs, new order statesmen seemed unsure how much of a challenge could be mounted against the customary, rural status quo or the Thammayut itself. This uncertainty is revealed in frank internal discussions.

During the war a series of cabinet meetings addressed the relation of Buddhism to secular power in the modern state, a discussion prompted by an admission of ignorance. The cabinet commissioned a report on the state of Buddhism in the country, submitted in January 1940, because of their lack of knowledge about the country's main cultural form. The participants—all senior People's Party members or supporters—wanted sweeping changes in rural religion and greater control over the order.[55] But the bold plans met the resistance of social reality. Commenting on the 1941 Act presented to the public as a landmark in Thai democracy, Thamrong Nawasawat, a leading government figure, wondered if the lay government had the legitimate authority to get as closely involved in internal relations of the Sangha as they had.[56] In the same vein of uncertainty, the cabinet floated ideas of temple abolition or consolidation, forcing monks into lay life, and seizing or at least closely scrutinizing temple wealth. The report commissioned by the government asserted that the estimated lay monk population ratio of seventy to one showed that the country had too many religious, and scattered over too large an area to control. The situation upcountry was extremely chaotic. Some places had many temples very near each other, elsewhere very few wats scattered far apart, and many of the latter being decrepit relics without custodians.

Wichit and Pridi however doubted that anything could be done. Temple razing or forcible defrocking were far too socially sensitive issues, and one participant asked whether the education ministry had the author- ity to dissolve wats. The answer from another was no and any decision would have to be made by local abbots, who were still the custodians of customary religion.[57] Moreover, an education ministry representative asserted that gaining control of temple assets was impossible. The big royally connected temples in Bangkok—all Thammayut—contained the vast majority of religious wealth. In 1934, the government had commis- sioned a report into temple finance but the outcome was inconclusive. The Thammayut refused and resisted any outside scrutiny of their assets, and the representative in the 1941 meeting further opined that 95 percent of all temple wealth nationwide could not be managed by the government because of social resistance to state interference.[58] The words of cabinet member Kat Songkhram form a fitting close to these discussions. In a spring 1941 meeting, Kat professed that the cabinet lacked a genuine understanding of how the religion operated in the country and that elite monks should be asked in to explain things to the government.[59]

And despite the changed political climate, and the backing of Phibun's military-populist state, the results of Mahanikai activism were opaque and short-lived. The Thammayut did not willingly submit to the new organization. The hoped-for national union of the two orders within a single entity was delayed and eventually killed. Contemplating such a merger, the Thammayut patriarch after World War II demanded that his disciples secede from the Sangha entirely rather than be drowned in a Mahanikai sea.[60] Faced with Thammayut resistance, in the late 1940s, Mahanikai activists repeatedly petitioned the government for fulfillment of the spirit and letter of the 1941 Sangha Act that was now obviously in danger of becoming meaningless.[61] By the early 1950s, Thammayut stubbornness, Mahanikai bitterness and state vacillation all seemed to have returned religious policy to the status quo of the early 1930s, when the Mahanikai movement began.

The pendulum had indeed swung back, and the conflict between the orders was exacerbated by the emergence of anti–People's Party national politics accompanied by royalist backing after the war. After three additional permanent (and one temporary) constitutions, twin military coups in 1957 and 1958 by Sarit Thanarat abolished constitutionalism and reelevated the monarchy as a focal point for national integration under a military dictatorship.[62] Ultimately in 1962, Sarit's government repealed the 1941 Sangha Act and issued a new law that restored the official separation of the orders and confirmed Thammayut dominance of the religion.[63]

Conclusion

Thailand's history wars have affected the study of 1932 in many historical fields. Studies of Sangha-state relations, like works on military politics or civilian democracy, have not been insulated from the question of whether 1932 was important to society (a revolution) or irrelevant (a coup). This chapter has shown the Promoters' relevance in an unlikely quarter. The People's Party was secular nationalists, motivated by a political ideology that promised freedom, prosperity, and education. They initially had no interest in the Sangha, and were content to let the old religious guard govern. Unintentionally, they inspired the Mahanikai to challenge the religious hierarchy. The Mahanikai movement forced the religious issue into national prominence in spite of the People's Party's ambivalence about intervening. And, while labor or schoolteachers similarly forced the Promoters to take action, in this case the Mahanikai had much more success.

Mahanikai monks succeeded partly because their push corresponded with the Promoters' consolidation of power, but also because they were a caste apart whose high social status and new view of history the secular state did not have the confidence to challenge. For the Mahanikai activists the tenets of "original" Buddhism and its codes of conduct, which they as much as the Thammayut authorities pledged to practice, governed a single order to which all monks belonged. While they acknowledged and indeed used the 1902 Sangha Act's protections, to them the system of hierarchy was open to abuse by unscrupulous monks and the rules of the discipline ignored because of the general privilege of the palace-founded Thammayut. They revised language current in the new regime to broaden the scope of democracy, from politics and the economy to religion, and from a narrow elite religious order's interpretation to a larger one.

The regime used a new word, *patiwat*, to explain the 1932 governmental change based on a concept of citizens with rights that superseded subjects solely bound by duty. The religious group posited the new political structure and events as a returning—to historical forms and social values that still had vitality and legitimacy but that were buried or tarnished by corrupting influences. The Mahanikai movement's "restoration" used *patisangkhon* to explain their interpretation of the unprecedented events of 1932 as offering—as Phra Jek said—a return to a presumably original ecclesiastical order and the harmony and purity that it supposedly had.[64]

Revolution and restoration legitimized the makers of the 1932 event and those whom they inspired. In these heady times, a group of educated men without money, possessions, or work greatly expanded the notion of democracy. Democracy—new beginning or return—was a legitimate and historically necessary development to the People's Party and the Mahanikai. The varied terms applied to events in the 1930s stemmed from the confusion of an unprecedented situation and its open-endedness, not from ignorant or willful misapplication of transparent (and transparently unsuitable) terms.

Others, however, viewed these 1930s conceptions as unsuitable. Within two decades revolution and restoration had been decoupled from notions of and aspirations for popular sovereignty in both secular and religious domains. Instead, Sarit Thanarat's 1958 *patiwat* meant a return to hierarchic authority, ultimately under monarchic power but mediated by a young cohort of military officers who had no interest in Western political philosophy.[65] Sarit's revolutionary autocracy illegitimized the older *patiwats* and *patisangkhons* and usurped the ground that these words had held. The 1962 Sangha Act, like the 1958 revolution, was conceived as a return to the harmonious and orderly Thai status quo ante before the detour into foreign-inspired politics and the resulting friction in society and the religious order. Indeed, Sarit told the Sangha elders that the supersession of the 1941 Act was intended to "reorganize the Sangha so that it would be as similar as possible to that pertaining in [*sic*] the Buddha's lifetime. . . ."[66] But the original revolution of 1932 and its positive interpretations did not disappear from public discourse. The simultaneously held view of democracy as a necessity both brand new for the state and socioreligiously very old, remained an inheritance from the 1930s.

Chapter Six

The Revolution Betrayed

Triumph and Tragedy in Assembly Politics

In the first year and a half of the revolution, new- and old-regime civil servants came to a tenuous compromise, which then crumbled in a political crisis that culminated in the bloody Bowondet rebellion of late 1933. Pridi believed that the military would give power to civilians after the royalist threat had been crushed,[1] but Phibun Songkhram's army cohort tightened their grasp of state power. With his group's immediate prospects dim, Pridi cooperated with Phibun's faction until the Pacific War. Civilians in the People's Party, Pridi included, at the same time expanded their network of alliances through the national assembly.

In this decade, elections were held for the parliament in 1933, about a month after the Bowondet rebellion, and then in 1937 and 1938. The first election returned seventy-eight representatives indirectly through electors. Ninety-one, directly chosen, made up the assembly in the second and third elections. All were men; one woman ran for the assembly in 1937, and two in 1938, but none gained seats.[2] All three elections returned a substantial number of local elites, outsiders to Bangkok of limited wealth, but considerable local authority and respect, and possessed of Western-style learning. They were not a generic lumpen group; marked differences existed among these outsiders. Around one-fifth came from old regional lordly families, mainly from the north, that lost power under the Bangkok reforms but still maintained prestige and influence. Another fifth represented central region Sino-Thai commercial and bureaucratic families with older roots in the country—the "good" Chinese who assimilated. Well over half were local officials, many of farming or petty merchant backgrounds, and the most vocal in the assembly came from the northeast, the poorest region of the country.[3] Assembly meetings were lively, and members challenged the maldistribution of wealth and power and defended the rule of law.

The tutelage principle constrained the assemblies, however. All three of the 1930s assemblies had an appointed portion, of an equal number of members, to restrain politics and hold to the state council's line. To the military's new elite especially, the post-1932 parliaments were not meant to represent the people, but the executive. Their vision for the assembly was not much different from that of the advisory bodies to the kings instituted from the fifth reign.[4] The appointed assemblymen rarely spoke; when they did, it was to caution elected members and to support the government. But civilian democracy remained a problem for Phibun's group. The assembly twice deposed the government and forced elections, in 1937 and 1938. General Phahon, the genial, senior military leader of the Promoters who became premier at the end of 1933, lost his position in 1937, regained it in the new government, and then lost it for good in 1938. The 1937 dissolution stemmed from assemblymen alleging that the government had improperly allowed sales of royal property to well-connected insiders. In 1938, assemblymen challenged the executive over the budget. After the faceoff the government reformed, and Phibun became premier. While both of these moves showed the adoption after 1932 of democratic checks and balances in a country without a history of parliamentary politics, the assembly had constantly to contend with irregular claims by the executive. From opaque insider fights over power, Phibun and his military cohort emerged.

As mentioned above, the largest groups returned by the three elections in the 1930s came from the provincial middle classes: tradespeople, lawyers, and local civil servants. There were no political parties, and local cliques coalesced around inspiring leaders and democratic idealism. Representatives from the northeast formed a core opposition to insider politics and in favor of civilian democracy. While the cohort around Choti Kumphan and Thephasadin na Ayudhaya were suspected soon after 1932 of attempting to topple the government, the executive did not level the same charge against regional assemblymen who worked to strengthen the assembly's hand in governance. Their time, unfortunately, would come later. Regional representatives faced Bangkok people who made up most type two assembly members, and who looked the elected, regional voices as naïve and inferior.[5] Isan men had no businesses to protect, and little binding them to Bangkok society. They resented being spoken down to and treated as second-class because of ethnicity and language.

In the 1930s and 1940s, the assembly opposition—largely but not entirely driven by northeastern representatives—targeted the aspects of growing antidemocratic politics most odious to them: the murky favoritism of insider politics, the growth in military spending, oppressive laws and the government's delay in allowing a fully elected assembly.

Activists Protest Corruption and the Growth of Military Budgets

In July and August 1937, insider dealing involving royal lands raised the ire of the elected assemblymen and forced the government to resign. The case became a public spectacle; large audiences packed the assembly gallery to watch the proceedings. The government dissolution paved the way for the first directly elected assembly members in November 1937. The land sales were shrouded in secrecy. Between the first and third weeks of July, the assembly learned that influential officials cheaply bought twenty-five plots of the king's land in Bangkok. From the middle of July, a recently enacted act on management of royal assets mandated that many royal assets would be transferred from the department of royal assets to the finance ministry, and their value reassessed. Senior government figures, aware of the opportunity presented, seized the chance to buy lands cheaply before the value changed.[6] Liang Chaiyakan, a representative from Ubon who was just shy of his thirty-fifth birthday, was the first to discover the case. Liang had a law degree attained from the justice ministry's law school in 1925. His legal education followed from exhaustion of the high school curriculum in Ubon, and then further study in Bangkok for a primary teaching and then high school teaching certificate. In both studies, Am Bunthai was one of his classmates and friends.[7] Liang was a commoner, but a well-known person because of his education. Not unusually, however, among the new intelligentsia he also had high status for other reasons. He was also a local personality because his wife's father was the last local lord of Ubon. Liang's father had helped Bangkok suppress the Holy Man's rebellion in 1902, the year Liang was born, and his funeral was a grand and expensive Ubon affair.[8]

In the land's scandal, Liang after some hesitation decided he must act. He wrote to Premier Phahon, the regency council and the assembly chair but did not receive a convincing answer. He then wrote to the newspapers, arguing that the wrongdoers should not only be removed from office but also banished from the kingdom for their shamelessness.[9] Among the beneficiaries of the sales were Premier Phahon's secretary; the secretary to Prince Aditya, one of the king's regents; Ronasit Phichai, the head of the publicity bureau; Ritthi Akhaney, the agriculture minister and one of the senior officers who had deposed Mano in 1933; the wife of an official in the king's secretariat; the secretary to defense minister Phibun; and a councillor in charge of the Bureau of the Royal Household. Thong-in Phuriphat, Liang's fellow Ubon assemblyman, and Tai Panikabutr, a Bangkok representative, supported Liang's position. Thinking him sympathetic, all three men went to see Ritthi Akhaney, and Ritthi indeed supported the three in bringing the case to the assembly floor.[10] In the assembly, Liang declared that the case was a moral, rather than a legal issue. The public had seen the corruption and the buyers should return the lands.[11] Thong-in contended that the king's council profited from the sales at the king's expense. Thong-in argued that as a minor, the boy king was excluded from the elite financial shenanigans, and in any case he was not even in Siam. The king was oblivious.[12] A confusing several days followed, what Sri Krung newspaper termed the "revolutionary week," with the regency and the government both resigning, and the military and police on edge and ready to quell public disorder. No one seemed to know what would come next.[13] Liang got police protection after he received a letter explaining that if he wanted to remain in the world he would give up the inquiry.[14]

Phahon became emotional when confronted by the accusations of impropriety, and stated that he wished he had more power to take responsibility. Phahon claimed that as premier he merely countersigned the king's order presented to him by the regents. Aditya and the other two regents resigned, as did the cabinet. Eventually, the regency re-formed, and then a new government formed on August 9th, the same cabinet reassembled and Phahon again became premier.[15]

The royal lands scandal came and went quickly, but set a dubious first as the original state corruption scandal in the constitutional era. Other government secrets produced larger storms in the assembly. Every year, the budgetary debates were contentious, and especially so because of the growth of military power after the Bowondet rebellion. The military withheld full disclosure at each budget hearing and claimed that release of defense figures jeopardized state security. In 1935, Phibun, then the minister of defense, spoke in an assembly meeting about the Japanese example. Defense spending always came first for Asia's superpower, according to Phibun, and any other country hoping to protect itself must follow Japan's lead. This approach was meant to silence the opposition, but it did not work. Yearly, the parliamentary opposition questioned the figures they were given and asked for more information. The opposition also wanted money to be spent for socioeconomic development. Thong-in Phuriphat at the same 1935 session argued for spending instead on the local economy and the development of local government. Thong-in also demanded funds for indigenous industrial development, claiming that silk and cotton manufacture in particular, two key industries that could fuel native industrial growth, were stunted by the government's preoccupation with the military.[16]

In the following year, Thong-in claimed in the assembly that common people benefited from only about one-tenth of budget outlays.[17] In a single sentence, he summarized a decade of skewed spending that favored the military and the administration. By 1937, culmination of a trend that began with the revolution, the military budget was about one-quarter of the total budget expenditure.[18] Thong-in lamented what the military's growing slice of the pie meant for local industry. Others decried the effects on schooling and agriculture. Sanit Charoenrath, another assemblyman from Ubon, accused the government of sacrificing education for weaponry, despite the vow made to the country about the importance of learning to democracy. Sanit further claimed that the military cohort completely ignored the peasantry and their work, the backbone of the country's wealth, since the budget allocated only 6 percent of spending on agricultural development.

Phra Phinit Thanakon of Chiang Mai, an entitled elected representative who frequently spoke in support of the Isan assemblymen, identified hidden budgetary processes as a problem that compounded the imbalance between national defense and socioeconomic welfare. Phra Pinich argued that the budgetary auditing committee was too lax in its work and that paperwork was improperly, or minimally, vetted. In short, the government made up figures without consulting the assembly.[19]

The military's backers in the executive found this too much to take. Prayun Phamonmontri in March 1937 went on the radio to criticize the assembly for questioning the military budgets and the military's secrecy about its funding. To Prayun, critics obstructed the nation's progress. Moreover, he gave an unequivocal answer to the question of new regime power's ultimate source. Prayun in his radio address said that the army brought the revolution to Siam, and they alone defended the constitution against its enemies.[20] The legacy of the Bowondet rebellion and threats of assassination against the People's Party senior leadership informed Prayun's position; readers can recall how he was questioned by royalists on the eve of the rebellion regarding where they should send his head after the People's Party were overthrown.

In the assembly, however, Thong-in voiced the displeasure of many at Prayun's attitude and implicit threat against the legislative branch. Phahon said that perhaps Prayun's headstrong speech came from his youth, and that Prayun did not understand fully how a democracy should work. Thong-in was not impressed; surely power came from the people as stated in the constitution, he countered, but Prayun was not interested in democracy.[21] Phibun's Lunar New Year speech to the nation that year presented the budgetary victors as its victims. He complained incorrectly that Siam could only spend 20 percent of its budget on the military, unlike Japan which spent 60 percent, according to Phibun. Phibun also admired Hitler, who he considered to be a great man making Germany great again, and used Germany to reiterate Prayun's point that only through the force of arms would the country prosper. And openly, like Prayun, he denied budgetary transparency; it was dangerous for too much of the military's affairs to be divulged and the assembly should not ask too many questions. Playing the role of the selfless strongman he said: "I could not afford to hold my peace any longer," seeing as how people are questioning the military and "intentionally obstructing its progress." Rather than the military, Phibun asked that people criticize the monarchy.[22] Phibun summed up perfectly the military's view of the three-way battle in state power: military first, with civilians and monarchy relegated to secondary roles.

An ugly incident in August 1938 showed authoritarianism winning the political battle that developed between the executive and the elected legislature. We can take a brief detour in period history before continuing with the budgetary issue of 1938. Liang Chaiyakan of the lands scandal was relaxing in the parliamentary tea room during a break between sessions on a Saturday morning. Several appointed members, including some military officers, entered the room and lifted the chair where he sat. Proceeded by another military officer beating a beer tray like a gong, the group carried Liang out of the building and unceremoniously dumped him and his chair into the pond that sat in the grounds of parliament. Thong-in Phuriphat and Tiang Sirikhan fished Liang out of the pond, and Thong-in condemned the incident in the subsequent assembly session.[23]

Liang's crime? During the Saturday morning session he had criticized Wichit Wathakan's pronouncements that week that compared the Chinese to Jews and advocated for their expulsion from Siam. Whether out of conviction or opportunism Wichit, whom we can recall from the nationalist party affair of 1933, jumped aboard the xenophobic bandwagon that the right-wing military faction used to pitch for public support. In a speech at Chulalongkorn University, he made the controversial remarks on the German Anschluss with Austria, which to Wichit showed the power and popularity of a proud ethnic majority. In the same weekend, an anonymous pamphlet appeared in Bangkok's streets that, after the standard invectives about the unassimilable and deceitful Chinese exploiting honest Thai people—and adding for good measure that all major newspapers were Chinese-supported—praised the men who gave Liang what he had coming to him. It added that it was time for "all to remember the brave example of those men and to get ready to exterminate the nation-sellers [i.e., the Chinese] so there are none left in the country."[24] Wichit at the time was a cabinet member and aside from his offensive language, Liang questioned the propriety of a government official espousing such ethnic policies. Wichit, it should be said, was not alone but tapped into a popular racism of the times.

A month after Liang's soaking, Thawin Udon introduced the motion that led to the government dissolution. Thawin, from Roi Et, entered the assembly in the late 1937 elections following the lands scandal. Born in 1909 to a comfortable merchant family, he was reputedly much different from his fellows. A bookish young man, Thawin was not interested in sports, intensely disliked gambling, and had a reputation for aloofness and arrogance. Thawin studied initially to mathayom five in Roi Et, the highest secondary-school level in the province, and then studied to mathayom eight at Suan Kulap in Bangkok.[25] Like Liang and others, he attended law school, and received his degree in 1931. At Suan Kulap and then the law school, Thong-in was his classmate. Thawin established a *ratsadon* school in Ubon in 1935. Thereafter, he worked as a lawyer in Bangkok and Ubon before a stint as an official in the prisons department and then a municipal inspector in Ubon before becoming a Roi Et assemblyman in 1937.[26] It was an impressive career to have by the age of thirty.

Eager to challenge the government, in the 1938 budgetary hearings, he sought to change the procedural rules so that the entire budget would be fully disclosed at first presentation. In a September assembly session that focused on his motion, Thawin said he fully sympathized with his fellow representatives who wasted lots of time and energy running around to various departments and ministries trying to get accurate budgetary figures that were rarely given.[27] The minister of finance countered that disclosing the full budget too early would lead to profiteering and corruption. The existing procedure traveled the sounder route, the minister added, since all figures were released by the close of the assembly discussion on the budget.[28] Thawin obviously disagreed with this conclusion. His motion succeeded by a forty-five to thirty-one vote, which shows that most of the assembly did not participate. Most second category members did not attend;[29] if they had, Thawin's move would have undoubtedly been defeated. Further, Thawin's initiative did not force the government's dissolution, according to the establishment *Bangkok Times* newspaper; rather, the government resorted to the constitutional stipulation for the king's declaration for a dissolution. At the time the king was a minor, the People's Party–controlled regency acted on his behalf, and hence the government plotted the move as a work-around to dissolve itself and reform.

Phahon declared that the budget proposals were unworkable, but that his Cabinet would resign if Thawin's move succeeded. The regency in fact rejected the Cabinet's resignation, arguing that it was too dangerous a time domestically and internationally and the country could not afford instability. Instead, the regency elected to dissolve the assembly first. The government made its position even clearer in its royal decree that dissolved the government. It stated, as the finance minister had previously, that the budget procedure worked well for the past five years, its flexibility was modeled on practices in many other (advanced) countries, and that some items must be kept secret. Now, the government said, the process would consume too much time; in any case the Thawin-led opposition was not interested in the budget per se, or in listening to reasoned arguments that the government put forward, but in scoring political points.[30] In any case, the elected legislature failed to effectively check the executive.

Following the September motion, Phibun replaced Phahon as premier in December 1938, and in the assembly only Thawin and Liang Chaiya-kan opposed his nomination. The *Bangkok Times* gloated over the young assemblymen's comeuppance, writing that "old Siam men [would] smile when they see how the Assembly has been put in its place,"[31] since "[t]he government did not go on their knees and *wai* [grovel] to the Assembly, begging that the body appoint new Ministers."[32] The paper also reiterated the government's position on the motivations of the assemblymen, arguing that they belonged to a "cult of obstructionism." Youth and inexperience, the paper claimed, drove the parliamentary cohort to speak intemperately.[33]

These sentiments exactly mirror the democratic paternalist attack on the young schoolteachers, young monks, and rabble-rousing labor activists. Politics should be left to the grown-ups.

The Center Responds: Special Courts and the Attack on Parliament

The creeping authoritarianism that kept budgetary secrets, won the battle over the assembly, and dumped renegades in the parliamentary pool also hanged people.

Regional assemblymen in February 1939 resisted the third special courts bill that allowed the tyranny of exceptional trials and that led the following year to the execution of eighteen "enemies." Again, among the most prominent critics was a northeastern representative, Chamlong Daoruang, born to a poor family in the Lao-speaking province of Mahasarakham. Called "ai khek" (the Indian) as a child because of his dark skin,[34] Chamlong studied to mathayom five in Roi Et at the same school as Thawin.[35] The poverty of education in his own province sent him to Roi Et, which gave him a great educational and social leg up. Chamlong reputedly held Thawin, his senior by one year, in high esteem and they formed a lifelong friendship. After finishing mathayom five in 1925 at age sixteen, family need sent him into the workforce.

Chamlong worked for a Chinese automotive store owner in Roi Et for fifty baht per month. The man, an ennobled Chinese entrepreneur, had met Chamlong at the temple where Chamlong lived while he was in high school. Chamlong impressed his soon to be patron.[36] Chamlong chauffeured and repaired cars, with his patron paying for repair instruction at a school in Bangkok. Later, after trying his hand at independent limousine service for a couple of years,[37] he roamed the left bank of the Mekhong boxing for money. At one successful bout, he came to the attention of the governor of Champassak, son of a Lao lord, who was impressed with his skill. Chamlong then worked for him in a similar driving and delivery business and in cross-river commercial traffic. Chamlong's language skill facilitated his work across the river, since he spoke Khmer, Vietnamese, and French. Many of the leaders of the Bowondet rebellion fled across the Mekhong into French Indochina. None returned. Unaffiliated others, however, like Chamlong suffered from the general climate of suspicion. A French official arrested him on suspicion that he was involved in the rebellion, on the pretext of "preserving the safety of the Siamese government."[38]

After his release he returned to Siam and taught in a *prachaban* school, and also as a clerk in the education department. He also became well known as a skilled debater in contests sponsored by the government,[39] akin to those mentioned in chapter 4 that gave people a chance to hone their skills of logical expression in apolitical subjects. In 1937 he set up a school in Mahasarakham, the first *ratsadon* school there, after resigning from a clerkship in the education department.[40] Like others, Chamlong's education initiatives served both to offer rural children their first opportunity to attend school and also served as good publicity for his parliamentary campaign.[41] He was elected as an assemblyman for Mahasarakham in the 1937 election at the age of twenty-seven. His election was supported by the governor of Mahasarakham and by the education official in his district whom he had worked for (both of these men later became parliamentarians in 1946). Like Tiang and Thong-in, he studied law at Thammasat and received a degree in 1946.

In the 1939 debates, Chamlong pointed out the special court's redundancy and subversion of the rule of constitutional law. The judiciary already had three levels of courts, he stated in the assembly, but these were avoided to impose a predetermined sentence that was the court's actual purpose. The accused had no rights. Chamlong said he thought that "court" and "justice" were an indissoluble pair, but now it was apparent that the former steered the country away from the latter.[42] Indra Singhanetra, a Chiang Mai representative who like Phra Pinich frequently spoke with the Isan MPs, said that the military's power over court appointed defense counsel completely undermined the rights of the accused. He claimed that no conscientious lawyer would seek appointment as defense counsel. Moreover, as we learned above, there was no right of appeal and court members were military men, and not necessarily justice ministry people. They would often not know anything about the law. The law, Indra concluded, would be a stain on the name of the constitutional government.[43]

For many assemblymen, local issues consumed their attention. The military's budgetary swindle that Thawin resisted meant a lack of money for farming or schooling, preferable ways to enhance people's prospects in life than, for example, an able-bodied man having to roam the borderlands boxing for prize money. But they also discovered and fought against the deadly game of Bangkok politics, which they witnessed close-up.

In late January special branch police began arresting people as rebels fomenting disorder and planning the assassination of important ministers. Commencing with pre-dawn gunfire at a Bangkok suspect's house on Sunday the 29th, where the police killed an army officer as they tried to apprehend him, the police sweep proceeded to arrest hundreds in the next few days, and they continued to arrest lesser accomplices until March.[44] Indra said that the government would sully its name with a new secret court. But the government had already tarnished itself by the time the assembly met. Moreover, the expansion of executive powers—as Thephasadin, Nimitmongkol, and others argued earlier in the decade—coarsened the spirit of constitutionalism. The cabinet saw the law as needed to meet the danger facing the state but, more concretely and urgently, because they had many people in jail they needed to try. Some of the arrested were military, and some civilian, and hence dividing legal jurisdiction would result in a longer process. Pridi, interior minister at the time, argued in the cabinet on the first of February that since the plots against the government included both civilians and military officers, they should be tried together under a special law.[45] Despite the protests of the northeastern MPs, it sailed through the assembly. The day after the cabinet discussed the bill, it was sent to the assembly. Three readings of the bill were held that same day and the act became law when it then appeared in the royal gazette.

The third special courts law came amid a wide-ranging crackdown on dissent in the latter half of the 1930s, a move that used the regular justice system as well as extraordinary measures.[46] The government refuted the charge that the courts were playing politics; instead they were saving constitutionalism from political factions. In the 1939 special courts cases, Phibun argued the following:

> We can easily see that those sentenced were plotting solely because of their own self interest. Why else would they seek to change the governmental system? The public entirely backs the regime. [The rebels] are acting for their own ends, and bringing in conspirators accordingly.[47]

Not least in the far-ranging conspiracy, the government suspected assemblymen of misusing the parliament to build their power. One of the intrigues in the 1939 trials centered on the suspected role of old-regime lords in advancing candidates for the 1937 and 1938 elections. The government alleged that lords' candidates, flush with cash, would build a network of lackeys and promise people that "they would not have to pay tax and would be happy as they were in old times."[48] If lords really bought votes, opposition would have emerged within the assembly. In the climate, however, the allegations spread doubt without much evidence, and soured the executive and the military cohort around Phibun against any representative politics as driven by hidden agendas. Three elected assemblymen were arrested in February 1939 and tried in the special court. Two had been recently elected, in the November 1938 elections, and one gained his seat in parliament in the prior election of November 1937 that came in the wake of the crown lands scandal. None had any relation to the northeastern MPs, but the government's act sent a chilling message.

The government suspected two of the accused—Phraya Wichitsarakrai and Phra Ratchayathiraksa—as Bowondet sympathizers. Wichitsarakrai in 1933 was the Chainat provincial governor, and he allegedly believed that the People's Party would fall to the rebels. According to the trial, he disbelieved government communiqués that the rebels were in retreat, and mobilized people in two Chainat districts, including the provincial capital, to aid the insurrection. The government released him in 1933 for lack of evidence, but Wichitsarakrai lost his governorship and became an outcast.[49] His return to politics via the assembly in 1937 brought him back into the government's sights. The other entitled assemblyman, Phra Ratchayathiraksa from Samut Songkhram province, was also a provincial governor, and then in 1937 an elected MP. He allegedly complained to a supporter (and government witness for the trial) in September 1938 that the recent assembly dissolution over the budget was a travesty. He claimed that while the government lost the vote that Thawin's motion brought, they blamed the assembly for acting wrongly and dissolved it. The government's pledge to legally enshrine rights and liberty—and thus enable the parliament to do its work—was a sham.[50]

The third victim—army lieutenant No Nen Talalaks—won his seat in 1938 as a Bangkok representative but had clashed with the People's Party government earlier in the decade. Like Wichitsarakrai, No Nen Talalaks lost a government position because of suspected treachery. The circumstances are unclear, but in 1936 No Nen was relieved of his work in the defense ministry and then detained at the ministry for nearly a month. After his release, he resigned his position.[51] His personal travails aside, No Nen apparently stated that he ran for the parliament to make people aware of the plight of poor workers and citizens. The government, he evidently asserted, had no sympathy for poor people and in fact mercilessly exploited them. Further, he supposedly contended that the government was clever, albeit only to a point: anticipating that people might see through their dictatorial ways, the cabinet chose a callow boy, Ananda, as king, upon Prajadhipok's 1935 abdication, in the belief that the royal mask to constitutional legitimacy would shield their true face.[52] His alleged comments ring true, since Thong-in in the lands scandal had made the similar point that the adolescent monarch had no influence over his ministers and regents. No Nen was executed later in 1939 along with seventeen others.

Outsiders Battle to Expand Democracy

Some members of the elected half of the parliament remained a thorn in the cabinet's side. Aside from demanding that existing democratic norms and procedures be kept, the assembly went further and clamored for their expansion. Like the forced government reshuffles and attempts at budgetary oversight, however, the assembly only partially succeeded in checking cabinet control of policy. The People's Party had promised to enlarge democracy to include a fully elected assembly. The permanent constitution of December 1932 had mandated that the assembly would become fully elected once one-half of the population had a primary education, or at a maximum of ten years hence. In 1940, much discussion in the assembly focused on whether to maintain or abolish an appointed portion of the house.

Both sides claimed to be fulfilling the People's Party promise to the *ratsadon* that, since 1932, the people were sovereign via a representative democracy. But backers of the status quo of appointed members presented the nonelected contingent as the ballast ensuring that the constitutional system stood for the people as a whole rather than particular interests. Those wanting a fully elected house accused the former group of patronizing and scorning the people as too stupid to succeed without them. The 1940 debate set the terms for the next eighty years over "demi"-democracy: was it better for national welfare and stability to have Bangkok guardians in charge or provincial representatives?

When a parliamentarian moved that the house vote to extend the tutelage period for another ten years, an impassioned Thong-in Phuriphat asserted that this assemblyman disempowered the people that elected him and hence "destroyed" (*thamlai*) them.[53] Thong-in argued during these debates that "we have to succeed with a mental revolution among the people,"[54] a transformation that he said was unfolding under the constitutional regime and that had reached the point where popular independence from state indoctrination was feasible. Thong-in identified three developments that had sustained the democratic movement: the popular vote, direct elections, and the expansion of local government. The first was an immediate product of the revolution: both men and women in Siam had the right to vote, an equal right that long-established democratic countries like France still lacked.[55] Second, from the 1933 elections, the citizens had elected one-half of the assembly.

But Thong-in was not a radical democrat. In common with all assemblymen and the People's Party, Thong-in envisioned indirect democracy led by the enlightened. He contended in the parliament that the standard for national political development should not be the outlook of workers and peasants, but the educated classes. The first group—the "backbone of the country"—wanted material improvement but were not interested in politics. The second engaged in politics, he asserted, as a part of their outlook on life. To them, the parliament especially owed a debt, and the proponent of the extension of the appointed members' term defamed his own class and the government.[56] The parliament should be the vehicle for the expansion, not contraction, of democracy but via the spokesmen. Thong-in's argument summarizes the absence of "organic" intellectuals in Siam at the time, even though he envisioned a spokesmen's democracy as aligning particular interests with popular interests. Somewhat implausibly, he claimed to embody popular will, and asserted that representatives were transparent vehicles for the masses' unarticulated needs.

Last, Thong-in's long appeal for a fully elected house rested on the success, as he argued, of local government over the past several years. The People's Party took pride in establishing institutionalized local councils—*thesaban*—as a way that people participated in governance. From legislation passed in 1934, the government allowed the formation of local assemblies at three ascending levels of population density. Each comprised a congress and a cabinet. Their progressive democratization matched exactly the national legislature's planned career. Initially, all assembly members were appointed, then half would be elected and half appointed, and finally all would elected by local people once education in the area had passed the 50 percent primary-school leaving threshold. As such, the People's Party government explained that in time all localities would obtain greater control over their affairs.

In a government text from the time explaining the system, Phraya Sunthonpipit, the director of the department of the interior, stated: "The *thesaban* system is modeled exactly on the constitutional system. Hence the *thesabans* are good primary schools where the population can learn the methods of constitutionalism. Future national parliamentarians will mostly come from the local councils."[57] The new regime's masters asserted in their explanation that *thesaban* democracy superseded the absolutist system's autocratic stranglehold on local administration. The old system, implemented by government fiat, vested all power with bureaucrats; the new system was "by the people and for the people."[58] The old system sought to control the population; the new to facilitate progress and popular well-being.

The differences between local administration under the old regime and local government under the new, however, are not as dramatic as the post-1932 government, or Thong-in, claimed. Central control blunted the democratic power of the *thesaban* system. And as in the educational curriculum, the constraints on teachers, and the new regime's democratic propaganda drive, the state offered with one hand what the other took away. *Thesaban* councils were banned from discussing politics or affairs outside of their locale. They could only manage local issues of material and moral welfare: public health, drinking water, local school administration, road maintenance, and the like. Moreover, ultimate power lay with the provincial governor, who was appointed by the center. With reason, the provincial governor could abolish the local assemblies, although how informative the explanation needed to be is not clear. In its ordinary activities, the assembly had the right to ask questions of the council about *thesaban* affairs, but the councilors reserved the right not to answer if they deemed the topic too sensitive.[59] Again, like the provincial governor's authority to dissolve the assembly, ambiguity surrounds where accountability to the citizenry ended.

Given these aspects of the new system of local government, Thong-in's faith in local government seems either naive or he is telling the appointed assemblymen what he thinks they want to hear. His idealism is apparent: "If we did not love to move forward, we would not have changed the government," he summarized.[60] At the same time, flattery of second category members does not match his stubbornness and independence on everything else about democracy's realization. His glowing tributes to *thesaban* works, moreover, occurred after the near demise of broader local politics which he well knew. In 1937, the national assembly nearly succeeded in abolishing provincial councils, which operated according to the same principle as the other levels. Officially begun in October 1936, just a few months later the provincial bodies came under attack. In July 1937, the assembly debated their elimination, and many members felt that the money to support them could be better used elsewhere. Type one representatives backed the provincial councils, however, and defeated the bill. Amid the growth of military power at the high levels of government, the provincial councils—and provincial officials generally in the climate of pending war and military power—became a civilian bulwark against the military.[61]

Northeastern assemblymen and their backers failed to abolish the tutelage period. In the end, Thong-in, Tiang Sirikhan from Sakon Nakhon province in the northeast, and Thawin Udon were the only ones to vote against the bill.[62] Assemblymen in favor of prolonging guided democracy also claimed the People's Party's mantle for their beliefs.[63] Kaeo Sing-hakhechen from Pichit province argued that none of the "people," educated or otherwise, were prepared to stand on their own. Targeting Thong-in and others who spoke out frequently in the assembly, Kaeo averred that the educated classes, including many MPs, were more interested in power than looking after the common people. Kaeo thus directly countered Thong-in's assertion that politics was a calling for people who sincerely wanted to serve the country, and his argument also echoed the way that party politics had been denigrated over the past decade. As for the uneducated, Kaeo cited very low education figures that he obtained from the 1937 census: he claimed that only about 22 percent of the population could read.[64] Kaeo argued that the People's Party inheritance would be squandered if the government allowed direct assembly voting by the people freed of appointees. Tiang Sirikhan retorted with dark humor: he said that Kaeo made it sound as if the People's Party was dead and buried.

Phibun himself, son of a market gardener now the guardian of Thai politics, spoke to the assembly at the closure of that parliamentary session in September. He claimed in effect that one of the six Promoters' principles—ensurement of public order and safety—overrode another—the fulfillment of full democracy. Faced, he said, with a global war and its corresponding threats to domestic peace, the tutelage period must be extended and the constitution amended despite what some people might see as an attack on the constitution's "sacrality."[65]

Democracy in the Pacific War: Autocracy's Brief Victory Unravels

Important outsiders formed an opposition to policy and practices that they claimed imperiled constitutionalism. They lost, however, the fights over insider trading, military expansion, and an assembly freed from executive control. If the story ended here, assembly politics under the new regime seems trapped in a cul de sac of good intentions, inspiring rhetoric and impotence. We could write a lament for what might have been. But the war brought by Japan's strike across Southeast Asia changed everything. In the first half of the war, pro-Japanese militarist nationalism—led by the army's seemingly clever alliance with the Asian superpower—trumped pursuit of democracy. But in the second half, pro-Allies feeling—led by state insiders and outsiders who saw in Japan's likely defeat the destruction of an Axis-aligned Thailand—enabled the assembly to take more control of state politics and reinvigorate democracy.

State outsiders' attempts to broaden Thai democracy by abolishing appointed assembly members occurred amid a popular war with France. Suppression of the 1933 rebellion, which paved the way for Phibun's rise to power, was very popular. And so was the reclamation of Lao lands in 1940 from France. After France's capitulation to Germany in June 1940, prewar colonial relations with Thailand changed quickly. That summer, Phibun pressed France to return territories the Thais claimed directly to them.[66] France refused and instead inflamed tension with a series of border provocations. Thammasat University students—guardians in training for the defense of democracy—rallied en masse against French claims. Chatchai Chunhavan, a young soldier at the time who served Phibun, recalled that the Thammasat rally prompted Phibun to invade the disputed territories.[67] Oppositional northeastern assemblymen also took heart from Phibun's stance, and toured the border region to see conditions firsthand.[68] War raged between France and Thailand from November 1940 into January 1941. Thailand successfully prosecuted the fight in both Cambodia and Laos but instead of a military conclusion, the fighting ended with a ceasefire in late January, and then a Japan-brokered peace treaty between the two sides in May 1941. Thailand gained right bank Mekhong lands in French Indochina that had been ceded to France by Chulalongkorn four decades earlier, as well as Battambang province and parts of Champasak and Siem Reap.[69]

Phibun attained the zenith of his popularity and power. His claim to "lost" territories echoed a long-standing emotional refrain in Thai public discourse.[70] Lao and Khmer lands especially occupied a special place in the hearts of nationalists, since they had long-standing political and cultural ties with Bangkok from the nineteenth century.[71] Phibun's victory seemed to end the trauma, and he capitalized on his successes. In the middle of

July that year the defense ministry proposed to the government that Phibun advance from lieutenant to full colonel. The chair of the regency council went one further, and enabled Phibun's promotion to field marshal, thus leapfrogging intermediary senior ranks.

Phibun's heady rise, according to people close to him, led him to fascism and a cult of personality. The head of the police special branch recalled that Phibun stopped listening to advice after the Indochina war, and Adun Decharat, the chief of police, added that Phibun had little interest in Nazism or fascism before becoming field marshal but then eagerly

Figure 6.1. Teaching the children about Phibun's new order. Schoolchildren visit an arts display commissioned by the government in the late 1930s. Photo courtesy of the National Archives of Thailand, Department of Fine Arts.

adopted the follow the leader ethos of Germany and Italy.[72] Moreover, his alliance with Japan from the end of 1941, despite a rocky beginning marked by confusion and fighting, spared Thailand the misery, killing, and destruction experienced in Burma, Malaya, and the Philippines. And as their ally Japan trounced colonial armies throughout the region, Phibun's choice seemed a winning move.

So far so good for Phibun's militarist populism. But a social backlash against the Japanese army's poor treatment of ordinary people, its hubris, and the changing wartime fortunes of the Japanese in Asia soon worked against Phibun and his government. By the second half of 1942, Phibun's government scrambled to deal with a deteriorating relationship between ordinary Thais and the Japanese army. Readers can recall the labor violence at Banpong in Central Thailand that turned many people against Japan. At the same time, high officials had serious misgivings about the alliance. By August 1943, the Japanese ambassador in Thailand wrote to his government that there was no pro-Japan faction in the Thai government, and that junior army officers showed an especially open hostility to the Japanese.[73] Doubt and dismay over the alliance changed Phibun's mind also. From early 1943, Phibun planned for Thailand's independent defense against an allied invasion, reasoning that the war had clearly turned against Japan.[74]

In the discussion of wartime labor, we learned that Chinese labor strongly resisted Japan. And that, after the war, Pridi and the civilians aligned with the Chinese movement to gain a broader social power base. But what of the civilian wing of the People's Party, or the parliamentary opposition to the government during the war itself? The conventional story reverses what really happened, and labels the Chinese as unimportant to the social struggle and the Thai civil service as the heroes.

In some accounts, a civilian resistance to military power predated the war and emerged amid the special court debacle of 1939. Chamkat Palangkun, later famous for dying on a mission to contact the Allies in China in 1943, wrote that he and like-minded patriots sought to form a resistance when they were studying at Oxford in the late 1930s: "I assembled many members to create a group that would resist (Phibun) and build a true democracy."[75] Chamkat studied in England on an education ministry scholarship and would have returned to work in the civil service upon graduation. His criticism of the government however stymied his civil service career: he displeased the authorities in a December 1938 article where he attacked the special court act as the work of a dictatorship.

On the day after the Japanese invasion of Southeast Asia, Chamkat met with Tiang Sirikhan, Thawin Udon, Thong-in Phuriphat, and Chamlong Daoruang to establish a Khana Kuchat (Save the Nation Party). The group sought to overthrow Phibun and/or establish a new government in the northeast. Forming the symbols of resistance was easy, the political and military structure difficult. The group could devise a flag, a pledge, or an anthem without trouble, but as Chamkat and Tiang discussed, men and materiel were scarce.[76]

Chamkat wrote that "[h]e looked for a leader [who could provide these things] and saw that only Pridi met the need. I thus immediately went to his house to speak to him."[77] That same day, when the Japanese army moved into Bangkok per their agreement with Phibun, "[t]he Thailanders [*sic*], shocked by the news of the surrender, wept as they stood dazed in the streets."[78] Pridi found Chamkat, Thawin and Tiang among many others awaiting him at his house when he returned from the cabinet meeting that confirmed the Japanese alliance. Pridi recalled that his friends voiced their dismay and itched for a fight against the Japanese and Phibun.[79] From that day, he says, Pridi committed to resist the Japanese.[80] A few days later in that decisive month, Pridi resigned under duress from his finance ministry position because he disagreed strongly with a Japanese demand for a loan.[81]

The reality of the times shows people's shock and dismay at the Japanese alliance, but also a largely impotent movement, with a lack of men, materiel, and strategy the primary obstacle to any meaningful resistance. Capitalizing on Chamkat and Tiang's plan, Pridi wanted to move a resistance force into northern Thailand that month to establish a resistance government, but he quickly abandoned the idea since the Japanese had already taken over the area.[82] To Somsak, the best informed critical historian of the times, Chamkat's early cohort had minimal power. So too the establishment of an anti-Japanese redoubt seems mainly idle talk among a few friends who met at Pridi's house, and who apparently naively thought that a few men could singlehandedly retake the north.[83]

Nineteen forty-two became a quiet year for any resistance, while an uncoordinated amalgam of groups emerged within Thailand and overseas: in Bangkok, the X.O. group under Pridi, which merged with Chamkat's Khana Kuchat, the Seri Thai under Seni Pramoj in Washington, DC, and in England a smattering of overseas Thais who joined Force 136, a covert Allied outfit working in Southeast Asia. Still, the Banpong violence in December 1942, the unpopularity of the Japanese by early 1943, and their losses in some key campaigns in Asia that year gave a political chance for a more integrated resistance to form. Pridi and the Bangkok group gave full political and material backing to Chamkat and authorized his journey to China to make contact with the allies in February 1943. With jewelry and valuables given by Tiang and his wife as emergency funds, and with Tiang's connections to Indochina, Chamkat set off to Hanoi and then to Chungking, China.[84] Poorly treated and isolated by the Chinese Nationalists, Chamkat did not make a connection with the Allies. Pridi and company lost contact with him, and Sanguan Tularaks, Pridi's man who had strongly criticized royalists in the early days of the revolution, traveled to China where he learned that Chamkat died in Chungking in October that year. Only later at the end of 1943 and into early 1944 did Pridi's group make contact with the Allies.[85]

The diverse elements that comprised the wartime resistance certainly acted out of pragmatism. We can be skeptical of Pridi's reply to a question about why he formed a resistance: "In the war, we had to fight those who were enemies of democracy according to our principles."[86] The democratic rule of law, as we saw, had already been trashed with Pridi's endorsement. Moreover, the coming together of a resistance occurred mainly through officialdom. Thawin, Tiang, Thong-in, and Chamlong all worked in their home provinces in the latter part of the war to spread the anti-Phibun resistance. They governed dictatorially; in a telling example, Tiang's force in Sakon Nakhon province dragooned villagers into serving the resistance effort, and executed a man for treason on flimsy evidence. Tiang shot the man himself, claiming that he had to set the example of how traitors fared. Thammasat University, just a few years earlier a source of Phibun's popularity during the Indochina dispute, now became a bastion of anti-Phibunism. The education ministry, too, was filled with Pridi backers. Moreover, an opportune turnaround among senior people in the cabinet and ministries who previously supported Phibun preserved bureaucratic power, and prevented social disorder, at an unstable time.[87]

And yet democratic principles survived, and especially first category national assemblymen tried to halt the budding autocracy through the war. And as previously, northeastern assemblymen and their friends used popular suffering as a way to upend the government. At the same time as the widespread Chinese labor strikes against the Japanese, a parliamentary defense of democracy merged with the sea change in feeling in the civil service and senior bureaucrats' reappraisal of the Thai position in the war to topple the Phibun government.

Northeastern representatives and their backers found a major weapon in the government's abuse of labor. Throughout the war, the government resorted to labor conscription. The policy brought criticism especially in the wake of the Banpong violence and the popular reaction to similar Japanese policies. National assembly members in the summer of 1944 set up a committee to investigate the hardship of two particular government projects: a new capital Phibun wanted built at Petchabun, and a new religious center nearby in Sayaburi. Prominent northeastern parliamentarians, representing provinces that supplied much of the labor for the projects, led the committee.[88]

The wartime government began building a new capital in Petchabun, at a remote, malarial site, and conceived it as a defensive redoubt from which the Phibun government could resist the Japanese as the war started to go badly for the Axis. By December 1943, and probably earlier, the government demanded labor for Petchabun.[89] The government's initial labor call relied on volunteers, but met little enthusiasm and hence "conscription was unavoidable" from the army's perspective.[90] As explained by the interior ministry, conscription (*kaen*) meant forced removal of people to go to work for the state, according to enforceable law. People who ignored the law were thus liable to criminal punishment.[91]

Bosses paid conscript labor at a rate that depended on working conditions and geographic area. Labor in a dangerous or unhealthy place garnered 2 or even 2.50 baht per day.[92] But problems soon developed in the government's scheme. Convincing people to work far from home, or in dangerous, inhospitable places, often required local Thai officials to pressure people to obey the summons.[93] A requisition generally depended on demand for a maximum percentage of labor from a locality, which varied depending on the work.[94] At other times, it meant the recruitment of much more labor than allowed by government regulations. Ostensibly, provincial governors decided what constituted 5 to 35 percent of the able-bodied, twenty to fifty years of age and not already engaged on a military project.[95] The rules governing conscript labor were widely ignored.[96] The government also reported common social abuse of the conscription demands. For example, unscrupulous middlemen, claiming to be government civil servants, extorted large cash payments from Chinese shop owners in the provinces, amounting to tens of thousands of baht; otherwise, the threatened would be sent to work in Petchabun.[97] As labor became scarce for the Petchabun project, the government sang the praises of the province in its attempts to woo workers through a public relations campaign. The land was fertile and abundant, and regional commerce vibrant, they claimed. The government's pitch aimed at both Thai and "trustworthy" Chinese workers as well,[98] preying in part on people's fear of Allied bombing in the city.[99] The government halted conscription within Petchabun itself in March 1944, because the labor drain undermined local agriculture.[100]

While modern laws and bureaucratic paperwork enabled conscription, the method for finding people to build a new capital in remote malarial forests seemed more like Ayutthaya-era despotism than twentieth-century administration. Thong-in Phuriphat exclaimed in the first assembly discussion on Petchabun that the forced labor was a death sentence for the workers.[101] And indeed many faced a grim fate. By a government estimate, 5,071 workers died at the Petchabun project.[102] Phibun told a journalist after the war that of all wartime policies, he most regretted the Petchabun labor scheme. The journalist likened Petchabun labor to slaves working for an Egyptian Pharaoh.[103]

Accompanying the Petchabun administrative capital plan, another grand plan for Buddhamonthon—the Buddha City—further stressed labor. In June 1944, the Phibun government decreed establishment of the religious city. The government took advantage of a parliamentary recess to have the act passed, although the constitution required the parliament at its next sitting to examine and approve the act. Coupled with the inquiry into the Petchabun labor crisis, the Buddhamonthon project brought down the Phibun government.

At the hearing Prayun Phamonmontri, the education minister at the time, presented the case for the holy site. The rush to pass the decree, he told the assembly, was based on a spiritual calculation. He explained that he consulted with Buddhist monks and determined that the auspicious timing of early June, when the kingdom according to the lunar calendar celebrated the Buddha's enlightenment (Visakha Puja), could not be missed.[104] Prayun said the government envisioned the city as a holy repository for Thai Buddhist artifacts from all over the kingdom and a new center for Sangha education and administration.[105]

In a wartime atmosphere of political turbulence and economic disruption, many parliamentarians criticized the government's move. The same cohort that attacked the Petchabun project weighed in on Buddhamonthon as a waste of money and, moreover, an unjust expropriation of smallholders' farms and property.[106] The local economy—markets and agricultural supply—would be destroyed. Thong-in argued that expropriating land was *abat* (immoral in Buddhist language). Any merit gained by building religious works would be overshadowed by the sin of taking people's land at an unfairly low price. Even worse, under the scheme farmers could rent land from the Sangha, an ill-intentioned idea that echoed feudalism.[107] Furthermore, Thong-in reported, since the Petchabun and Buddhamon-thon proposals wealthy landowners began buying up land and created a speculative market that eliminated poor farmers.[108]

Not only outspoken democracy advocates demanded Phibun resign as a result of these projects, but second-category assemblymen, many from the army, also sided with the civilians against Phibun in the no-confidence motion of July 1944.[109] The patriotic resistance to Phibun became politically successful only when the war's outcome was apparent, and when Phibun's main supporters in the military and police abandoned him.[110]

The Heady Confusion of Postwar Democracy

The end of the Phibun government, and then the end of the war, presented opportunity and danger for the democratic movement in the assembly. The outcome of the war seemed to validate civilian democracy and the outsiders' efforts: the war was a victory for freedom against tyranny, for democracy against dictatorship. Pridi emerged as the most important national political figure.[111] His followers and allies in the Seri Thai, now in a strong position in state politics, pushed their agenda. In the ensu-ing years, however, conflicts internal to Pridi's faction, and the outsiders from the northeast he brought in to the government, emerged and were accompanied by a strong backlash against civilian democracy.

A government under Thawi Bunyaket as premier formed on Sep-tember 1, 1945, and pledged above all to make Thailand a democratic country and an ally of international liberalism. The military was cast out of politics, and Phibun's army badly treated. Thousands who had been sent into Burma in 1943 to expand Thai territory were forced to walk home in late 1945; the Seri Thai commandeered upcountry transport for their own people to demobilize. At the end of September 1945, 8,000 Seri Thai marched in a grand parade in Bangkok down Ratchadamnern Avenue and around the Democracy Monument, commissioned by Phibun as one of his great architectural monuments to constitutionalism in 1941. Pridi presided as the master of ceremonies for the celebration.[112] Two days after the parade, a war crimes bill was introduced into the assembly. Pridi and Seni Pramoj, the wartime liaison to the US in the Seri Thai, and premier after Thawi's short-lived cabinet, pushed for the bill. Thais learned of the possible war criminality of their leaders on Radio San Francisco. Phibun, Wichit Wathakan (Thai ambassador to Tokyo at the time), and Prayun Phamonmontri, the minister of education, were all named.[113] The victorious allies seemed to suggest that the Thais could be tried in a criminal case overseas.

Seni's premiership, meanwhile, continued the democratic tenor of government rhetoric. Thawi's pledge to be a good international partner gained a spur from the threat the country seemed to face. Pridi advanced Seni as premier because of the latter's Washington connections and as a way to prevent a second infringement of Thai sovereignty, after the Japanese period, by having its citizens tried overseas. The drafters defined a war criminal broadly, and those convicted faced execution and asset seizure.[114] Phibun and senior figures in his cohort were arrested. Sanguan Tularaks—one of the government's representatives in the trials, an original Promoter, and the publisher of a newspaper that readers may recall Mano termed the *Pravda* of Siam—remarked in the assembly in 1946 that a small country like Thailand did not need an army in any case. The entire wartime period should be forgotten.

Postwar democratic euphoria soon faced a gritty reality. Inflation, scarcity, British demands for war reparations and low cost rice for its colonies created household uncertainty and hardship. Violence enabled by the widespread availability of guns made daily life more dangerous than during the war. The demobilization of 120,000 Japanese troops, a British Indian army of 17,000 tasked with handling the Japanese but that seemed more like an occupying force, and an angry military all had to be confronted, handled, or accepted.[115] Over all of this, a revolving door of cabinets tried to govern; from August 1945 to November 1947, cabinets averaged four months, with seven in all.[116]

Popular hardship brought the fall of one of these cabinets when northeasterners in the assembly challenged the government's inability to handle the economic crisis. In March 1946, Thong-in Phuriphat proposed a bill to control living expenses. The draft law called for a triple structure of central, provincial, and district committees that would examine consumer costs and fix prices. Citizens' groups of at least 100 people had the right to petition their committee if they found prices too high or unfair. Vendors who did not clearly display prices or overcharged faced stiff penalties, including jail time.[117] Like Liang Chaiyakan during the lands scandal, Thong-in asserted that the government must act for moral reasons.

Thong-in argued in the discussion for solidarist ethics of mutual obligation and help, which he combined with the four requisites in Buddhism: food, shelter, clothing, and medicine. At times in his speech, Thong-in spoke ominously of a pending revolution should selfishness expand the wealth gap between rich and poor; in other places he spoke of people's natural goodness and proclivity to help each other.

On the one hand, he argued that the political turmoil since the war's end led to profiteering; on the other, he contended that no black market would emerge with the new regulations since people were good Buddhists.[118] The government's backers argued that supply and demand economics, and hands-off liberalism were the best ways to spread wealth; people would never be economically equal, nor should they since price controls were an infringement of personal liberty. Thong-in responded that many other countries used price controls, including the United States, but that Thailand "prefers liberalism beyond boundaries."[119] Tiang Sirikhan added that laissez-faire policy, allowing markets free rein, would result in everyone starving.[120]

On the grounds that they could not execute such a policy of control, the government resigned. A Pridi-driven government formed, and drafted a new constitution that went much further in enshrining rights and freedoms than the 1932 charter. Three articles in the 1946 constitution banned civil servants from both houses of parliament and also from the cabinet. These created a politics unprecedentedly free of bureaucratic insider influence; the "civil service assembly" of the 1930s disappeared. Amid the political turbulence, Thailand made a great leap forward when political parties formed. But a main tragedy of the period immediately emerged: the introduction of a freewheeling political party system helped to kill democracy.

This odd outcome of democracy's advance stems from the royalist reaction against Pridi and company, fuelled by bitterness at their political exile over the prior decade and a half. From the end of 1945, parties formed, even though their legal status remained unclear.[121] Unlike the fraught legal status of parties in 1932 and 1933, this time no opposition to party formation stood in the way. The following year, the 1946 constitution drafted by Pridi's people explicitly allowed political parties to form; gone was the vague language allowing "associations" that had confused many people in the early days of the People's Party.[122]

Two of the first political parties were the royalist Progress and Democrat parties. The brothers Seni and Kukrit Pramoj—minor royals descended from King Rama II (r. 1809–1824)—pioneered the next generation attack on commoner democracy. The Pramojs had never served the absolutist state. The British-educated Seni had been ambassador to the United States during the war and a leader of the Seri Thai movement in that country. He returned to Thailand in 1945, briefly served as premier after Thawi, and also played a lead role in the peace negotiations with the allied victors. In 1946, during the government that Thong-in's bill ended, Seni falsely accused Pridi of embezzling Seri Thai funds, a charge that led to an investigating committee that called in OSS and Force 136 witnesses. Pridi was cleared of the charges but the bad feeling Seni introduced poisoned politics.[123] Seni publicly spread the idea that Pridi and his followers did not warrant any credit for the Seri Thai's contribution to the allied effort.[124] He wrote that: "Pridi's Free Thai Movement soldiers appeared to be a sort of Gestapo that would intimidate rival politicians and regiment the people. . . . We could never get over the suspicion that Pridi was a Communist."[125] In forming the Progress party in late 1945, Seni's brother Kukrit declared that his aim would be "anti the Promoters of 1932 by all means" and wrote a newspaper article where he declared himself a royalist.[126] He combined with Nimitmongkol Navarat and other prisoners from the 1930s—released under an amnesty in 1944 after the fall of Phibun's government[127]—and used their hard experience to exploit grievances against the People's Party. These Thai prisoners felt like many others the world over: imprisoned by hatred posing as justice, and aggrieved as "hostile to the past, impatient of the present and cheated of the future."[128] But they had a way to make up for lost time, and perhaps redeem what lay ahead, as the Progress Party became the "champion of the Bang Khwang prison group."[129] Kukrit's Progress Party soon folded itself into the Democrat Party, whose leading members then included his brother Seni, Choti Kumphan, and Phraya Thephasadin na Ayutthaya.

In addition to these men, Louis Girivat and Luen Saraphaiwanich from the Siam Free Press group that attacked the People's Party, both of whom also went to prison in the 1930s, wrote influential newspaper articles and books criticizing the Promoters. Louis Girivat fondly recalled Mano and the royalists who drafted the December 1932 constitution, men who prevented radical politicians from taking over. Indeed "politician" meant to him a smooth-tongued deceiver, like Pridi.[130] In 1949, he described the prior seventeen years not "as a time of the education in building democratic institutions so much as 17 years of destruction by politicians who seized the honorable seat (of governance) and turned it into theatre . . . this is a pitiful democracy and a fearful danger, where people choose the low and stupid as their representatives."[131] He despised and disparaged the symbols of the revolution. He deplored the constitutional defense memorial at Laksi, with which Phibun as premier honored the soldiers who defeated the Bowondet rebellion in 1933, as a testimony to vengeance not bravery. To Girivat, the unmemorable memorial could not compare to the kingly sites around the country, and even paled in comparison to Vajiravudh's commemorative site for his loyal canine. (Indeed, the Laksi memorial, like many others, has been forgotten; it was initially moved from Laksi in 2016, and then vanished altogether at the end of 2018.) The animal knew loyalty and gratitude, at least.[132] Girivat also poked fun at the June 24 plaque that Phibun established. Its words: "At this spot the People's Party established the Constitution for the progress of the nation," and "24 June 1932, Dawn" should be replaced, he said. Girivat lampooned the real meaning as here Phahon fostered the revolt. "The pig dressed in lion skins sat on the throne instead" and fooled the armed forces into rebellion.[133]

Pridi-linked groups, however, had far more electoral success than the royalist parties. The largest party to officially form was the *Sahachip*, or Cooperative party, which mobilized from discussions among northeastern representatives in September 1945. Socialism, rural welfare, and popular democracy comprised their platform. The Isan ministers who followed Thong-in Phuriphat became prime movers in the party. Others came from a longer alliance with Pridi: Sanguan Tularaks helped the party to organize.[134] The *Naeo Rathathammanun* (Constitutional Front) also formed and entered government in 1946 as a pro-Pridi group.[135] Thongplaeo Chonlaphumi, who coordinated aid to urban workers after the war, as we learned in chapter 2, and who also helped establish Sahachip, became Naeo Rathathammanun's party secretary. Ninety-six assemblymen sat in January 1946 after the national elections, and men from these two parties accounted for the majority. In by-elections held seven months later in August 1946, Pridi people won three-fourths of eighty-two seats available.[136]

The radicalism of the communist-directed wartime movement—and, the consummate triumph, the legalization of the Thai Communist Party in 1946 and its resulting public profile—influenced the parties linked to Pridi and his cohort.[137] In the early postwar years, as one outcome, the peasantry became a target for communist-affiliated or influenced activists, and the communist influence hence spread beyond what we discussed as a urban movement in an earlier chapter, and far beyond the original *lukjin* focus. Sahachip emerged out of this intellectual milieu as a type of new people's party, and practiced a much more assertive rural interest on the ground than Pridi's officially sanctioned solidarism. Throughout the late 1940s and 1950s, the left-wing People's Party members and the communists developed the same ideology, which was reliant on Marxism-Leninism; the same social analysis, that Thailand was still bound by colonial and residual "feudal" forces (i.e., big landlords and royals); and the same ethos, to serve the people.[138] Sahachip members aligned with the communists, and published in *Mahachon*, the party paper, what the American government termed "heavy blasts against American imperialism."[139]

But the wild rhetoric from royalists undermined what had been only recently gained. While Pridi was premier from June 1946, he immediately faced rumors that implicated him in King Ananda's death on June 9. He banned media reporting about the king's death and established an official inquiry into the case, but this failed to calm the situation. In the aftermath of the August election, a resounding victory for Pridi, Seni and Khuang Aphaiwong interrupted government business by raising suspicions about Pridi.[140] Pridi resigned from the premiership and Thamrong Nawasawat, a naval officer, prominent People's Party original, and leader of Naeo Rathathammanun, became premier.

Postwar society was rapidly spinning to a climax. Banditry and lawlessness—in Bangkok and everywhere else it seemed—created insecurity. Banditry had been a challenge to the absolutist state as it expanded its power. Now, after the relative peace and security of the People's Party government of the 1930s, outlawry returned to the country and city alike. The Chinese population divided between KMT and Communist Party sympathizers. In late 1945, fighting in Chinatown erupted between Chinese and the police. The government cracked down harshly on the Chinese and spoke of them in nakedly racist terms.[141] There was a thriving gun market in Bangkok and the Indochinese border provinces. The military and police benefited from the illegal trade, not only of guns, but drugs and basic commodities. Many Isan representatives sold Seri Thai weapons to the Lao and Khmer independence movements fighting the French.[142]

The end of the People's Party era came with a successful and then a failed coup that presaged many more in the vicious cycle of late-twentieth- and early-twenty-first-century Thai politics. A November 8, 1947 military coup ended civilian democracy. This fascinating and complex episode shows a new generation of military officers working with Phibun in alliance with old-regime stalwarts and the younger generation of royalists against the Pridi faction.[143] It stemmed from two main causes: the Democrat Party's opposition to Pridi and the assertion of Ananda's death as Pridi directed; and the military's opposition to the Seri Thai movement and their public humiliation at the end of the war.[144]

Like the Bowondet rebellion fourteen years earlier, the leaders of the coup group were nonserving officers forced out of their positions. Also like the Bowondet group, the coup group of 1947 spread bogus rumors of a republican plot to end the monarchy.[145] They claimed to have solid evidence that Pridi was involved in the king's death and that he also planned the murder of Bhumibol.[146] In late November a royal senior senator wrote in the newspaper that "Pridi . . . is an anarchist. He has no morals. He thinks to kill anyone who gives more importance to the king than himself. He wants to kill Bhumibol but has not succeeded."[147] Seni Pramoj likewise claimed that the November 9 coup prevented a republican bloodbath planned for the end of the month.[148]

A new government formed, with the military's approval, under the Democrat Party and Khuang Aphaiwong.[149] Khuang directed the interior ministry in cooperation with the military to arrest alleged republican conspirators, which meant Pridi supporters. Between late November and late December the police took many into custody, including Thong-in Phuriphat, Tiang Sirikhan, Thongplaeo Chonlaphumi, Duen Bunnag, and Thawi Bunyaket. The police claimed that Wichit Lulitanon, a Pridi colleague who served in the Seri Thai, was tasked with giving a great deal of money to a republican party.[150] From elite insiders to prisoners and back again to power: many royalists and figures imprisoned or cast into the political wilderness after 1932 gained cabinet positions. These included Kukrit and Seni Pramoj, Phraya Sriwisanwaja, Prince Sittiphon Kridakon, Luen Saraphaiwanich, and Thephasadin na Ayutthaya.[151] Important royalists drafted a new constitution. Prince Rangsit, the regent to the young king Bhumibol after the latter's brother's death, immediately approved the coup and endorsed a draft constitution. Rangsit's return to power was especially poignant: he had been sentenced to death in the 1939 special court trial and then stripped of his royal titles.

The constitution introduced a Supreme Council of State, like Prajadhipok's of the 1920s, that returned management of royal affairs to the palace for the first time since 1932. Rangsit named himself head of the council, and appointed Prince Dhani Nivat along with two other princes and Adun Decharat as the remainder. Adun—perhaps chosen as a sop to the People's Party—never attended council meetings.[152] All laws were to be countersigned by the supreme councillors not by the cabinet or premier as under the People's Party charters. The new constitution vested in the head of the supreme council, not the national assembly chair, the power over martial law declarations, foreign treaties, appointment of the senate, and the premier. The charter also restored to the king veto power over legislation.[153] The American ambassador to Thailand wrote to his secretary of state that the constitution provided "only nominal and partial curbing of the powers enjoyed by an absolute monarchy."[154] The ambassador was correct in that the constitution was antidemocratic, only it was not the young King Bhumibol who really held power but the senior princes in the supreme council.

In January 1948, the further rollback of the People's Party revolution employed constitutionalism. Amendments to the 1947 constitution raised the minimum age of assembly candidates to thirty-five from twenty-three, as specified in the 1946 and 1932 constitutions, and enlarged an assembly-man's electorate to 200,000 citizens from 100,000. With the first proviso, many young assemblymen from the 1946 elections lost their chance of participating in politics. The amendments also revoked the freedom to form political parties.[155] The government charged many northeastern representatives with various crimes, thus eliminating them from politics. Through such machinations, the Democrats obtained the majority in the parliament in January elections, something they failed to accomplish before the military helped them into power.[156] Most of the appointed senate, produced by the 1947 constitution, featured an overwhelming royal-noble elite cohort. Seni indeed remarked that: "Our senate is an assembly from the days of yore (*sapha prawatisat*). In reading the names of the assembly members, it sounds like you are reading from the pages of a Thai dynastic chronicle."[157] Residual anti-Pridi sentiment was fomented further when Khuang's government appointed Phra Pinitchonkadi, Seni's brother-in-law and a former police officer, to pursue the investigation into Ananda's death.

But the days of yore had not returned. In a peaceful "coup by letter,"[158] the military suggested that Khuang should step down and he obeyed in April. The military, like Phibun and his group had after the fall of the Mano government in 1933, installed military officers in the unelected section of the parliament and Phibun himself returned as premier. Kukrit claimed in a 1951 newspaper column that the Khuang government's acceptance of their weakness showed the spirit of democracy. In fact, as Suthachai clarifies what this tortured logic really meant, while the postwar royalist renaissance legitimized the army's political role anew, it also made the monarchy dependent on the service.[159]

While the coup group struck back against its royal partners, 1948 was not a complete loss for royalists. Prince Rangsit commenced drafting yet another constitution in July and Seni was appointed chief drafter. The resulting constitution of May 1949 reinforced rule by senior princes. Continuing the power regained by senior princes in 1947, chair of the nine-member Privy Council that superseded the supreme council of state had to countersign and ratify the king's actions.[160] Moreover, senators chosen in 1947 remained senators under the stipulation of the 1949 charter, what Pridi termed "mutual back-scratching between the coup group and the old order."[161] The king's party in any case also gained the power of plebiscite whereby the monarch could bypass the government and poll the citizenry on proposed constitutional changes. Finally, the privy council alone ratified succession to the throne, not the parliament. The royalist intellectual Prince Dhani's notion of the king as gaining the throne through popular acclaim, thus becoming the "Great Elect," buttressed the renaissance of royal power after the war and threw a gauzy cover over history. As Paul Handley put it, Prince Dhani's elected monarchy did exist. But the electors lived in the palace.[162]

February 1949: The Idealists' Desperate Gamble

In a reckless gamble born of frustration and anger that had been building since the November 1947 coup, Pridi-allied groups staged a rebellion on February 26, 1949. The alliance of Pridi-aligned state insiders and outsiders waged a confused fight against the resurgent conservative forces, and then collapsed. Pridi called the group the February 26 Democratic Movement.[163] Contrary to the clarity suggested by Pridi's label, the rebels formed a hodgepodge of dissatisfied elements, and notably the leading northeastern assemblymen did not play a part. After the 1947 coup, some assemblymen clamored for a revolt, but a changed balance of forces stymied their plans. In 1947, Thong-in Phuriphat, the industry minister in Thamrong's precoup civilian government, met with some conspirators to plan a putsch that would install him as the new premier. Others, however, demurred, and military sympathizers' lack of support killed the idea.[164] Adun Decharat, among others—naval officers most prominently—blamed the northeastern ministers who held strong influence in the Thamrong government for the civilian regime's corruption.[165] The 1947 coup, moreover, scattered the northeastern contingent. Tiang Sirikhan returned to

Sakon Nakhon where he pledged to set up an independent authority to await a "genuine people's government" in Bangkok. As he had during the war, Tiang armed villagers to defend his territory.[166] Tiang was arrested on treason charges but released for lack of evidence. Thong-in and Chamlong Daoruang tried to run in elections held in 1948. The government declared them ineligible, but they attended the first assembly meeting anyway in February 1948 and were arrested. Like Tiang, they soon were released, but also like Tiang they enjoyed only a short-lived, harried freedom.

Mainly because he saw them as too controversial, Pridi did not include the Isan MPs in the scheme to topple the government. Meanwhile, the 1949 rebellion proceeded. Pridi and some conspirators, who had been overseas, returned in early February and assembled arms for their cause. The government learned what was planned and declared a state of emergency. Police arrested many conspirators, and the police chief claimed if they were a day late, senior Thai government officials would suffer the sorry fate of Aung San in Burma who had been assassinated the previous year.[167]

With echoes of the propaganda war that raged around the Bowondet rebellion years earlier, around 10:00 p.m. on the night of the 26th, the rebels seized the Phaya Thai radio station and announced a new government of People's Party civilians. Thammasat became the headquarters of the revolt. Heavy fighting took place on the evening of the 26th and into the morning of the following day. Fierce tank and artillery exchanges marked the early and mid-morning of the 27th at the Ratchaprasong intersection in central Bangkok. Initially, the rebels had the advantage as the government leaders scattered and became isolated. But the army fought back. Sarit Thanarat—destined to rule as a tyrant—followed Phibun's 1933 example of turning military victory into political advantage. He carried the day when he attacked the palace near Thammasat where the rebels established a defense. Pridi fled from here across the river into Thonburi. In all, seven people were killed in the revolt and thirty-one injured. Like the Bowondet rebellion and the 1939 special court executions, however, the political and psychological effect of the fratricide far exceeded the existential cost. The People's Party civilian wing and the Seri Thai veterans' network were destroyed. At Thammasat and the palace, police arrested anyone associated with Pridi, whether involved in the rebellion or not.

Between May and October 1949 the government charged twenty-four people with revolt, all of whom were associated with Thammasat and the Seri Thai. Among others, the police hammer fell on the four Isan ministers who did not take part in the rebellion. Thong-in, Chamlong, and Thawin were arrested in Bangkok, and Thongplaeo, on his arrival at Don Mueang from Penang. Police nabbed Tiang in Sakon Nakhon and brought him to Bangkok. They also issued warrants for eighteen other alleged conspirators, including Pridi, who fled for his life overseas and never returned to Thailand.[168] In early March, police killed Thong-in, Thongplaeo, Thawin, and Chamlong, whom they held in custody, but claimed that Malay bandits murdered the men in an ambush of the transport carrying the prisoners between detention sites.[169] A witness to the killings of Thong-in and the others in early 1949, recalled the police cars' lights going out on a dark stretch of road outside Bangkok where they stopped. The witness heard a man plead for mercy, as a father and husband, from the back of the police station wagon, where the three were shackled, then saw a policeman shoot all of them. The victims were dragged from the car, while a police commander told his men to turn the car headlights on to make sure the men were dead. Just before then, a couple of the police had remarked: "They are rebels against the country, why are they still alive?"[170] Police released Tiang Sirikhan but never forgot about him. After a government committee meeting in late 1952, a few police officers asked Tiang to accompany them to the special branch station. Some of Tiang's associates had vanished in recent days, and he worried for their safety. Tiang told a political ally to seek out the chief of police, Phao Siyanon, if he did not return from the special branch headquarters. And he did not. Phao met with some of Tiang's colleagues in the legislature canteen for lunch a few days later and denied harming Tiang. Phao explained that it was unthinkable that Phao's men would hurt Tiang, since Tiang's wife was Phao's relative and he always tried to help the couple. A few days later, however, in a meeting Phao denounced Tiang as a communist and traitor. Tiang's wife never saw her husband again.[171]

Conclusion

The dizzying pace of political change at the close of the war seems like anarchy—a melee that emerged as elite and popular interests pulled and repelled each other in a hypercharged political force field. A blooming, buzzing confusion reigned at the time and our story of the first phase of Thai democracy comes to a close. That democracy collapsed when it had seemed at its most robust is the consummate irony of the People's Party years. The Promoters' consolidation of their power enabled Thammasat to flourish, and a social movement like the Mahanikai to succeed. And as we have seen in this chapter, outsiders attained legislative and political power far beyond their most fervent dreams in the regime's early years. The once relatively clear divisions between insiders and outsiders blurred, as many merged into a new elite that helped to build democracy.

The revolution, coupled with the conflicts introduced or exacerbated by the Pacific War, also however eventually split the Promoters and bred darker forces that actively sought to undermine sociopolitical reform and turn the clock back to a regime akin to the oligarchy of yore—but one with a much better armed and viciously energetic police force. While democracy strengthened as the line blurred between insiders and outsiders, it also became rapidly enfeebled as the once-clear opposition of radical commoners and conservative monarchists muddied. After the 1947 coup, new generation military commoners allied with monarchy. More than any other group, this alliance dismantled the post-1932 consensus of constitutional legitimacy—public approval for the Promoters' moral claim to be creating a better society. The dual structure of their power, and of Thai politics generally, seemed to have submitted to the singular force of an iron fist. One historian declared that violence was the common political currency of the 1940s and 1950s, and no group could maintain power in any other way.[172]

If we read history backward from this depressing perspective, the democratic ideals and efforts of the progressive generation born at the turn of the twentieth century are trivialized—their hopes naive fantasies and their efforts to make democracy completely futile. Such reading also deepens the amnesia of contemporary Thai politics, its lack of a sense of history. Remembering that Liang Chaiyakan exposed the insider lands scandal in 1937, or that Thong-in Phuriphat argued idealistically for extending direct elections and abolishing appointed assemblymen in 1940 challenges the status quo of forgetting in service of autocracy—as does remembering the hardship of workers dragooned into the ill-conceived wartime construction plan that angered the parliamentary opposition and led to the removal of Phibun, and remembering also summons the contingency and fleetingness of people's lives, the real subject of history. A gesture, a plea, the moments of pain and fear before the abrupt loss of the living that people at the time immediately felt resonate still, as in the cases of the northeastern ministers described all too briefly above.

To be sure, the Promoters' regime was discriminatory, and eventually undermined not only by circumstances beyond its makers' control—like the Japanese occupation and King's Ananda's death—but also by their internal conflicts, which paved the way for the royalist resurgence after the war. And like Phibun's Pharaohnic building project in the wilds of Petchabun, the febrile dreams of Pridi's agricultural utopia and Thong-in's assertion of a rural Buddhist-infused solidarism, they clung to abstract visions, chimeras that did not match the reality of most people's lives and exposed a disconnection between the revolutionaries and the masses. All of this should be remembered when thinking about the period. But to be historically accurate, the palimpsest of the lives of people who made democracy in the period, and those caught up in the maelstrom, must be traced. In this chapter, the record shows political activism on a range of issues that aimed to uphold democracy—a coincidence of motives and means that shaped the era.

Conclusion

History beyond Royalism

Figure C.1. An accident of circumstance. Tree, ruined bicycle, smashed car, and young observer, 1930s. Photo courtesy of the National Archives of Thailand, Department of Fine Arts.

The junta that took power in 2014 toppled the country's last democracy and unleashed a wave of protests that hoisted symbols from the Thai past. Iconography from the 1932 revolution, as after the 2006 coup, rose to prominence as people asserted that democracy mattered and demanded its return. In the most recent wave of protests, in late 2020 a group of activists embedded a new 1932 plaque at the Sanam Luang grounds to commemorate the People's Party and prayed for their souls.[1] Exactly as a great historian of Europe described how the historical imagination makes the past a living reality, in Thailand once the emotional chord had been struck, the line between the present and the past could not be reduced to a merely mathematical chronology.[2] To remind people of the importance of the past today, the protesters have also used ideas and gestures from Western media, new and old, from Hollywood film to classic literature. Among the latter icons, antidictatorship protesters frequently staged silent public readings of George Orwell's *1984*. The book's popularity exploded. A main source of the appeal lay with the seeming descent of Thailand into Orwell's nightmare of an oligarchy that surveils everyone, disappears many of them, and perverts language to control their thoughts and convince them that reality is different from what they are experiencing. In rereading this perennial favorite recently for the umpteenth time, I was struck by the resonance of these aspects of the novel to Thailand today, but even more moved by Orwell's focus on historical memory as a source of political entrapment.

The lovers Winston and Julia retreat to their rented bedroom refuge atop, appropriately enough, an antique store filled with junk from a forgotten time before Big Brother. It is a shoddy, dangerous place, and a haven for human feelings, thoughts, and words forbidden in their society. At one point, lying on their bed stripped bare on a baking-hot afternoon, Winston remarks: "History has stopped. Nothing exists except an endless present in which the Party is always right." A sense of history, as necessary a part of human fulfillment as togetherness and a belief in freedom, vanishes along with these latter qualities. In the counterfeit rebel document that Winston reads in the doomed lovers' sanctuary, the author explains that the point of falsifying history is to rob people of any point of comparison, and so to accept any present politics as natural and its conditions as acceptable. The mutability of the past is a pillar of the "Oceania" regime's power.

The assault in recent years on the architectural remains and memorials of the People's Party era ultimately asserts that royalist autocracy is the eternally suitable and just way for the country to be governed. In proclaiming adherence to a timeless Thai style of rule, the twenty-first-century regimes have returned to a belief first constructed in the late nineteenth century, and then revived and expanded at times of crisis when sociopolitical conflict—reality, in other words—has threatened to topple the house of cards founded on historical myths and ideologies.

Historical contingency allowed the Chakri dynasty to modernize the country within the confines of a semicolonial relationship to the Western imperial powers that surrounded Siam. But a series of crises produced an intellectual panic that drove the creation of new historical myths.[3] The 1893 French demands that the king cede his claims over Lao territory led to the first great rethink of the Thai story. Under King Chulalongkorn (r. 1868–1910), the young absolutist state reinvented Thai political and cultural history, and portrayed the monarchic regime as a transmission from antiquity, one that preserved customs of popular kingship, high civilization, and age-old national independence. While the birth of the new history came from an anticolonial position, its founding myths endured long after the threat from any European power vanished, and served thereafter to blunt domestic criticism of absolutism and ignore social change.

King Vajiravudh (r. 1910–1925) gave the most articulate defense of Thai kingly tradition in circumstances much changed from the issues his father had to face. Following the failed republican revolt in the military of the early teens, he used the opportunity to dismiss the public interest in socialism and other -isms' "imitationism" (lathi ao yang).[4] Implicit is a denial of intellectual maturity to most people. Many alternative forms of political activism or self-making could be dismissed this way.[5] The monarchs' status as national saviors, and as the wise men introducing the best of the modern world while keeping out bad influences, established an iconic durability for kingship that hid absolutism's fragility and newness. The attitude also proved to be long lived and simmered in the background during the political conflicts of the 1930s and 1940s. We can recall the amusement of the Bangkok Times at Thawin Udon's demand for the executive to make the budget transparent; to the establishment he was a naive upstart, whom the kingdom's founding fathers would have patted on the head and dismissed for not knowing his place. A bit later and with acute venom, Vajiravudh's intellectual heirs, the reactionaries of the late 1940s, lambasted the Promoters as dreamers and theoretical revolutionaries, whose lust for power upended Thai tradition and sowed social chaos. They demanded the restoration of kingly autocracy, and that the Promoters' regime be forgotten.

In explaining the People's Party era, veneration for monarchy and hatred of the Promoters has led royalists down two opposing paths. On the one hand, King Prajadhipok is hailed as bestowing democracy on a grateful nation. Such a political feat has been memorialized forever in the famous photo of the king handing the signed constitution down to his subject in the December 1932 ceremony that legitimized the charter. This impressive mental contortion removes the People's Party from the picture, as well as the longer trajectory of social tension and criticism over what state building produced, and elevates Prajadhipok as the true democratic hero.[6] But a further, contradictory interpretation holds that his supposedly natural inclination for democracy was stymied by the People's Party's impatience.[7] Prajadhipok here is a tragic, defeated figure betrayed by young hotheads who permanently destabilized the political system. As with everything buttressing monarchic power, this contradictory nonsense aims above all at memorializing a highborn figure, who is supposedly a representative of a timeless political culture. It ignores the genuine aspirations and contributions of many more people in shaping Thai history in concrete historical circumstances. The People's Party revolution and its social resonance demonstrate that the path to modernity did not proceed smoothly along the royalist high road.

The tasks of silencing and forgetting that are now so urgent thus began decades ago. The royalist historical ideology is a clever trick or, as conjured by the rulers of Orwell's Oceania, a self-convincing "doublethink" that has two parts. It is a conscious falsification, which serves to ensure precision in the creation of a national story, and it also becomes unconsciously believed, and thus prevents any guilt for perpetuating a sham.

History more worthy of the name exposes the fragility of the myths begun at the end of the nineteenth century, and also shows the ways that 1932's true importance has been warped to fit into the monarchic national biography. For one thing, leading figures in the dynasty have always been forced by their political weakness to seek global knowledge. Aspects of liberalism became central tools of royal ideology. The kingly administrations supplemented their invention of Thai tradition with rule by bourgeois law as cornerstone of their claims to legitimacy, which they pitched simultaneously to domestic and international audiences. The royal-aristocratic class selected tools of modernity to use for social control (and sometimes to enjoy as hobbies), and excluded other aspects on the grounds of social unsuitability and potential radicalism. The royal a priori determination of which Western political or social ideas and practices were good for the nation and which were harmful denied validity to representative democracy.

Second, prior to 1932, politics rotated on a brittle axis of royal autocracy. The majority of the population had no relation to or interest in the Bangkok monarchy. Among the talented minority on the high road of middle-class ambition, revolutionary ideas fermented. The June 1932 toppling of kingly autocracy grew from and furthered the activism of a large section of middle-class society; it was much more than a palace and bureaucratic tangle. The young, educated generation in interwar Siam experienced profound social and intellectual change. The influx of new ideas, rapid economic change, and the psychological effect of post-World War I nationalisms around the world all challenged an idealized social hierarchy and the monarchy. Pressure accumulated for the introduction of a modern liberal political system among people who grew to maturity in a very young absolutist state.

Third, the revolution—a turning point in history where the past and future collided—was fundamentally conflicted. The Khana Ratsadon's June 1932 takeover did not destroy the neotraditionalist paternalism embedded in absolutist outlooks. In some ways, it amplified them. The upper bureaucracy still constituted the domain of state insiders. The bureaucracy throughout this period, and well into the latter decades of the twentieth century, offered the most attractive careers for young people, and especially men. Male students in law, administration, and military science committed to state careers early in their lives as a means to relative wealth and social respect. The People's Party is a local example of a wider social phenomenon in Southeast Asia in the early twentieth century. Like others, the young Thai civil servants formed a vital and growing educated minority who quickly perceived the advantages of the new centrally controlled state and hoped to capture it rather than bolster an older order. But while the Promoters' revolution promised a better life for Thai citizens, it ignored or discriminated against people it did not value. The regime offered little to women and to the Chinese, and indeed in the latter case tried to take away what they had.

And yet, in the dialectic between old and new "tradition" or stubborn prejudices met their match in the new ways of being Thai that emerged. The revolution allowed greater participation in public affairs and inspired more people to imagine the country's political destiny. It contributed to an ever-more complex debate about governance and social and personal well-being. The People's Party ended the absolute monarchy, but it claimed also that the termination of the old regime entailed more than an institutional change. It was a beginning as well, for the emergence of new social relations and outlooks. The Promoters' revolution, in spite of its conservatism, allowed a new freedom from inherited customs and authority. No country boys like Chamlong Daoruang or Thong-in Phuriphat would ever have risen to national importance in the old regime.

Outsiders to the upper civil service, from a range of backgrounds, acted on this conception of a new beginning. Their legitimizing claims span a range of positions that do not form a single reaction to the revolution. Indeed, without political parties or much associational life beyond the village, and given the compression of political development under the absolute monarchy, it would have been difficult to form such coherent plans. But that does not negate the genuine contribution to post-1932 politics that they made. More social equality, material improvement, popular religion as part of village democracy, local education, and a voice for the provinces in national administration all constituted parts of their aspiration. All of these aspirations are still part of Thai public discourse, and the revolution is their source.

The social importance of the 1932 revolution is genuine and is reflected by the Mahanikai movement, Thawatt's labor movement, political party formation, regional clamor for material development, and among all the passion and idealism to fashion their own story. Perhaps the formula absolutist state + modernizing reforms + rising bureaucratic frustration = revolution has value on some level to frame the structure of this period of Thai history. But such an approach also fails to account for the inspirational, or willed aspect, of the social uptake of the People's Party message. It also airbrushes the lives and passions of those involved out of the picture. Viewing the 1932 revolution as an outcome of larger social and intellectual forces shows that a far larger cast of characters made the revolution than the usual suspects bound by the patrimonial ties of kingship and its career networks. Rescuing schoolteacher activism from obscurity, or that of the Mahanikai, puts educated society into the story as an active agent in 1930s political history, and can lead us to better understand the revolution and its democracy by conceiving of the abrupt end of the absolute monarchy as producing an arena of contest. The People's Party's striving for hegemony in a new language of popular sovereignty opened communication with wider society rather than, as Thai state politics are often seen to do, slamming the door shut.

Excitement about the promise of the new regime philosophy is clear. Social agency and institutional structure then were not separate forces, in which the latter predictably overwhelmed and crushed the former. The assertion of conflicting and yet interconnected ideas linked the two poles of activity and produced a sociopolitical dynamism.

Empirically, we can put common people back into prewar history, and morally we must, as vital players in the emergence of democracy. In any other country, this would be taken for granted. Siam is not unique in its history. Had the Promoters merely tried and failed to perfect the illusion that Thai democracy existed? And has Thai political culture now swung back to a natural state of despotism? No, the pendulum has not swung back, and then been arrested in place. There cannot be a restoration of a hypostatized, eternal authority, since one never existed and because the revolution changed everything. As in any country, political and social modernity has generated a desire for popular sovereignty and for recognition of the individual and collective dignity that universal human rights demand.

Notes

Introduction

1. Suthachai Yimprasert, "Rueang khon rai 'na sai' khamoi mut," *Prachathai*, April 26, 2017.

2. "Uprooting Democracy: The War of Memory and the Lost Legacy of the People's Party," *Prachathai*, December 19, 2019; "Ruamlis moradok Khana Ratsadon thi hai pai," *Prachathai*, March 26, 2020; "No Explanation: Democratic Revolt Leaders Statues Gone Missing," *Khaosod*, January 27, 2020; "1932 Revolt Purge: Statue Removed from Military Academy," *Khaosod*, January 28, 2020.

3. See, for example, *Military, Monarchy and Repression: Assessing Thailand's Authoritarian Turn. Journal of Contemporary Asia* 46, no. 3 (2016): 371–537.

4. Kevin Hewison, "Thailand's Conservative Democratization," in *East Asia's New Democracies: Deepening, Reversal, Non-liberal Alternatives*, Yin-wah Chu and Siu-lun Wong, eds. (Abingdon, Oxon, UK: Routledge, 2010), 122.

5. Thongchai Winichakul, "Prawatisat Thai baep rachachatniyom: chak yuk ananikhom amphrang su rachachatniyom mai rue latthi sadet pho khun krathumphi Thai nai patchuban" [Royalist-Nationalist History: From the Era of Crypto-Colonialism to the New Royalist-Nationalism, or the Contemporary Thai Bourgeois Cult of Rama V]. *Silapa Wathanatham* 23, no. 1 (November 2001): 56–65.

6. Phraya Sriwisanwaja, "The Revolution of 1932," in *Anuson nai kanphraratchathan phloengsop phan ek Phraya Sriwisanwaja* [Royal Cremation Volume for Phraya Sriwisanwaja] (Bangkok: Samnakngan Thep Sriris, 1968), 119–25.

7. Nattapoll Chaiching, "Khwamchop duai rabawp" [Regime Legitimation], in Nattapoll, *Khofanfai nai fan an luea chuea: Khwamkhlueanwai khong khabuankanpatipaks patiwat Siam (pho. so. 2475–2500)* [An Unbelievable Dream: The Resistance Movement against the Siamese Revolution, 1932–1957] (Bangkok: Fadiokan, 2013), 79–81; Dhani Nivat, "The Old Siamese Conception of the Monarchy," *Journal of the Siam Society* 36, no. 2 (1947): 91–104. Reprinted in *Collected Articles by H. H. Prince Dhani Nivat. Bangkok: Siam Society, 1969.

8. The best-known writings that criticized the People's Party on these

grounds are: Louis Girivat, *Prachathipatai 17 pi* [Seventeen Years of Democracy] (Bangkok: Odeon Store, 1949); Malaengwi (pseud., Seni Pramoj) *Bueanglang prawatisat* [Behind History] (Bangkok: Publishing Cooperative, 1947); Luen Saraphaiwanich, *Fanrai khong khappajao* [My Nightmare] (Bangkok: Saraphai, 1969); Nimitmongkol Navarat, *The Dreams of an Idealist*, trans. David Smyth (Chiang Mai, Thailand: Silkworm Books, 2009); Phayap Rotchanawiphat, *Yuk thamin* [The Barbarous Age] (Bangkok: So Sethabut, 1972 (1946); Chamlong Ittharong, *Lakhon kanmueang* [Political Theater] (Bangkok: Publishing Cooperative, 1948); Free Press (pseud., Wichai Prasangsit), *Nak kanmueang sam kok* [Politicians of the Three Kingdoms] (Bangkok: Sahakit, 1950); Kukrit Pramoj, *Four Reigns*, trans. Tulachandra (Chiang Mai, Thailand: Silkworm Books, 1999); and Chai-Anan Samudvanija, Setthapon Khusripitak and Sawaeng Rattanamongkholmas, eds. *Sat kanmueang* [Political Animals] (Bangkok: Thai Watana Panich, 1971).

9. Matthew Phillips, *Thailand in the Cold War* (Abingdon, Oxon: Routledge, 2016), 1–2.

10. Fred W. Riggs, *Thailand: The Modernization of a Bureaucratic Polity* (Honolulu: East-West Center Press, 1966), 148–65; 180–82.

11. Benedict R. O'G. Anderson, "Studies of the Thai State, the State of Thai Studies," in *Exploration and Irony in Studies of Siam over Forty Years* (Ithaca, NY: Cornell University Southeast Asia Program Publications, 2014), 39.

12. Nakharin Mektrairat, *Khwamkhit, khwamru lae amnat thang kanmueang nai kanpatiwat Siam 2475* [Thought, Knowledge and Political Power in the Siamese Revolution of 1932] (Bangkok: Fadiokan, 2003); Nakharin, *Kanpatiwat Siam pho. So. 2475* [The 1932 Siamese Revolution] (Bangkok: Fadiokan, 2010); Patrick Jory, "Republicanism in Thai History," in *A Sarong for Clio, Essays on the Intellectual and Cultural History of Thailand*, ed. Maurizio Peleggi (Ithaca, NY: Cornell Southeast Asia Program, 2013), 97–117.

13. Matthew Copeland, "Contested Nationalism and the Overthrow of the Thai Absolute Monarchy" (PhD Diss., Australian National University, 1993); Charnvit Kasetsiri, *Kanpatiwat Siam*. Also see the comparison of Charnvit's study with Nakharin's two books above, in Benjamin A. Batson, "Review," *Journal of Southeast Asian Studies* 24, no. 2 (1993): 374–77.

14. Nattapoll, *Khofanfai*; Somsak Jeamteerasakul, *Prawatisat thi phueng sang: Ruam botkhwam kiaokap karani 14 Tula lae 6 Tula* [The History Just Constructed: Collected Articles on 14 October and 6 October] (Bangkok: Samnakphim 6 Tula Ramleuk, 2001); Nattapoll Chaiching, "The Monarchy and the Royalist Movement in Modern Thai Politics, 1932–1957," in *Saying the Unsayable, Monarchy and Democracy in Thailand*, eds. Soren Ivarsson and Lotte Isager (Copenhagen: NIAS Press, 2010), 147–78.

15. Charnvit Kasetsiri and Thamrongsak Petchlert-anan, *Patiwat 2475* [1932 Revolution in Siam] (Bangkok: The Foundation for the Promotion of Social Sciences and Humanities Textbooks Project, 2001); Puli Fuwongcharoen,

"Khana kanmueang" lang kanpatiwat siam: pholawat, patthanakan lae chathakam khong rabop rai phak ["Political Parties" after the Siamese Revolution: Dynamics, Development and Fate of the No Party System] (Bangkok: Thammasat University, 2017).

16. Chatri Prakitnonthakan, *Silapa sathapatchyakam Khana Ratsadon: Sanyalak thang kanmueang nai choeng udomkan* [Art-Architecture of the People's Party: Political Symbolism of Principles] (Bangkok: Matichon, 2009); Puli Fuwongcharoen, " 'Long Live Rathathammanun!': Constitution Worship in Revolutionary Siam," *Modern Asian Studies* 52, no. 2 (March 2018): 609–44; Lawrence Chua, "The Aesthetic Citizen: Translating Modernism and Fascism in Mid Twentieth Century Thailand," in *Southeast Asia's Modern Architecture: Questions of Translation, Epistemology and Power*, eds. Jiat Hwee-Chang and Imran bin Tajrudeen (Singapore: NUS Press, 2019), 58–84; Saranyu Thepsongkhro, "Mong samneuk ponlamueang yuk khana ratsadon phan anusawari rathathammanun nai Isan" (Examining Popular Consciousness in the People's Party Age through Constitutional Monuments in the Northeast), *Silapa Wathanatham* 39, no. 8 (2018): 74–105.

17. Chatri Prakitnonthakan, "Khana Ratsadon lang rathaprahan 19 Kanya" (The People's Party after the 19 September Coup), *Aan* 4, no. 4 (2013): 18–39; Suthachai Yimprasert and Thipaphon Thantisunthon, eds. *Jak 100 pi ro. so. 130 thueng 80 pi prachathipatai* [From 100 Years Since 1912 to 80 Years of Democracy] (Bangkok: Institute of Public Policy Studies, 2012); Thanavi Chotpradit, "Revolution versus Counter-Revolution: The People's Party and the Royalist(s) in Visual Dialogue" (PhD diss., Birkbeck, University of London, 2016).

18. Pamela Pilbeam, *The Middle Classes in Europe, 1789–1914: France, Germany, Italy and Russia* (London: Macmillan, 1990), 1.

19. The king's government rewarded civil servants with ranks, which enabled many commoners to rise through the system. Ennobled ranks bestowed by the king in ascending order were: Khun, Luang, Phra, Phraya, and Chaophraya. The People's Party leaders came especially from the bureaucracy's middle tier, and hailed from the central provinces where the bureaucratic network put down the deepest roots in the latter nineteenth century. See David K. Wyatt, "Family Politics in Nineteenth Century Thailand," in *Studies in Thai History: Collected Articles* (Chiang Mai, Thailand: Silkworm Books, 1994), 106–30.

20. Harry J. Benda, "Non-Western Intelligensias [*sic*] as Political Elites," in *Continuity and Change in Southeast Asia: Collected Journal Articles of Harry J. Benda* (New Haven, CT: Yale University Southeast Asian Studies, 1972), 100.

21. Eric Hobsbawm, *The Age of Empire, 1875–1914* (New York: Pantheon Books, 1987), 79.

22. Nakharin Mektrairat, *Kanpatiwat Siam*, 75–118; Tony Day, *Fluid Iron: State Formation in Southeast Asia* (Honolulu: University of Hawai'i Press, 2002), 166–227.

23. Lynn Hunt, *Politics, Culture and Class in the French Revolution* (Berkeley: The University of California, 1984), 11–13; 180–81; 187–88; 214.

24. See, for example, Narit Charatchanyawong, "Anuson ngansop samachik Khana Ratsadon" [Funeral Volumes of the People's Party Members], *Silapa Wathanatham* 38, no. 8 (2017): 70–113.

25. Raymond Williams, *Keywords: A Vocabulary of Culture and Society*, rev. ed. (New York: Oxford University Press, 1983), 152.

26. Thawatt Mokarapong, *History of the Thai Revolution: A Study in Political Behaviour* (Bangkok: Chalermnit, 1972).

27. Williams, *Keywords*, 154.

28. Antonio Gramsci, "Notes on Italian History," in *Selections from the Prison Notebooks*, eds. Quinton Hoare and Geoffrey Nowell-Smith (New York: International Publishers, 1972), 55–60. Gramsci's hegemony is explained in Perry Anderson, "The Antinomies of Antonio Gramsci," *New Left Review* 100 (1976): 3–78.

Gramsci's ideas have been applied all over the world to understand modern politics, but there are particularly intriguing parallels between his Italy and Siam that make Gramsci's insights especially useful here. Both modern states emerged in the late nineteenth century via an internal or "passive" revolution directed from above that allowed the state bureaucracy to partially colonize society by bringing in new social groups to state service. In both Siam and Italy as a result class interests did not mature into national interests via political parties. Instead politics featured a stunted "transformism," whereby elements in the state in effect became the dominant political party but without reaching a stable control. See Gramsci, "Notes on Politics," in *Selections from the Prison Notebooks*, 227–28. The Thai comparison to Italy is made in John Girling, "Thailand in Gramscian Perspective," *Pacific Affairs* 57, no. 3 (1984), especially 396–97.

29. The paradox, within the contexts of more recent Thai history, is explained by Michael Kelly Connors, *Democracy and National Identity in Thailand* (Copenhagen: NIAS Press, 2007).

30. Wasana Wongsurawat, *The Crown and the Capitalists: The Ethnic Chinese and the Founding of the Thai Nation* (Seattle: University of Washington Press, 2019), 24–33; 140–41.

31. Marc Bloch, *The Historian's Craft*, trans. Peter Putnam (New York: Vintage Books, 1953), 59.

32. Tamara Loos, *Subject Siam: Family, Law and Colonial Modernity in Thailand* (Ithaca, NY: Cornell University Press, 2006), 110.

33. Karl Marx, "The German Ideology, Part I," in *The Marx-Engels Reader*, 2nd ed., ed. Robert C. Tucker (New York: W. W. Norton, 1972), 173.

34. Gramsci, "State and Civil Society," in *Selections from the Prison Notebooks*, 263.

Chapter One

1. Sompop Manarungsan, "The Rice Economy of Thailand in the 1930s Depression," in *Weathering the Storm: The Economies of Southeast Asia in the 1930s Depression*, eds. Peter Boomgaard and Ian Brown (Singapore: ISEAS, 2000), 189–97.

2. Nai Honhuay (pseud. Silapachai Chanchalerm), *Thahan rua patiwat* [The Navy in the Revolution] (Bangkok: Matichon, [1947]) 2012, 23.

3. Thamrongsak Petchlert-anan, *2475 lae nueng pi lang kanpatiwat* [1932 and One Year after the Revolution], in Charnvit and Thamrongsak, *Patiwat 2475*, 148–50.

4. Phao Sriyanon, "Hetkan kon kanplianpleng kanpokhrong lae kanching amnat rawang phu kokan" [Events before the Change of Government and the Struggle for Power among the Promoters], in Samakhom Nakkhao haeng Prathet Thai, comp. *Bueangraek prachathipatai: Banthuek khwamsongjam khong phu yu nai hetkan samai pho. so. 2475–2500* [Democracy's First Phase: Record of the Memories of Those Involved in the Events of 1932–1957] (Bangkok: Samakhom Nakkhao haeng Prathet Thai, 2007), 150; "The Curse that Haunted Bangkok 150 Years—Until Now?" *Khaosod*, April 21, 2017.

5. Yasukichi Yatabe, *Banthuek khong thut Yipun hen hetkan patiwat 2475, kanpatiwat lae kanplianpleng nai Prathet Siam* [Account of the Japanese Ambassador in Siam who saw the 1932 Revolution, Revolution and Change in Siam], trans. Eiji Murashima and Nakharin Mektrairat (Bangkok: Matichon, 2007), 25.

6. Thamronsak Petchlert-anan, *2475 lae nueng pi lang*, 153.

7. Murashima, "Democracy and Political Parties in Thailand"; Nakharin, *Kanpatiwat Siam*.

8. Pridi Banomyong, "Some Aspects of the Establishment of the People's Party and Democracy," in *Pridi by Pridi: Selected Writings on Life, Politics, Economy*, trans. Chris Baker and Pasuk Phongpaichit (Chiang Mai, Thailand: Silkworm Books, 2000), 124; Thamrongsak, *2475 lae nueng pi lang*, 105.

9. "Introduction," "The Banomyong Family" and "Excerpts from: Some Experiences and Opinions of Senior Statesman Pridi Banomyong (1981)," in *Pridi by Pridi*, 3, 12–13, 20–21.

10. Charnvit Kasetsiri, Thamrongsak Petchlert-anan, and Vigal Phongpanitanon, eds., *Jomphol pho. Phibun Songkhram kap kanmueang Thai samai mai* [Field Marshal Phibunsongkhram and Modern Thai Politics] (Bangkok: The Foundation for the Promotion of Social Sciences and Humanities Textbooks Project, 2001), 19–20.

11. Kulap Saipradit, *Bueanglang kanpatiwat 2475* [Behind the 1932 Revolution] (Bangkok: Mingmit, [1941] 2000), 29–33.

12. Prayun Phamonmontri, *Chiwit 5 phaendin* [Life over Five Reigns] (Bangkok: Bannakit, 1975), 134.

13. Thamgrongsak, *2475 lae nueng pi lang*, 112–13.

14. Thawatt, *History*, 28.

15. Phao, "Hetkan kon kanplianpleng kanpokhrong," 194.

16. Phraya Song Suradet, "The Revolution of June 24, 1932," in *Thai Politics: Extracts and Documents 1932–1957*, ed. and trans. Thak Chaloemtiarana (Bangkok: The Social Science Association of Thailand, 1978), 78–86.

17. Thawatt, *History*, 35.

18. "What Happened inside the Regency Council," in *Pridi by Pridi*, 218.

19. Prasert Patthamasukhon, *Rathasapha Thai nai rop sisipsong pi (2475–2517)* [The Thai Parliament over 42 Years (1932–1974)] (Bangkok: Munithi Thanakhan Krungthep, 1983), 9.

20. Yasukichi, *Banthuek khong thut Yipun*, 29.

21. Thamrongsak, *2475 lae nueng pi lang*, 154–55.

22. Phao, "Hetkan kon kanplianpleng kanpokhrong," 195–99.

23. "Announcement of the People's Party No. 1," in *Pridi by Pridi*, 70–72.

24. "Announcement of the People's Party," 72.

25. "Announcement of the People's Party," 72.

26. "Announcement of the People's Party," 72.

27. Hereafter he will be referenced as Prince Boriphat.

28. Thamrongsak, *2475 lae nueng pi lang*, 157.

29. Thamrongsak, *2475 lae nueng pi lang*, 160–63.

30. Thamrongsak, 166.

31. English language letter from King Prajadhipok to Prince Chula, August 1932, in Prince Chula Chakrabongse, *Lords of Life* (London: Alvin Redman, 1960), 312.

32. King Prajadhipok letter in Chula Chakrabongse, *Lords of Life*, 312.

33. "Provisional Constitution of the Kingdom of Siam, 1932," in *Pridi by Pridi*, 73–79.

34. Prasert, *Rathasapha Thai*, 17, 20–22.

35. "Some Aspects of the Establishment of the People's Party," in *Pridi by Pridi*, 124–25.

36. Prince Wan, "The Future of Siam," *Bangkok Times*, February 27, 1933.

37. Sombat Chandrawong, *Phasa thang kanmueang: Pattanakan khong naeo athibai kanmueang lae sap kanmueang nai ngankhian praphet sarakhadi thang kanmueang khong Thai, pho. so. 2475–2525* [Political language: Development of Political Explanations and Vocabulary in Thai Political Documents, 1932–1982] (Bangkok: Thai Khadi Institute, 1990), 40–42.

38. The consolidation of an absolutist, centralizing state in the decades after the Bowring Treaty is the best studied topic in Thai history. See the vivid summary of the late nineteenth and early twentieth centuries in B. J. Terwiel, *Thailand's Political History* (Bangkok: River Books, 2011), 146–229.

39. On education see David K. Wyatt, *The Politics of Reform: Education in the Reign of King Chulalongkorn* (New Haven, CT: Yale University Press, 1969); on upcountry administration, Tej Bunnag, Tej Bunnag, *Prince Damrong and the Provincial Administration of Thailand, 1892-1915* (Oxford: Oxford University, 1976); on national territorial modernization, Thongchai Winichakul, *Siam Mapped* (Hawaii: University of Hawai'i Press, 1994); on the military, Noel Alfred Battye, "The Military, Government and Society in Siam, 1868-1910: Politics and Military Reform during the Reign of King Chulalongkorn" (PhD diss., Cornell University, 1974); on law, Loos, *Subject Siam*; on the economy, Chaiyan Rajchagool, *The Rise and Fall of the Thai Absolute Monarchy* (Bangkok: White Lotus, 1994); on the civil service, Kullada Kesbunchoo Mead, *The Rise and Decline of Thai Absolutism* (London: RoutledgeCurzon, 2004).

40. Eiji Murashima, "The Origin of Modern Official State Ideology in Thailand," *Journal of Southeast Asian Studies* 19, no. 1 (1988): 80–96.

41. In Gray's fine analysis, Kings Mongkut and Chulalongkorn reasonably skillfully handled the antinomy problem because the modern economy was undeveloped. With the socioeconomic challenges of the twentieth century, however, Kings Vajiravudh and Prajadhipok faced much more difficult challenges. With his inability to handle the Great Depression, the "antinomy issue hit Prajadhipok full force." Christine Gray, "Thailand: The Soteriological State in the 1970s" (PhD diss., University of Chicago, 1986), 8–14; 255–66; 276–80; 312–19; 329–37.

42. Kullada, *The Rise and Decline of Thai Absolutism*, 104.

43. UK Foreign Office document, quoted in Kullada, 104.

44. "Banmueang khong rao" [Our Homeland], *Sayam Riwiw*, September 11, 1927, in Copeland, "Contested Nationalism," 152.

45. Anderson, "Studies of the Thai State," 39.

46. Kullada, *The Rise and Decline of Thai Absolutism*, 111–25.

47. For the geopolitics of Siamese territorial claims see Thongchai, *Siam Mapped* and Shane Strate, *The Lost Territories: Thailand's History of National Humiliation* (Honolulu: University of Hawai'i Press, 2015).

48. Tej Bunnag, *Kabot Ro. So. 121* [The Revolts of 1902] (Bangkok: The Foundation for the Promotion of Social Sciences and Humanities Textbooks Project, 2008).

49. Thamsook Numnonda, *Yang Terk runraek: Kabot ro. so. 130* [The First Generation of Young Turks: The 1912 Revolt] (Bangkok: Saitharn Publication House, 2002).

50. Yasukichi, *Banthuek khong thut Yipun*, 14–15.

51. Phraya Song Suradet, "Kanpatiwat 24 Mi.y. 75 jak banthuek Phraya Song Suradet" [The Revolution of 24 June 1932, from the Memoirs of Phraya Song Suradet], in *Bueangraek prachathipatai*, vol. 1, 117.

52. Kulap, *Bueanglang kanpatiwat*, 55.

53. *Sri Krung*, July 12, 1932.

54. I have adapted Nakharin's social scheme from his *Kanpatiwat Siam*, 3–200, esp. 14–28.

55. Sorasak Ngamcachonkulkid, *Free Thai: The New History of the Seri Thai Movement* (Bangkok: Chulalongkorn University, 2010); 11; 27–95; and in more detail Sorasak Ngamcachonkulkid, "The Seri Thai Movement: The First Alliance against Military Authoritarianism in Modern Thai History" (PhD diss., University of Wisconsin-Madison, 2005).

56. Nakharin, *Kanpatiwat Siam*, 82, 76.

57. Ministry of Finance, Department of General Statistics, *Statistical Year Book of the Kingdom of Siam*, no. 16, 1930–1931, 52. Hereafter, this series will be abbreviated to SYB, followed by the volume number, year and relevant pages.

58. Ministry of Finance, *Statistical Year Book of the Kingdom of Siam*, 58. SYB, no. 16 (1930–1931): 52.

59. Khana Thamngan Prawat Kanphim nai Prathet Thai, *Sayamphimphakan: Prawatisat kanphim nai Prathet Thai* [Sayamphimphakan: The History of Publishing in Thailand] (Bangkok: Matichon, 2006), 90–91.

60. Khana Thamngan Prawat Kanphim, *Sayamphimphakan*, 484–99. The figure includes all types of print. Around twenty-five daily newspapers appeared after 1932. Supaphan Bunsa-at, *Prawat nangsuephim nai Prathet Thai* [History of the Newspaper in Thailand] (Bangkok: Bhannakij Trading, 1974), 79–83.

61. Marc Bloch, *Strange Defeat, a Statement of Evidence Written in 1940*, Gerard Hopkins, trans. (New York: W. W. Norton), 162–63.

62. Thamsook Numnonda, *Lakhon kanmueang: 24 Mithuna 2475* [Political Theater: 24 June 1932] (Bangkok: Samakhom Prawatisat), 44–49; Thamrongsak, *2475 lae nueng pi lang*, 240–71.

63. Yasukichi, *Banthuek khong thut Yipun*, 42–44.

64. Suphot Dantrakun and Pricha Suwannathat, *Khotheching thang prawatisat lae phraratchabanyat thammanun kanpokhrong phaendin Siam chua khrao chabap 27 Mithunayon 2475* [Real Facts about History and the Temporary Siamese Constitution of 27 June 1932] (Bangkok: Sathaban Pridi Banomyong, 2007).

65. "Provisional Constitution of the Kingdom of Siam, 1932," in *Pridi by Pridi*, 73. I have slightly changed the translation.

66. *Nawikasat*, August 1932, quoted in Thamrongsak, *2475 lae nueng pi lang*, 290.

67. Thamrongsak, 296–97.

68. Thamrongsak, 200–10; Nattapoll, "Khwamchop duai rabawp," especially 71–74. As Nattapoll explains, the supposed compatibility between Thai and British customary kingships was highly selective.

69. Mano, quoted in Thamrongsak, *2475 lae nueng pi lang*, 205.

70. See Nattapoll, "Khwamchop duai rabawp," 3–63.

71. Thamrongsak, *2475 lae nueng pi lang*, 208.

72. "Constitution of the Kingdom of Siam B.E. 2475," in Thak, *Thai Politics*, 96.

73. Charnvit Kasetsiri, *Prawat kanmueang Thai Siam pho. so. 2475–2500* [A Political History of Thailand-Siam 1932–1957] (Bangkok: The Foundation for the Promotion of Social Sciences and Humanities Textbooks Project, 2008), 124–28. The government changed formal English translations of political offices and groups over the decade. Later the authorities fixed *khana rathamontri* as "Council of Ministers," *nayok rathamontri* as "President of the Council," and *rathamontri* as a "Minister of State." *Bangkok Times*, "New Translation of Familiar Terms," January 2, 1937. Studies of the period use a confusing welter of terms. For clarity and simplicity, throughout this book I will use cabinet or state council for the *khana rathamontri*, premier for *nayok rathamontri*, and minister for *rathamontri*. The *sapha phuthen ratsadon* is similarly translated in different ways, for example "House of the People's Representatives," or "Assembly of the People's Representatives." I will term it the national assembly, house or parliament, and its members *assemblymen* or *representatives*. *Assemblymen* is specifically chosen since there were no women in the assembly until after the People's Party period ended.

74. Scot Barmé, *Luang Wichit Wathakan and the Creation of a Thai Identity* (Singapore: ISEAS, 1993), 71.

75. NA, SR.0201.16/28, letter to government, August 26, 1932.

76. NA, SR.0201.16/23, letter to government, September 23, 1932.

77. "Place of the People's Society," *Bangkok Times*, July 2, 1932.

78. "The New Siam, Gifts by the King," *Bangkok Times*, June 30, 1932.

79. Draft regulations on the People's Party Association, in NA, S.B.3.10/1, *Samakhom Khana Ratsadon pho. so. 2475* (February 1933-June 1935).

80. Puli, *Khana kanmueang*, 64.

81. NA, SB.3.10/1, People's Party Association Charter, June 1935; "Kho-bangkhap samoson Khana Ratsadon," April 29, 1934.

82. "The New Society," *Bangkok Times*, August 25, 1932.

83. Puli, *Khana kanmueang*, 47–48.

84. Puli, 71–81.

85. Thamrongsak, *2475 lae nueng pi lang*, 300.

86. Puli, *Khana kanmueang*, 66–69.

87. Puli, *Khana kanmueang*, 81–86.

88. Puli, 86.

89. *Bangkok Daily Mail*, July 3, 1932, quoted in Eiji Murashima, "Democracy and the Development of Political Parties in Thailand 1932–1945," in Murashima, Nakharin Mektrairat and Somkiat Wanthana, *The Making of Modern Thai Political Parties* (Tokyo: Institute of Developing Economies, 1991), 14.

90. Barmé, *Luang Wichit Wathakan*, 75, 78.

91. Barmé, 40.

92. Barmé, 42–43.

93. NA, SR.0201/28; Nakharin, *Kanpatiwat Siam*, 328; Copeland, "Contested Nationalism," 207–11.

94. Phraya Thonawanikamontri, quoted in Nakharin, *Kanpatiwat Siam*, 28.

95. Sorasak Ngamcachonkulkid, *Free Thai: The New History of the Seri Thai Movement* (Bangkok: Institute of Asian Studies, Chulalongkorn University, 2010), 60–61.

96. Puli, *Khana kanmueang*, 115.

97. Nakharin, *Kanpatiwat Siam*, 340.

98. Puli, *Khana kanmueang*, 142–44.

99. Withet Korani, *Khwampenma haeng rabawp prachathipatai khong Thai* [The Origins of the Thai Democratic Regime] (Bangkok: Panfa Phitya, 1968), 871; Suphot Dantrakun, "Pu Nguan kap prawatisat Thai yuk mai" [Grandfather Nguan and the Modern History of Thailand], in *Anuson ngan phraratchathan phloengsop Nai Sanguan Tularaks* (Royal Cremation Volume for Sanguan Tularaks) (Bangkok, 1995), 201–2.

100. *Sajjang*, January 25, 1933, quoted in Murashima, "Democracy and the Development of Political Parties," 16.

101. Ferrara, *The Political Development of Modern Thailand* (Cambridge, UK: Cambridge University Press, 2015), 92.

102. The letter is central to his mythology. See Somsak Jeamteerasakul and Prajak Kongkirati, "Phra ratchahatalekha salarat R. 7: Chiwaprawat khong ekkasan chabap nung [The Seventh King's Abdication Letter: Biography of a Document], in Somsak, *Prawatisat thi phueng sang*, 20–30; Nakharin Mektrairat, *Karani ro. 7 song sala ratchasombat* [The Case of the Seventh King's Abdication] (Bangkok: Kobfai Publishing Project, 2007).

103. Puli, *Khana kanmueang*, 147.

104. In 1926, the king commissioned the government adviser Francis Sayre and Phraya Sriwisanwaja, a senior government official, to present government reform plans. Their outline would have centralized power in the king but added some advisory bodies comprised of elite royals and aristocrats. Hardly a democratic revolution, Prajadhipok endorsed their opinions and wrote in a letter to Sayre: "Is this country ready to have some sort of representative Government? . . . My personal opinion is an emphatic NO." King Prajadhipok, "The Problems of Siam," Memorandum to Dr. Sayre, July 23, 1926, in *Siam's Political Future: Documents from the End of the Absolute Monarchy,* comp. and ed. Benjamin A. Batson (Ithaca, NY: Cornell University Southeast Asia Program, 1974), 15.

105. Nattapoll, "Khwam patiwat," 33–40.

106. Murashima, "Democracy and the Development of Political Parties," 17–18.

107. Puli, *Khana kanmueang*, 152.

108. Puli, 159.

109. Puli, 162–68.

110. Chula Chakrabongse, *Lords of Life*, 319.

111. Nattapoll Chaiching, *Kabot Bowondet: Bueangraek patipaks patiwat Siam 2475* [The Bowondet Rebellion: The First Counterrevolution against 1932] (Bangkok: Matichon, 2016), 34.

112. Prajadhipok, letter of March 1, 1933 to Prince Chirasak Suphrapat, in Nattapoll, "Khwam patiwat," 18.

113. The coup did not show, as one might assume, unanimity among the People's Party that the revolution must be saved from its enemies. Mano's attack on the People's Party and the constitutional system was a genuine motivation. But Mano's end also resulted from a tangled web of relations among and between the People's Party military leadership and Mano, with Mano's support sought from some of the People's Party leaders for their own ends. Above all, this complicated series of maneuvers pitted one senior military figure, Song Suradet, against his junior, Phibun Songkhram, for control of the army. In the end, Phibun's star rose within the government and Song essentially left politics. See Thamrongsak, *2475 lae nueng pi lang*, 399–450; Momchao Suphasawatwongsanit Sawatiwat, *1 satawat Suphasawat* [One Century of Suphasawat] (Bangkok: Suphasawat Family, 2000), 98–102.

114. Barmé, *Luang Wichit Wathakan*, 83.

115. Chongkon Krairoek, *Yu yang suea: Banthuek chiwit kantosu thang kanmueang yuk bukboek pho. so. 2500* [Live like a Tiger: Records of a Life of Political Struggle in Its First Phase, 1957] (Chiang Mai, Thailand: The Knowledge Center, [1969] 2003), 88–89.

116. Chaiwat Yonpiam, *Fanrai khong Mueang Thai* [Thailand's Nightmare] (Bangkok: Chaophraya, 1983), 11–13.

117. The prince studied artillery and engineering in Britain in the fifth reign and then became military commander in Nakhon Rajasima. He left the military to become Thai plenipotentiary in Europe at the end of Chulalongkorn's reign. He returned to the army under Chulalongkorn's son Vajiravudh, and then in the seventh reign Bowondet became the minister of war. He resigned from the army in the late 1920s when the king vetoed his promotion and salary increase scheme during the Great Depression. Nakharin, *Kanpatiwat Siam*, 375–76.

118. Nattapoll, *Kabot Bowondet*, 69.

119. Suphasawatwongsanit, *1 Satawat Suphasawat*, 103.

120. See especially Nattapoll, *Kabot Bowondet* and Chaiwat, *Fanrai*.

121. NA, SR.0201.1/1, Srisitthi to Phahon, October 11, 1933.

122. Nattapoll, *Kabot Bowondet*, 82–85.

123. NA, SR.0201.1/1, Bowondet to Phahon, October 13, 1933.

124. Barmé, *Luang Wichit Wathakan*, 91–92.

125. NA, SR.0201.1/2, "The Situation," *Bangkok Times*, October 15, 1933. *The Times* of London found the government's initial news blitz to be "too full of contradictions, naïve explanations and possible suppressions of the truth to be entirely successful," "The Fighting in Siam," November 17, 1933, NA, SR.0201.1/7.

126. One US dollar in 1933 equaled about 2.68 baht at the Treasury par rate. The baht's dollar value fluctuated over the decade, with a low of 2.81 baht

in 1932, and a high of 2.20 baht in 1936. James C. Ingram, *Economic Change in Thailand, 1850-1970* (Stanford, CA: Stanford University Press, 1971), 336-37.

127. "The Revolt, 10,000 Ticals Reward Offered," *Bangkok Times*, October 13, 1933.

128. NA, SR.0201.1/7, manager of Bamrungnukulakit printing to cabinet secretary, November 17, 1933; *Thai Mai* newspaper editor to cabinet secretary, November 22, 1933; *Prachachat* newspaper editor Kulap Saipradit to cabinet secretary, November 22, 1933.

129. "The Situation, Further Fighting Outside Bangkok," *Bangkok Times*, October 16, 1933.

130. Nattapoll, *Kabot Bowondet*, 115-16.

131. Nattapoll, 146.

132. Nattapoll, *Kabot Bowondet*, 211-21.

133. Nakharin, *Kanpatiwat Siam*, 389.

134. Nattapoll, *Kabot Bowondet*, 50.

135. Nakharin, *Kanpatiwat Siam*, 395.

136. Nattapoll, *Kabot Bowondet*, 125.

137. NA, SR.0201.1.3/9.

138. "The Situation," *Bangkok Times*, November 13, 1933.

139. "The Situation," *Bangkok Times*, October 18, 1933.

140. "The Situation," *Bangkok Times*, October 17, 1933.

141. "The Situation," *Bangkok Times*, October 18, 1933.

142. NA, SR. 0201.1.3/4 (folder one of two), letter from Thai Labour Association to premier Phahon, December 25, 1933. On labor support for the government during Bowondet more broadly, Nattapoll, *Kabot Bowondet*, 178-88.

143. NA, SR.0201.1.3/8, cabinet secretary to chief warrant officer Phriksuwan, October 18, 1933.

144. NA, SR.0201.1.3/8, Uttaradit provincial group to cabinet secretary, October 24, 1933; premier to Trang provincial group, October 31, 1933.

145. NA, SR.0201.1/7, Letters to government, October 16, 1933 and October 19, 1933.

146. NA, SR.0201.1.3/8, Run Kriang to Phahon, November 10, 1933.

147. In addition to the above, see the diverse offers in NA, SR.0201.1.3/9.

148. Nattapoll, *Kabot Bowondet*, 275-77.

149. See for example, NA, SR.0201.25/50, Bunchuay Sompong to the Promoters, June 28, 1932. Bunchuay, a Bangkok teacher advised that city schools were heavily staffed by royalists, and singled out Ratchinee school for girls and Wachirawut boys school as particular sites of widespread anti-People's Party sentiment. Bunchuay appended a list of names of new regime supporters who could help spread the People's Party message. So too another civilian wrote to the government in amazement that an ultraroyalist and wealthy Ayuthaya resident openly expressed his contempt for the new regime, and forbade his employees at the large ferry pier on the Chaophraya River there for having a day off on new

order holidays. See NA, SR.0201.16/27, letter to People's Party, December 1932. Others warned of black magic being used against the People's Party, and assassination plots against the leading members. On the former, see NA, SR.0201.10/14, Yun Seniwong na Ayuthaya to People's Party, January 1933; on the latter NA, SR.0201.16/26, Som Saiyawibul to People's Party, July 11, 1932.

150. "Anusawari prap kabot Bowondet hai kueap pi khana thi chue "Bowondet-Srisitthi Songkhram phlo pen teuk nai hong tho.bo.," *Prachathai*, October 19, 2019.

151. Pho. tho. Luang Ronasit Phichai, *Siang withayu* [Radio Sound] (Bangkok: Thai Kasem, 1934); Nattapoll, *Kabot Bowondet*, 248.

152. Nattapoll, *Kabot Bowondet* 247. In the end, only a single volume appeared, which described the sequence of events and collected government documents.

153. Nakharin, *Kanpatiwat Siam*, 387.

154. Murashima, "Democracy and Political Parties," 26–28.

155. "The Situation," *Bangkok Times*, October 31, 1933.

156. Phuthorn Phumadhon, "Kansueksa San Piset (Pho. So. 2476, 2478, 2481)" [A Study of the Special Courts of 1933, 1935 and 1938] (master's thesis, Chulalongkorn University, 1977), 29–30.

157. Charnvit, *Prawat kanmueang*, 159–60.

158. *Bangkok Times*, October 30, November 12 and 23, 1933.

159. Luen Saraphaiwanich, *Fanching khong khappajao* [My Real Dream] (Bangkok: Saraphai, 1969), 138; Virginia Thompson, *Thailand: The New Siam* (New York: Paragon Books Reprint, [1941] 1967), 71.

160. Luen Saraphaiwanich, *Fanrai*, 16–17.

161. Luen, *Fanrai*, 44–47. The story of when the king took flight, the successful Siamese version of a flight to Varennes, is told by those on the journey. See, for example, Punpisamai Disakul, *Sing thi khappajao phop hen: Prawatisat plianpleng kanpokhrong 2475* [The Things I Have Seen: History of the Change of Rule 1932] (Bangkok: Matichon, 2008), 136–49.

162. Luen, *Fanrai*, 95–102.

163. Luen, 106–13.

164. Luen, 228–31.

165. NA, SR.0201.15/12, *Khadikhwam tang tang* (Various cases, Choti Kumphan and others).

166. NA, SR.0201.8/14, *Suan bukkhon Chao Thai* (Thai People).

167. English transliterations of his surname vary. The *Bangkok Times* used below, for example, spelled his name Devahastin.

168. Stefan Hell, *Siam and World War I: An International History* (Bangkok: River Books, 2017), 145–55.

169. Sorasak, *Free Thai*, 60.

170. NA, SR.0201.15/12.

171. NA, SR.0201.15/16, Phraya Thephasadin na Ayutthaya case.

172. The Sinhalese William Alfred G. Tilleke emigrated to Siam in 1890 from Ceylon, and became acting attorney general for Chulalongkorn's government during the period of administrative reforms. In 1906, the Briton Ralph Gibbins arrived in Siam and joined with Tilleke to establish the firm. Arnold Wright and Oliver T. Breakspear, *Twentieth Century Impressions of Siam* (London: Lloyd's Greater Britain Publishing, 1908), 96; John Hoskin, *Wise Counsel: A History of Tilleke & Gibbins, Thailand's Oldest Law Firm* (Bangkok: Tilleke & Gibbins International, 2010).

173. "The Case against Phya Devahastin," *Bangkok Times*, October 10, 1934; NA, SR.0201.15/12.

174. "Phya Devahastin States his Case," *Bangkok Times*, September 10, 1934.

175. "Phya Devahastin," *Bangkok Times*, December 26, 1934.

176. "Phya Devahastin, Details of New Judgment," *Bangkok Times*, January 31, 1935.

177. "Phya Devahastin and the Police," *Bangkok Times*, November 3, 1937.

178. Thawatt, *History of the Thai Revolution*, 223.

179. Krom khosanakan, *Thalaengkan rueang phrabatsomdet phraparamin maha Prajadhipok Phrapokklao chaoyuha songsala ratchasombat* [Official Report on King Prajadhipok's Abdication] (Bangkok, 1935).

180. "What Happened Inside the Regency Council," in *Pridi by Pridi*, 210–17. Ananda reached his majority in September 1945 at his twentieth birthday. Aside from considering the internal relations of the extended royal family, Pridi said the cabinet chose to propose Ananda to the assembly since Ananda's father "conducted himself as a democrat," 215.

181. Nai Honhuay (pseud. Silapachai Chanchalerm), *Kabot nai sip 2478* [The 1935 Non-commissioned Officers' Revolt] (Bangkok: Matichon, 2000), 55. Phibun's rise, Song's fall, and intra-army conflict are explained in Thamrongsak, *2475 lae nueng pi lang*, 271–78.

182. "That Conspiracy on the Part of Non-coms," *Bangkok Times*, September 9, 1935.

183. Nai Honhuay, *Kabot nai sip*, 64, 80–81.

184. "Attempted Assassination of Minister of Defence," *Bangkok Times*, February 26, 1935.

185. Judith Stowe, *Siam becomes Thailand, a Story of Intrigue* (Honolulu: University of Hawai'i Press, 1991), 105–6.

186. Krom khosanakan, *Khamphiphaksa san piset phutthasakarat 2482 rueang kabot* [Verdict of the 1939 Special Court on Rebellion].

187. Phraya Thephasadin, "Khappajao mai dai pen kabot" (I did not foment rebellion), in *Bueangraek prachathipatai*, vol. 1, 280.

188. Phraya Thephasadin, 281–85.

189. Krom khosanakan, *Khamphiphaksa*, 7–8.

190. Krom khosanakan, 11 and 77–81.

191. Phraya Thephasadin, "Khappajao mai dai pen kabot," 285.

192. Jo. So., "Khappajao hen kanyingphao" [I Saw the Shooting], in *Bueang-raek prachathipatai, vol. 1*, 261–304.

193. Nai Chantana, *Banthuek jomphol*, 32–34.

194. Nimitmongkol Navarat, "A Victim of Two Political Purges," in Nimit-mongkol, *The Dreams of an Idealist*, trans. David Smyth (Chiang Mai, Thailand: Silkworm Books, 2009), 210–12.

195. Nimitmongkol, 216–17.

196. Nimitmongkol, 225–26.

197. Nimitmongkol, 245.

198. Nimitmongkol, 243–55.

199. Nimitmongkol, 264.

200. Nimitmongkol, 260–61.

201. Nimitmongkol, 268.

202. Murashima, "Democracy and the Development of Political Parties," 52; Suphasawatwongsanit, *1 satawat Suphasawat*, 83.

203. Gramsci, "The Modern Prince," in *Selections from the Prison Notebooks*, 169–70.

204. Albert Camus, *The Rebel, An Essay on Man in Revolt*, trans. Anthony Bower (New York: Vintage Books, 1956), 118.

205. Terwiel, *Thailand's Political History*, 268; Charnvit et al., *Jomphol pho. Phibun Songkhram*, 243.

Chapter Two

1. Batson, *The End of the Absolute Monarchy*, 239. Prince Boriphat report-edly had 300 million baht—roughly 112 million dollars—stashed away; his giving away of his residence Bangkhunphrom Palace to the government before leaving for exile in the Dutch East Indies contributed to suspicion that the luxurious palace was a drop in his financial bucket. Prince Kamphaengphet, another royal councillor to King Prajadhipok, possessed 167 million, 100 million of which he deposited in Switzerland. *Lak Mueang*, July 11, 1932, related in Thamrongsak, *2475 lae nueng pi lang*, 309–10.

2. SYB, no. 20 (1938–1939): 283; 294; 297.

3. NA, SR.0201.25/62, Robert Silpin to government, September 9, 1932. The writer opined that "seeing as how much of Siam's wealth is tied up in private hands" (i.e., with royals and the entitled elite), the government should set up a "death" (written in English) tax on those with 50,000 baht or more in assets. The new regime did institute an inheritance tax in 1935, but the sums formed a tiny contribution to national income. SYB, 1938–1939, no. 20: 278.

4. Nakharin, *Kanpatiwat Siam*, 46.

5. For example, "The Assembly, the Budget Again," *Bangkok Times*, Febru-ary 14, 1936. Thong-in Phuriphat on that occasion argued that just over a tenth

of the budget was for common people; much of the rest was for the civil service and the military.

6. "The University Salary Rates," *Bangkok Times*, November 28, 1935.

7. NA, SR.0201.25/38, Anonymous letter, July 11, 1932. He argued that the defense ministry above all paid far too much to senior officers.

8. NA, SR.0201.25/14, Anonymous letter, September 11, 1932.

9. NA, SR.0201.25/13, Chamras's letter, September 3, 1932.

10. Porphant Ouyyanont, "Bangkok's Population and the Ministry of the Capital in Early 20th Century Thai History," *Journal of Southeast Asian Studies* 35, no. 2 (1997): 247–49.

11. SYB, 1933–1935, no. 18: 9; 88.

12. Porphant Ouyyanont, *A Regional Economic History of Thailand* (Singapore: ISEAS, 2017), 40.

13. Porphant, 41.

14. G. William Skinner, *Chinese Society in Thailand: An Analytical History* (Ithaca, NY: Cornell University Press, 1957), 91–125.

15. Quoted in Skinner, *Chinese Society in Thailand*, 88.

16. Skinner, *Chinese Society in Thailand*, 178.

17. Skinner, *Chinese Society in Thailand*, 165–71.

18. Wasana Wongsurawat, "Thailand and the Xinhai Revolution: Expectation, Reality and Inspiration," in *Sun Yat-Sen, Nanyang and the 1911 Revolution*, eds. Lee Lai To and Lee Hock Guan (Singapore: ISEAS, 2011), 130–47.

19. Eiji Murashima, *Kanmueang Jin Siam: Kankhlueanwai thang kanmueang khong chao Jin phontale nai Prathet Thai kho. So. 1928–1941* [Chinese Politics in Siam: The Political Movement of the Overseas Chinese in Thailand, 1928–1941], trans. and ed. Worasak Mahathanobol (Bangkok: Asian Studies Institute, Chulalongkorn University, 1996), 1–23; Khana Thamngan Prawat Kanphim, *Sayamphimphakan*, 93–95; 116–17.

20. Skinner, *Chinese Society in Thailand*, 157–58. For the changes in Chinese business and capitalists in the period, see Suehiro Akira, *Capital Accumulation in Thailand, 1855–1985* (Chiang Mai, Thailand: Silkworm Books, 1996), 71–90.

21. Skinner, *Chinese Society in Thailand*, 183. The numbers of immigrants dropped quickly in the early 1930s because of the worsening economy, and between 1931 and the end of the Pacific War around 80 percent of new arrivals had returned to China. Skinner, 176.

22. Skinner, *Chinese Society in Thailand*, 198–204.

23. Prince Purachatra, in Batson, *The End*, 86. Prajadhipok responded that if the Chinese did not spread commerce along the lines, "maybe no one would . . ." 118.

24. Charnvit Kasetsiri, "2475 Kanpatiwat Siam" [The 1932 Siamese Revolution], in Charnvit and Thamrongsak, *Patiwat 2475*, 59–62.

25. King Prajadhipok, "Democracy in Siam," in *Siam's Political Future*, 48.

26. Batson, *The End*, 84–86.

27. Skinner, *Chinese Society*, 242.

28. Bunsong Wijarana, "Khothaeching kiaokap kabuankan raengngan Thai jak saha achiwa kammakon theung kammakon 16 nuai" [Facts about the Thai Labor Movement from the Labor Union to the Group of 16 Labor Organization] in *Prawatisat raengngan Thai* [Thai Labor History], eds. Chalong Soontravanich et al. (Bangkok: Labor Museum, 1998), 253.

29. Sirot Khlampaiboon, *Rengngan wijan jao* [Labor Criticizes the Lords] (Bangkok: Matichon, 2004), 72.

30. Kevin Hewison, "Forgotten Facts: Industrial Development, Labour and Rural Life in Thailand, 1850–1942." Unpublished research paper, 1986, 19–26.

31. Jongjairak Pokpattanakul, "Nyobai khong rathaban Thai kiaokap kammakon rawang pho. so. 2475–2499" [Thai Government Labor Policy, 1932–1956], in Chalong, *Prawatisat raengngan Thai*, 155–61.

32. David Strand, *Rickshaw Beijing: City People and Politics in the 1920s* (Berkeley: University of California, 1989), 20–64.

33. James F. Warren, *Rickshaw Coolie: A People's History of Singapore, 1880–1940* (Singapore: Oxford University Press, 1986); Tam Lang, "I Pulled a Rickshaw," in *The Light of the Capital: Three Modern Vietnamese Classics*, trans. Greg Lockhart and Monique Lockhart (Kuala Lumpur: Oxford University Press, 1996).

34. Panni Bualek, *Kuli lakrot kap prawatisat raengngan Thai* [Rickshaw Coolies and the History of Thai Labor] (Bangkok: Panthakit, 2003), 152–54, 113, 146.

35. Panni, *Kuli lakrot*, 147–51.

36. Panni, 151.

37. Panni, 154–55.

38. Panni, 156.

39. Panni, 159.

40. Virginia Thompson, *Labor Problems in Southeast Asia* (New Haven, CT: Yale University Press, 1947), 249.

41. See Nattapoll Chaiching, "Kabot ro. so. 130" [The 1912 Revolt], in Suthachai and Thipaphon, *Jak 100 pi ro. so. 130*.

42. Panni, *Kuli lakrot*, 165.

43. Panni, *Kuli lakrot*, 167.

44. Sirot, *Raengngan wijan jao*, 21.

45. Copeland, "Contested Nationalism," 71–72.

46. Sirot, *Raengngan wijan jao*, 22–23.

47. Quoted in Saichon Satyanurak, *Prawatisat rat Thai lae sangkhom Thai* [History of the Thai State and Thai Society] (Chiang Mai, Thailand: Chiang Mai University Press, 2015), 130.

48. Sirot, *Raengngan wijan jao*, 41.

49. Sirot, 41.

50. Sungsidh, *Kantosu*, 38.

51. Sungsidh, *Kantosu*, 39.

52. "Kamakan Khana Ratsadon nat pai wan thi 23," *Thai Noi*, July 18, 1932.

53. "Phra Suwaphan ja tong yai wiman laeo," *Thai Noi*, July 31, 1932.

54. Sungsidh, *Kantosu*, 141.

55. NA, (2)SR.0201.75/3, January 17, 1933 letter.

56. Ichiro Kakizaki, *Trams, Buses and Rails: The History of Urban Transport in Bangkok, 1886–2010* (Chiang Mai, Thailand: Silkworm Books, 2014), 91–94. As Ichiro explains, traffic congestion, not economic nationalism, led to the end of the SEC's concession later in the decade.

57. NA, (2)SR.0201.75/3, March 1, 1933 letter to the state council secretary.

58. Pridi, "Outline Economic Plan (1933)," in *Pridi by Pridi*, 107.

59. See King Prajadhipok's written response in *Ekkasan kanmueang-kan-pokhrong Thai pho. so. 2417-2477* [Thai Political and Administrative Documents, 1874–1934], eds. Chai-anan Samudvanija and Khattiya Kannasut (Bangkok: Khrongkan Tamra Sangkhomsat lae Manusayasat, 1975), 277–356.

60. "Minutes of a Meeting of a Committee to Consider a National Economic Policy at Paruskawan Palace, March 12, 1933," in Thak, *Thai Politics: Extracts and Documents*, 161–85.

61. Nattapoll, *Khofanfai*, 251–55.

62. "Phraboroma winitchai khong Phra Pokklao" [King Prajadhipok's Criticism of Pridi's Economic Plan], in Duen Bunnag, *Than Pridi rataburut awuso phu wangphaen settakit Thai khon raek* [Senior Statesman Pridi, First Thai Economic Planner] (Bangkok: Saitharn Publication House, 2009), 201.

63. Sirot, *Raengngan wijan jao*, 94–105. Sirot presents this fascinating episode as an example of Thawatt's working-class heroism and democratic virtue. Somsak's analysis changes the frame from Thawatt's bravery to the difficulty limiting kingly power in the constitutional era. It is not clear why Thawatt approached the assembly. The third article of the December constitution stated that the king's person was sacred and inviolable, suggesting that he was not subject to, or was above, the law. See "Constitution of the Kingdom of Siam B.E. 2475," in Thak, 98. But Thawatt may have been thinking of Pridi's temporary constitution of June 27 that had stipulated in its sixth article that the king cannot be charged in a criminal court, but that if warranted the assembly could judge him. "Provisional Constitution of the Kingdom of Siam, 1932," in Pridi, 74. As Somsak explains, the December constitution's third article is not clear in its intent, and the drafters of the December charter may have intended a meaning closer to the provisional constitution's sixth clause. Somsak Jeamteerasakul, "Korani Thawatt Rittidej fong Phrapokklao" [The Case of Thawatt Rittidej Charging King Prajadhipok], October 16, 2006, at http://somsakwork.blogspot.com.au/2006/10/. It seems likely that the vagueness was intentional and sought to placate the king, who as we have seen played a key role in drafting the permanent constitution. Conflict over the actual political role versus the legal status, of the king, and indeed of all kings since Prajadhipok, is among the central destabilizing factors in modern Thai

history. Among many others, see Thongchai, *Khamhaipon prachathipatai baep lang 14 Tula* [Getting past Democracy of the Post-October 14 Type] (Bangkok: 14 October Foundation, 2005).

64. Phraya Udompong Phensawat to Phahon, September 18, 1933, quoted in Somsak, "Korani Thawatt Rittidej."

65. Sirot, *Raengngan wijan jao*, 100. Mangkon's motivations are not clear. A Sino-Thai entrepreneur, Mangkon was an economic nationalist who criticized preferential treatment of well-connected businesspeople. He presented his own economic plan to the government. Earlier during the rickshaw strikes he voiced sympathy with the coolies. Despite his lèse majesté case on behalf of the king, it is not evident how pro-monarchy or "establishment" Mangkon's political opinions were.

66. NA, (2)SR.0201.75/3, interior minister to cabinet secretary, March 1, 1933.

67. NA, (2)SR.0201.75/3, letter from interior minister to premier Phahon, November 19, 1933.

68. Sirot, *Raengngan wijan jao*, 75.

69. NA, (2)SR.0201.75/18, January 14, 1934 letter.

70. NA, (2)SR.0201.75/18, January 20, 1934 letter.

71. Virginia Thompson, *Labor Problems in Southeast Asia* (New Haven, CT: Yale University Press, 1947), 240.

72. Thompson, *Labor Problems*, 242.

73. NA, (2)SR.0201.75/18, letter of February 9, 1934.

74. NA, (2)SR.0201.75/18, letter of March 12, 1934.

75. Sirot, *Raengngan wijan jao*, 75–77.

76. Thompson, *Labor Problems*, 230–41. Five-year-olds, as an example, continued to work in Bangkok match factories.

77. Thompson, 241.

78. Landon, *The Chinese in Thailand*, 215.

79. Landon, *The Chinese in Thailand*, 242.

80. In January 1939, the education ministry allowed only Thai food hawkers on its premises. Many other ministries and offices soon followed its lead. The government aimed to get Thai people to become vendors and to set an example for young people to learn the new trade. In one high-profile piece of publicity, the mayor of Thonburi across the river from Bangkok had a photo of himself proudly manning a hawker's cart published in a daily newspaper. The act disrupted the lives of thousands of Chinese food vendors, greatly inconvenienced businesses, government departments and schools dependent on the Chinese food carts, but did not appreciably change the overall trade. Landon, *The Chinese in Thailand*, 180; 220–23.

81. Thompson, *Labor Problems*, 228. The new economic planning of the late 1930s will be discussed more in the next chapter.

82. Sirot, *Raengngan wijan jao*, 109–10.

83. The frequent rotation of Japanese officers, their irregular record-keeping, the frequency of labor abandoning the work, and the postwar bonfires of relevant documents by the Japanese all make determining the numbers of laborers difficult. Yoshikawa Toshiharu, *Thangrotfai sai Thai-Phama nai samai songkhram maha Asia burapha* [The Thai-Burma Railway in the Time of the Great East Asian War], trans. Athon Fungthammasan, Trithip Rattanaphaisan and Marasi Miyamoto, ed. Saichon Satanyanurak (Bangkok: Amarin, 1995), 356–58.

84. NA, Bo.Ko. Sungsut, 2.6.8/3, government report, December 15, 1943.

85. At one early enlistment, nearly 6,000 men and women workers sought the 1,000 jobs that the Japanese advertised. That the Japanese offered about 13 percent higher wages than comparable manual labor for the Thai government certainly helped. Chainarong Phanpracha, "Kansang thangrotfai sai morana: Phonkrathop to phumiphak tawantok khong Prathet Thai" [The Construction of the Death Railway: Its Impact on the Western Region of Thailand] (master's thesis, Silpakorn University, 1987), 62–64.

86. Chainarong, "Kansang thangrotfai," 64.

87. Chainarong, "Kansang thangrotfai," 64–65.

88. For Photaram, see NA, Bo.Ko. Sungsut, 2.7.3.2/58; for Banpong see NA, Bo.Ko.Sungsut 2.7.6/7 and Charnvit Kasetsiri, ed., *Mae: Klap jak Banpong thueng Paknam* [Mother: Back from Banpong to Paknam] (Bangkok: Charnvit Kasetsiri, 2010), 119–51.

89. NA, Bo.Ko. Sungsut, 2.7.6/7, Ratburi governor to interior ministry, December 22, 1942.

90. "Magic" Summary no. 284, January 4, 1943, in Paul H. Kratoska, ed., *The Thailand-Burma Railway: Documents and Selected Writings*, vol. 2 (London: Routledge, 2006), 3. The message was sent December 23, 1942.

91. "Magic" Summary no. 295, January 15, 1943, in Kratoska, *Thailand-Burma Railway*, vol. 2, 5.

92. E. Bruce Reynolds, *Thailand and Japan's Southern Advance, 1940–1945* (New York: St. Martin's Press, 1994), 139.

93. The Petchburi governor reported in August 1943 that trains from Singapore daily brought Chinese and Malays up to Kanchanaburi for work. Many, however, fled immediately upon disembarking from the trains and became destitute wretches begging in provincial markets and causing public disorder. Provincial report, related in Yoshikawa, *Thangrotfai sai Thai-Phama*, 321. Many preferred begging in the market to what lay ahead. By an Allied estimate, between April and July 1943, an astounding 41 percent of the 70,000 Malaya-resident workers brought up to the rail line perished. SEATIC report, summarized in Yoshikawa, *Thangrotfai sai Thai-Phama*, 207.

94. Murashima, *Kanmueang Jin Siam*, 129–30.

95. Skinner, *Chinese Society in Thailand*, 272.

96. Landon, *The Chinese in Thailand*, 289.

97. Murashima, *Kanmueang Jin Siam*, 136–43.

98. Landon, *The Chinese in Thailand*, 284–85, 288–89.

99. Skinner, *Chinese Society in Thailand*, 267. Beginning in 1941, well before the Thai alliance with Japan, the Phibun government established several upcountry areas as zones prohibited to foreigners. The main victims were China-born Chinese. The state banned foreigners from residing in key eastern seaboard provinces, commercial hubs in the northeast, and then after the Banpong violence, in the north as well. In the eastern seaboard, Prachinburi and Lopburi provinces, and the naval district of Satthahip in Chonburi province. In September 1941, the districts of Khorat, Ubon, and Warinchamrap in the northeast, all important nodes of commerce and transportation, were similarly declared off limits to foreigners. Skinner, *Chinese Society in Thailand*, 270–71. In January 1943 in the north, foreigners had to leave six provinces: Chiang Mai, Lampun, Lampang, Chiang Rai, Phrae, and Uttaradit. Eiji Murashima, "The Thai-Japanese Alliance and the Chinese of Thailand," in *Southeast Asian Minorities in the Wartime Japanese Empire*, ed. Paul H. Kratoska (London: RoutledgeCurzon, 2002), 203–4. Exclusion of noncitizens obviously included the Japanese or Europeans resident in the areas, but neither were forced to leave. Moreover, Phibun soon offered a way around the policy by opening a special path for Chinese nationals to obtain Thai citizenship; by the middle of 1943 naturalization gave safety and security. Murashima, "The Thai-Japanese Alliance," 195. Over 6,000 resident Chinese applied for naturalization and nearly half gained legitimate status in 1943. Panni Bualek, "Kammakon Jin kap kansang thang rotfai sai morana rawang Songkhram Lok khrang thi 2" [Chinese Labor and the Building of the Death Railway during World War II], in *Prawatisat raengngan Thai*, 274–75.

100. The first two enlistments in 1943 targeted construction labor and the second two the following year maintenance and repair of the railway. Panni, "Kammakon Jin," 211–12; 215; 216–19.

101. Panni, "Kammakon Jin," 231.

102. Yoshikawa, *Thangrotfai sai Thai-Phama*, 198, 202, 207, 208.

103. Panni, "Kammakon Jin," 231.

104. NA, Bo.Ko. Sungsut, 2.4.1.2/12, March 25,1943 report; Bo.Ko. Sungsut, 2.4.1.2/12, March 30, 1943 letter, supreme commander to army field headquarters.

105. Yoshikawa, *Thangrotfai sai Thai-Phama*, 293–94.

106. NA, Bo.Ko. Sungsut, 2.4.1.2/12, Allied Liaison Office meeting, March 31, 1943.

107. NA, Bo.Ko. Sungsut, 2.4.1.2/12, police department report, April 5, 1943. The report states that Tan Siao Meng, the chair of the chamber, met with Japanese representatives on the third of April.

108. Panni, "Kammakon Jin," 204.

109. E. Bruce Reynolds, "'International Orphans': The Chinese in Thailand during World War II," *Journal of Southeast Asian Studies* 28, no. 2 (September 1997): 376; Reynolds, "History, Memory, Compensation, and Reconciliation: The Abuse of Labor along the Thailand-Burma Railway," in *Southeast Asian Minorities in the Wartime Japanese Empire*, 332.

110. Reynolds, "International Orphans," 376.

111. NA, Bo.Ko. Sungsut, 2.6.8/1, meeting on Japanese proposal to establish maximum wage in Bangkok, April 30, 1943.

112. NA, S.Th. Interior ministry meeting report, April 21, 1943. The Thais determined that Chinese laborers should be taken from Bangkok, Thonburi, Suphanburi, Nakhon Pathom, and Ratchburi. Of these, the vast majority should come from Bangkok and Thonburi. But an unknown number acted under duress, having recently been forced from exclusion zones in northern Thailand as non-citizens. Reynolds, "History, Memory, Compensation," 332; Reynolds, "International Orphans," 377.

113. Panni, "Kammakon Jin," 205.

114. Panni, "Kammakon Jin," 206–9.

115. Somsak, "The Communist Movement," chapter 3.

116. Batson, *The End of the Absolute Monarchy*, 145, 165–72; Kasian, *Commodifying Marxism*, 18–20.

117. King Prajadhipok's commentary in *Siam's Political Future*, 64. The full communist document is "Draft Statement Analyzing the Government and Economy of Siam, and Procedures for the Association, Approved by the Special Enlarged Committee, March 20" (Translation from Chinese), in *Siam's Political Future*, 66–71.

118. Murashima, *Kanmueang Jin Siam*, 101–2; Kasian, *Commodifying Marxism*, 20–21.

119. *Bangkok Times*, October 3 and October 10, 1932.

120. Murashima, *Kanmueang Jin Siam*, 100–18.

121. Kasian, *Commodifying Marxism*, 26–34.

122. Kasian, *Commodifying Marxism*, 43, 45–46.

123. Kasian, *Commodifying Marxism*, 46, 51–52.

124. Information summarized from Sungsidh, *Kantosu*, 149–52.

125. Damri Ruangsutham, *Khabuankan raengngan Thai nai kantotan kongthap Yipun nai Songkhram Lok khrang thi 2* [The Thai Labor Movement in the anti-Japanese Resistance during World War II] (Bangkok: Sukhaphapchai, 2001), 95–97.

126. This summary of Jit's life taken from Damri, *Khabuankan raengngan Thai*, 95–96; and Murashima, *Kanmueang Jin Siam*, 122–23.

127. Kasian, *Commodifying Marxism*, 53–54.

128. Kasian, *Commodifying Marxism*, 55. The Seri Thai did not publish anything, but needed to show the Allies the extent of popular resistance to Phibun and the Japanese. The growing alliance with the communists during the war enabled Pridi and company to present the Allies with the Thai version of *Mahachon*.

129. Damri, *Khabuankan raengngan Thai*, 94.

130. Tho Phianwitthaya, "An internal history of the Communist Party of Thailand," Chris Baker, trans. *Journal of Contemporary Asia*, 33, no. 4 (2003): 521.

131. Somsak, "The Communist Movement," 134.

132. Bunsong, "Khotheching kiaokap khabuankan raengngan Thai," 257–58.

133. Somsak, "The Communist Movement," 132; Damri, *Khabuankan raengngan Thai*, 233–38.

134. Somsak, "The Communist Movement," 129.

135. Damri, *Khabuankan raengngan Thai*, 132–33.

136. Damri, 132.

137. Damri, 198–201.

138. Damri, 178.

139. Damri, 161–62.

140. Damri, 166–70.

141. Somsak, "The Communist Movement," 3.

142. Bunsong, "Khotheching kiaokap khabuankan raengngan Thai," 259–60.

143. Sungsidh, *Kantosu*, 181–82; Bunsong, "Khotheching kiaokap khabuankan raengngan Thai," 262.

144. "Panha samkhan chapona khong prathet rao!" (The Important Problem Facing Our Country!), *Mahachon*, June 11, 1946.

145. Sungsidh, *Kantosu*, 192.

146. Sungsidh, *Kantosu*, 190–93.

147. Chiap Amphunan, *Mahawitthayalai khong khappajao* [My University] (Bangkok: Ruamsan Press, 1958), 496.

148. Chiap, *Mahawitthayalai*, 464–71.

149. Of all of the Allied powers, Britain most sought to punish Thailand for allying with the Japanese, and to exploit the country's rice trade. Initially, in 1945 and 1946 Britain demanded free rice and then after a fraught Thai-British negotiation in 1947, gained Thai rice at a low price for the UK. See Direk Chaiyanam, *Thailand and World War II*, ed. Jane Keyes (Chiang Mai, Thailand: Silkworm Books, 2008), 208–25, 317–29.

150. Chiap, *Mahawitthayalai*, 498–500.

151. Chiap, *Mahawitthayalai*, 501.

152. Chiap, *Mahawitthayalai*, 503–5.

153. Thamrongsak Petchlert-anan, "Thongplaeo Chonlaphumi: Chiwit lae ngan" [Thongplaeo Chonlaphumi: Life and Work], in *Pridi Banomyong lae 4 rathamontri Isan + 1* [Pridi Banomyong and 4 Isan Ministers + 1], Charnvit

Kasetsiri and Thamrongsak Petchlert-anan, eds. (Bangkok: The Foundation for the Promotion of Social Sciences and Humanities Textbooks Project, 2001), 262–65.

154. Chiap, *Mahawitthayalai* 505–8.

155. Chiap, *Mahawitthayalai*, 505.

156. Sungsidh, *Kantosu*, 157–161.

157. Chiap, *Mahawitthayalai*, 493.

158. Pridi, "Some Aspects of the Founding of the People's Party," quoted in Charnvit, *Prawatisat kanmueang*, 44.

159. "The People's Party and the Democratic Revolution of 24 June 1932" (1982), in *Pridi by Pridi*, 169.

160. "The People's Party and the Democratic Revolution," 168.

Chapter Three

1. Prajadhipok writing in 1927, related in Nattapoll, "Khwam Patiwat," 9; Chula Chakrabongse, *Lords of Life*, 216–67.

2. David K. Wyatt, *The Politics of Reform: Education in the Reign of King Chulalongkorn* (New Haven, CT: Yale University Press, 1969), 385.

3. Hong Lysa, *Thailand in the Nineteenth Century: Evolution of the Economy and Society* (Singapore: ISEAS, 1984), 4–5.

4. See Tej, *Prince Damrong and the Provincial Administration of Thailand*; Thongchai, *Siam Mapped*; Loos, *Subject Siam*.

5. Thongchai, "Siam's Colonial Conditions and the Birth of Thai History," in *Southeast Asian Historiography, Unraveling the Myths: Essays in Honour of Barend Jan Terwiel*, Volker Grabowsky, ed. (Bangkok: River Books, 2011), 23–45.

6. Sawai Suthipithak, *Doktoe Pridi Phanomyong* (Bangkok: Khlet Thai, 1983).

7. Description of Morden Carthew's Rotary Club talk is related in Batson, *The End of the Absolute Monarchy*, 108. The Baron Lapomarede, the French Indochinese official, identified Chinese and half-Chinese troublemakers as behind the revolution. *Bangkok Times*, April 24, 1934.

8. Purposefully difficult to pinpoint in time, a vanished golden age served conservative interests during decades of socioeconomic change. Elite royals and foreign advisers who directed the great administrative changes undertaken by the absolute kings waxed eloquently about old Siam even as they dismantled it. Prince Damrong, architect of state administrative modernization in the 1890s, wrote glowingly of rural simplicity and self-sufficiency in the northeast while his reforms rendered them obsolete.

Josiah Crosby, a longtime British diplomat in Bangkok commented during the 1940s on the deepening commercialism in the central plains. He wrote with an unabashed wistfulness for a society he did not experience. "[There] is a kind of mass culture which is common, as regards its outward attributes, at any rate, to the generality of mankind. . . . Nowadays the stamp of uniformity is being impressed upon the population everywhere. . . . Romance, in fact, has flown out at the window as modern progress has come in at the door." Despite Crosby's laments, modernity did not banish the "charms" of old Siam—poverty and isolation—but exacerbated them.

9. Landon, *The Chinese in Thailand*, 243.

10. Categories of labor varied and were applied differently in different surveys. For 1929, I have added four major occupations: farming, rice farming, various farming, and sundry garden cultivation. "Rice farming" alone is insufficient, with the number only totaling a bit over 61,000. The largest category is "farming," which is given as over 5.6 million. See *Thesaphiban* 30, no. 6 (1929): 383. In the 1937 census, "agriculture and fishing" is the general category for more than 6 million people. SYB, no. 20 (1937–1938 and 1938–1939): 57.

11. Ingram, *Economic Change in Thailand*, 44–45.

12. Chris Baker and Pasuk Phongpaichit, *Thailand, Economy and Politics* (Oxford: Oxford University Press, 2002), 22.

13. Baker and Pasuk, 19–20.

14. Baker and Pasuk, 63.

15. Carle C. Zimmerman, *Siam, Rural Economic Survey, 1930–31* (Bangkok: White Lotus Press, [1931] 1999), 176–77; James M. Andrews, *Siam, 2nd. Rural Economic Survey, 1934–1935* (Bangkok: W. H. Mundie, 1935), 333.

16. Landon, *The Chinese in Thailand*, 131.

17. Andrews, *2nd. Rural Economic Survey*, 308–10.

18. Zimmerman, *Rural Economic Survey*, 165, 174–75.

19. Chatthip et al., *The Political Economy of Siam, 1851–1910*, 4. This process had begun much earlier. King Mongkut in the 1860s noted that central plains people preferred imported cotton clothing to homespun, because the former was much cheaper. In 1906, van der Heide stated that not only cotton and silk manufactures, but metalwork, paper, earthenware, and other home industries had similarly been extinguished in the central plains. J. Homan van der Heide, "The Economical Development of Siam during the Last Half Century," *Journal of the Siam Society* 3 (1906): 85–87, 96–99.

20. Banditry and lawlessness also marked the growth of central plains agriculture. Large bands of forty to fifty armed brigands herding stolen cattle formed a common sight in the center around the turn of the century. *Bangkok Times* article of February 22, 1893, quoted in Johnston, "Rural Society and the Rice Economy," 169. From the beginnings of the Rangsit development, crime and unrest accompanied the anarchic settlement patterns of immigrants. Government concern that a lack of control over settlements led to unrest persisted in later decades. A report on the area in the late 1920s explained that individual families were wary of settling there because of thieves and general insecurity. Johnston, "Rural Society and the Rice Economy," 118.

The initial phase of state expansion into the provinces in the late nineteenth century revealed that local crime lords governed. These bosses' protection alone brought peace, and the Bangkok state had to use them to consolidate its rule. Prince Damrong Rajanuphap, *Thesaphiban* [Control over Territory] (Bangkok: Matichon, [1925] 2002), 53.

21. Zimmerman, *Rural Economic Survey*, 174.

22. The figures are 78 percent and 94 percent, respectively. Zimmerman, 18, 25.

23. Eighty-four percent in Zimmerman's survey, 18. The Rangsit story—and central plains irrigation plans in the early twentieth century—can be found in Johnston, "Rural Society and the Rice Economy" and Ian Brown, *The Elite and the Economy in Siam, 1890–1920* (Oxford: Oxford University Press, 1988), chapter 1. Hans ten Brummelhuis describes the grand plans and disappointing career of J. Homan van der Heide, a Dutchman from Java hired to develop an irrigation network in the early 1900s, in *King of the Waters: Homan van der Heide and the Origin of Modern Irrigation in Siam* (Leiden, The Netherlands: KITLV Press, 2005).

24. Chatthip et al., *The Political Economy of Siam, 1910–1932*, 4–5.

25. Central plains farmers used buffaloes to thresh grain rather than flails. David Feeny, *The Political Economy of Productivity: Thai Agricultural Development, 1880–1975* (Vancouver, Canada: University of British Columbia Press, 1982), 39.

26. Chatthip Nartsupha, *The Thai Village Economy in the Past*, trans. Chris Baker and Pasuk Phongphaichit (Chiang Mai, Thailand: Silkworm Books, 1999), 17.

27. Zimmerman, *Rural Economic Survey*, 153. Ungreased axles served a spiritual purpose as well. In common with other parts of Southeast Asia, Thai peasants believed that the noise of carts and tools kept evil spirits away from their fields.

28. "Raingan prajampi khong monthon Nakhon Ratchasima" [Annual Report on Nakhon Ratchasima Circle], *Thesaphiban* 30, no. 11 (1931): 742.

29. *Thesaphiban*, 757–59, 762.

30. *Thesaphiban*, 765.

31. *Thesaphiban*, 733.

32. *Thesaphiban*, 766–67.

33. *Thesaphiban*, 53, 37.

34. Nakharin, *Kanpatiwat Siam*, 172.

35. "Some Experiences and Opinions," in *Pridi by Pridi*, 23–27.

36. Quoted in Batson, *The End of the Absolute Monarchy*, 105.

37. Kevin Hewison, *Bankers and Bureaucrats: Capital and the Role of the State in Thailand* (New Haven, CT: Yale University Southeast Asia Studies, 1989), 65.

38. "Rueang rang phraratchabanyat samruat lae ha withi chuai luea khwamthuk khong ratsadon pho so. 2478 khong Phra Phinit Thanakon," *Raingan kanprachum sapha phuthen ratsadon*, no. 6, June 1935 (Bangkok: Samnakngan lekhathikan sapha phuthen ratsadon), 456–503.

39. *Raingan* (1935), 466.

40. Liang Chaiyakan, "Pathakatha rueang saphap changwat Ubon Rajathani" [Lecture on the State of Ubon Rajathani Province], in *Pathakata khong phuthen ratsadon rueang saphap khong changwat tangtang* [Assembly Representatives' Lectures on the State of Various Provinces, 1933–34] (Bangkok: Thai Club of Japan, 1996), 23. Liang here updated a claim from Young Siam—Chulalongkorn's network. The first Thai prince to gain a doctorate, Chulalongkorn's son Dilok Nabarath, wrote in his 1908 University of Tubingen PhD that until the Bangkok era, "rural people and their profession were simply regarded as an inexhaustible supply of food for the higher classes of the population." Prince Dilok Nabarath, *Siam's Rural Economy under King Chulalongkorn*, Walter E. J. Tips, trans. (Bangkok: White Lotus, 2000), 169. The skimming operation, Dilok wrote, blocked any agricultural development. Liang said the same thing twenty years later.

41. Liang in "Rueang rang phraratchabanyat samruat," 468.

42. Liang, 477.

43. *Raingan kanprachum sapha phuthen ratsadon*, no. 4 (1936): 162–64.

44. "Khrathutham khong Nai Thong-in Phuriphat rueang kiaokae rokruen rueang kiaokae nisai nakthot rueang kiaokae prap fin lae rueang thang luang nai phak Isan," *Raingan kanprachum sapha phuthen ratsadon*, no. 9, 1933, 381–92.

45. *Raingan* (1933), 173–75.

46. *Raingan* (1933), 176.

47. *Raingan* (1933), 167–69.

48. Constance Wilson, *Thailand: A Handbook of Historical Statistics* (Boston: G. K. Hall, 1983), 161, 171.

49. "The Tyranny of Proximity: Power and Mobility in Colonial Cambodia, 1863–1954," *Journal of Southeast Asian Studies* 37, no. 3 (October 2006): 421–43. In addition to their supposed spatial immobility, Edwards explains that the French viewed the Cambodians as living in a time warp. To the French, nothing had changed in the Cambodian mentality since twelfth-century Angkor. "The Cambodians . . . were seen as time travellers, albeit ones stuck in a degenerate, medieval groove," 424.

50. Phraya Sarakham Khanaphibal and Thongmuan Attakon, "Pathakatha rueang saphap changwat Mahasarakham," in *Pathakata khong phuthen ratsadon*, 117.

51. NA, SR.0201.8/13, "Khwamhen samrap monthon Udon doichapo," letter to Thammasakmontri, national assembly president, July 14, 1932, 2.

52. NA, SR.0201.8/13, letter to Mano, September 10, 1932, 2–3 of letter.

53. Letter to Mano, 1.

54. NA, SR.0201.8/13, "Khwamhen samrap monthon Udon doichapo."

55. NA, SR.0201.8/13, "Banthuek khwamhen bettalet," letter to Mano, August 17, 1932, 2–3 of letter.

56. *Anuson mo.cho. Sitthiphon Kridakon, botkhwam khong lae kiaokap mo.cho. Sitthiphon Kridakon* [Memorial Volume for Prince Sitthiphon Kridakon, Articles

by and about Prince Sitthiphon Kridakon] (Bangkok: Social Science Association of Thailand, 1971).

57. Chaiyasri Samudvanija, "Prawat nai Am Bunthai," in Am Bunthai, *Kridakan bon thi rap sung* [Might on the High Plains] (Bangkok: Thai Club of Japan, [1933] 2000), 12.

58. *Thai Mai*, March 29, 1936, quoted in Phuthorn, "San Piset," 191.

59. "Lakkan lae kanjat sahakon" [Principles and Establishment of Cooperatives], in *Sahakon, Anuson nai ngan phraratchathan phloengsop Chaophraya Wongsanuprapat (Mom Ratchawong Sathan Sanitwongse)* [Sahakon, Royal Cremation Volume for Chaophraya Wongsanuphrapat] (Bangkok: Rongphim Sophonphiphanthanakon, 1941), 5–6; Landon, *Siam in Transition*, 75.

60. Am Bunthai, *Kridakan bon thi rap sung*, 71.

61. Am, 101.

62. Murashima, "Democracy and the Development of Political Parties in Thailand 1932–1945," 3.

63. Murashima, 3.

64. See e.g., Chongkon, *Yu yang suea.*

65. For example, Saneh Chamarik, *Kanmueang Thai kap pathanakan rathathammanun* [Thai Politics and Constitutional Development] (Bangkok: The Foundation for the Promotion of Social Sciences and Humanities Textbooks Project, 2006), 130–31.

66. *Raingan kanprachum sapha phuthen ratsadon*, no. 6 (June 1935): 467. Government ministers also sometimes attended parliamentary sessions.

67. *Raingan* (1935), 472.

68. *Raingan* (1935), 460.

69. *Raingan* (1935), 373–74.

70. *Raingan* (1935), 196.

71. The king bears a heavy responsibility for politicizing the plan. He commissioned its publication and dissemination as a way to discredit the People's Party.

72. Somsak Jeamteerasakul, "The Communist Movement," 88–89, 90–101.

73. Somsak, 93.

74. Khuang gave his recollection at a Teachers' Association speech in 1963; Pridi was not amused. See Pridi, Appendix 1 in Pridi Banomyong, *Bang rueang kiaokap phraboromawongsanuwong nai rawang Songkhram Lok krang thi 2* [Some Issues concerning the Royal Family during World War II] (Bangkok: Pridi-Phoonsuk Foundation, [1972] 2000), 60.

75. Quoted in Prayun, *Banthuek rueang kanplianpleng kanpokhrong*, 66.

76. Prayun, 102.

77. "Outline Economic Plan (1933)" in *Pridi by Pridi*, 82–123.

78. "Outline Economic Plan," 114.

79. Solidarism in law and politics is most associated with Leon Bourgeois and Léon Duguit. See Joseph Charmont, "Solidarism," in A. Fouillée et al. *Modern French Legal Philosophy*, trans. Mrs. Franklin W. Scott and Joseph P. Cham-

berlain (Boston: Boston Book Co., 1916), 82–98; Duguit, "Social Solidarity," in *Modern French Legal Philosophy*, 258–85; and Duguit, *Law in the Modern State*, trans. Harold Laski (New York: B. W. Huebsch, 1919). For an overview of Third Republic legal philosophy, see Martti Koskenniemi, *The Gentle Civilizer of Nations: The Rise and Fall of International Law 1870—1960* (Cambridge, UK: Cambridge University Press, 2002), 288–302. For more on Pridi, see Thapanan Nipithakul, *Pharadoraphapniyom (Solidarisme) khong Pridi Banomyong* [Pridi Banomyong's Solidarism] (Bangkok: Pridi Banomyong Institute, 2006).

80. "Outline Economic Plan," 106.

81. "Outline Economic Plan," 99.

82. "Outline Economic Plan," 99.

83. "Outline Economic Plan," 94.

84. Quoted in Somsak, "The Communist Movement," 111.

85. "Outline Economic Plan," 114.

86. "Outline Economic Plan," 108.

87. "Outline Economic Plan," 99.

88. Somsak, "The Communist Movement," 91.

89. "Outline Economic Plan," 113.

90. Cabinet meeting of March 12, 1933, in Duen, *Than Pridi rataburut awuso*, 126.

91. "The People's Party and the Democratic Revolution of 24 June," in *Pridi by Pridi*, 169.

92. Somsak, "The Communist Movement," 116–17.

93. Charles Gide, *Consumers' Co-operative Societies*, trans. Co-operative Reference Library Dublin (New York: Alfred A. Knopf, 1922), 279.

94. Somsak, "The Communist Movement," 117–19.

95. Somsak, "The Communist Movement," 138–43.

96. The economic orthodoxy of the absolutist period and British influence is studied in Ian Brown, *The Elite and the Economy in Siam, 1890-1920* (Singapore: Oxford University Press, 1988).

97. See Nakharin, "Kansawaengha rabop setthakit mai nai chuang nung thosawat phai lang kanpatiwat Siam 2475" [The Search for a New Economic System in the Decade after the 1932 Thai Revolution], in Nakharin, *Khwamkhit, khwamru lae amnat thang kanmueang*, 340–42.

98. NA, (2)SR.0201.22/3, "Khrongkan sethakit samai Phraya Mano pen nayok rathamontri," March 16, 1933.

99. NA, (2)SR.0201.22/3, "Khrongkan sethakit samai Phraya Mano," September 13, 1933.

100. NA, (2)SR.0201.22/3, "Khrongkan sethakit samai Phraya Mano," English language letter, August 11, 1934.

101. Vichitvong na Pombhejara, *Pridi Banomyong and the Making of Thailand's Modern History* (Bangkok: Committee for Centennial Anniversary of Pridi Banomyong, Senior Statesman, 2001 (1983), 112–20, 126–32.

102. Landon, *The Chinese in Thailand*, 174.

103. Landon, *The Chinese in Thailand*, 168–72; 182–86; 209–10.

104. Suehiro, *Capital Accumulation in Thailand*, 122–34.

105. Quoted in Landon, *The Chinese in Thailand*, 245.

106. Kasian, *Commodifying Marxism*, 38.

Chapter Four

1. The Royal Secretariat, as Batson described it, stood "(B)etween the king and the world" (*The End of the Absolute Monarchy*, 48). It handled all correspondence addressed to the monarch. Chaophraya Mahithon's comments on Dhani's letter show Prajadhipok's opinion.

2. NA, R.7, "Kansueksa," Chaophraya Mahithon to Nakhon Sawan, June 1, 1932. Dhani's letter to Mahithon is dated May 26, 1932. Mahithon also noted that constitutional monarchy was the only way to halt the institution's further loss of respect. He said that a Mussolini-type dictatorship was impossible in Siam, partly because foreigners would view Siam as uncivilized. Mahithon argued that the Italians did not have to worry about foreign opinion (because they were Europeans? or because he saw them as a military power?).

3. "Announcement of the People's Party No. 1" and "Provisional Constitution, 1932" in *Pridi by Pridi*, 72 and 75.

4. *Thesaphiban* 30, no. 6 (1929): 383; SYB, no. 20 (1937–1938, 1938–1939): 57.

5. Nakharin, using the SYB, *Khwamkhit, khwamru lae amnat thang kanmueang*, 154.

6. Pendulums were common images at the time, and one wonders whether the Siamese adopted the image from Britain, whose intellectual life profoundly influenced the Thai elite. When in metaphorical doubt, as Raymond Williams wrote, the English used the pendulum. *Culture and Society, 1780–1950* (New York: Harper & Row Publishers, 1958), 53.

7. NA, SR.0201.27/8, Li Sukriket and group to Phahon, August 9, 1933.

8. At the time the government grouped several provinces into a "circle" (monthon) for administrative ease. Pitsanulok was both a province and the central authority of some northern provinces at the time; Phra Sawat would have been responsible for Pichit.

9. NA, SR.0201.27/8, Pichit teachers group to Phahon, July 30, 1933. "Phra" was Sawat's ennobled rank.

10. Pichit group to Phahon, August 18, 1933.

11. Thammasakmontri cited this report in exchanges with Phahon.

12. NA, SR.0201.27/8, Khun Witayawuti et al. to Phahon, August 9, 1933.

13. NA, SR.0201.27/8, letter of August 24, 1933.

14. NA, SR.0201.27/8.

15. "Petitions by Ministry Officials," *Bangkok Times*, September 13, 1933.

16. It is ironic that the Christian schools contributed to the growth of absolutist moral authority. For one thing, their ethos and worldview directly in many ways contradicted the hierarchy taught by elite Buddhism. Second, there was no political or economic incentive to become a Christian, unlike in neighboring European colonies, and hardly any elites converted. Still, the missionary schools centrally contributed to Thai state building with their modern pedagogy and foreign language skill.

17. Kullada, *The Rise and Decline of Thai Absolutism*, 66–92.

18. Nakharin, *Kanpatiwat Siam*, 125, 467.

19. See Warunee Osatharom, "Kansueksa nai sangkhom Thai pho. so. 2411–2475. [Education in Thai Society 1868–1932] (master's thesis: Chulalongkorn University, 1981).

20. Warunee, "Kansueksa," 231 and 229.

21. Wyatt, *The Politics of Reform*, 136–40. A senior figure in British education, Morant was a close adviser of Prince Damrong Rajanuphap, and also a government education inspector and tutor to Crown Prince Vajirunhis. Vajirunhis would likely have become the sixth king except that he died prematurely, thus making room for Vajiravudh to ascend the throne in 1910 on Chulalongkorn's death.

22. According to Wyatt, Thammasakmontri's ability around this time attracted Chula's attention and he replaced Wisut as the king's favored educational adviser, 363–67.

23. "Chiwaprawat" (Biography), in *Botphrapan bang rueang khong Khru Thep, phim nai ngan phraratchathan phloengsop phana than so. Thammasakmontri Thephasadin na Ayutthaya* [Some Writings of Khru Thep, Printed on the Occasion of the Royal Cremation of Thammasakmontri na Ayutthaya] (Bangkok, 1943), i–xviii.

24. In 1916, he pointed out that British Burma spent about seven times more, and the Philippines twelve times, the amount spent in Siam on education. In that year, Siam had 3,134 primary schools with 135,162 students, compared to more than twice as many schools and four times the pupils in Burma, and 4,000-plus primary schools and four times the students in the Philippines. Siam spent just under 2 percent of its budget on education in that year, compared to 17 percent in the Philippines. In 1918, he found 10 percent of school-age children attended school, compared to 98.5 percent in Japan. Thammasakmontri's opinions in a meeting of provincial viceroys and secretaries, May 1919, translated in Chatthip, et al. *The Political Economy of Siam, 1910–1932*, 116–18.

25. Chatthip, 113–16. The meeting is also covered in Warunee, "Kansueksa," 236–41.

26. "Outline Economic Plan (1933)," in *Pridi by Pridi*, 87–88, 98.

27. "Outline Economic Plan (1933)," 97.

28. "His Majesty King Prachathipok's Comments on Pridi's Economic Plan," in Thak, *Thai Politics*, 195 and 207.

29. Warunee, "Kansueksa," 242.

30. NA, ST9.2/253, "Huakho thammanun kanpokkhrong phaendin siam samrap pen khumer khong khru chai son nakrian chan prathom."

31. NA, ST9.2/253, "Laksut chan mathayom 5 thueng 8."

32. See Oliver Wolters, *History, Culture and Region in Southeast Asian Perspectives* (Singapore: ISEAS, 1982).

33. Riggs, *Bureaucratic Polity*, 181–82.

34. And still today political crises stymie liberal transitions and reveal the bureaucratic elite's hostility toward popular democratic activism.

35. "Kot krasuang thammakan, ok tam khwam nai phraratchabanyat prathomseuksa phutthasakarat 2478 (chabap thi 2)," *Rajanukitchabeksa* 54 (May 17, 1937): 441–42.

36. "Phraratchabanyat prathomseuksa hhutthasakarat 2478," *Rajanukitch-abeksa* 25 (November 24, 1935): 1591–616. The act called for all children aged eight to fifteen to be enrolled.

37. SYB, no. 20 (1937–1938, 1938–1939): 390–91.

38. Most municipal schools grew out of older *prachaban* schools. Landon, *The Chinese in Thailand*, 264.

39. SYB, no. 20 (1937–1938, 1938–1939): 392.

40. NA, M.R7, RL.20, Thammasakmontri to royal secretary Chaophraya Mahithon, May 17, 1926, with appended report "Sangkhep khrongkansueksa khong rao kap suan thi jat pai laeo." Also see Raluek Thani, *Wiwatthanakan nai kanjat kansueksa phak bangkhap khong Thai (Pho. So. 2475–503)* [Development of the Establishment of Thai Compulsory Education, 1932–1960] (Bangkok: Thai Watana Panich, 1984), 22–25.

41. By 1932, nearly 89 percent of townships nationally had some form of compulsory education. Warunee, "Kansueksa," 378. The government established roughly 1,300 new schools between 1923 and 1932, bringing the total number in the kingdom to about 6,330 (*SYB*, 1938–1939, 392). The education ministry estimated that in 1921, 90 percent of the population was illiterate. By 1931, the figure had dropped to 37 percent. In 1921, about 923,000 boys and girls could read and write basic Thai; ten years later the figure had jumped to 6.895 million. NA, So. Th. 4/168, 1932 report from krom sueksatikan [Education Department].

42. By 1939, there were about 11,500 schools; student enrolment reached nearly 1.446 million; and teachers numbered more than 32,000. SYB, no. 20 (1937–1938, 1938–1939): 392.

43. Thompson, *The New Siam*, 683; Barmé, *Woman, Man, Bangkok*, 248.

44. Landon, *Siam in Transition*, 98.

45. SYB, no. 20 (1937–1938, 1938–1939): 393, 402.

46. Of these, about 84 percent were less than eighteen years old; the majority were aged fifteen to seventeen. NA, SR.0201.24/4, "Banthuek khwamhen khong jaonathi khong krasuang thammakan kromwichakan," March 1941.

47. Murashima, *Kanmueang Jin Siam*, 34; Phao, "Hetkan kon kanpliangpleng kanpokhrong," 141.

48. Landon, *The Chinese in Thailand*, 204.

49. Landon, *The Chinese in Thailand*, 266–67.

50. SYB, no. 20 (1937–1938, 1938–1939): 413.

51. Landon, *The Chinese in Thailand*, 268.

52. Landon, 276–77.

53. Skinner, *Chinese Society in Thailand*, 229–30.

54. Landon, *The Chinese in Thailand*, 289.

55. Landon, 271–73.

56. Landon, 272.

57. Skinner, *Chinese Society in Thailand*, 229.

58. Murashima, *Kanmueang Jin Siam*, 36.

59. SYB, no. 20 (1937–1938, 1938–1939): 412; Skinner, *Chinese Society in Thailand*, 230.

60. Landon, *The Chinese in Thailand*, 278.

61. Kasian, *Commodifying Marxism*, 61.

62. NA, S.B. 3.7/3, "The University of Moral and Political Sciences Act B.E. 2476" (English translation).

63. Duen Bunnag, *Kham athibai kotmai rathathammanun, lem 1* [Explanation of Constitutional Law, vol. 1] (Bangkok: Nitisat, 1934), 157.

64. Sawai, *Doktoe Pridi*, 459. Prior to the army's use of the land, the river-front property was the Front Palace: the hallowed ground from which the "second king" launched his doomed challenge to King Chulalongkorn in 1874–1875. The outcome was Young Siam's triumph over the main obstacle to absolutism.

65. Sawai, 461–62.

66. "University City," *Bangkok Times*, July 5, 1935.

67. This group included Pridi, J. F. Hutchesson from Britain, and L. Duplatre, H. Eygoût and Guyon from France. The brothers Waithayakon, Princes Wan and Sakol, accounted for the nonlawyers among the group, and both were educated in Britain (NA, S.B. 3.7/3). Thammasat divided professors into two groups, ordinary and extraordinary (five in the first group, four in the second). Government papers always referred to the foreign professors' first name by initial only, and doctors of law were always styled "docteur en droit" although it is not clear that all of them studied in France. Practicing lawyers in Siam always were referred to by the English designation of "barrister-at-law."

68. SYB, no. 20, 1938–1944, 417.

69. NA, S.B.3.7/3 gives the figure as 7,550 students in the first year. Another Thammasat document, from the opening ceremony of the university in June

1934, reported the number as 7,094. Possibly the discrepancy is that the first figure includes enrollment in both semesters for 1934. The second figure quoted in Bunyen, *Mahawithayalai wicha Thammasat lae Kanmueang: Kamnert lae khwamkiaophan kap rabop prachathipatai* [Thammasat University: Origins and Relation to the Democratic System] (Bangkok: Samnakwichai, Sathaban Banthit Patthana Borihansat, 1969), 44.

70. SYB, no. 20 (1937–1938, 1938–1939): 416. The Chula student body grew to 873 in 1936, 976 in 1937 and 1,124 in 1938.

71. Tunsiri Vichai, "The Social Background and the Legislative Recruitment of the Thai Members of Parliament and their Political Consequences" (PhD diss., Indiana University, 1971), 56.

72. Suksanti Chirachariyawech, ed., *Nangsue thi raluek khrop rop 84 Achan Sanya Dharmasakdi* (Bangkok 1991); Nitisat Paisal, "Fuekfon tua eng" [Training the Self] in *Anuson nai phraratchathanplergnsop Nitisat Paisal* [Royal Cremation Volume for Nitisat Paisal] (Bangkok 1967).

73. Federico Ferrara, "Unfinished Business," in *'Good Coup' Gone Bad: Thailand's Political Developments since Thaksin's Downfall*, ed. Pavin Chachavalpongpun (Singapore: ISEAS, 2014), 27.

74. SYB, 1938–1944, 416.

75. Thompson, *The New Siam*, 683.

76. SYB, no. 20 (1937–1938, 1938–1939): 417.

77. Barmé, *Woman, Man, Bangkok*, 232.

78. Barmé, 232, 248.

79. John B. Haseman, *The Thai Resistance Movement During World War II* (Chiang Mai, Thailand: Silkworm Books, 2002), 98.

80. Suthachai Yimprasert, ed. *Saithan haeng adit* [Streams of History] (Bangkok: Chulalongkorn University, 2007), 78–81.

81. Nattapoll, *Kabot Bowondet*, 390.

82. Murashima, "Democracy and Political Parties," 27.

83. Murashima, 27–28.

84. Samruat Kanchanasit, *Tho. So. Chaokhun Song Suradet*, related in Thamrongsak, *2475 lae nueng pi lang*, 114.

85. NA, (2)SR.0201.18/3, "Khambanyai rabiap ratchakan khong samnakngan khosanakan," August 21, 1935.

86. NA, (2)SR.0201.18/3, "Kitchakan khong samnakngan khosanakan," September 2, 1934.

87. Suwimon Phonlajan, "Krom khosanakan kap kankhosana udomkan thang kanmueang khong rat, 2476–2487" [The Propaganda Department and Dissemination of State Political Principles, 1933–1944] (master's thesis, Thammasat University, 1988).

88. Puli Fuwongcharoen, "Long Live Rathathammanun!"

89. Carol Gluck, *Japan's Modern Myths: Ideology in the Late Meiji Period* (Princeton, NJ: Princeton University Press, 1985).

90. NA, (2)SR.0201.18/7, "Kanpaitham kansadaeng pathakata nai khet changwat Chachoengsao, Prachinburi lae Nakhon Nayok," June 28, 1939.

91. NA, (2)SR.0201.18, "Khambanyai rabiap ratchakan."

92. NA, SR.0201.16/46, Khun Inthongphakdi to cabinet secretary, December 30, 1933. The Lamphun representative's experience prompted an effort to publicize the work of the various ministries. The publicity bureau argued internally that governmental transparency was key to the success of democracy, but the plea fell on deaf ears. Publicity officials lamented the unwillingness of the ministries (especially defense) to share information. The exchange between the publicity bureau and the cabinet took place in 1935. See the letters in NA, SR.0201.16/47.

93. NA, SR.0201.16/46, interior ministry to cabinet secretary, June 11 and July 11, 1934. The same file shows a similar problem in Chiang Mai; Chiang Mai provincial committee letter to deputy interior minister, July 6, 1934. Also publicity bureau to cabinet secretary, May 1934 in NA, SR.0201.18/7.

94. Pairoj Chaiyanam, *Pathakata khosana phak thi ha: Rueang sithi le nathi khong phonlamueang* [Propaganda Lectures Part Five: Rights and Duties of the Citizenry] (Songkhla Provincial Committee, 1935), 2.

95. Fung Charoenwit, *Sithi lae nathi phonlamueang tam rabawp pra-chathipatai* [Rights and Duties of Citizens according to the Democratic Regime] (Chachoengsao Provincial Committee, 1934), 18.

96. NA, (2)SR.0201.18/9, "Lak haeng kansadaeng pathakata." Undated, this document is probably from 1934.

97. Lecturers followed the stipulations of Articles 12 to 15 of the December 10, 1932 permanent constitution.

98. Tej, *Khabot ro. so.* 121.

99. NA, (2)SR.0201.18/9, "Lak haeng kan sadaeng pathakata."

100. Charnvit and Thamrongsak, *Pridi Banomyong lae 4 rathamontri Isan + 1*, 29.

101. NA, (2)SR.0201/18, "Kho sangket bang yang thi dai jak kanpai ratcha-kan thi changwat Ubon," and "Khwampenpai khong phuthen," both June 1934; and "Kho sangketkan neuang nai kanpai sadaeng pathakata thi changwat Ubon," October 1934.

102. "Ekaraj," *Siam Ukhos*, August 21, 1938.

103. NA, (2)SR.0201.18/3, Sakon's report of July 21, 1933 and Ronasit's radio address, September 2, 1934. The number doubled in two years. By one count, in 1931 there were about 11,000 radios in the kingdom. Suwimon, "Krom khosanakan," 12.

104. Suwimon, "Krom khosanakan," 36. War and right-wing nationalism spurred investment in capacity. The government set up stations in Phra Ta Bong

(Battambang), Srisophon and Siam Rat (Siem Reap) when the Thais took these provinces from the French in 1940, and also additional stations in the northeast, 33–34.

105. "Pathakata rueang saphap khong changwat Chiang Mai" [Lecture on the Topic of the State of Chiang Mai Province], in *Pathakata khong phuthen ratsadon*, 31–37.

106. Khun Prajet Darunaphan, "Pathakatha rueang saphap khong changwat Pitsanulok" [Lecture on the State of Pitsanulok Province], in *Pathakata khong phuthen ratsadon*, 100–2.

107. Luang Natha Nithithada, "Pathakatha rueang saphap changwat Chaiyaphum" [Lecture on the State of Chaiyaphum Province], in *Pathakata khong phuthen ratsadon*, 98.

108. Liang, "Pathakatha rueang saphap changwat Ubon Ratchathani" [Lecture on the State of Ubon Rajathani Province], in *Pathakata khong phuthen ratsadon*, 23.

109. Only those of *parian* (a religious educational rank) five or higher could lecture and initially the speakers came only from Bangkok and Thonburi due to the difficulty upcountry monks had traveling to Phraya Thai.

110. NA, (2)SR.0201.18, "Khambanyai rabiap ratchakan," August 21, 1935. Under pressure, monks praised the government. During his incarceration at Bang Khwang prison after 1932, Luen Saraphai avoided Sunday sermons at all costs. He described them as naked government propaganda that attacked the old regime and all government enemies. *Fanrai*, 89.

111. Wichit Wathakan is the best-known figure of the self-help movement. See Barmé, *Luang Wichit Wathakan*.

112. "Nayok sang kae kho wathi," *Krungthep Warasap*, August 10, 1935.

113. "To wathi thi Krom Silpakorn meua wan athit sanuksanan thang 3 rueang phu fang lon rong," *Krungthep Warasap*, August 20, 1935; "Phuying nai adit di kwa patchuban?," *Mitthraphap*, November 1935.

114. "Kanto wathi," *Krungthep Warasap*, November 21, 1935.

115. See, for example, Mr. Ratburi in "Kho khot khuan khit," *Krungthep Warasap*, March 1936; "Withayu krajai siang khong rao khuan prapprung hai krachap kwa thi thamkan yu thuk wanni," *Thert Rathammanun*, February 13, 1936; and "The Radio," *Bangkok Times*, March 13, 1937.

116. See Peleggi, *Lords of Things*.

117. Puli, "Long Live Rathathammanun!," 6.

118. Puli, 17.

119. Puli, 28.

120. "Speech by Luang Pradit Manudham," in *Pridi by Pridi*, 196.

121. Netr Phunwiwat, quoted in Puli, "Long Live Rathathammanun!," 29.

122. December 11, 1934 letter, quoted in Puli, 28.

123. Puli, 20 and 26.

124. Sarawut Wisaphrom, *Ratsadon saman lang kanpatiwat 2475* [Commoners after the 1932 Revolution] (Bangkok: Matichon, 2016).

125. NA, SR.0201.16/38, "Kamnotkan kanngan chalong rathathammanun," December 7, 1934.

126. NA, SR.0201.16/38.

127. Barmé, *Woman, Man, Bangkok*, 233–36.

128. Barmé, 235.

129. "Thesaban pen prakan prachathipatai," *Siam Ukhos*, August 21, 1938.

Chapter Five

1. Paul T. Cohen, "Charismatic Monks of Lanna and Isan," in *Charismatic Monks of Lanna Buddhism*, ed. Paul T. Cohen (Copenhagen: NIAS Press, 2017), 59.

2. NA, SR.0201.8/20, Phra Suriyanuwat, July 1932 letter to Bangkok. On Srivichai's career and tangle with the authorities, see: NA, SR.0201.8/20; and NA, SR.0201.10/61; Charas Mosanand, *Phra Khruba Jao Srivichai, ariyasongh haeng Lanna* (Khruba Srivichai, Noble Monk of Lanna) (Bangkok: Phueangfa, 2006); Katherine A. Bowie, "Of Buddhism and militarism in northern Thailand: Solving the puzzle of the saint Khruubaa Srivichai," *Journal of Asian Studies* 73, no. 3 (2014): 711–32.

3. See Narin Phasit, *Thalaengkan rueang samaneri Wat Nariwong* [Announcements on the Issue of the Female Novices of Wat Nariwong] (Bangkok: Thai-Japanese Friendship Association [1929] 2001); NA, R.6/R.7 files; Sakdina Chatrakun na Ayutthaya, *Chiwit, naeokhit lae kantosu khong "Narin klung" ru Narin Phasit, khon khwang lok* [Life, Thought and Struggles of "Narin Klung" or Narin Phasit, the Person who Blocked the World] (Bangkok: Matichon, 1993); Peter Koret, *The Man who Accused the King of Killing a Fish: The Biography of Narin Phasit of Siam (1874–1950)* (Chiang Mai, Thailand: Silkworm Books, 2012).

4. Chit Phibanthen, *Chiwit lae ngan khong Phutthathat* [Life and works of Buddhadasa] (Bangkok 1977), 48. On Buddhadasa's life and society, see among others: Buddhadasa Bhikkhu, *Lao wai meua wai sonthaya, attachiwaprawat khong than Phutthathat* [Recalling Life at Twilight, the Autobiography of Buddhadasa], interviewer Phra Pracha Phasanuthammano (Bangkok: Komol Thong Foundation, 1985); Kamala Tiyavanich, *Sons of the Buddha: The Early Lives of Three Extraordinary Thai Masters* (Boston: Wisdom Publications, 2007), Tomomi Ito, *Modern Thai Buddhism and Buddhadasa Bhikkhu: A Social History* (Singapore: NUS Press, 2012); and Peter A. Jackson, *Buddhadasa: Theravada Buddhism and Modernist Reform in Thailand* (Chiang Mai, Thailand: Silkworm Books, 2003).

5. The figure of 55,000 is in Ito, *Modern Thai Buddhism*, 19, referencing Phra Maha Thongsup in *Thammajaksu* 20, no. 3 (December 1934): 259–74. Maha

Thongsup was a *parian* nine scholar, director of Mahamakuta Academy's textbook division and a committed rationalist. He became a friend of Buddhadasa and in 1937 adopted one of Buddhadasa's writings in the curriculum. Ito, *Modern Thai Buddhism*, 54.

6. Thompson, *The New Siam*, 641–42.

7. Yoneo Ishii, *Sangha, State and Society: Thai Buddhism in History* (Honolulu: University of Hawai'i Press, 1986); Somboon Suksamran, *Buddhism and Politics in Thailand* (Singapore: ISEAS, 1982); Khanuengnit Chantrabut. *Kankhlueanwai khong yuwasong Thai run rek pho. so. 2477-2484* [The Movement of the First Generation of Young Thai Monks, 1934–1941] (Bangkok: Textbooks Project, 1985); Krajang Nanthapo, *Mahanikai-Thammayut: Khwamkhatyaeng phai nai khong Khanasong Thai* [Mahanikai and Thammayut: Conflict in the Thai Sangha] (Bangkok: Santitham, 1985); Jim L. Taylor, *Forest Monks and the Nation-state: An Anthropological and Historical Study in Northeastern Thailand* (Singapore: ISEAS, 1993).

8. Prasert, *Rathasapha Thai*, 36–37.

9. Justin McDaniel, *Gathering Leaves & Lifting Words: Histories of Buddhist Monastic Education in Laos and Thailand* (Chiang Mai, Thailand: Silkworm Books, 2009).

10. *Acts on the Administration of the Buddhist Order of Sangha* (Bangkok: The Mahamakuta Educational Council, the Buddhist University, 1963).

11. Wachirayan's name is transliterated in different ways. In this book I have used a commonly used English spelling. In the bibliography, his works are listed under Vajirananavarorasa, a rarer English form of his name, since this spelling appears in a bilingual textbook he compiled that was published by the Sangha.

12. *Thalaengkan khanasong pakh piset*, no. 23 (1935).

13. Khanuengnit, *Kankhlueanwai*, 81–82.

14. Khanuengnit, *Kankhlueanwai*; Krajang, *Mahanikai-Thammayut*, 47–115.

15. Premwit Tokaeo, "Kankotang le khayai tua khong Thammayut nikai nai phak tawanok chiang neuea (pho. so. 2394-2473)" [Establishment and expansion of the Thammayut order in the northeast, 1851–1930] (master's thesis, Chulalongkorn University, 1991); Kamala Tiyavanich, *Forest Recollections: Wandering Monks in Twentieth-Century Thailand* (Honolulu: University of Hawai'i Press, 1997), 172–97.

16. Thanissaro, "The Traditions of the Noble Ones: An Essay on the Thai Forest Tradition and Its Relationship with the Dhammayut Hierarchy." Paper presented at Ninth International Thai Studies Conference, Northern Illinois University, Dekalb, IL, available at https://www.accesstoinsight.org/lib/authors/thanissaro/customs.html; Taylor, *Forest Monks*, 40–73.

17. Taylor, *Forest Monks*, 133.

18. Craig Reynolds, "The Buddhist Monkhood in Nineteenth Century Siam" (PhD diss., Cornell University, 1972), 236, 245–50.

19. Because of divisions and seniority issues in the Sangha, between 1851 and 1910 the position of supreme patriarch was vacant for a total of thirty-one years. On his accession in 1851, Mongkut stepped back from his leadership of the Thammayut, and to ensure Sangha harmony appointed someone who would bring a degree of unity. He first appointed his uncle, Prince Paramanuchit, a Mahanikai monk. Paramanuchit held the position for two years until his death in 1853, when the position fell vacant for twenty-one years. Prince Pawaret (Thammayut) was supreme patriarch from 1874 until he died in 1892, although his official status was slightly lower than his predecessor until 1891, just before his death, purposefully so perhaps to maintain harmony with the Mahanikai (Reynolds, "The Buddhist Monkhood," 121–23). Sa, Pawaret's successor and also Thammayut, held the position until he died in 1900. The position was then vacant again for a decade. The discontinuity stems from King Chulalongkorn's reliance on Prince Wachirayan to advance educational reforms using monasteries as fulcra for a new school system. Wachirayan, born in 1860, was only in his early thirties when the reforms began in the 1890s, and was seen as too young to become supreme patriarch. He did not take the position until the sixth king took the throne in 1910 (Reynolds, "The Buddhist Monkhood," 113–25). In late 1937 the first Mahanikai supreme patriarch since 1853 was elected to lead the Sangha. Somdet Phra Wannarat (Phe Tissathera) of Wat Suthat took the position after the death of Prince Chinaworasit, the latter a member of the extended royal family who had been supreme patriarch since Wachirayan's death in 1921.

20. Ishii, *Sangha, State and Society*.

21. This was a longer-term aspect of textual religion. Surveys of provincial Buddhism from early in the twentieth century conducted by the Sangha had noticed the positive effect of learning on practice: the more books there were in a locale, the more disciplined were the monks. Reynolds, "The Buddhist Monkhood," 258.

22. Khanuengnit, *Kankhlueanwai*, 70–71.

23. The group rejected two of Prince Wan's neologisms, *patiwat* and *patirup* ("reformist"), partly because to them the terms had overly worldly associations.

24. Khanuengnit, *Kankhlueanwai*, 106.

25. In part the group sent messages through a "monk's bowl post" (*praisani bat*) to maintain secrecy. Khaneungnit, 108.

26. Later abolished, *monthon* were administrative divisions that grouped together several provinces. The system was an inheritance from the absolutist state used for several years after the revolution.

27. NA, SR.0201.10/33, "Rueang phrasong ampher Wang Krajom changwat Nakhon Nayok klaothot Phra Muni Nayok lae Phra Ratchakawi," Sangha committee to Phra Sarasas Prapan, December 3, 1934. Ban Na and Pakpli were the other two districts. By their description, the Mahanikai were those of the "left side rolled and uncovered" (*muan sai chai waek*), referring to the exposed left

shoulder that marked the Mahanikai. Thammayut monks generally wear their robes to cover both shoulders.

28. *Naktham* courses were preparatory to *parian* exams, and qualifications for the instructors were less advanced than for the higher exams.

29. A preceptor in the Theravada lineage is a monk qualified to ordain a layperson or novice into the order.

30. The 1902 Sangha Act patterned ecclesiastical administration on the civil service hierarchy. Power in the Sangha spread downward from the Council of Elders in Bangkok to heads of *monthon*, provinces, districts (*khweng* or *amphoe*), townships (*tambon*) and individual temples. See Somboon, *Buddhism and Politics*, 37–40.

31. NA, SR.0201.10/33, Sangha committee to Phra Sarasas Prapan, December 3, 1934.

32. NA, SR.0201.10/33, Sangha committee to Phra Sarasas Prapan, December 3, 1934.

33. This practice is confirmed in the 1902 Sangha Act, article 12. The district Sangha head called a meeting among local monks and laypeople.

34. NA, SR.0201.10/33, Sangha committee to Phra Sarasas Prapan, December 3, 1934, 9–10 letter.

35. Letter to education minister, April 3, 1935, in Khanuengnit, *Kankhlueanwai*, 287; emphasis added.

36. NA, SR.0201.10.43, "Rueang rang phraratchabanyat laksana pokhrong khanasong pho. so. 2477."

37. NA, SR.0201.10.43; February 25 and March 5, 1935 letters. The fourteen provinces spanned the country: Bangkok, Thonburi Ayuthaya, Nakhon Pathom, Suphanburi, Nakhon Sri Thammarat, Ratchaburi, Samut Prakan, Chachoengsao, Nakhon Nayok, Saraburi, Khon Kaen, Pijit, and Surat.

38. The highest profile case centered on Phra Thammapidok (Phuean) a venerated Mahanikai head of the Ratchburi *monthon* Sangha. Council of Elders chair Phra Phutthakosajan thought he was attempting to spread the party's influence in his area through a recent promotion of another Mahanikai monk under his supervision as a *tambon* head in place of a Thammayut monk who lived too far away to be effective. At the beginning of 1936, Thammapidok resigned his position. Khanuengnit, *Kankhlueanwai*, 128–31.

39. NA, SR.0201.10/43; February 3, 1936 letter.

40. NA, SR.0201.10/76, "Phra Rajakawi jao khana monthon Prachinburi klaothot Phra Wimonmettajan jao khana changwat Trat," Wimonmettajan to deputy education minister, January 18, 1937.

41. NA, SR.0201.10/76, January 25, 1937 letter to the elders' chair.

42. NA, SR.0201.10/76, February 1, 1937 letter from Phra Ratchakawi to elders' chair.

43. NA, SR.0201.10/76, education minister to Phra Ratchakawi, April 30, 1937.

44. Khanuengnit, *Kankhlueanwai*, 140–48.

45. Khanuengnit, 117–19.

46. Parliamentary minutes, referenced in Khanuengnit, *Kankhlueanwai*, 149–55.

47. Prasert, *Rathasapha Thai*, 302–5.

48. Charnvit et al., *Jomphol pho. Phibun Songkhram*, 228–350; Chatri, *Silapa sathapatchyakam Khana Ratsadon*, 118–63.

49. Prasert, *Rathasapha Thai*, 317–18.

50. *Rajanukitchanubeksa* 58 (October 1941): 1391–1410. Also see Ishii, *Sangha, State and Society*, 103–4.

51. Narit Charatchanyawong, "Lom nikai, mahasanghakam khana ratsadon upasombot Phraya Phahon pho. so. 2484" [Joining the Orders, the People's Party's Great Sangha Work and the Ordination of Phraya Phahon], *Silapa Wathanatham* 39, no. 8 (2018): 108–29.

52. Lawrence Chua, "Building Siam: Race, Leisure and Nationalism in Modern Thai Architecture, 1910–1973" (PhD diss., Cornell University, 2012), 185–97.

53. NA, SR.0201.46, "Wat Phra Sri Mahathat," Wichit to cabinet secretary, April 22, 1941 and latter's reply, May 1, 1941.

54. Kamala, *Forest Recollections*, 189–90.

55. NA, SR.0201.10/101, May and June 1941 cabinet meetings.

56. NA, SR.0201.10/101, August 18, 1941 cabinet meeting.

57. NA, SR.0201.10/101, January 30, 1940 and April 10, 1941 cabinet meetings.

58. NA, SR.0201.10/101, Phra Chamnan in June 16, 1941 cabinet meeting.

59. NA, SR.0201.10/101, Kat Songkhram in March 27, 1941 cabinet meeting.

60. Jackson, Buddhism, *Legitimation and Conflict: The Political Functions of Urban Thai Buddhism* (Singapore: ISEAS, 1989), 73–76.

61. Ishii, *Sangha, State and Society*, 107–113.

62. Thak, *Thailand: The Politics of Despotic Paternalism* (Chiang Mai, Thailand: Silkworm Books, 2007).

63. Ishii, *Sangha, State and Society*, 113–19.

64. The 1932 revolution also was construed as a return, rather than an eruption of something new. Songsujarit Nawarat termed the 1932 event a reformation, using both words in the title of his 1937 book (*Siam rathapatiwat* in Thai, *Siam Reformation* in English). Songsujarit alleged return to a democracy that existed before Ayutthaya and Bangkok-era absolutism. See Nakharin, *Khwamkhit, khwamru lae amnat thang kanmueang*, 15–17.

65. Thak, *The Politics of Despotic Paternalism*, 98–109; 134–35.

66. Office of the Prime Minister announcement, October 1960, quoted in Somboon, *Buddhism and Politics*, 47.

Chapter Six

1. M. Sivaram, *The New Siam in the Making* (Bangkok: Stationer's Printing Press, 1936).

2. Thompson, *The New Siam*, 683–84.

3. Sorasak Ngamcachonkulkid, *Free Thai*, 81–95.

4. Sorasak Ngamcachonkulkid, "The Seri Thai Movement: The First Alliance against Military Authoritarianism in Modern Thai History" (PhD diss., University of Wisconsin-Madison, 2005), 301.

5. Dararat Mettarikanon, *Kanmueang song fang Khong* [The Politics of Two Sides of the Mekhong River] (Bangkok: Matichon, 2003), 209.

6. Sathuean Suphasophon, *Chiwit thang kanmueang khong pho. o. Phraya Ritthi Akhaney* [The Political Life of Ritthi Akhaney] (Bangkok: Samnakphim Wacharin, 1971), 267.

7. *Anuson ngan phraratchathan phloengsop nai Liang Chaiyakan po.mo. tho. cho.* [Royal Cremation Volume for Nai Liang Chaiyakan] (Bangkok, 1986), vol. 1, n.p.; vol. 3, 3, 5–6. Liang, like many prominent commoners, was cremated and honored at the democracy temple, Wat Phra Sri Mahathat.

8. *Anuson ngan phraratchathan phloengsop nai Liang Chaiyakan*, vol. 3, 4.

9. Sathuean, *Ritthi Akhaney*, 276.

10. Sathuean, 277–78.

11. Sathuean, 290.

12. "The Lands Scandal," *Bangkok Times*, July 29, 1937.

13. Sathuean, *Ritthi Akhaney*, 319–22.

14. Sathuean, 297–98.

15. "The Lands Scandal," *Bangkok Times*, August 4 and August 10, 1937.

16. "The Assembly, a Better Navy Needed," *Bangkok Times*, April 2, 1935.

17. "The Assembly, the Budget Again," *Bangkok Times*, February 14, 1936.

18. "New Year's Budget Estimates," *Bangkok Times*, February 5, 1937. Total expenditures rose from around 70.2 million baht in 1932–1933 to about 110.7 million by 1938–1939. In this time, the military's share rose from about 13 million baht to 28 million. SYB, vol. 20 (1938–1939): 273, 284.

19. "Siam's Budget Debated," *Bangkok Times*, February 8, 1937.

20. "A Broadcast Address," *Bangkok Times*, March 24, 1937.

21. "The Government's Assurance Regarding Broadcasting in Siam," *Bangkok Times*, March 24, 1937.

22. "Armed Strength, its Importance for Siam," *Bangkok Times*, April 3, 1937.

23. "Assembly Rag, Member Ducked in Pond," *Bangkok Times*, August 8, 1938; "Saturday's Incident," *Bangkok Times*, August 9, 1938.

24. NA, S.B. 9.2.3/5, anonymous pamphlet, August 8, 1938. The police brought Wichit in for questioning after the pamphlet appeared, but the results were inconclusive. "Luang Wichit thuk tamruat chern pai tai saona," *Pramuan Wan*, August 16, 1938; "Sang hai santiban suepsuan khadi baipleo thuean to pai ik," *Prachamit*, September 9, 1938.

25. Hat Daoruang, *Chiwit lae ngan khong si adit rathamontri* [Life and Works of the Four Former Ministers] (Bangkok: Aksonsan, 1965), 396–97, 400–1.

26. Hat, 402.

27. Hat, 412. Thawin's September motion is reproduced on 409–64.

28. "Politics in Siam," *Bangkok Times*, September 12, 1938.

29. "The Assembly," *Bangkok Times*, September 12, 1938.

30. "Royal Decree," *Bangkok Times*, September 12, 1938.

31. "Politics in Siam," *Bangkok Times*, September 12, 1938.

32. "The Assembly," *Bangkok Times*, September 12, 1938.

33. "Obstructionist Tactics," *Bangkok Times*, September 12, 1938.

34. Hat, *Chiwit lae ngan*, 108.

35. Hat, 123–26.

36. Hat, 129.

37. His business ended when his vehicle broke down and was too expensive to repair. A talented boxer from a young age, he then boxed for money to support his family. Hat, 132–36.

38. Hat, 140–44.

39. Hat, 147–48.

40. Thirawat Pranatasutja, "Naeokhwamkhit lae botbat thang kanmueang khong Nai Chamlong Daoruang" [Political Thought and Role of Chamlong Daoruang], in *Pridi Banomyong lae 4 Rathamontri Isan + 1*, 150.

41. Thirawat, "Nai Chamlong," 152.

42. *Raingan kanprachum sapha phuthen ratsadon*, "Rueang rang phraratchya-banyat san piset phutthasakarat 2481," 378–81.

43. "Rang phraratchyabanyat san piset," 383–87.

44. Sathuean, *Ritthi Akhaney*, 416–38.

45. Phuthorn, "San piset," 209.

46. Phuthorn, "San piset."

47. Quoted in Phuthorn, 196.

48. Krom khosanakan, "Khamphiphaksa," 73.

49. Krom khosanakan, 349.

50. Krom khosanakan, 281; 283–84. The government then alleged that Phra Ratchayathiraksa joined a plot with Song Suradet and others to topple the government and bring back Prajadhipok as king. Krom khosanakan, 282–84.

51. Krom khosanakan, 190.

52. Krom khosanakan, 193.

53. *Raingan kanprachum sapha phuthen ratsadon* 2/8, 1940, 376.

54. *Raingan* (1940), 378.

55. *Raingan* (1940), 378.

56. *Raingan* (1940), 378.

57. Phraya Sunthonpipit, "Thesaban Prathet Siam" [Siamese Local Government] in Momchao Sakon Wannakon Worawan and Phraya Sunthonpipit, *Sakon thesaban* [Local Government around the World] (Bangkok: Thai Club of Japan, 2004 (1935)), 163–64.

58. Phraya Sunthonpipit, 205.

59. "Phraratchabanyat jat rabiap phutthasakarat 2476," articles 18 and 19. Reprinted in Phraya Sunthonpipit, 220.

60. *Raingan* (1940), 376 and 378.

61. Thompson, *The New Siam*, 253–54.

62. *Raingan* (1940), 270.

63. *Raingan* (1940), 386–95.

64. *Raingan* (1940), 391.

65. Prasert, *Rathasapha Thai*, 329.

66. Direk Chaiyanam, "Border Dispute and Peace Agreement between Thailand and French Indochina," in *Thailand and World War II*, 25.

67. "Pathakata nam khong pho. no. Phon Ek Chatchai Chunhavan" [Introduction by Colonel Chatchai Chunhavan], in *Jomphon pho. Phibun Songkhram*, 11.

68. Benjamin A. Batson, "The Fall of the Phibun Government, 1944," *Journal of the Siam Society* 62, no. 2 (July 1974): 92.

69. Direk, "Border Dispute," 33–46.

70. Shane Strate, *The Lost Territories*, 37–63.

71. Charnvit, *Prawatisat kanmueang Thai*, 423–24.

72. Suthachai Yimprasert, *Phaenching Chat Thai:Wa duai rat lae kantotan rat samai jomphon pho. Phibun Songkhram khrang thi song (pho. so. 2491–2500* [The Plan to Steal the Nation: On the State and Resistance to the State in the Second Time of Field Marshal Phibun Songkhram, 1948–1957] (Bangkok: 6 Tula Raluek, 2010), 29–31.

73. Murashima, "The Thai-Japanese Alliance," 203.

74. Murashima, 192.

75. Quoted in Nai Chanthana (pseud. Malai Chupinit), *X.O. Group: Rueangrao phai nai khabuankan Seri Thai* [X.O. Group: Stories from within the Seri Thai] (Bangkok: Krathom Po. Lo., [1946] 2001), 54.

76. Nai Chanthana, 56.

77. Nai Chanthana, 56.

78. *Washington Times Herald*, December 18, 1941, quoted in "Establishment of the Anti-Japan Resistance Movement and the Seri Thai," in *Pridi by Pridi*, 197.

79. "Establishment of the Anti-Japan Resistance Movement," 197.

80. Pridi, "The Organisation of the Seri Thai Movement," in Thak, *Thai Politics: Extracts and Documents*, 373.

81. Thawi Bunyaket, "Additional Facts on the Situation in Thailand during World War II," in *Thailand and World War II*, 141–42.

82. Nai Chanthana, *X.O. Group*, 44–45.

83. Somsak, "The Communist Movement," 140–42.

84. Nai Chanthana, *X.O. Group*, 58, 63–76.

85. Haseman, *The Thai Resistance Movement*, 43–79.

86. In Thak, *Thai Politics: Extracts and Documents*, 377.

87. Somsak, "The Communist Movement," 156.

88. NA, (3)SR.0201.41.1/28, parliamentary secretary to the government, July 20, 1944.

89. NA, (3)SR.0201.41.1/28, December 25, 1943, supreme commander's instruction of removal of government to Petchabun.

90. NA, (3)SR.0201.41.1/28, January 17, 1944 secretary of army, field office to cabinet secretary.

91. NA, (3)SR.0201.41.1/28, January 11, 1944 minister of the interior to cabinet secretary.

92. NA, Bo.Ko. Sungsut, 2.6.8/3, interior minister letter to army field commander, January 23, 1944. These latter rates were high by peacetime standards, but still lower than the Japanese paid.

93. NA, Bo.Ko. Sungsut, 2.6.8/3, letter from interior ministry to provincial governors, November 18, 1944.

94. NA, (3)SR.0201.41.1/58, interior ministry to provincial work committees, March 16, 1944.

95. NA, (3)SR.0201.41.1/58, Rabiap kanjatha raengngan nai khwam amnuai kan khong krasuang mahathai [System for finding labour in the administration of the interior ministry], February 15, 1944.

96. The government relied on two absolutist era laws to obtain conscript labor: a 1914 martial law act and a 1923 civilian assistance to the military act. The king's government introduced the first law at the beginning of World War I to prevent social unrest among foreign communities in Siam. The second law sought to legalize drafting people into large-scale military construction projects in peacetime. The interior ministry, tasked with raising conscript labor during World War II, resisted both of these laws. Mainly the ministry felt that having military officers dragooning people into service would diminish respect and support for the military. NA, Bo.Ko. Sungsut, 2.6.8/3, November 24, 1944 letter from interior minister to provincial governors.

97. Two to four hundred baht per demand was common. NA, (3) SR.0201.41.1/28, July 15 and July 20, 1944 government reports.

98. NA, (2) SR.0201.41.1/30, interior minister to provincial governors, January 22, 1944.

99. NA, (2) SR.0201.41.1/30, interior ministry labor announcement, January 24, 1944.

100. NA, (3)SR.0201.41.1/28, Phibun letter, March 11, 1944.

101. Suthachai, *Phaenching Chat Thai*, 38.

102. NA, (3)SR.0201.41.1/58 July 26, 1947 letter from interior ministry to cabinet secretary.

103. Nai Chanthana (pseud. Malai Chupinit), *Banthuek jomphol* [The Field Marshal's Memoirs] (Bangkok: Krathom Po. Lo., [1945] 2001), 62.

104. Hat Daoruang, *Chiwit lae ngan*, 249–50.

105. Hat, 248–53.

106. Hat, 252.

107. Hat, 256.

108. Hat, 259–260.

109. Suthachai, *Phaenching Chat Thai*, 37–38; Sorasak, *Tamnan Seri Thai*, 189–90.

110. Sangh Pathanothai, *Khwamneuk nai krongkhang* [Thoughts in Prison] (Bangkok: Klang Withaya, 1956), 481; Somsak, "The Communist Movement," 153–54.

111. Somsak, "The Communist Movement," 162.

112. Charnvit, *Prawatisat kanmueang Thai*, 410.

113. Withet Korani, *Khwampenma haeng rabawp prachathipatai khong Thai* [The Origins of the Thai Democratic Regime] (Bangkok: Panfa Phitya, 1968), 811–12.

114. Withet, 813–16.

115. Sukhin, *Rathaprahan 2490*, 30–47; Charnvit, *Prawatisat kanmueang*, 405–8.

116. Sukhin, *Rathaprahan 2490*, 57.

117. "Phratchaybanyat khumkhrong khachajai khong prachachon nai phawa khopkhan phutthasakarat 2489," in Hat, *Chiwit lae ngan*, 270–76.

118. Hat, *Chiwit lae ngan*, 281–87.

119. Withet, *Khwampenma haeng rabawp prachathipatai*, 1055.

120. Hat, *Chiwit lae ngan*, 371.

121. Prasert, *Rathasapha Thai*, 502–3.

122. "Constitution of Siam, 1946" in Thak, *Thai Politics: Extracts and Documents*, 506.

123. Suphasawatwongsanit, "A Memorandum on a Certain Aspect of the Siamese Politics," in *1 satawat Suphasawat*, 543–44.

124. Suphasawatwongsanit's letter to his wife, May 20, 1946 in *1 satawat Suphasawat*, 495.

125. Jayanta Kumar Ray, *Portraits of Thai Politics* (New Delhi: Orient Longman, 1972), 171.

126. Suthachai, *Phaenching Chat Thai*, 47.

127. Prasert, *Rathasapha Thai*, 443, 445–46.

128. Albert Camus, *The Plague*, trans. Stuart Gilbert (New York: Vintage International, 1975), 73.

129. Suphasawatwongsanit's letter to his wife, May 16, 1946, in *1 satawat Suphasawat*, 494.

130. Girivat *Prachathipatai 17 pi*, 158–59, 164.

131. Girivat, 186.

132. Girivat, 225–30. Recent royalist hagiography also has elevated dogs over citizens.

133. Girivat, 297, 229.

134. Dararat, *Kanmueang song fang*, 360–61.

135. Sukhin, *Rathaprahan*, pp. 20–23.

136. Ferrara, *Political Development*, 128.

137. Kasian, *Commodifying Marxism*, 56–58.

138. Somsak, "The Communist Movement," 9–10; 216–19.

139. Thanet Aphornsuvan, "The United States and the Coming of the Coup of 1947 in Siam," *Journal of the Siam Society* 75 (1987): 199.

140. Handley, *The King Never Smiles*, 86–87.

141. Wasana, *The Crown and the Capitalists*, 141–44; Prasert, *Rathasapha Thai*, 482–87.

142. Chalong Soontravanich, "Small Arms, Romance, Crime and Violence in Post-WWII Thai Society," *Journal of Southeast Asian Studies* 43, no. 1 (June 2005): 26–46.

143. See Suthachai's superb analysis, *Phaenching Chat Thai*, esp. 103–32.

144. Suthachai, 129.

145. Suthachai, 115–18.

146. Handley, *The King Never Smiles*, 88.

147. Prince Chalermsri Chantrathat in *Thai Kasem*, Novemember 20, 1947, quoted in Suthachai, *Phaenching Chat Thai*, 117.

148. Malaengwi, *Bueanglang prawatisat*, 77.

149. Prince Dhani Nivat, the last education minister under the old regime and strongly anti-People's Party, apparently demanded of the military group that Khuang be named prime minister. Handley, *The King Never Smiles*, 89.

150. Suthachai, *Phaenching Chat Thai*, 116.

151. Suthachai, 105–6.

152. Handley, *The King Never Smiles*, 89.

153. Kobkua Suwannathat-Pian, *Kings, Country and Constitutions* (London: RoutledgeCurzon, 2004), 50.

154. Quoted in Kobkua, 50.

155. "Some Aspects of the Establishment of the People's Party," in *Pridi by Pridi*, 146–47.

156. Suthachai, *Phaenching Chat Thai*, 118–19.

157. Malaengwi, *Bueanglang prawatisat*, 85.

158. Thamrongsak Petchlert-anan, *"Kho Ang" kanpatiwat-rathaprahan, kabot nai kanmueang Thai patchuban: Botwikhro lae ekasan* ["Reason" for Coups in Modern Siam/Thailand: Document and Analysis] (Bangkok: The Foundation for the Promotion of Social Science and Humanities Textbooks Project, 2007), 127–29.

159. Suthachai, *Phaenching Chat Thai*, 132.

160. "Some Aspects of the Establishment of the People's Party," in *Pridi by Pridi*, 148.

161. "Uphold the Aim for Full Democracy of the Heroes of 14 October," in *Pridi by Pridi*, 246.

162. Handley, *The King Never Smiles*, 92.

163. Suthachai, *Phaenching Chat Thai*, 167–68.

164. Suthachai, 167–68.

165. Suthachai, 168.

166. Suthachai, 169, 171.

167. Suthachai, 185.

168. Suthachai, *Phaenching Chat Thai*, 184–94.

169. *Bangkok Post*, February 28, March 1, March 3, and March 4, 1949.

170. Hat, *Chiwit lae ngan*, 484–85.

171. Hat, 28–31.

172. Thak, *The Politics of Despotic Paternalism*, 44.

Conclusion

1. "Protesters install 'new plaque' at Sanam Luang," *Bangkok Post*, September 12, 2020.

2. Bloch, *The Historian's Craft*, 37.

3. Thongchai, "Siam's Colonial Conditions."

4. King Vajiravudh, "Lathi ao yang," in *Royal Cremation Volume for Luang Anukan Ratchaphat* (Bangkok, 1963), 1–9.

5. Prince Pithayalongkorn, another leading royal intellectual, in 1932 broadly dismissed interest in foreign ideas as faddish misunderstandings, and indirectly criticized the revolutionaries on these grounds. See his "Phawa yangrai no thi riak wa siwilai" (What Are the Conditions of What Is Called Civilized), *Prachum pathakata khong krommeun Pithayalongkorn* [Collected Lectures of Prince Pithayalongkorn] (Bangkok: 1970), 429–72.

6. The long-standing appeal of the idea of Prajadhipok as the democratic king is well described by Prajak Kongkirati, *Lae laeo khwamkhlueanwai ko prakot: Kanmueang wathanatham khong naksuksa lae panyachon kon 14 Tula* [And then the Movement Emerged: Student and Intellectuals' Cultural Politics before 14

October] (Bangkok: Thammasat University, 2005), esp. 486–519. The actual story is best explained by Nattapoll. See his "Khwam Patiwat—Khon Khana Ratsadon."

7. Prajak, *Khwamkhlueanwai*; Chai-Anan Samudvanija, Setthapon Khusripitak and Sawaeng Rattanamongkholmas, eds. *Sat kanmueang* [Political Animals] (Bangkok: Thai Watana Panich, 1971).

Bibliography

National Archives of Thailand Files

Krasuang sueksathikan, S.Th. (Ministry of Education)
Krasuang mahathai, Mo.Tho (Ministry of the Interior)
Samnak nayok ratthamontri, SR (Office of the Premier)
Suan bukkhon chao Thai, S.B. (Personal Papers)
Ratchakan thi 7, R.7 (Seventh Reign Archives)
Ratchakan thi 6, R.6 (Sixth Reign Archives)
Kong banchakan thahan sungsut, Bo.Ko. Sungsut (Supreme Command of the Armed Forces)

Other Sources

Acts on the Administration of the Buddhist Order of Sangha. Bangkok: The Mahamakuta Educational Council, The Buddhist University, 1963.

Adas, Michael. *The Burma Delta: Economic Development and Social Change on an Asian Rice Frontier, 1852–1941*. Madison: University of Wisconsin Press, 1974.

A. K. Rungsaeng. *Pho. 27 sailap phrapokklao* [P. 27 King Prajadhipok's Secret Agent]. Bangkok: Thaikasem, 1978.

Am Bunthai. *Kridakan bon thi rap sung* [Might on the High Plains]. Bangkok: Thai Club of Japan, 2000 (1933).

Anderson, Benedict R. O'G. "Studies of the Thai State: The State of Thai Studies." In *Exploration and Irony in Studies of Siam over Forty Years*, 15–45. Ithaca, NY: Cornell Southeast Asia Program Publications, 2014.

Anderson, Perry. "The Antinomies of Antonio Gramsci." *New Left Review* 100 (1976): 3–78.

Andrews, James M. *Siam 2nd. Rural Economic Survey, 1934–1935*. Bangkok: W. H. Mundie, 1935.

Anuson ngan phraratchathan phloengsop nai Liang Chaiyakan po. mo. tho. cho. [Royal Cremation Volume for Nai Liang Chaiyakan]. Bangkok, 1986.

Anuson ngan phraratchathan phloengsop nai Sanguan Tularaks [Royal Cremation Volume for Sanguan Tularaks]. Bangkok, 1995].

Anuson nai ngan phraratchathan phloengsop phon ruea ek Sindhu Songkhramchai [Royal Cremation Volume for Admiral Sindhu Songkhramchai]. Bangkok: Department of Naval Information, 1977.

Anuson mo.cho. Sitthiphon Kridakon, botkhwam khong lae kiaokap mo.cho. Sitthiphon Kridakon [Memorial Volume for Prince Sitthiphon Kridakon, Articles by and about Prince Sittiphon Kridakon]. Bangkok: Social Science Association of Thailand, 1971.

Anuson nai ngan phraratchathan phloengsop Nitisat Paisal [Royal Cremation Volume for Nitisat Paisal]. Bangkok, 1967.

Baker, Chris, and Pasuk Phongpaichit. *A History of Thailand.* Chiang Mai, Thailand: Silkworm Books, 2006.

Barmé, Scot. *Luang Wichit Wathakan and the Creation of a Thai Identity.* Singapore: ISEAS, 1993.

———. *Woman, Man, Bangkok.* Chiang Mai, Thailand: Silkworm Books, 2006.

Batson, Benjamin A. *The End of the Absolute Monarchy in Siam.* Oxford: Oxford University Press, 1984.

———. "The Fall of the Phibun Government, 1944." *Journal of the Siam Society* 62, no. 2 (July 1974): 89–120.

———, ed. and compiler. *Siam's Political Future: Documents from the End of the Absolute Monarchy.* Ithaca, NY: Cornell University Southeast Asia Program, 1974.

Battye, Noel. "The Military, Government and Society in Siam, 1868–1910: Politics and Military Reform during the Reign of King Chulalongkorn." PhD diss., Cornell University, 1974.

Benda, Harry J. "Non-Western Intelligensias [sic] as Political Elites." In *Continuity and Change in Southeast Asia: Collected Journal Articles of Harry J. Benda,* 93–106. New Haven, CT: Yale University Southeast Asian Studies, 1972.

Bloch, Marc. *The Historian's Craft.* Translated by Peter Putnam. New York: Vintage Books, 1953.

———. *Strange Defeat: a Statement of Evidence Written in 1940.* Translated by Gerard Hopkins. New York: W. W. Norton, 1968.

Bowie, Katherine A. "Of Buddhism and Militarism in Northern Thailand: Solving the Puzzle of the Saint Khruubaa Srivichai." *Journal of Asian Studies* 73, no. 3 (2014): 711–32.

Brown, Ian. *The Elite and the Economy in Siam, 1890–1920.* Oxford, UK: Oxford University Press, 1988.

ten Brummelhuis, Hans. *King of the Waters: Homan van der Heide and the Origin of Modern Irrigation in Siam.* Leiden: KITLV Press, 2005.

Buddhadasa Bhikkhu. *Lao wai muea wai sonthaya, attachiwaprawat khong Than Phutthathat* [Recalling life at twilight, the autobiography of Buddhadasa]. Interviewed by Phra Pracha Phasanuthammano. Bangkok: Komol Thong Foundation, 1985.

Bot phrapan bang ruang khong Khru Thep, phim nai ngan phraratchathan phloengsop phana than so. Thammasakmontri Thephasadin na Ayutthaya [Some Writings of Khru Thep, Printed on the Occasion of the Royal Cremation of Thammasakmontri Thephasadin na Ayutthaya]. Bangkok: n.p., 1943.

Chai-anan Samudvanija, Setthapon Khusripitak, and Sawaeng Rattanamongkholmas, eds. *Sat kanmueang* [Political Animals]. Bangkok: Thai Watana Panich, 1971.

Chai-anan Samudvanija, and Khattiya Kannasut, eds. *Ekkasan kanmueang-kanpokhrong Thai pho. so. 2417–2477* [Thai Political and Administrative Documents, 1874–1934]. Bangkok: Khrongkan Tamra Sangkhomsat lae Manussyasat, 1975.

Chainarong Phanpracha. "Kansang thangrotfai sai morana: Phonkrathop to phumiphak tawantok khong Prathet Thai" [The Construction of the Death Railway: Its Impact on the Western Region of Thailand]. MA thesis, Silpakorn University, 1987.

Chaiwat Yonpiam. *Fanrai khong Mueang Thai* [Thailand's Nightmare]. Bangkok: Chaophraya, 1983.

Chaiyan Rajchagool. *The Rise and Fall of the Thai Absolute Monarchy: Foundations of the Modern Thai State from Feudalism to Peripheral Capitalism.* Bangkok: White Lotus Press, 1994.

Chalong Soontravanich. "Small Arms, Romance, Crime and Violence in Post-WWII Thai Society." *Journal of Southeast Asian Studies* 43, no. 1 (June 2005): 26–46.

Chalong Soontravanich, Suwimon Rungcharoen, Sakdina Chatrakun na Ayutthaya, and Saman Chaemburi, eds. *Prawatsat raengngan Thai* [Thai Labor History]. Bangkok: Labor Museum, 1998.

Chamlong Ittharong. *Lakhon kanmueang* [Political Theater]. Bangkok: Publishing Cooperative, 1948.

Chamras Mosanand. *Phra Khruba Jao Srivichai, ariyasongh haeng Lanna* [Khruba Srivichai, Noble Monk of Lanna]. Bangkok: Phueangfa, 2006.

Charnvit Kasetsiri. *Prawat kanmueang Thai Siam pho. so. 2475–2500* [A Political History of Thailand-Siam 1932–1957]. Bangkok: Foundation for the Promotion of Social Science and Humanities Textbooks Project, 2008.

———, ed. *Mae: Klap jak Banpong thueng Paknam* [Mother: Back from Banpong to Paknam]. Bangkok: Charnvit Kasetsiri, 2010.

Charnvit Kasetsiri, and Thamrongsak Petchlert-anan. *Patiwat 2475* [1932 Revolution in Siam]. Bangkok: The Foundation for the Promotion of Social Science and Humanities Textbooks Project, 2004.

————, eds. *Pridi Phanomyong lae 4 Rathamontri Isan + 1* [Pridi Banomyong and 4 Isan Ministers + 1]. Bangkok: Foundation for the Promotion of Social Science and Humanities Textbooks Project, and Thammasat Archives Project, 2001.

Charnvit Kasetsiri, Thamrongsak Petchlert-anan, and Vigal Phongpanitanon, eds., *Jomphol pho. Phibun Songkhram kap kanmueang Thai samai mai* [Field Marshal Phibunsongkhram and Modern Thai Politics]. Bangkok: The Foundation for the Promotion of Social Science and Humanities Textbooks Project, 2001.

Chatri Prakitnonthakan. *Silapa sathapatchyakam Khana Ratsadon: Sanyalak thang kanmueang nai choeng udomkan* [Art-Architecture of the People's Party: Political Symbolism of Principles]. Bangkok: Matichon, 2009.

————. "Khana Ratsadon lang Rathaprahan 19 Kanya" [The People's Party after the 19 September Coup], *Aan* 4, no. 4 (2013): 18–39.

Chatthip Nartsupha. *The Thai Village Economy in the Past*. Translated by Chris Baker and Pasuk Phongphaichit. Chiang Mai, Thailand: Silkworm Books, 1999.

Chatthip Nartsupha, and Suthy Prasartset, eds. *The Political Economy of Siam, 1851–1910*. Bangkok: Social Science Association of Thailand, 1978.

Chatthip Nartsupha, Suthy Prasartset, and Montri Chenvidyakarn, eds. *The Political Economy of Siam, 1910–1932*. Bangkok: Social Science Association of Thailand, 1978.

Chiap Amphunan. *Mahawitthayalai khong khappajao* [My University]. Bangkok: Ruamsan Press, 1958.

Chit Phibanthen. *Chiwit lae ngan khong Phutthathat* [Life and Works of Buddhadasa]. Bangkok, 1977.

Chongkon Krairoek. *Yu yang suea: Banthuek chiwit kantosu thang kanmuang yuk bukboek pho. So. 2500* [Live like a Tiger: Records of a Life of Political Struggle in Its First Phase, 1957]. Chiang Mai, Thailand: The Knowledge Center, 2003 (1969).

Cohen, Paul T., ed. *Charismatic Monks of Lanna Buddhism*. Copenhagen, Denmark: NIAS Press, 2017.

Chua, Lawrence. "The Aesthetic Citizen: Translating Modernism and Fascism in Mid-Twentieth Century Thailand." In *Southeast Asia's Modern Architecture: Questions of Translation, Epistemology and Power*, edited by Jiat Hwee-Chang and Imran bin Tajrudeen, 58–84. Singapore: NUS Press, 2019.

————. "Building Siam: Race, Leisure and Nationalism in Modern Thai Architecture, 1910–1973." PhD diss., Cornell University, 2012.

Chula Chakrabongse. *Lords of Life*. London: Alvin Redman, 1960.

Chuli Saranusit. *Daen hok* [Division Six]. Bangkok, n.d.

Copeland, Matthew. "Contested Nationalism and the Overthrow of the Thai Absolute Monarchy." PhD diss., Australian National University, 1993.

Crosby, Josiah. *Siam: The Crossroads*. London: Hollis and Carter, 1945.

Damri Ruangsutham. *Khabuankan raengngan Thai nai kantotan kongthap Yipun nai Songkhram Lok khrang thi 2* [The Thai Labor Movement in the anti-Japanese Resistance during World War II]. Bangkok: Sukhaphapchai, 2001.

Damrong Rajanuphap. *Nithan borankhadi* [Ancient Tales]. Bangkok: Dokya, 2002 (1944).

———. *Thesaphiban* [Control over Territory]. Bangkok: Matichon, 2002 (1925).

Dararat Mettarikanon. *Kanmueang song fang Khong* [The Politics of Two Sides of the Mekhong River]. Bangkok: Matichon, 2003.

Day, Tony. *Fluid Iron: State Formation in Southeast Asia* Honolulu: University of Hawai'i Press, 2002.

Dhani Nivat. "The Old Siamese Conception of the Monarchy," *Journal of the Siam Society* 36, no. 2 (1947). Reprinted in *Collected Articles by H. H. Prince Dhani Nivat*. Bangkok: Siam Society, 1969.

Dilok Nabarath, Prince. *Siam's Rural Economy under King Chulalongkorn.* Translated by Walter E. J. Tips. Bangkok: White Lotus, 2000.

Direk Chaiyanam. *Thailand and World War II.* Edited by Jane Keyes. Chiang Mai, Thailand: Silkworm Books, 2008.

Duen Bunnag, *Than Pridi rathaburut awuso phu wangphaen setthakit Thai khon raek* [Senior Statesman Pridi, First Thai Economic Planner]. Bangkok: Saitharn Publication House, 2009.

Duen Bunnag, and Pairoj Chayanam. *Kham athibai kotmai rathathammanun, lem 2* [Explanation of Constitutional Law, vols. I and II]. Bangkok: Nitisat, 1934.

Duguit, Léon. *Law in the Modern State.* Translated by Harold Laski. New York: B. W. Huebsch, 1919.

Edwards, Penny. "The Tyranny of Proximity: Power and Mobility in Colonial Cambodia, 1863–1954." *Journal of Southeast Asian Studies* 37, no. 3 (October 2006): 421–43.

———. *Kanmueang Jin Siam: Kankhlueanwai thang kanmueang khong chao Jin phontale nai Prathet Thai kho. so. 1928–1941* [Chinese Politics in Siam: The Political Movement of the Overseas Chinese in Thailand, 1928–1941]. Edited and translated by Worasak Mahathanobol. Bangkok: Asian Studies Institute, Chulalongkorn University, 1996.

———. "The Origin of Modern Official State Ideology in Thailand," *Journal of Southeast Asian Studies* 19, no. 1 (1988): 80–96.

Feeny, David. *The Political Economy of Productivity: Thai Agricultural Development, 1880–1975.* Vancouver: University of British Columbia Press, 1982.

Ferrara, Federico. *The Political Development of Modern Thailand.* Cambridge, UK: Cambridge University Press, 2015.

Fouillée, Alfred, J. Charmont, L. Duguit, and R. Demogue. *Modern French Legal Philosophy.* Translated by Mrs. Franklin W. Scott and Joseph P. Chamberlain. Boston, MA: Boston Book Co., 1916.

Free Press [pseud., Wichai Prasangsit]. *Nak kanmueang sam kok* [Politicians of the Three Kingdoms]. Bangkok: Sahakit, 1950.

Fung Charoenwit. *Sithi le nathi phonlamueang tam rabawp prachathipatai* [Rights and Duties of Citizens According to the Democratic System]. Chachoengsao Provincial Committee, 1934.

Gide, Charles. *Consumers' Co-operative Societies.* Translated by the Co-operative Reference Library Dublin. New York: Alfred A. Knopf, 1922.

Girivat, Louis. *17 pi prachathipatai* [17 Years of Democracy]. Bangkok: Odeon, 1949.

Girling, John. "Thailand in Gramscian Perspective." *Pacific Affairs* 57, No. 3 (Autumn 1984): 385–403.

Gluck, Carol. *Japan's Modern Myths: Ideology in the Late Meiji Period.* Princeton, NJ: Princeton University Press, 1985.

Gramsci, Antonio. *Selections from the Prison Notebooks.* Quinton Hoare and Geoffrey Nowell-Smith, eds. New York: International Publishers, 1972.

Gray, Christine. "Thailand: The Soteriological State in the 1970s." PhD diss., University of Chicago, 1986.

Handley, Paul. *The King Never Smiles.* New Haven, CT: Yale University Press, 2006.

Haseman, John B. *The Thai Resistance Movement during World War II.* Chiang Mai, Thailand: Silkworm Books, 2002.

Hat Daoruang. *Chiwit lae ngan khong sii adit rathamontri* [The Lives and Work of the Four Former Ministers]. Bangkok: Aksonsan, 1965.

van der Heide, J. Homan. "The Economical Development of Siam during the Last Half Century," *Journal of the Siam Society* 3 (1906): 85–99.

Hell, Stefan. *Siam and World War I: An International History.* Bangkok: River Books, 2017.

Hewison, Kevin. *Bankers and Bureaucrats: Capital and the Role of the State in Thailand.* New Haven, CT: Yale University Southeast Asia Studies, 1989.

———. "Forgotten Facts: Industrial Development, Labour and Rural Life in Thailand, 1850–1942." Unpublished research paper, 1986.

———. "Thailand's Conservative Democratization." In *East Asian's New Democracies: Deepening, Reversal, Non-liberal Alternatives,* edited by Yin-wah Chu and Siu-lun Wong, 122–40. Abingdon, Oxon, UK: Routledge, 2010.

Hobsbawm, Eric. *The Age of Empire, 1875–1914.* New York: Pantheon Books, 1987.

Hong Lysa. *Thailand in the Nineteenth Century: Evolution of the Economy and Society.* Singapore: ISEAS Press, 1984.

Hoskin, John. *Wise Counsel: A History of Tilleke & Gibbins, Thailand's Oldest Law Firm.* Bangkok: Tilleke & Gibbins International, 2010.

Hunt, Lynn. *Politics, Culture and Class in the French Revolution.* Berkeley: University of California Press, 1984.

Ingram, James C. *Economic Change in Thailand, 1850–1970.* Stanford, CA: Stanford University Press, 1971.

Ito Tomomi. *Modern Thai Buddhism and Buddhadasa Bhikkhu: A Social History.* Singapore: NUS Press, 2012.

Jackson, Peter A. *Buddhadasa: Theravada Buddhism and Modernist Reform in Thailand.* Chiang Mai, Thailand: Silkworm Books, 2003.

———. *Buddhism, Legitimation and Conflict.* Singapore: ISEAS, 1983.

Johnston, David B. "Rice Cultivation in Thailand: The Development of an Export Economy by Indigenous Capital and Labor." *Modern Asian Studies* 15, no. 1 (1981): 107–26.

———. "Rural Society and the Rice Economy in Thailand, 1880–1930." PhD diss., Yale University, 1975.

Jory, Patrick. "Republicanism in Thai History." In *A Sarong for Clio, Essays on the Intellectual and Cultural History of Thailand*, edited by Maurizio Peleggi, 97–117. Ithaca, NY: Cornell Southeast Asia Program, 2013.

Journal of Contemporary Asia. Military, Monarchy and Repression: Assessing Thailand's Authoritarian Turn 46, no. 3 (2016): 371–37.

Kakizaki Ichiro. *Laying the Tracks: The Thai Economy and its Railways, 1885–1935.* Kyoto, Japan: Kyoto University Press, 2005.

———. *Trams, Buses and Rails: The History of Urban Transport in Bangkok, 1886–2010.* Chiang Mai, Thailand: Silkworm Books, 2014.

Kamala Tiyavanich. *Forest Recollections: Wandering Monks in Twentieth-Century Thailand.* Honolulu: University of Hawai'i Press, 1997.

———. *Sons of the Buddha: The Early Lives of Three Extraordinary Thai Masters.* Boston, MA: Wisdom Publications, 2007.

Kasian Tejapira. *Commodifying Marxism.* Kyoto, Japan: Kyoto University Press, 2001.

Khana Thamngan Prawat Kanphim nai Prathet Thai. *Siamphimphakan: Prawatisat Kanphim nai Prathet Thai* [Siamphimphakan: The History of Publishing in Thailand]. Bangkok: Matichon Books, 2006.

Khanuengnit Chantrabut. *Kankhlueanwai khong yuwasong Thai run raek pho. so. 2477–2484* [The Movement of the First Generation of Young Thai Monks, 1934–1941]. Bangkok: Textbooks Project, 1985.

Krajang Nanthapo. *Mahanikai–Thammayut: Khwamkhatyaeng phai nai khong khanasong Thai* [Mahanikai and Thammayut: Conflict in the Thai Sangha]. Bangkok: Santitham, 1985.

Kobkua Suwannathat-Pian. *Kings, Country and Constitutions.* London: Routledge-Curzon, 2004.

Koret, Peter. *The Man Who Accused the King of Killing a Fish: The Biography of Narin Phasit of Siam (1874–1950).* Chiang Mai, Thailand: Silkworm Books, 2012.

Koskenniemi, Martti. *The Gentle Civilizer of Nations: The Rise and Fall of International Law 1870–1960.* Cambridge, UK: Cambridge University Press, 2002.

Kratoska, Paul, ed. *The Thailand—Burma Railway, 1942–1946: Documents and Selected Writings* [six volumes]. London: Routledge, 2006.

Krom khosanakan. *Khamphiphaksa san piset phuttasakarat 2482 rueang kabot* [1939 Special Court Verdict on Rebellion]. Bangkok, 1939.

———. *Thalaengkan rueang phrabatsomdet phraparamin maha Prajadhipok phrapokklao chaoyuhua songsala ratchasombat* [Official Report on King Prajadhipok's Abdication]. Bangkok, 1935.

Kukrit Pramoj. *Four Reigns*. Translated by Tulachandra. Chiang Mai, Thailand: Silkworm Books, 1999.

Kulap Saipradit. *Bueanglang kanpatiwat 2475* [Behind the Revolution of 1932]. Bangkok: Mingmit, [1941] 1999.

Kullada Kesbunchoo Mead. *The Rise and Decline of Thai Absolutism*. London: Routledge, 2004.

Kruger, Rayne. *The Devil's Discus*. London: Cassell, 1964.

Landon, Kenneth Perry. *The Chinese in Thailand*. London: Oxford University Press, 1941.

———. *Siam in Transition: A Brief Survey of Cultural Trends in the Five Years since the Revolution of 1932*. New York: Greenwood Press, [1939] 1968.

Larsson, Tomas. *Land and Loyalty: Security and the Development of Property Rights in* Thailand. Ithaca, NY: Cornell University Press, 2012.

Lockhart, Greg, and Monique Lockhart, trans. *The Light of the Capital: Three Modern Vietnamese Classics*. Kuala Lumpur, Malaysia: Oxford University Press, 1996.

Loos, Tamara. *Subject Siam: Family, Law and Colonial Modernity in Thailand*. Ithaca, NY: Cornell University, 2006.

Luen Saraphaiwanich. *Fanrai khong khappajao* [My Nightmare]. Bangkok: Saraphai, 1969.

———. *Fanjing khong khappajao* [My Real Dream]. Bangkok: Saraphai, 1969.

Mahamakut rajawithayalai 100 pi [100 Years of Mahamakut College]. Bangkok: Mahamakut Rajawithayalai, n.d.

Malaengwi [pseud., Seni Pramoj]. *Bueanglang prawatisat* [Behind History]. Bangkok: Publishing Cooperative, 1947.

Marx, Karl. "The German Ideology, Part I." In *The Marx-Engels Reader*, 2nd ed. Robert C. Tucker, ed., 146–200. New York: W. W. Norton, 1972.

Mazower, Mark. *The Dark Continent: Europe's Twentieth Century*. New York: Vintage Books, 2000.

McDaniel, Justin. *Gathering Leaves and Lifting Words: Histories of Buddhist Monastic Education in Laos and Thailand*. Seattle: University of Washington Press, 2008.

Murashima Eiji. "Democracy and the Development of Political Parties in Thailand, 1932–1945." In *The Making of Modern Thai Political Parties*, Eiji Murashima, Nakharin Mektrairat and Somkiat Wanthana, 1–100. Tokyo: Institute of Developing Economies, 1991.

Nai Chanthana [pseud. Malai Chupinit]. *Banthuek jomphol* [The Field Marshal's Memoirs]. Bangkok: Krathom Po. Lo., [1945] 2001.

———. *X.O. Group: Rueangrao phai nai khabuankan Seri Thai* [X.O. Group: Stories from within the Seri Thai]. Bangkok: Krathom Po. Lo., [1946] 2001.

Nai Honhuay [pseud. Silapachai Chanchalerm]. *Kabot nai sip 2478* [The 1935 Non-commissioned Officers' Revolt]. Bangkok: Matichon, 2000.

———. *Thahan ruea patiwat* [The Navy in the Revolution]. Bangkok: Matichon, [1947] 2012.

Nakharin Mektrairat. *Kanpatiwat Siam 2475* [The Revolution in Siam 1932]. Bangkok: Fadiokan, [1992] 2010.

———. *Khwamkhit khwamru lae amnat thang kanmueang nai patiwat Siam 2475* [Thought, Knowledge and Political Power in the Siamese Revolution of 1932]. Bangkok: Fadiokan, 2003.

———. *Karani ro. 7 song sala ratchasombat* [The Case of the Seventh King's Abdication]. Bangkok: Kobfai Publishing Project, 2007.

Narin Phasit. *Thalaengkan rueang samaneri wat nariwong* [Announcements on the Issue of the Female Novices of Wat Nariwong]. Bangkok: Thai-Japanese Friendship Association, [1929] 2001.

Narit Charatchanyawong. "Anuson ngansop samachik Khana Ratsadon" [Funeral Volumes of the People's Party Members]. *Silapa Wathanatham* 38, no. 8 (2017): 70–113.

———. "Lom nikai, mahasanghakam Khana Ratsadon upasombot Phraya Phahon pho. so. 2484" [Joining the Orders, the People's Party's Great Sangha Work and the Ordination of Phraya Phahon]. *Silapa Wathanatham* 39, no. 8 (2018): 108–29.

Nattapoll Chaiching. *Kabot Bowondet: Bueangraek patipaks patiwat Siam 2475* [The Bowondet Rebellion: The First Counterrevolution against 1932]. Bangkok: Matichon, 2016.

———. *Khofanfai nai fan anluea chuea: Khwamklueanwai khong khabuankanpatipaks patiwat Siam [pho. so. 2475–2500]* [An Unbelievable Dream: The Resistance Movement against the Siamese Revolution, 1932–1957]. Bangkok: Fadiaokan, 2013.

———. "The Monarchy and the Royalist Movement in Modern Thai Politics, 1932–1957." In *Saying the Unsayable, Monarchy and Democracy in Thailand*, edited by Soren Ivarsson and Lotte Isager, 147–78. Copenhagen, Denmark: NIAS Press, 2010.

Netr Khemayothin. *Ngan taidin khong phan ek Yothi, lem 3* [The Underground Work of General Yothi, vol. 3]. Bangkok: Kasem Bannakit, 1967.

Ngern Hongladarom. *Jomphol nai thatsana khong khapajao* [My Viewpoint on the Field Marshal]. Bangkok: Ratchadarom, 1949.

Nimitmongkol Navarat. *The Dreams of an Idealist*. Translated by David Smyth. Chiang Mai, Thailand: Silkworm Books, 2009.

Nithi Eoseewong. *Pen and Sail: Literature and History in Early Bangkok*. Translated by Chris Baker et al. Chiang Mai, Thailand: Silkworm Books, 2006.

Orwell, George. *1984*. New York: The New American Library, 1961.

Pairoj Chaiyanam. *Pathakata khosana phak thi ha: Rueang sithi lae nathi khong phonlamueang* [Propaganda Lectures Part Five: Rights and Duties of the Citizenry]. Songkhla Provincial Committee, 1935.

Paisan Silapasat, Phra [Chaophraya Thammasakmontri]. *Thammachariya*, vol. 4. Bangkok: Aksorniti, 1912.

Paisan Silapasat, Phra [Chaophraya Thammasakmontri], and Luang Anukit Withun. *Thammachariya*, vol. 1. Bangkok: Aksorniti, 1909.

———. *Thammachariya*, vol. 2. Bangkok: Aksorniti, n.d.

Panni Bualek. *Kuli lakrot kap prawatisat raengngan Thai* [Rickshaw Coolies and the History of Thai Labor]. Bangkok: Panthakit, 2003.

Pasuk Phongpaichit, and Chris Baker. *Thailand, Economy and Politics*, 2nd ed. Selangor, Malaysia: Oxford University Press, 2002.

Pathakata khong phuthen ratsadon rueang saphap khong changwat tangtang [Parliamentary Representatives' Lectures on the State of Various Provinces]. Bangkok: Thai Club of Japan, 1996.

Pavin Chachavalpongpun, ed. *'Good Coup' Gone Bad: Thailand's Political Developments since Thaksin's Downfall*. Singapore: ISEAS, 2014.

Peleggi, Maurizio. *Lords of Things: The Fashioning of the Siamese Monarchy's Modern Image*. Honolulu: University of Hawai'i Press, 2002.

Phayap Rotchanawiphat. *Yuk thamin* [The Barbarous Age]. Bangkok: So Sethabut, [1946] 1972.

Pithayalongkorn, Phra. *Prachum pathakata khong krommuen Pithayalongkorn* [Collected Lectures of Prince Pithayalongkorn]. Bangkok, n.p., 1970.

Phillips, Matthew. *Thailand in the Cold War*. Abingdon, Oxon, UK: Routledge, 2016.

Phuthorn Phumadhon. "Kansueksa san piset [pho. so. 2476, 2478, 2481]" [A Study of the Special Courts of 1933, 1935 and 1938]. MA thesis, Chulalongkorn University, 1977.

Pilbeam, Pamela. *The Middle Classes in Europe, 1789–1914: France, Germany, Italy and Russia*. London: Macmillan, 1990.

Porphant Ouyyanont. "Bangkok's Population and the Ministry of the Capital in Early 20th Century Thai History." *Southeast Asian Studies* 35, no. 2 (1997): 240–60.

———. "Physical and Economic Change in Bangkok, 1851–1925." *Southeast Asian Studies*, 36, no. 4 (1999): 437–74.

———. *A Regional Economic History of Thailand* Singapore: ISEAS, 2017.

Prajak Kongkirati. *Lae laeo Khwamkhlueanwai ko prakot: Kanmueang wathanatham khong naksueksa lae panyachon kon 14 Tula* [And then the Movement Emerged: Student and Intellectuals' Cultural Politics before 14 October]. Bangkok: Thammasat University, 2005.

Prasert Patthamasukhon. *Rathasapha Thai nai rop sisipsong pi [2475–2517]* [The Thai Parliament over 42 Years (1932–1974)]. Bangkok: Munithi Thanakhan Krungthep, 1983.

Prayun Phamonmontri. *Chiwit 5 phaendin* [Life over Five Reigns]. Bangkok: Bannakit, 1975.

———. *Banthuek rueang kanplianpleng kanpokhrong pho. so. 2475 waduai kamnert khwammungmai kanpatiwat khwamsamret lae khwamlomlaeo* [Record of the Governance Change of 1932, on Birth, Aims, Revolution, Success and Failure]. Bangkok: Bhannakij Trading, 1974.

Premwit Towkaew. "Kankotang lae khayaitua khong Thammayut nikai nai phak tawanok chiang nuea [pho. so. 2394–2473]" [The Establishment and Expansion of the Dhammayuttikanikaya in the Northeast, 1851–1930]. MA thesis, Chulalongkorn University, 1991.

Pridi Banomyong. *Pridi by Pridi: Selected Writings on Life, Politics, Economy*. Translated by Chris Baker and Pasuk Phongpaichit. Chiang Mai, Thailand: Silkworm Books, 2000.

———. *Bang ruang kiaokap phraboromawongsanuwong nai rawang songkhram lok krang thi 2* [Some Issues concerning the Royal Family during World War II]. Bangkok: Pridi-Phoonsuk Foundation, 2000 (1972).

Puli Fuwongcharoen. "*Khana kanmueang*" *lang kanpatiwat siam: pholawat, pathanakan lae chathakam khong rabop rai phak* ["Political Parties" after the Siamese Revolution: Dynamics, Development and Fate of the No Party System]. Bangkok: Thammasat University, 2017.

———. "Long Live Rathathammanun! Constitution Worship in Revolutionary Siam." *Modern Asian Studies* 52, no. 2 (March 2018): 609–44.

Punpisamai Disakul. *Sing thi khappajao phop hen: Prawatisat plianpleng kanpokhrong 2475* [The Things I Have Seen: History of the Change of Rule 1932]. Bangkok: Matichon, 2008 (1943).

Raluek Thani. *Wiwathanakan nai kanjat kansueksa phak bangkhap khong Thai [pho. so. 2475–2503]* [Course of the Establishment of Thai Compulsory Education, 1932–1960]. Bangkok: Thai Watana Panich, 1984.

Ray, Jayanta K. *Portraits of Thai Politics*. Delhi: Orient Longman, 1972.

Reynolds, Craig. "The Buddhist Monkhood in Nineteenth Century Thailand." PhD Diss., Cornell University, 1972.

Riggs, Fred W. *Thailand: The Modernization of a Bureaucratic Polity*. Honolulu: University of Hawai'i Press, 1966.

Ronasit Phichai, Pho. tho. Luang. *Siang withayu* [Radio Sound]. Bangkok: Thai Kasem, 1934.

Royal Thai Government, Ministry of Finance, Department of General Statistics. *Statistical Year Book of the Kingdom of Siam*. Bangkok, 1929–1944.

Sahakon, Anuson nai ngan phraratchathan phloengsop Chaophraya Wongsanuprapat (Mom Ratchawong Sathan Sanitwongse) [Sahakon, Royal Cremation Volume

for Chaophraya Wongsanuprapat]. Bangkok: Rongphim Sophonphiphanthanakon, 1941.

Saichon Satyanurak. *Prawatisat rat Thai lae sangkhom Thai* [History of the Thai
State and Thai Society]. Chiang Mai, Thailand: Chiang Mai University
Press, 2015.

———. *10 panyachon Siam, lem 2* [10 Siamese Intellectuals, vol. 2]. Bangkok:
Openbooks, 2014.

Sakdina Chatrakun na Ayutthaya. *Chiwit, naeokhit lae kantosu khong "Narin
klung" ru Narin Phasit, khon khwang lok* [Life, Thought and Struggles of
Narin Klung or Narin Phasit, the Person who Blocked the World]. Bangkok:
Matichon, 1993.

Sakon Wannakon Worawan, Momchao, and Phraya Sunthonpipit. *Sakon thesaban*
[Local Government Around the World] [Bangkok: Thai Club of Japan,
[1935] 2004.

Samakhom Nakkhao haeng Prathet Thai, compiler. *Bueangraek prachathipatai:
Banthuek khwamsongjam khong phu yu nai hetkan samai pho. so. 2475–2500*
[Democracy's First Phase: Record of the Memories of those involved in
the events of 1932–1957, two vols.] Bangkok: Samakhom Nakkhao haeng
Prathet Thai, 2007.

Samnakngan lekhathikan sapha phuthen ratsadon. *Raingan kanprachum sapha
phuthen ratsadon* [Minutes of Meetings of the Assembly of the People's
Representatives]. Bangkok: Samnakngan lekhathikan sapha phuthen ratsadon, 1932–1944.

Saneh Chamarik. *Kanmueang Thai kap pathanakan rathathammanun* [Thai Politics
and Constitutional Development], 3rd ed. Bangkok: Textbooks Project, 2006.

Sangh Pathanothai. *Khwamnuek nai krongkhang* [Thoughts in Prison]. Bangkok:
Klang Withaya, 1956.

Saranyu Thepsongkhro. "Mong samnuek ponlamueang yuk khana ratsadon phan
anusawari rathathammanun nai isan" [Examining Popular Consciousness in
the People's Party Age through Constitutional Monuments in the Northeast].
Silapa Wathanatham 39, no. 8 (2018): 74–105.

Sarawut Wisaphrom. *Ratsadon saman lang kanpatiwat 2475* [Commoners after
the 1932 Revolution]. Bangkok: Matichon, 2016.

Sathuean Suphasophon. *Chiwit thang kanmueang khong pho. o. Phraya Ritthi
Akhaney* [The Political Life of Ritthi Akhaney]. Bangkok: Samnakphim
Wacharin, 1971.

Sawai Suthipithak. *Doktoe Pridi Phanomyong* [Doctor Pridi Banomyong]. Bangkok:
Khlet Thai, 1983.

Sirot Khlampaiboon. *Raengngan wijan jao* [Labor Criticizes the Lords]. Bangkok:
Matichon, 2004.

Sivaram, M. *The New Siam in the Making*. Bangkok: Stationer's Printing Press, 1936.

Skinner, G. William. *Chinese Society in Thailand: An Analytical History*. Ithaca, NY: Cornell University Press, 1957.

Sombat Chandrawong. *Phasa thang kanmueang: Pathanakan khong naeo athibai kanmueang lae sap kanmueang nai ngankhian phraphet sarakhadi thang kanmueang khong Thai, pho. so. 2475–2525* [The Language of Politics: The Development of Political Explanations and Vocabulary in Thai Political Treatises, 1932–1982]. Bangkok: Thai Khadi Research Institute, 1990.

Somboon Suksamran. *Buddhism and Political Legitimacy*. Bangkok: Chulalongkorn University, 1993.

———. *Buddhism and Politics in Thailand*. Singapore: ISEAS, 1982.

Sompop Manarungsan. "The Rice Economy of Thailand in the 1930s Depression." In *Weathering the Storm: The Economies of Southeast Asia in the 1930s Depression*, edited by Peter Boomgaard and Ian Brown, 189–97. Singapore: ISEAS, 2000.

Somsak Jeamteerasakul. "The Communist Movement in Thailand." PhD diss., Monash University, 1991.

———. *Prawatisat thi phueng sang: Ruam botkhwam kiaokap karani 14 Tula lae 6 Tula* [The History Just Constructed: Collected Articles on 14 October and 6 October]. Bangkok: Samnakphim 6 Tula Ramleuk, 2001.

———. "Korani Thawatt Rittidej fong Phrapokklao" [The Case of Thawatt Rittidej Charging King Prajadhipok], October 16, 2006, http://somsakwork. blogspot.com.au/2006/10/.

Sorasak Ngamcachonkulkid. "The Seri Thai Movement: The First Alliance against Military Authoritarianism in Modern Thai History." PhD diss., University of Wisconsin-Madison, 2005.

———. *Free Thai: The New History of the Seri Thai Movement*. Bangkok: Chulalongkorn University, 2010.

———. *Tamnan mai khong khabuankan Seri Thai: Rueangrao khong kantosu phuea ekarat santiphap lae prachathipatai yang thaeching* [A New Legend of the Free Thai Movement: A Story of the Struggle for Independence, Peace and True Democracy]. Bangkok: Chulachomklao Military Academy, 2012.

So. Wisut Bussayakul. *Tiang Sirikhan, wirachon nakprachathipatai khunphol phuphan* [Tiang Sirikhan, Democratic Hero, Phuphan Commander]. Bangkok: Mae Khamfang, 2010.

Sriwisanwaja, Phraya. "The Revolution of 1932." In *Anuson nai kanphraratchathan phloengsop phan ek Phraya Sriwisanwaja* [Royal Cremation Volume for Phraya Sriwisanwaja]. Bangkok: Samnakngan Thepsiris, 1968.

Stowe, Judith. *Siam becomes Thailand: A Story of Intrigue*. Honolulu: University of Hawai'i Press, 1991.

Strand, David. *Rickshaw Beijing: City People and Politics in the 1920s*. Berkeley: University of California, 1989.

Strate, Shane. *The Lost Territories: Thailand's History of National Humiliation*. Honolulu: University of Hawai'i Press, 2015.

Subrahmanyan, Arjun. "Buddhism, Democracy and Power in the 1932 Thai Revolution." *Asian Studies Review* 41, no. 1 (2017): 40–57.

———. "Education, Propaganda and the People: Democratic Paternalism in 1930s Siam." *Modern Asian Studies* 49, no. 4 (2015): 1122–42.

Suehiro Akira. *Capital Accumulation in Thailand, 1855–1985*. Chiang Mai, Thailand: Silkworm Books, 1996.

Sukhin Tantikul. *Rathaprahan pho. so. 2490* [The 1947 Coup] Bangkok: Matichon, [1972] 2014.

Suksanti Chirachariyawech, ed. *Nangsue thi raluek khrop rop 84 Achan Sanya Dharmasakdi* [Honorary Volume for the Seventh Cycle of Sanya Dharmasakdi]. Bangkok: Munithi Nitisat, Thammasat University, 1991.

Sungsidh Piriyarangsan. *Kantosu khong kammakon Thai* [The Struggle of Thai Labor]. Bangkok: Chulalongkorn University Social Research Institute, 1986.

———. *Thunniyom khun nang Thai, pho. so. 2475–2503* [Thai Bureaucratic Capitalism, 1932–1960]. Bangkok: Sangsan, 1983.

Sunthonpipit, Phraya. "Thesaban Prathet Siam" [Siamese Local Government]. In Momchao Sakon Wannakon Worawan and Phraya Sunthonpipit, *Sakon thesaban* [Local Government around the World]. Bangkok: Thai Club of Japan, [1935] 2004.

Suphaphan Bunsa-at. *Prawat nangsuephim nai Prathet Thai* [History of the Newspaper in Thailand]. Bangkok: Bhannakij Trading, 1974.

Suphasawatwongsanit Sawatiwat, Momchao. *1 satawat Suphasawat* [One Century of Suphasawat]. Bangkok: Suphasawat Family, 2000.

Suphot Dantrakun. *Khothaeching kiaokap karani suwannakhot* [The Facts about the King's Death]. Bangkok, 1974.

Suphot Dantrakun and Pricha Suwannathat. *Khotheching thang prawatisat lae phraratchabanyat thammanun kanpokhrong phaendin Siam chuea khrao chabap 27 Mithunayon 2475* [Real Facts about History and the Temporary Siamese Constitution of 27 June 1932]. Bangkok: Sathaban Pridi Banomyong, 2007.

Suthachai Yimprasert. *Phaenching Chat Thai: Wa duai rat lae kantotan rat samai jomphon pho. Phibun Songkhram khrang thi song (pho. so. 2491–2500* [The Plan to Steal the Nation: On the State and Resistance to the State in the Second Time of Field Marshal Phibun Songkhram, 1948–1957]. Bangkok: 6 Tula Raluek, 2010.

———, ed. *Saithan haeng adit* [Streams of History]. Bangkok: Chulalongkorn University, 2007.

Suthachai Yimprasert, and Thipaphon Thantisunthon, eds. *Jak 100 pi ro. so. 130 thueng 80 pi prachathipatai* [From 100 Years since 1912 to 80 Years of Democracy]. Bangkok: Institute of Public Policy Studies, 2012.

Suwimon Phonlajan. "Krom khosanakan kap kankosana udomkan thang kanmueang khong rat, 2476–2487" [The Propaganda Department and Dissemination of State Political Principles, 1933–1944]. MA thesis, Thammasat University, 1988.

Taylor, Jim L. *Forest Monks and the Nation-State: An Anthropological and Historical Study in Northeastern Thailand.* Singapore: ISEAS, 1993.

Tej Bunnag. *Kabot ro. so. 121* [The Revolts of 1903]. Bangkok: Foundation for the Promotion of Social Sciences and Humanities Textbooks Project, [1968] 2008.

———. *The Provincial Administration of Siam 1892–1915: The Ministry of the Interior under Prince Damrong Rajanubhab.* Kuala Lumpur, Malaysia and London: Oxford University Press, 1977.

Terwiel, B. J. *Thailand's Political History.* Bangkok: River Books, 2011.

Thaemsuk Numnonda. *Kabot ro. so. 130, yangterk runraek* [The Revolt of 1912, the First Generation of Young Turks]. Bangkok: Saitharn Publishing House, 2002.

———. *Lakhon kanmueang, 24 Mithuna 2475* [Political Theater, June 24, 1932]. Bangkok: Samakhom Prawatisat, 2002.

Thak Chaloemtiarana. *Thailand: The Politics of Despotic Paternalism.* Chiang Mai, Thailand: Silkworm Books, 2007.

———, ed. and trans. *Thai Politics: Extracts and Documents 1932–1957.* Bangkok: Social Science Association of Thailand, 1978.

Thammasakmontri, Chaophraya. *Thammachariya,* vol. 5. Bangkok: Aksorniti, 1921.

Thamrongsak Petchlert-anan. *2475 lae nueng pi lang kanpatiwat* [1932 and One Year after the Revolution]. In Charnvit Kasetsiri and Thamrongsak Phetlert-anand, *Patiwat 2475* [1932 Revolution in Siam]. Bangkok: The Foundation for the Promotion of Social Science and Humanities Textbooks Project, 2004.

———. *"Kho Ang" kanpatiwat-rathaprahan, kabot nai kanmueang Thai patchu-ban: botwikhro lae ekasan* ["Reason" for Coups in Modern Siam/Thailand: Document and Analysis]. Bangkok: The Foundation for the Promotion of Social Science and Humanities Textbooks Project, 2007.

Thanavi Chotpradit. "Revolution versus Counter-Revolution: The People's Party and the Royalist[s] in Visual Dialogue." PhD Diss., Birkbeck, University of London, 2016.

Thanet Aphornsuvan. "The United States and the Coming of the Coup of 1947 in Siam." *Journal of the Siam Society,* 75 (1987): 187–214.

Thanissaro Bhikkhu. "The Customs of the Noble Ones." Accessed June 7, 2010, http://www.accesstoinsight.org/lib/authors/thanissaro/customs.html.

Thapanan Nipithakul. *Pharadoraphapniyom [solidarisme] khong Pridi Banomyong* [Pridi Banomyong's Solidarism]. Bangkok: Pridi Banomyong Institute, 2006.

Thawatt Mokarapong. *History of the Thai Revolution: A Study in Political Behaviour.* Bangkok: Chalermnit, 1972.

Thompson, E. P. *The Making of the English Working Class.* New York: Vintage, 1966.

Thompson, Virginia. *Labor Problems in Southeast Asia.* New Haven, CT: Yale University Press, 1947.

———. *Thailand: The New Siam.* New York: Paragon Book Reprint, [1941] 1967.

Thongchai Likitpornasawan. *Samutphap Phraya Phahon Phonphayuhasena phak nueng* [General Phraya Phahon Phonphayuhasena: A Photographic Album. vol. 1]. Bangkok: Tonchabap, 2013.

———. *Samutphap Phraya Phahon Phonphayuhasena phak song: Prap kabot pho. so. 2476* [General Phraya Phahon Phonphayuhasena: A Photographic Album Volume 2]. Bangkok: Tonchabap, 2015.

———. *Samutphap Siam yuk prachathipatai* [Siam Photographic Album, the Democratic Age]. Bangkok: Tonchabap, 2015.

Thongchai Winichakul. "Siam's Colonial Conditions and the Birth of Thai History." In *Southeast Asian Historiography, Unraveling the Myths: Essays in Honour of Barend Jan Terwiel*, edited by Volker Grabowsky, 23–45. Bangkok: River Books, 2011.

———. *Khamhaiphon prachathipatai baep lang 14 Tula* [Getting past Democracy of the Post-October 14 Type]. Bangkok: 14 October Foundation, 2005.

———. "Prawatisat thai baep rachachatniyom: chak yuk ananikhom amphrang su rachachatniyom mai rue latthi sadet pho khun krathumphi thai nai patchuban" [Royalist-Nationalist History: From the Era of Crypto-Colonialism to the new Royalist-Nationalism, or the Contemporary Thai Bourgeois Cult of Rama V]. *Silapa Wathanatham* 23, no. 1 (November 2001): 56–65.

———. "The Quest for Siwilai: A Geographical Discourse of Civilizational Thinking in Late Nineteenth and Early Twentieth-Century Siam." *Journal of Asian Studies* 59, no. 3 (August 2000): 528–49.

———. *Siam Mapped: A History of the Geo-Body of a Nation*. Honolulu: University of Hawai'i Press, 1994.

Tho Phianwitthaya. "An Internal History of the Communist Party of Thailand." Translated by Chris Baker. *Journal of Contemporary Asia* 33, no. 4 (2003): 510–41.

Tunsiri Vichai. "The Social Background and the Legislative Recruitment of the Thai Members of Parliament and their Political Consequences." PhD thesis, Indiana University, 1971.

Turton, Andrew. "Northern Thai Peasant Society: Twentieth Century Transformations in Political and Jural Structures." *Journal of Peasant Studies* 3, no. 3 (April 1976): 267–98.

Urban Dharma. 2013. The Agganna Sutta. Urban Dharma website. Accessed November 29, 2018, http://www.urbandharma.org/pdf/AggannaSutta.pdf.

Vajirananavarorasa, Somdet Phra Maha Samanachao Kromphraya. *Praprawat tras lao* [Autobiography]. Bangkok: Khurusapha, 1971.

———, compiler. *Navakovada, laksut naktham chan tri, phra niphon Somdet Phra Maha Samanajao Krom Phraya Wachirayan Waroros* [Navakovada, Instructions for Newly-ordained Bhikkus and Samaneras (Standard Text for the Dhamma Student, 3rd Grade)]. Bangkok: Mahamakut Rajavidyalaya, 1999.

Vajiravudh, King. "Lathi ao yang" [Imitationism]. In *Royal Cremation Volume for Luang Anukan Ratchaphat*, 1–9. Bangkok, 1963.

Vichitvong na Pombhejara. *Pridi Banomyong and the Making of Thailand's Modern History*. Bangkok: Committees on the Project for the National Celebration on the Occasion of the Centennial Anniversary of Pridi Banomyong, Senior Statesman, 2001.

Warren, James F. *Rickshaw Coolie: A People's History of Singapore, 1880–1940*. Singapore: Oxford University Press, 1986.

Warunee Osatharom. "Kansueksa nai sangkhom Thai pho. so. 2411–2475" [Education in Thai Society 1868–1932]. MA thesis, Chulalongkorn University, 1981.

Wasana Wongsurawat. *The Crown and the Capitalists: The Ethnic Chinese and the Founding of the Thai Nation*. Seattle: University of Washington Press, 2019.

———. "Thailand and the Xinhai Revolution: Expectation, Reality and Inspiration." In *Sun Yat-Sen, Nanyang and the 1911 Revolution*, edited by Lee Lai To and Lee Hock Guan, 130–47. Singapore: ISEAS, 2011.

Wibha Senanan. *Kamnert nawaniyai nai Prathet Thai* [Birth of the Novel in Thailand]. Bangkok: Dokya, 1997.

Wichit Wathakan, Luang. *Kanmuang kanpokhrong khong Siam* [Siamese Politics and Administration]. Bangkok, Thailand: Thai Mai, 1932.

Williams, Raymond. *Culture and Society, 1780–1950*. New York: Harper & Row, 1958.

———. *Keywords*. Oxford, UK: Oxford University Press, 1984.

Wilson, Constance. *Thailand: A Handbook of Historical Statistics*. Boston: G. K. Hall, 1983.

Wimon Wiriyawit, compiler. *Free Thai: Personal Recollections and Official Documents*. Bangkok: White Lotus, 1997.

Withet Korani, *Khwampenma haeng rabawp prachathipatai khong Thai* [The Origins of the Thai Democratic Regime]. Bangkok: Panfa Phitya, 1968.

Wolters, Oliver. *History, Culture and Region in Southeast Asian Perspectives*. Singapore: ISEAS, 1982.

Wright, Arnold, and Oliver T. Breakspear. *Twentieth Century Impressions of Siam*. London: Lloyd's Greater Britain Publishing, 1908.

Wyatt, David K. *The Politics of Reform in Thailand: Education in the Reign of King Chulalongkorn*. New Haven, CT: Yale University Press, 1969.

———. "Family Politics in Nineteenth Century Thailand." In *Studies in Thai History: Collected Articles*, 106–30. Chiang Mai, Thailand: Silkworm Books, 1994.

Yasukichi Yatabe. *Bantheuk khong thut Yipun hen hetkan patiwat 2475, kanpatiwat lae kanplianpleng nai Prathet Siam* [Account of the Japanese Ambassador in Siam who saw the 1932 Revolution, Revolution and Change in Siam]. Translated by Eiji Murashima and Nakharin Mektrairat. Bangkok: Matichon, [1936] 2007.

Yoneo Ishii. *Sangha, State and Society: Thai Buddhism in History*. Honolulu: University of Hawai'i Press, 1986.

Yoshikawa Toshiharu. *Thangrotfai sai Thai-Phama nai samai songkhram maha Asia burapha* [The Thai-Burma Railway in the Time of the Great East Asian

War]. Translated by Athon Fungthammasan, Trithip Rattanaphaisan, and Marasi Miyamoto, edited by Saichon Satanyanurak. Bangkok: Amarin, 1995.

Zimmerman, Carle C. *Siam Rural Economic Survey, 1930–1931*. Bangkok: White Lotus Press, [1931] 1999.

Index

www.ingramcontent.com/pod-product-compliance
Lightning Source LLC
Chambersburg PA
CBHW031408270326
41929CB00010BA/1369